The Ultimate PBSAA Guide

Copyright © 2017 *UniAdmissions*. All rights reserved.

ISBN 978-0-9935711-5-2

No part of this publication may be reproduced or transmitted in any form or by any means, electronic or mechanical, including photocopying, recording, or by any information retrieval system without prior written permission of the publisher. This publication may not be used in conjunction with or to support any commercial undertaking without the prior written permission of the publisher.

Published by *RAR Medical Services Limited*
www.uniadmissions.co.uk
info@uniadmissions.co.uk
Tel: 0208 068 0438

This book is neither created nor endorsed by PBSAA. The authors and publisher are not affiliated with PBSAA. The information offered in this book is purely advisory and any advice given should be taken within this context. As such, the publishers and authors accept no liability whatsoever for the outcome of any applicant's PBSAA performance, the outcome of any university applications or for any other loss. Although every precaution has been taken in the preparation of this book, the publisher and author assume no responsibility for errors or omissions of any kind. Neither is any liability assumed for damages resulting from the use of information contained herein. This does not affect your statutory rights.

The Ultimate PBSAA Guide

550 Practice Questions

Dr Rohan Agarwal

About the Author

Rohan is the **Director of Operations** at *UniAdmissions* and is responsible for its technical and commercial arms. He graduated from Gonville and Caius College, Cambridge and is a fully qualified doctor. Over the last five years, he has tutored hundreds of successful Oxbridge and Medical applicants. He has also authored twenty books on admissions tests and interviews.

Rohan has taught physiology to undergraduates and interviewed medical school applicants for Cambridge. He has published research on bone physiology and writes education articles for the Independent and Huffington Post. In his spare time, Rohan enjoys playing the piano and table tennis.

The Basics 6
General Advice 7

SECTION 1A: Critical Thinking 11
Critical Thinking Questions 14
SECTION 1A: Problem Solving 46
Problem Solving Questions 48

SECTION 1B 82
SECTION 1B: Biology 83
Biology Questions 84
SECTION 1B: Maths 100
Maths Questions 101

SECTION 1C: Reading Comprehension 114
Reading Comprehension Questions 118

SECTION 2: Writing Task 178
Annotated Essays 184

Answer Key 200
Worked Answers 203

Final Advice 281
Your Free Book 283

The Basics

What is the PBSAA?
The Psychological and Behavioural Sciences Admissions Assessment (PBSAA) is a two hour written exam for prospective Cambridge applicants for Physcholgy and Behavioural Sciences (PBS).

What does the PBSAA consist of?

Section	Timing	FORMAT	Questions	Mandatory
ONE	80 Minutes	1A: Thinking Skills 1B: Mathematics and Biology 1C: Reading Comprehension	22 MCQs 30 MCQs 24 MCQs	Must complete Section 1A and either 1B or 1C
TWO	40 Minutes	Essay Task	One Essay from a choice of Four	Must Complete Section 2

Why is the PBSAA used?
Cambridge applicants tend to be a bright bunch and therefore usually have excellent grades. The vast majority of applicants score greater than 90% in all of their A level subjects. This means that competition is fierce – meaning that the universities must use the PBSAA to help differentiate between applicants.

When do I sit PBSAA?
The PBSAA takes place in the first week of November every year. The date for 2017 is 2nd November.

Can I resit the PBSAA?
No, you can only sit the PBSAA once per admissions cycle.

Where do I sit the PBSAA?
You can usually sit the PBSAA at your school or college (ask your exams officer for more information). Alternatively, if your school isn't a registered test centre or you're not attending a school or college, you can sit the PBSAA at an authorised test centre.

Do I have to resit the PBSAA if I reapply?
Yes - you cannot use your score from any previous attempts.

How is the PBSAA Scored?
In section 1, each question carries one mark and there is no negative marking. In section 2, your answer will be assessed based on the argument and also its clarity.

How is the PBSAA used?
Different Cambridge colleges will place different weightings on different components so its important you find out as much information about how your marks will be used by emailing the college admissions office.

In general, the university will interview a high proportion of realistic applicants so the PBSAA score isn't vital for making the interview shortlist. However, it can play a huge role in the final decision after your interview

General Advice

Start Early
It is much easier to prepare if you practice little and often. Start your preparation well in advance; ideally by mid September but at the latest by early October. This way you will have plenty of time to complete as many papers as you wish to feel comfortable and won't have to panic and cram just before the test, which is a much less effective and more stressful way to learn. In general, an early start will give you the opportunity to identify the complex issues and work at your own pace.

Prioritise
Some questions in sections 1A + 1B can be long and complex – and given the intense time pressure you need to know your limits. It is essential that you don't get stuck with very difficult questions. If a question looks particularly long or complex, mark it for review and move on. You don't want to be caught 5 questions short at the end just because you took more than 3 minutes in answering a challenging multi-step biology question. If a question is taking too long, choose a sensible answer and move on. Remember that each question carries equal weighting and therefore, you should adjust your timing in accordingly. With practice and discipline, you can get very good at this and learn to maximise your efficiency.

Positive Marking
There are no penalties for incorrect answers in the PBSAA; you will gain one for each right answer and will not get one for each wrong or unanswered one. This provides you with the luxury that you can always guess should you absolutely be not able to figure out the right answer for a question or run behind time. Since each question provides you with 4 to 6 possible answers, you have a 16-25% chance of guessing correctly. Therefore, if you aren't sure (and are running short of time), then make an educated guess and move on. Before 'guessing' you should try to eliminate a couple of answers to increase your chances of getting the question correct. For example, if a question has 5 options and you manage to eliminate 2 options- your chances of getting the question increase from 20% to 33%!

Avoid losing easy marks on other questions because of poor exam technique. Similarly, if you have failed to finish the exam, take the last 10 seconds to guess the remaining questions to at least give yourself a chance of getting them right.

Practice
This is the best way of familiarising yourself with the style of questions and the timing for this section. You are unlikely to be familiar with the style of questions when you first encounter them. Therefore, you want to be comfortable at using this before you sit the test.

Practising questions will put you at ease and make you more comfortable with the exam. The more comfortable you are, the less you will panic on the test day and the more likely you are to score highly. Initially, work through the questions at your own pace, and spend time carefully reading the questions and looking at any additional data. When it becomes closer to the test, **make sure you practice the questions under exam conditions**.

Past Papers
The PBSAA is a very new exam so there aren't many sample papers available. Specimen papers are freely available online at **www.uniadmissions.co.uk/PBSAA**. Once you've worked your way through the questions in this book, you are highly advised to attempt them.

Repeat Questions

When checking through answers, pay particular attention to questions you have got wrong. If there is a worked answer, look through that carefully until you feel confident that you understand the reasoning, and then repeat the question without help to check that you can do it. If only the answer is given, have another look at the question and try to work out why that answer is correct. This is the best way to learn from your mistakes, and means you are less likely to make similar mistakes when it comes to the test.

The same applies for questions which you were unsure of and made an educated guess which was correct, even if you got it right. When working through this book, **make sure you highlight any questions you are unsure of**, this means you know to spend more time looking over them once marked.

No Calculators

You aren't permitted to use calculators in the PBSAA – thus, it is essential that you have strong numerical skills. For instance, you should be able to rapidly convert between percentages, decimals and fractions. You will seldom get questions that would require calculators but you would be expected to be able to arrive at a sensible estimate. Consider for example:

Estimate 3.962 x 2.322:
3.962 is approximately 4 and 2.323 is approximately $2.33 = 7/3$.

Thus, $3.962 \times 2.322 \approx 4 \times \frac{7}{3} = \frac{28}{3} = 9.33$

Since you will rarely be asked to perform difficult calculations, you can use this as a signpost of if you are tackling a question correctly. For example, when solving a physics question, you end up having to divide 8,079 by 357- this should raise alarm bells as calculations in the PBSAA are rarely this difficult.

> ***Top tip!*** In general, students tend to improve the fastest in section 1B and slowest in section 1C; section 1A usually falls somewhere in the middle. Thus, if you have very little time left, it's best to prioritise section 1B (assuming you've chosen it over section 1C!).

Choose Wisely

You have a choice of doing section 1B or section 1C which require markedly different skills. In most cases it will be immediately obvious to you which section will suit you best. Generally, applicants with a scientific predisposition will tend towards section 1B whilst those with a humanities background will prefer section 1C.

If you're unsure, take the time to review the content of both sections and try out some questions so you can get a better idea of the style and difficulty of the questions. In general, section 1B tends to be more time pressured but easier to improve in whilst section 1C requires skills that take more time to develop.

A word on timing...

You have 80 minutes to complete section one which consists of Section 1A and either Section 1B or 1C. Whilst in theory it's possible to spend unequal amounts of time on different sections, it's generally a good idea to split your time evenly i.e. 40 minutes on section 1A and 40 minutes on section 1B/C.

This means that you will do around 46 – 52 questions in 80 minutes which means you have around 95 seconds per question; this may sound like a lot but given that you're often required to read and analyse passages or graphs- it can often not be enough. Some questions in this section are very tricky and can be a big drain on your limited time. **The people who fail to complete section 1 are those who get bogged down on a particular question**.

Therefore, it is vital that you start to get a feel for which questions are going to be easy and quick to do and which ones should be left till the end. The best way to do this is through practice and the questions in this book will offer extensive opportunities for you to do so.

"If you had all day to do your PBSAA, you would get 100%. But you don't."

Whilst this isn't completely true, it illustrates a very important point. Once you've practiced and know how to answer the questions, the clock is your biggest enemy. This seemingly obvious statement has one very important consequence. **The way to improve your PBSAA score is to improve your speed.** There is no magic bullet. But there are a great number of techniques that, with practice, will give you significant time gains, allowing you to answer more questions and score more marks.

Timing is tight throughout the PBSAA – **mastering timing is the first key to success**. Some candidates choose to work as quickly as possible to save up time at the end to check back, but this is generally not the best way to do it. PBSAA questions can have a lot of information in them – each time you start answering a question it takes time to get familiar with the instructions and information. By splitting the question into two sessions (the first run-through and the return-to-check) you double the amount of time you spend on familiarising yourself with the data, as you have to do it twice instead of only once. This costs valuable time. In addition, candidates who do check back may spend 2–3 minutes doing so and yet not make any actual changes. Whilst this can be reassuring, it is a false reassurance as it is unlikely to have a significant effect on your actual score. Therefore it is usually best to pace yourself very steadily, aiming to spend the same amount of time on each question and finish the final question in a section just as time runs out. This reduces the time spent on re-familiarising with questions and maximises the time spent on the first attempt, gaining more marks.

It is essential that you don't get stuck with the hardest questions – no doubt there will be some. In the time spent answering only one of these you may miss out on answering three easier questions. If a question is taking too long, choose a sensible answer and move on. Never see this as giving up or in any way failing, rather it is the smart way to approach a test with a tight time limit. With practice and discipline, you can get very good at this and learn to maximise your efficiency. It is not about being a hero and aiming for full marks – this is almost impossible and very much unnecessary (even Oxbridge will regard any score higher than 7 as exceptional). It is about maximising your efficiency and gaining the maximum possible number of marks within the time you have.

> ***Top tip!*** Ensure that you take a watch that can show you the time in seconds into the exam. This will allow you have a much more accurate idea of the time you're spending on a question. In general, if you've spent >120 seconds on a question move on regardless of how close you think you are to solving it.

Use the Options

Some questions may try to overload you with information. When presented with large tables and data, it's essential you look at the answer options so you can focus your mind. This can allow you to reach the correct answer a lot more quickly. Consider the example below:

The table below shows the results of a study investigating antibiotic resistance in staphylococcus populations. A single staphylococcus bacterium is chosen at random from a similar population. Resistance to any one antibiotic is independent of resistance to others.

Calculate the probability that the bacterium selected will be resistant to all four drugs.

A   1 in 10^6
B   1 in 10^{12}
C   1 in 10^{20}
D   1 in 10^{25}
E   1 in 10^{30}
F   1 in 10^{35}

Antibiotic	Number of Bacteria tested	Number of Resistant Bacteria
Benzyl-penicillin	10^{11}	98
Chloramphenicol	10^9	1200
Metronidazole	10^8	256
Erythromycin	10^5	2

Looking at the options first makes it obvious that there is **no need to calculate exact values**- only in powers of 10. This makes your life a lot easier. If you hadn't noticed this, you might have spent well over 90 seconds trying to calculate the exact value when it wasn't even being asked for.

In other cases, you may actually be able to use the options to arrive at the solution quicker than if you had tried to solve the question as you normally would. Consider the example below:

A region is defined by the two inequalities: $x - y^2 > 1$ and $xy > 1$. Which of the following points is in the defined region?

A. (10,3)
B. (10,2)
C. (-10,3)
D. (-10,2)
E. (-10,-3)

Whilst it's possible to solve this question both algebraically or graphically by manipulating the identities, by far **the quickest way is to actually use the options**. Note that options C, D and E violate the second inequality, narrowing down to answer to either A or B. For A: $10 - 3^2 = 1$ and thus this point is on the boundary of the defined region and not actually in the region. Thus the answer is B (as 10-4 = 6 > 1.)

In general, it pays dividends to look at the options briefly and see if they can be help you arrive at the question more quickly. Get into this habit early – it may feel unnatural at first but it's guaranteed to save you time in the long run.

Keywords

If you're stuck on a question; pay particular attention to the options that contain key modifiers like "**always**", "**only**", "**all**" as examiners like using them to test if there are any gaps in your knowledge. E.g. the statement "arteries carry oxygenated blood" would normally be true; "All arteries carry oxygenated blood" would be false because the pulmonary artery carries deoxygenated blood.

SECTION 1A: Critical Thinking

This is the first section of the PBSAA and as you walk in, it is inevitable that you will feel nervous. Make sure that you have been to the toilet because once it starts you cannot simply pause and go. Take a few deep breaths and calm yourself down. Remember that panicking will not help and may negatively affect your marks- so try and avoid this as much as possible.

Whilst section 1 of the PBSAA is renowned for being difficult to prepare for, there are powerful shortcuts and techniques that you can use to save valuable time on these types of questions.

PBSAA Critical thinking questions require you to understand the constituents of a good argument and be able to pick them apart. The majority of PBSAA Critical thinking questions tend to fall into 3 major categories:

1. Identifying Conclusions
2. Identifying Assumptions + Flaws
3. Strengthening and Weakening arguments

Having a good grasp of language and being able to filter unnecessary information quickly and efficiently is a vital skill at oxbridge – you simply do not have the time to sit and read vast numbers of textbooks cover to cover, you need to be able to filter the information and realise which part is important and this will contribute to your success in your studies. You need to be able to pick out key information so getting to grips with verbal reasoning goes a long way - do not underestimate its importance.

Only use the Passage

Your answer must only be based on the information available in the passage. Do not try and guess the answer based on your general knowledge as this can be a trap. For example, if the passage says that spring is followed by winter, then take this as true even though you know that spring is followed by summer.

> *Top tip!* Though it might initially sound counter-intuitive, it is often best to read the question *before* reading the passage. Then you'll have a much better idea of what you're looking for and are therefore more likely to find it quicker.

Take your time

Unlike the problem solving questions, critical thinking questions are less time pressured. Most of the passages are well below 300 words and therefore don't take long to read and process (unlike the UKCAT in which you should skim read passages). Thus, your aim should be to understand the intricacies of the passage and identify key information so that you don't miss key information and lose easy marks.

Identifying Conclusions

Students struggle with these type of questions because they confuse a premise for a conclusion. For clarities sake:

- A **Conclusion** is a summary of the arguments being made and is usually explicitly stated or heavily implied.
- A **Premise** is a statement from which another statement can be inferred or follows as a conclusion.

Hence a conclusion is shown/implied/proven by a premise. Similarly, a premise shows/indicates/establishes a conclusion. Consider for example: *My mom, being a woman, is clever as all women are clever.*

Premise 1: My mom is a woman + **Premise 2:** Women are clever = **Conclusion:** My mom is clever.

This is fairly straightforward as it's a very short passage and the conclusion is explicitly stated. Sometimes the latter may not happen. Consider: *My mom is a woman and all women are clever.*
Here, whilst the conclusion is not explicitly being stated, both premises still stand and can be used to reach the same conclusion.

You may sometimes be asked to identify if any of the options cannot be "reliably concluded". This is effectively asking you to identify why an option **cannot** be the conclusion. There are many reasons why but the most common ones are:

1. Over-generalising: *My mom is clever therefore all women are clever.*
2. Being too specific: All kids like candy thus my son also likes candy.
3. Confusing Correlation vs. Causation: *Lung cancer is much more likely in patients who drink water. Hence, water causes lung cancer.*
4. Confusing Cause and Effect: *Lung cancer patients tend to smoke so it follows that having lung cancer must make people want to smoke.*

Note how conjunctives like hence, thus, therefore and it follows give you a clue as to when a conclusion is being stated. More examples of these include: "it follows that, implies that, whence, entails that".
Similarly, words like "because, as indicated by, in that, given that, due to the fact that" usually identify premises.

Assumptions and Flaws

Other types of critical thinking questions may require you to identify assumptions and flaws in a passage's reasoning. Before proceeding it is useful to define both:

- An assumption is a reasonable assertion that can be made on the basis of the available evidence.
- A flaw is an element of an argument which is inconsistent to the rest of the available evidence. It undermines the crucial components of the overall argument being made.

Consider for example: *My mom is clever because all doctors are clever.*

Premise 1: Doctors are clever. **Assumption:** My mom is a doctor. **Conclusion:** My mom is clever.

Note that the conclusion follows naturally even though there is only one premise because of the assumption. The argument relies on the assumption to work. Thus, if you are unsure if an option you have is an assumption or not, just ask yourself:

1) *Is it in the passage?* If the answer is **no** then proceed to ask:
2) *Does the conclusion rely on this piece of information in order to work?* – If the answer is **yes** – then you've identified an assumption.

You may sometimes be asked to identify flaws in an argument – it is important to be aware of the types of flaws to look out for. In general, these are broadly similar to the ones discussed earlier in the conclusion section (over-generalising, being too specific, confusing cause and effect, confusing correlation and causation). Remember that an assumption may also be a flaw.

For example consider again: *My mom is clever because all doctors are clever.*

What if the mother was not actually a doctor? The argument would then breakdown as the assumption would be incorrect or **flawed**.

Strengthening and Weakening Arguments:

You may be asked to identify an answer option that would most strengthen or weaken the argument being made in the passage. Normally, you'll also be told to assume that each answer option is true. Before we can discuss how to strengthen and weaken arguments, it is important to understand "what constitutes a good argument:

1. **Evidence:** Arguments which are heavily based on value judgements and subjective statements tend to be weaker than those based on facts, statistics and the available evidence.
2. **Logic**: A good argument should flow and the constituent parts should fit well into an overriding view or belief.
3. **Balance:** A good argument must concede that there are other views or beliefs (counter-argument). The key is to carefully dismantle these ideas and explain why they are wrong.

Thus, when asked to strengthen an argument, look for options that would: Increase the evidence basis for the argument, support or add a premise, address the counter-arguments.

Similarly, when asked to weaken an argument, look for options that would: decrease the evidence basis for the argument or create doubt over existing evidence, undermine a premise, strengthen the counter-arguments.

In order to be able to strengthen or weaken arguments, you must completely understand the passage's conclusion. Then you can start testing the impact of each answer option on the conclusion to see which one strengthens or weakens it the most i.e. is the conclusion stronger/weaker if I assume this information to be true and included in the passage.

Often you'll have to decide which option strengthens/weakens the passage most – and there really isn't an easy way to do this apart from lots of practice. Thankfully, you have plenty of time for these questions.

> *Top tip!* Don't get confused between premises and assumptions. A **premise** is a statement that is explicitly stated in the passage. An **assumption** is an inference that is made from the passage.

Critical Thinking Questions

Question 1-6 are based on the passage below:

People have tried to elucidate the differences between the different genders for many years. Are they societal pressures or genetic differences? In the past it has always been assumed that it was programmed into our DNA to act in a certain more masculine or feminine way but now evidence has emerged that may show it is not our genetics that determines the way we act, but that society pre-programmes us into gender identification. Whilst it is generally acknowledged that not all boys and girls are the same, why is it that most young boys like to play with trucks and diggers whilst young girls prefer dollies and pink?

The society we live in has always been an important factor in our identity, take cultural differences; the language we speak the food we eat, the clothes we wear. All of these factors influence our identity. New research finds that the people around us may prove to be the biggest influence on our gender behaviour. It shows our parents buying gendered toys may have a much bigger influence than the genes they gave us. Girls are being programmed to like the same things as their mothers and this has lasting effects on their personality. Young girls and boys are forced into their gender stereotypes through the clothes they are bought, the hairstyle they wear and the toys they play with.

The power of society to influence gender behaviour explains the cases where children have been born with different external sex organs to those that would match their sex determining chromosomes. Despite the influence of their DNA they identify to the gender they have always been told they are. Once the difference has been detected, how then are they ever to feel comfortable in their own skin? The only way to prevent society having such a large influence on gender identity is to allow children to express themselves, wear what they want and play with what they want without fear of not fitting in.

Question 1:
What is the main conclusion from the first paragraph?
A. Society controls gender behaviour.
B. People are different based on their gender.
C. DNA programmes how we act.
D. Boys do not like the same things as girls because of their genes.

Question 2:
Which of the following, if true, points out the flaw in the first paragraph's argument?
A. Not all boys like trucks.
B. Genes control the production of hormones.
C. Differences in gender may be due to an equal combination of society and genes.
D. Some girls like trucks.

Question 3:
According to the statement, how can culture affect identity?
A. Culture can influence what we wear and how we speak.
B. Our parents act the way they do because of culture.
C. Culture affects our genetics.
D. Culture usually relates to where we live.

Question 4:
Which of these is most implied by the statement?
A. Children usually identify with the gender they appear to be.
B. Children are programmed to like the things they do by their DNA.
C. Girls like dollies and pink because their mothers do.
D. It is wrong for boys to have long hair like girls.

Question 5:
What does the statement say is the best way to prevent gender stereotyping?
A. Mothers spending more time with their sons.
B. Parents buying gender-neutral clothes for their children.
C. Allowing children to act how they want.
D. Not telling children if they have different sex organs.

Question 6:
What, according to the statement is the biggest problem for children born with different external sex organs to those which match their sex chromosomes?
A. They may have other problems with their DNA.
B. Society may not accept them for who they are.
C. They may wish to be another gender.
D. They are not the gender they are treated as which can be distressing.

SECTION 1A: CRITICAL THINKING — QUESTIONS

Questions 7-11 are based on the passage below:

New evidence has emerged that the most important factor in a child's development could be their napping routine. It has come to light that regular napping could well be the deciding factor for determining toddlers' memory and learning abilities. The new countrywide survey of 1000 toddlers, all born in the same year showed around 75% had regular 30-minute naps. Parents cited the benefits of their child having a regular routine (including meal times) such as decreased irritability, and stated the only downfall of occasional problems with sleeping at night. Research indicating that toddlers were 10% more likely to suffer regular night-time sleeping disturbances when they regularly napped supported the parent's view.

Those who regularly took 30-minute naps were more than twice as likely to remember simple words such as those of new toys than their non-napping counterparts, who also had higher incidences of memory impairment, behavioural problems and learning difficulties. Toddlers who regularly had 30 minute naps were tested on whether they were able recall the names of new objects the following day, compared to a control group who did not regularly nap. These potential links between napping and memory, behaviour and learning ability provides exciting new evidence in the field of child development.

Question 7:
If in 100 toddlers 5% who did not nap were able to remember a new teddy's name, how many who had napped would be expected to remember?
A. 8
B. 9
C. 10
D. 12

Question 8:
Assuming that the incidence of night-time sleeping disturbances is the same in for all toddlers independent of all characteristics other than napping, what is the percentage of toddlers who suffer regular night-time sleeping disturbances as a result of napping?
A. 7.5%
B. 10%
C. 14%
D. 20%
E. 50%

Question 9:
Using the information from the passage above, which of the following is the most plausible alternative reason for the link between memory and napping?
A. Children who have bad memory abilities are also likely to have trouble sleeping.
B. Children who regularly nap, are born with better memories.
C. Children who do not nap were unable to concentrate on the memory testing exercises for the study.
D. Parents who enforce a routine of napping are more likely to conduct memory exercises with their children.

Question 10:
Which of the following is most strongly indicated?
A. Families have more enjoyable meal times when their toddlers regularly nap.
B. Toddlers have better routines when they nap.
C. Parents enforce napping to improve their toddlers' memory ability.
D. Napping is important for parents' routines.

Question 11:
Which of the following, if true, would strengthen the conclusion that there is a causal link between regular napping and improved memory in toddlers?
A. Improved memory is also associated with regular mealtimes.
B. Parents who enforce regular napping are more inclined to include their children in studies.
C. Toddlers' memory development is so rapid that even a few weeks can make a difference to performance.

D. Among toddler playgroups where napping incidence is higher and more consistent memory performance is significantly improved compared to those that do not.

Question 12:

Tom's father says to him: 'You must work for your A-levels. That is the best way to do well in your A-level exams. If you work especially hard for Geography, you will definitely succeed in your Geography A-level exam'.

Which of the following is the best statement Tom could say to prove a flaw in his father's argument?
A. 'It takes me longer to study for my History exam, so I should prioritise that.'
B. 'I do not have to work hard to do well in my Geography A-level.'
C. 'Just because I work hard, does not mean I will do well in my A-levels.'
D. 'You are putting too much importance on studying for A-levels.'
E. 'You haven't accounted for the fact that Geography is harder than my other subjects.'

Question 13:

Today the NHS is increasingly struggling to be financially viable. In the future, the NHS may have to reduce the services it cannot afford. The NHS is supported by government funds, which come from those who pay tax in the UK. Recently the NHS has been criticised for allowing fertility treatments to be free, as many people believe these are not important and should not be paid for when there is not enough money to pay the doctors and nurses.

Which of the following is the most accurate conclusion of the statement above?
A. Only taxpayers should decide where the NHS spends its money.
B. Doctors and nurses should be better paid.
C. The NHS should stop free fertility treatments.
D. Fertility treatments may have to be cut if finances do not improve.

Question 14:

'We should allow people to drive as fast as they want. By allowing drivers to drive at fast speeds, through natural selection the most dangerous drivers will kill only themselves in car accidents. These people will not have children, hence only safe people will reproduce and eventually the population will only consist of safe drivers.'

Which one of the following, if true, most weakens the above argument?
A. Dangerous drivers harm others more often than themselves by driving too fast.
B. Dangerous drivers may produce children who are safe drivers.
C. The process of natural selection takes a long time.
D. Some drivers break speed limits anyway.

SECTION 1A: CRITICAL THINKING — QUESTIONS

Question 15:
In the winter of 2014 the UK suffered record levels of rainfall, which led to catastrophic damage across the country. Thousands of homes were damaged and even destroyed, leaving many homeless in the chaos that followed. The Government faced harsh criticism that they had failed to adequately prepare the country for the extreme weather. In such cases the Government assess the likelihood of such events happening in the future and balance against the cost of advance measures to reduce the impact should they occur versus the cost of the event with no preparative defences in place. Until recently, for example, the risk of acts of terror taking was low compared with the vast cost anticipated should they occur. However, the risk of flooding is usually low, so it could be argued that the costs associated with anti-flooding measures would have been pre-emptively unreasonable. Should the Government be expected to prepare for every conceivable threat that could come to pass? Are we to put in place expensive measures against a seismic event as well as a possible extra-terrestrial invasion?

Which of the following best expresses the main conclusion of the statement above?
A. The Government has an obligation to assess risks and costs of possible future events.
B. The Government should spend money to protect against potential extra-terrestrial invasions and seismic events.
C. The Government should have spent money to protect against potential floods.
D. The Government was justified in not spending heavily to protect against flooding.
E. The Government should assist people who lost their homes in the floods.

Question 16:
Sadly the way in which children interact with each other has changed over the years. Where once children used to play sports and games together in the street, they now sit alone in their rooms on the computer playing games on the Internet. Where in the past young children learned human interaction from active games with their friends this is no longer the case. How then, when these children are grown up, will they be able to socially interact with their colleagues?

Which one of the following is the conclusion of the above statement?
A. Children who play computer games now interact less outside of them.
B. The Internet can be a tool for teaching social skills.
C. Computer games are for social development.
D. Children should be made to play outside with their friends to develop their social skills for later in life.
E. Adults will in the future play computer games as a means of interaction.

Question 17:
Between 2006 and 2013 the British government spent £473 million on Tamiflu antiviral drugs in preparation for a flu pandemic, despite there being little evidence to support the effectiveness of the drug. The antivirals were stockpiled for a flu pandemic that never fully materialised. Only 150,000 packs were used during the swine flu episode in 2009, and it is unclear if this improved outcomes. Therefore this money could have been much better spent on drugs that would actually benefit patients.

Which option best summarises the author's view in the passage?
A. Drugs should never be stockpiled, as they may not be used.
B. Spending millions of pounds on drugs should be justified by strong evidence showing positive effects.
C. We should not prepare for flu pandemics in the future.
D. The recipients of Tamiflu in the swine flu pandemic had no difference in symptoms or outcomes to patients who did not receive the antivirals.

Question 18:
High BMI and particularly central weight are risk factors associated with increased morbidity and mortality. Many believe the development of cheap, easily accessible fast-food outlets is partly responsible for the increase in rates of obesity. An unhealthy weight is commonly associated with a generally unhealthy lifestyle, such a lack of exercise. The best way to tackle the growing problem of obesity is for the government to tax unhealthy foods so they are no longer a cheap alternative.

Why is the solution given, to tax unhealthy foods, not a logical conclusion from the passage?
A. Unhealthy eating is not exclusively confined to low-income families.
B. A more general approach to unhealthy lifestyles would be optimal.
C. People do not only choose to eat unhealthy food because it is cheaper.
D. People need to take personal responsibility for their own health.

Question 19:
As people are living longer, care in old age is becoming a larger burden. Many people require carers to come into their home numerous times a day or need full residential care. It is not right that the NHS should be spending vast funds on the care of people who are sufficiently wealthy to fund their own care. Some argue that they want their savings kept to give to their children; however this is not a right, simply a luxury. It is not right that people should be saving and depriving themselves of necessary care, or worse, making the NHS pay the bill, so they have money to pass on to their offspring. People need to realise that there is a financial cost to living longer.

Which of the following statements is the main conclusion of the above passage?
A. We need to take a personal responsibility for our care in old age.
B. Caring for the elderly is a significant burden on the NHS.
C. The reason people are reluctant to pay for their own care is that they want to pass money onto their offspring.
D. The NHS should limit care to the elderly to reduce their costs.
E. People shouldn't save their money for old age.

Question 20:
There is much interest in research surrounding production of human stem cells from non-embryo sources for potential regenerative medicine, and a huge financial and personal gain at stake. In January 2014, a team from Japan published two papers in *Nature* that claimed to have developed totipotent stem cells from adult mouse cells by exposure to an acidic environment. However, there has since been much controversy surrounding these papers. Problems included: inability by other teams to replicate the results of the experiment, an insufficient protocol described in the paper and issues with images in one of the papers. It was dishonest of the researchers to publish the papers with such problems, and a requirement of a paper is a sufficiently detailed protocol, so that another group could replicate the experiment.

Which statement is most implied?
A. Research is fuelled mainly by financial and personal gains.
B. The researchers should take responsibility for publishing the paper with such flaws.
C. Rivalry between different research groups makes premature publishing more likely.
D. The discrepancies were in only one of the papers published in January 2014.

Question 21:
The placebo effect is a well-documented medical phenomenon in which a patient's condition undergoes improvement after being given an ineffectual treatment that they believe to be a genuine treatment. It is frequently used as a control during trials of new drugs/procedures, with the effect of the drug being compared to the effect of a placebo, and if the drug does not have a greater effect than the placebo, then it is classed as ineffective. However, this analysis discounts the fact that the drug treatment still has more of a positive effect than no action, and so we are clearly missing out on the potential to improve certain patient conditions. It follows that where there is a demonstrated placebo effect, but treatments are ineffective, we should still give treatments, as there will therefore be some benefit to the patient.

Which of the following best expresses the main conclusion of this passage?
- A. In situations where drugs are no more effective than a placebo, we should still give drugs, as they will be more effective than not taking action.
- B. Our current analysis discounts the fact that even if drug treatments have no more effect than a placebo, they may still be more effective than no action.
- C. The placebo effect is a well-recognised medical phenomenon.
- D. Drug treatments may have negative side effects that outweigh their benefit to patients.
- E. Placebos are better than modern drugs.

Question 22:
The speed limit on motorways and dual carriageways has been 70mph since 1965, but this is an out-dated policy and needs to change. Since 1965, car brakes have become much more effective, and many safety features have been introduced into cars, such as seatbelts (which are now compulsory to wear), crumple zones and airbags. Therefore, it is clear that cars no longer need to be restricted to 70mph, and the speed limit can be safely increased to 80mph without causing more road fatalities.

Which of the following best illustrates an assumption in this passage?
- A. The government should increase the speed limit to 80mph.
- B. If the speed limit were increased to 80mph, drivers would not begin to drive at 90mph.
- C. The safety systems introduced reduce the chances of fatal road accidents for cars travelling at higher speeds.
- D. The roads have not become busier since the 70mph speed limit was introduced.
- E. The public want the speed limit to increase.

Question 23:
Despite the overwhelming scientific proof of the theory of evolution, and even acceptance of the theory by many high-ranking religious ministers, there are still sections of many major religions that do not accept evolution as true. One of the most prominent of these in western society is the Intelligent Design movement, which promotes the religious-based (and scientifically discredited) notion of Intelligent Design as a scientific theory. Intelligent Design proponents often point to complex issues of biology as proof that god is behind the design of human beings, much as a watchmaker is inherent in the design of a watch.

One part of anatomy that has been identified as supposedly supporting Intelligent Design is fingerprints, with some proponents arguing that they are a mark of individualism created by God, with no apparent function except to identify each human being as unique. This is incorrect, as fingerprints do have a well documented function – namely channelling away of water to improve grip in wet conditions – in which hairless, smooth skinned hands otherwise struggle to grip smooth objects. The individualism of fingerprints is accounted for by the complexity of thousands of small grooves. Development is inherently affected by stochastic or random processes, meaning that the body is unable to uniformly control its development to ensure that fingerprints are the same in each human being. Clearly, the presence of individual fingerprints does nothing to support the so-called-theory of Intelligent Design.

Which of the following best illustrates the main conclusion of this passage?
A. Fingerprints have a well-established function.
B. Evolution is supported by overwhelming scientific proof.
C. Fingerprints do not offer any support to the notion of Intelligent Design.
D. The individual nature of fingerprints is explained by stochastic processes inherent in development that the body cannot uniformly control.
E. Intelligent design is a credible and scientifically rigorous theory.

Question 24:
High levels of alcohol consumption are proven to increase the risk of many non-infectious diseases, such as cancer, atherosclerosis and liver failure. James is a PhD student, and is analysing the data from a large-scale study of over 500,000 people to further investigate the link between heavy alcohol consumption and health problems. In the study, participants were asked about their alcohol consumption, and then their medical history was recorded. His analysis displays surprising results, concluding that those with high alcohol consumption have a *decreased* risk of cancer. James decides that those carrying out the study must have incorrectly recorded the data.

Which of the following is **NOT** a potential reason why the study has produced these surprising results?
A. Previous studies were incorrect, and high alcohol consumption does lower the risk of cancer.
B. The studies didn't take account of other cancer risk factors in comparing those with high and low alcohol consumption.
C. James has made some errors in his analysis, and thus his conclusions are erroneous.
D. The participants involved in the study did not truthfully report their alcohol consumption, leading to false conclusions being drawn.
E. The studies control group data was mixed up with the test group data.

SECTION 1A: CRITICAL THINKING — QUESTIONS

Question 25:
A train is scheduled to depart from Newcastle at 3:30pm. It stops at Durham, Darlington, York, Sheffield, Peterborough and Stevenage before arriving at Kings Cross station in London, where the train completes its journey. The total length of the journey between Newcastle and Kings Cross was 230 miles, and the average speed of the train during the journey (including time spent stood still at calling stations) is 115mph. Therefore, the train will complete its journey at 5:30pm.

Which of the following is an assumption made in this passage?
A. The various stopping points did not increase the time taken to complete the journey.
B. The train left Newcastle on time.
C. The train travelled by the most direct route available.
D. The train was due to end its journey at Kings Cross.
E. There were no signalling problems encountered on the journey.

Question 26:
There have been many arguments over the last couple of decades about government expenditure on healthcare in the various devolved regions of the UK. It is often argued that, since spending on healthcare per person is higher in Scotland than in England, that therefore the people in Scotland will be healthier. However, this view fails to take account of the different needs of these 2 populations of the UK. For example, one major factor is that Scotland gets significantly colder than England, and cold weakens the immune system, leaving people in Scotland at much higher risk of infectious disease. Thus, Scotland requires higher levels of healthcare spending per person simply to maintain the health of the populace at a similar level to that of England.

Which of the following is a conclusion that can be drawn from this passage?
A. The higher healthcare spending per person in Scotland does not necessarily mean people living in Scotland are healthier.
B. Healthcare spending should be increased across the UK.
C. Wales requires more healthcare spending per person simply to maintain population health at a similar level to England.
D. It is unfair on England that there is more spending on healthcare per person in Scotland.
E. Scotland's healthcare budget is a controversial topic.

Question 27:
Vaccinations have been hugely successful in reducing the incidence of several diseases throughout the 20th century. One of the most spectacular achievements was arguably the global eradication of Smallpox, once a deadly worldwide killer, during the 1970s. Fortunately, there was a highly effective vaccine available for Smallpox, and a major factor in its eradication was an aggressive vaccination campaign. Another disease that is potentially eradicable is Polio. However, although there is a highly effective vaccine for Polio available, attempts to eradicate it have so far been unsuccessful. It follows that we should plan and execute an aggressive vaccination campaign for Polio, in order to ensure that this disease too is eradicated.

Which of the following is the main conclusion of this passage?
A. Polio is a potentially eradicable disease.
B. An aggressive vaccination campaign was a major factor in the eradication of smallpox.
C. Both Polio and smallpox have been eradicated by effective vaccination campaigns.
D. We should execute an aggressive vaccination campaign for Polio.
E. The eradication of smallpox remains one of the most spectacular achievements of medical science.

SECTION 1A: CRITICAL THINKING — QUESTIONS

Question 28:
The Y chromosome is one of 2 sex chromosomes found in the human genome, the other being the X chromosome. As the Y chromosome is only found in males, it can only be passed from father to son. Additionally, the Y chromosome does not exchange sections with other chromosomes (as happens with most chromosomes), meaning it is passed on virtually unchanged through the generations. All of this makes the Y chromosome a fantastic tool for genetic analysis, both to identify individual lineages and to investigate historic population movements. One famous achievement of genetic research using the Y chromosome provides further evidence of its utility, namely the identification of Genghis Khan as a descendant of up to 8% of males in 16 populations across Asia.

Which of the following best illustrates the main conclusion of this passage?
A. The Y chromosome is a fantastic tool for genetic analysis.
B. Research using the Y chromosome has been able to identify Genghis Khan as the descendant of up to 8% of men in many Asian populations.
C. The Y chromosome does not exchange sections with other chromosomes.
D. The Y chromosome is a sex chromosome.
E. Genghis Khan had a staggering number of children.

Question 29:
In order for a bacterial infection to be cleared, a patient must be treated with antibiotics. Rachel has a minor lung infection, which is thought by her doctor to be a bacterial infection. She is treated with antibiotics, but her condition does not improve. Therefore, it must not be a bacterial infection.

Which of the following best illustrates a flaw in this reasoning?
A. It assumes that a bacterial infection would definitely improve after treatment with antibiotics.
B. It ignores the other potential issues that could be treated by antibiotics.
C. It assumes that antibiotics are necessary to treat bacterial infections.
D. It ignores the actions of the immune system, which may be sufficient to clear the infection regardless of what has caused it.
E. It assumes that antibiotics are the only option to treat a bacterial infection.

Question 30:
The link between smoking and lung cancer has been well established for many decades by overwhelming numbers of studies and conclusive research. The answer is clear and simple, that the single best measure that can be taken to avoid lung cancer is to not smoke, or to stop smoking if one has already started. However, despite the overwhelming evidence and clear answers, many smokers continue to smoke, and seek to minimise their risk of lung cancer by focusing on other, less important risk factors, such as exercise and healthy eating. This approach is obviously severely flawed, and the fact that some smokers feel this is a good way to reduce their risk of lung cancer shows that they are delusional.

Which of the following best illustrates the main conclusion of this passage?
A. Many smokers ignore the largest risk factor, and focus on improving less important risk factors by eating healthily and exercising.
B. Some smokers are delusional.
C. The biggest risk factor of lung cancer is smoking.
D. Overwhelming studies have proven the link between smoking and lung cancer.
E. The government should ban smoking in order to reduce the incidence of lung cancer.

SECTION 1A: CRITICAL THINKING — QUESTIONS

Question 31:
The government should invest more money into outreach schemes in order to encourage more people to go to university. These schemes allow students to meet other people who went to university, which they may not always be able to do otherwise, even on open days.

Which of the following is the best conclusion of the above argument?
A. Outreach schemes are the best way to encourage people to go to university.
B. People will not go to university without seeing it first.
C. The government wants more people to go to university.
D. Meeting people who went to a university is a more effective method than university open days.
E. It is easier to meet people on outreach schemes than on open days.

Question 32:
The illegal drug cannabis was recently upgraded from a class C drug to class B, which means it will be taken less in the UK, because people will know it is more dangerous. It also means if people are caught, possessing the drug they will face a longer prison sentence than before, which will also discourage its use.

Which **TWO** statements if true, most weaken the above argument?
A. Class C drugs are cheaper than class B drugs.
B. Upgrading drugs in other countries has not reduced their use.
C. People who take illegal drugs do not know what class they are.
D. Cannabis was not the only class C drug before it was upgraded.
E. Even if they are caught possessing class B drugs, people do not think they will go to prison.

Question 33:
Schools with better sports programmes such as well-performing football and netball teams tend to have better academic results, less bullying and have overall happier students. Thus, if we want schools to have the best results, reduce bullying and increase student happiness, teachers should start more sports clubs.

Which one of the following best demonstrates a flaw in the above argument?
A. Teachers may be too busy to start sports clubs.
B. Better academic results may be a precondition of better sports teams.
C. Better sports programmes may prevent students from spending time with their family.
D. Some sports teams may be seen to encourage internal bullying.
E. Sport teams that do not perform well lead to increase bulling.

Question 34:
The legal age for purchasing alcohol in the UK is 18. This should be lowered to 16 because the majority of 16 year olds drink alcohol anyway without any fear of repercussions. Even if the police catch a 16-year-old buying alcohol, they are unable to enforce any consequences. If the drinking limit was lowered the police could spend less time trying to catch underage drinkers and deal with other more important crimes. There is no evidence to suggest that drinking alcohol at 16 is any more dangerous than at 18.

Which one of the following, if true, most weakens the above argument?
A. Most 16 year olds do not drink alcohol.
B. If the legal drinking age were lowered to 16, more 15 year olds would start purchasing alcohol.
C. Most 16 year olds do not have enough money to buy alcohol.
D. Most 16 year olds are able to purchase alcohol currently.

Question 35:

There has been a recent change in the way the government helps small businesses. Whilst previously small businesses were given non-repayable grants to help them grow their profits, they can now only receive government loans that must be repaid with interest when the business turns a certain amount of profit. The government wants to support small businesses but studies have shown they are less likely to prosper under the new scheme as they have been deterred from taking government money for fear of loan repayments.

Which one of the following can be concluded from the passage above?

A. Small businesses do not want government money.
B. The government cannot afford to give out grants to small businesses anymore.
C. All businesses avoid accumulating debt.
D. The action of the government is more likely to do more harm than good to small businesses.
E. Big businesses do not need government money.

SECTION 1A: CRITICAL THINKING QUESTIONS

Questions 36-41 are based on the passage below:

Despite the numerous safety measures in place within the practice of medicine, these can fail when the weaknesses in the layers of defence aligns to create a clear path leading to often disastrous results. This is known as the 'Swiss cheese model of accident causation'. One such occurrence occurred where the wrong kidney was removed from a patient due to a failure in the line of defences designed to prevent such an incident occurring.

When a kidney is diseased it is removed to prevent further complications, this operation, a 'nephrectomy', is regularly performed by experienced surgeons. Where normally the consultant who knew the patient would have conducted the procedure, in this case he passed the responsibility to his registrar, who was also well experienced but had not met the patient previously. The person who had copied out the patient's notes had poor handwriting had accidentally written the 'R' for 'right' in such a way that it was read as an 'L' and subsequently copied, and not noticed by anyone who further reviewed the notes.

The patient had been put asleep before the registrar had arrived and so he proceeded without checking the procedure with the patient, as he normally would have done. The nurses present noticed this error but said nothing, fearing repercussions for questioning a senior professional. A medical student was present whom, having met the patient previously in clinical, tried to alert the registrar to the mistake he was about to make. The registrar shouted at the student that she should not interrupt surgery; she did not know what she was talking about and asked her to leave. Consequently the surgery proceeded with the end result being that the patient's healthy left kidney was removed, leaving them with only their diseased right kidney, which would eventually lead to the patient's unfortunate death. Frightening as these cases appear what is perhaps scarier is the thought of how those reported may be just the 'tip of the iceberg'.

When questioned about his action to allow his registrar to perform the surgery alone, the consultant had said that it was normal to allow capable registrars to do this. 'While the public perception is that medical knowledge steadily increases over time, this is not the case with many doctors reaching their peak in the middle of their careers.' He had found that his initial increasing interest in surgery had enhanced his abilities, but with time and practice the similar surgeries had become less exciting and so his lack of interest had correlated with worsening outcomes, thus justifying his decision to devolve responsibility in this case.

Question 36:
Which of the following, if true, most weakens the argument above?

A. If incidences are severe enough to occur they will be reported.
B. Doctors undergo extensive training to reduce risks.
C. Thousand of operations happen every year with no problems.
D. Some errors are unavoidable.
E. The patient could have passed away even if the operation had been a complete success.

Question 37:
Which one of the following is the overall conclusion of the statement?

A. The error that occurred was a result of the failure of safety precautions in place.
B. Surgeries should only be performed by surgeons who know their patients well.
C. The human element to medicine means errors will always occur.
D. The safety procedures surrounding surgical procedures need to be reviewed.
E. Some doctors are overconfident.

SECTION 1A: CRITICAL THINKING — QUESTIONS

Question 38:
Which of the following is attributed as the original cause of the error?

A. The medical student not having asserted herself.
B. The poor handwriting in the chart.
C. The hierarchical system of medicine.
D. The registrar not having met the patient.
E. The patient being asleep.
F. The lack of the surgical skill possessed by the registrar.
G. The registrar's poor attitude.

Question 39:
What does the 'tip of the iceberg' refer to in the passage?

A. Problems we face every day.
B. The probable large numbers of medical errors that go unreported.
C. The difficulties of surgery.
D. Reported medical errors.
E. Problems within the NHS.

You may use the graphs below once, more than once, or not at all.

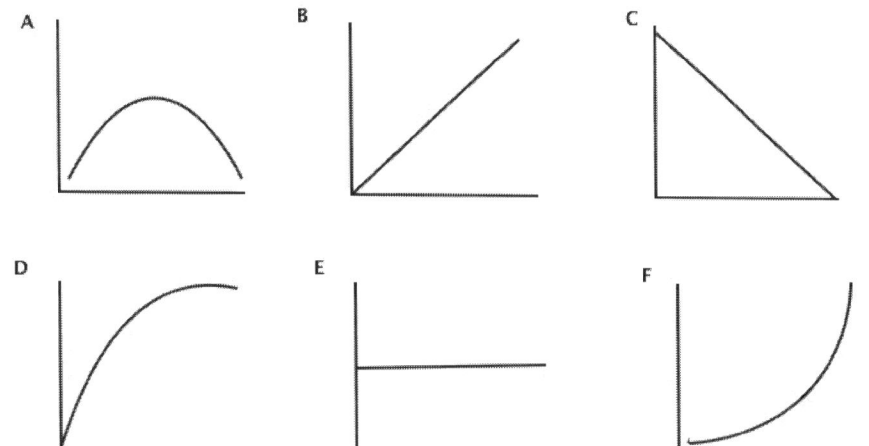

Question 40:
Which graph best describes the consultants' performance versus emotional arousal over his career?

A. A B. B C. C D. D E. E F. F

Question 41:
Which graphs best describe the medical knowledge acquired over time?

Option	Public Perception	Consultant's Perception
A	B	B
B	B	D
C	B	F
D	D	B
E	D	D
F	D	F
G	F	B
H	F	D
I	F	F

SECTION 1A: CRITICAL THINKING — QUESTIONS

Question 42:
Sadly, in recent times, the lack of exercise associated with sedentary lifestyles has increased in the developed world. The lack of opportunity for exercise is endemic and these countries have also seen a rise of diseases such as diabetes even in young people. In these developed countries, bodily changes such as increased blood pressure, that are usually associated with old age, are rapidly increasing. These are however still uncommon in undeveloped countries, where most people are physically active throughout the entirety of their lives.

Which one of the following can be concluded from the passage above?
A. Exercise has a greater effect on old people than young people.
B. Maintenance of good health is associated with lifelong exercise.
C. Changes in lifestyle will be necessary to cause increased life expectancies in developed countries.
D. Exercise is only beneficial when continued into old age.
E. Obesity and diabetes are the result of lack of exercise.

Questions 43 - 45 are based on the passage below:
'Midwives should now encourage women to, as often as possible, give birth at home. Not only is there evidence to suggest that normal births at home are as safe those as in hospital, but it removes the medicalisation of childbirth that emerged over the years. With the increase in availability of health resources we now, too often, use services such as a full medical team for a process that women have been completing single-handedly for thousands of years. Midwives are extensively trained to assist women during labour at home and capable enough to assess when there is a problem that requires a hospital environment. Expensive hospital births must and should move away from being standard practice, especially in an era where the NHS has far more demands on its services that it can currently afford.'

Question 43:
Which one of the following is the most appropriate conclusion from the statement?
A. People are over dependent on healthcare.
B. Some women prefer to have their babies in hospital.
C. Having a baby in hospital can actually be more risky than at home.
D. Childbirth has been over medicalised.
E. Encouraging women to have their babies at home may relieve some of the financial pressures on the NHS.
F. We should have more midwives than doctors.

Question 44:
Which one of the following if true most weakens the argument presented in the passage above?
A. Some women are scared of home births.
B. Home births are associated with poorer outcomes.
C. Midwives do not like performing home visits.
D. Some home births result in hospital births anyway.

Question 45:
Which one of the following describes what the statement cites as the cause for the 'medicalisation of childbirth'?
A. Women fear giving birth without a full medical team present.
B. Midwives are incapable of aiding childbirth without help.
C. Giving birth at home is not as safe as it used to be.
D. Excessive availability of health services.
E. Women only used to give birth at home because they could not do so at hospital.

SECTION 1A: CRITICAL THINKING — QUESTIONS

Question 46:
We need to stop focussing so much attention on the dangers of fires. In 2011 there were only 242 deaths due to exposure to smoke, fire and flames, while there were 997 deaths from hernias. We need to think more proportionally as these statistics show that campaigns such as 'fire kills' are not necessary as comparison with the risk from the death from hernias clearly shows that fires are not as dangerous as they are perceived to be.

Which of the following statements identify a weakness in the above argument?
1. More people may die in fires if there were no campaigns about their danger and how to prevent them.
2. The smoke of a fire is more dangerous than it flames.
3. There may be more people with hernias than those in fires.

A. 1 only
B. 2 only
C. 3 only
D. 1 and 2 only
E. 1 and 3 only
F. 2 and 3 only
G. 1, 2 and 3

Question 47:
A survey of a school was taken to find out whether there was any correlation between the sports students played and the subjects they liked. The findings were as follows: some football players liked Maths and some of them liked History. All students liked English. None of the basketball players liked History, but all of them, as well as some rugby players liked Chemistry. All rugby players like Geography.

Based on the findings, which one of the below must be true?
A. Some of the footballers liked Maths and History.
B. Some of the rugby players liked three subjects.
C. Some rugby players liked History.
D. Some of the footballers liked English but did not like Maths and History.
E. Some basketball players like more than 3 subjects.

Question 48:
The control of illegal drug use is becoming increasingly difficult. New 'legal highs' are being manufactured which are slightly changed molecularly from illegal compounds so they are not technically illegal. These new 'legal drugs' are being brought onto the street at a rate of at least one per week, and so the authorities cannot keep up. Some health professionals therefore believe that the legality of drugs is becoming less relevant as to the potentially dangerous side effects. The fact that these new compounds are legal may however mean that the public are not aware of their equally high risks.

Which of the following are implied by the argument?
1. Some health professionals believe there is no value in making drugs illegal.
2. The major problem in controlling illegal drug use is the rapid manufacture of new drugs that are not classified as illegal.
3. The general public are not worried about the risks of legal or illegal highs.
4. There is no longer a good correlation between risk of drug taking and the legal status of the drug.

A. 1 only
B. 2 only
C. 1 and 4
D. 2 and 4
E. 2 and 3
F. 1,2,3 and 4

SECTION 1A: CRITICAL THINKING — QUESTIONS

Question 49:
WilderTravel Inc. is a company which organises wilderness travel holidays, with activities such as trekking, mountain climbing, safari tours and wilderness survival courses. These activities carry inherent risks, so the directors of the company are drawing up a set of health regulations, with the aim of minimising the risks by ensuring that nobody participates in activities if they have medical complications meaning that doing so may endanger them. They consider the following guidelines:

'Persons with pacemakers, asthma or severe allergies are at significant risk of heart attack in low oxygen environments'. People undertaking mountain climbing activities with WilderTravel frequently encounter environments with low oxygen levels. The directors therefore decide that in order to ensure the safety of customers on WilderTravel holidays, one step that must be taken is to bar those with pacemakers, asthma or allergies from partaking in mountain climbing.

Which of the following best illustrates a flaw in this reasoning?

A. Participants should be allowed to assess the safety risks themselves, and should not be barred from activities if they decide the risk is acceptable.
B. They have assumed that all allergies carry an increased risk of heart attack, when the guidelines only say this applies to those with severe allergies.
C. The directors have failed to consider the health risks of people with these conditions taking part in other activities.
D. People with these conditions could partake in mountain climbing with other holiday organisers, and thus be exposed to danger of heart attack.

Question 50:
St John's Hospital in Northumbria is looking to recruit a new consultant cardiologist, and interviews a series of candidates. The interview panel determines that 3 candidates are clearly more qualified for the role than the others, and they invite these 3 candidates for a second interview. During this second interview, and upon further examination of their previous employment records, it becomes apparent that Candidate 3 is the most proficient at surgery of the 3, whilst Candidate 1 is the best at patient interaction and explaining the risks of procedures. Candidate 2, meanwhile, ranks between the other 2 in both these aspects.

The hospital director tells the interviewing team that the hospital already has a well-renowned team dedicated to patient interaction, but the surgical success record at the hospital is in need of improvement. The director issues instructions that therefore, it is more important that the new candidate is proficient at surgery, and patient interaction is less of a concern.

Which of the following is a conclusion that can be drawn from the Directors' comments?

A. The interviewing team should hire Candidate 2, in order to achieve a balance of good patient relations with good surgical records.
B. The interviewing team should hire Candidate 1, in order to ensure good patient interactions, as these are a vital part of a doctor's work.
C. The interviewing team should ignore the hospital director and assess the candidates further to see who would be the best fit.
D. The interviewing team should hire Candidate 3, in order to ensure that the new candidate has excellent surgical skills, to boost the hospital's success in this area.

SECTION 1A: CRITICAL THINKING — QUESTIONS

Question 51:

Every winter in Britain, there are thousands of urgent callouts for ambulances in snowy conditions. The harsh conditions mean that ambulances cannot drive quickly, and are delayed in reaching patients. These delays cause many injuries and medical complications, which could be avoided with quicker access to treatment. Despite this, very few ambulances are equipped with winter tyres or special tyre coverings to help the ambulances deal with snow. Clearly, if more ambulances were fitted with winter tyres, then we could avoid many medical complications that occur each winter.

Which of the following is an assumption made in this passage?
A. Fitting winter tyres would allow ambulances to reach patients more quickly.
B. Ambulance trusts have sufficient funding to equip their vehicles with winter tyres.
C. Many medical complications could be avoided with quicker access to medical care.
D. There are no other alternatives to winter tyres that would allow ambulances to reach patients more quickly in snowy conditions.

Question 52:

Vaccinations have been one of the most outstanding and influential developments in medical history. Despite the huge successes, however, there is a strong anti-vaccination movement active in some countries, particularly the USA, who claim vaccines are harmful and ineffective.

There have been several high-profile events in recent years where anti-vaccine campaigners have been refused permission to enter countries for campaigns, or have had venues refuse to host them due to the nature of their campaigns. Many anti-vaccination campaigners have claimed this is an affront to free speech, and that they should be allowed to enter countries and obtain venues without hindrance. However, although free speech is desirable, an exception must be made here because the anti-vaccination campaign spreads misinformation to parents, causing vaccination to rates to drop.

When this happens, preventable infectious diseases often begin to increase, causing avoidable deaths of innocent members of the community, particularly so in children. Thus, in order to protect innocent people, we must continue to block the anti-vaccine campaigners from spreading misinformation freely by pressuring venues not to host anti-vaccination campaigners.

Which of the following best illustrates the principle that this argument follows?
A. Free speech is always desirable, and must not be compromised under any circumstances.
B. The right of innocent people to protection from infectious diseases is more important than the right of free speech.
C. The right of free speech does not apply when the party speaking is lying or spreading misinformation.
D. Public health programmes that achieve significant success in reducing the incidence of disease should be promoted.

Question 53:

In order for a tumour to grow larger than a few centimetres, it must first establish its own blood supply by promoting angiogenesis. Roger has a tumour in his abdomen, which is investigated at the Royal General Hospital. During the tests, they detect newly formed blood vessels in the tumour, showing that it has established its own blood supply. Thus, we should expect the tumour to grow significantly, and become larger than a few centimetres. Action must be taken to deal with this.

Which of the following best illustrates a flaw in this reasoning?
A. It assumes that the tumour in Roger's abdomen has established its own blood supply.
B. It assumes that a blood supply is necessary for a tumour to grow larger than a few centimetres.
C. It assumes that nothing can be done to stop the tumour once a blood supply has been established.
D. It assumes that a blood supply is sufficient for the tumour to grow larger than a few centimetres.

Question 54:

In this year's Great North Run, there are several dozen people running to raise money for the Great North Air Ambulance (GNAA), as part of a large national fundraising campaign. If the runners raise £500,000 between them, then the GNAA will be able to add a new helicopter to its fleet. However, the runners only raise a total of £420,000. Thus, the GNAA will not be able to get a new helicopter.

Which of the following best illustrates a flaw in this passage?
A. It has assumed that the GNAA will not be able to acquire a new helicopter without the runners raising £500,000.
B. It has assumed that that GNAA wishes to add a new helicopter to its fleet.
C. It has assumed that the GNAA does not have better things to spend the money on.
D. It has assumed that some running in the Great North Run are raising money for the GNAA.

Question 55:

Many courses, spanning Universities, colleges, apprenticeship institutions and adult skills courses should be subsidised by the government. This is because they improve the skills of those attending them. It has been well demonstrated that the more skilled people are, the more productive they are economically. Thus, government subsidies of many courses would increase overall economic productivity, and lead to increased growth.

Which of the following would most weaken this argument?
A. The UK already has a high level of growth, and does not need to accelerate this growth.
B. Research has demonstrated that higher numbers of people attending adult skills courses results in increased economic growth.
C. Research has demonstrated that the cost of many courses (to those taking them) has little effect on the number of people undertaking the courses.
D. Employers often seek to employ those with greater skill-sets, and appoint them to higher positions.

Question 56:

Pluto was once considered the 9th planet in the solar system. However, further study of the planet led to it being reclassified as a dwarf planet in 2006. One key factor in this reclassification was the discovery of many objects in the solar system with similar characteristics to Pluto, which were also placed into this new category of 'Dwarf Planet'. Some astronomers believe that Pluto should remain classified as a planet, along with the many entities similar to Pluto that have been discovered. Considering all of this, it is clear that if we were to reclassify Pluto as a planet, and maintain consistency with classification of astronomical entities, then the number of planets would significantly increase.

Which of the following best illustrates the main conclusion of this passage?
A. If Pluto is classified as a planet, then many other entities should also be planets, as they share similar characteristics.
B. Some astronomers believe Pluto should be classified as a planet.
C. Pluto should not be classified as a Planet, as this would also require many other entities to be classified as planets to ensure consistency.
D. If Pluto is to be classified as a planet, then the number of objects classified as planets should increase significantly.

SECTION 1A: CRITICAL THINKING — QUESTIONS

Question 57:
2 trains depart from Birmingham at 5:30 pm. One of the trains is heading to London, whilst the other is heading to Glasgow. The distance from Birmingham to Glasgow is three times larger than the distance from Birmingham to London, and the train to London arrives at 6:30 pm. Thus, the train to Glasgow will arrive at 8:30pm.

Which of the following is an assumption made in this passage?
A. Both trains depart at the same time.
B. Both trains depart from Birmingham.
C. Both trains travel at the same speed.
D. The train heading to Glasgow has to travel three times as far as the train heading to London.

Question 58:
Carcinogenesis, oncogenesis and tumorigenesis are various names given to the generation of cancer, with the term literally meaning 'creation of cancer'. In order for carcinogenesis to happen, there are several steps that must occur. Firstly, a cell (or group of cells) must achieve immortality, and escape senescence (the inherent limitation of a cell's lifespan). Then they must escape regulation by the body, and begin to proliferate in an autonomous way. They must also become immune to apoptosis and other cell death mechanisms. Finally, they must avoid detection by the immune system, or survive its responses. If a single one of these steps fails to occur, then carcinogenesis will not be able to occur.

Which of the following is a conclusion that can be reliably drawn from this passage?
A. Several steps are essential for carcinogenesis.
B. If all the steps mentioned occur, then carcinogenesis will definitely occur.
C. The immune system is unable to tackle cells that have escaped regulation by the body.
D. There are various mechanisms by which carcinogenesis can occur.
E. The terminology for the creation of cancer is confusing.

Question 59:
P53 is one of the most crucial genes in the body, responsible for detecting DNA damage and halting cell replication until repair can occur. If repair cannot take place, P53 will signal for the cell to kill itself. These actions are crucial to prevent carcinogenesis, and a loss of functional P53 is identified in over 50% of all cancers. The huge importance of P53 towards protecting the cell from damaging mutations has led to it deservedly being known as 'the guardian of the genome'. The implications of this name are clear – any cell that has a mutation in P53 is at serious risk of developing a potentially dangerous mutation.

Which of the following **CANNOT** be reliably concluded from this passage?
A. P53 is responsible for detecting DNA damage.
B. Most cancers have lost functional P53.
C. P53 deserves its name 'guardian of the genome'.
D. A cell that has a mutation in P53 will develop damaging mutations.
E. None of the above.

SECTION 1A: CRITICAL THINKING — QUESTIONS

Question 60:
Sam is buying a new car, and deciding whether to buy a petrol or a diesel model. He knows he will drive 9,000 miles each year. He calculates that if he drives a petrol car, he will spend £500 per 1,000 miles on fuel, but if he buys a diesel model he will only spend £300 per 1,000 miles on fuel. He calculates, therefore, that if he purchases a Diesel car, then this year he will make a saving of £1800, compared to if he bought the petrol car.

Which of the following is **NOT** an assumption that Sam has made?
A. The price of diesel will not fluctuate relative to that of petrol.
B. The cars will have the same initial purchase cost.
C. The cars will have the same costs for maintenance and garage expenses.
D. The cars will use the same amount of fuel.
E. All of the above are assumptions.

Question 61:
In the UK, cannabis is classified as a Class B drug, with a maximum penalty of up to 5 years imprisonment for possession, or up to 14 years for possession with intent to supply. The justification for drug laws in the UK is that classified drugs are harmful, addictive, and destructive to people's lives. However, available medical evidence indicates that cannabis is relatively safe, non-addictive and harmless. In particular, it is certainly shown to be less dangerous than alcohol, which is freely sold and advertised in the UK. The fact that alcohol can be freely sold and advertised, but cannabis, a less harmful drug, is banned highlights the gross inconsistencies in UK drugs policy.

Which of the following best illustrates the main conclusion of this passage?
A. Cannabis is a less dangerous drug than alcohol.
B. Alcohol should be banned, so we can ensure consistency in the UK drug policy.
C. Cannabis should not be banned, and should be sold freely, in order to ensure consistency in the UK drug policy.
D. The UK government's policy on drugs is grossly inconsistent.
E. Alcohol should not be advertised in the UK.

Question 62:
Every year in Britain, there are thousands of accidents at people's homes such as burns, broken limbs and severe cuts, which cause a large number of deaths and injuries. Despite this, very few households maintain a sufficient first aid kit equipped with bandages, burn treatments, splints and saline to clean wounds. If more households stocked sufficient first aid supplies, many of these accidents could be avoided.

Which of the following best illustrates a flaw in this argument?
A. It ignores the huge cost associated with maintaining good first aid supplies, which many households cannot afford.
B. It implies that presence of first aid equipment will lead to fewer accidents.
C. It ignores the many accidents that could not be treated even if first aid supplies were readily available.
D. It neglects to consider the need for trained first aid persons in order for first aid supplies to help in reducing the severity of injuries caused by accidents.

Question 63:
Researchers at SmithJones Inc., an international drug firm, are investigating a well-known historic compound, which is thought to reduce levels of DNA replication by inhibiting DNA polymerases. It is proposed that this may be able to be used to combat cancer by reducing the proliferation of cancer cells, allowing the immune system to combat them before they spread too far and become too damaging. Old experiments have demonstrated the effectiveness of the compound via monitoring DNA levels with a dye that stains DNA red, thus monitoring the levels of DNA present in cell clusters. They report that the compound is observed to reduce the rate at which DNA replicates. However, it is known that if researchers use the wrong solutions when carrying out these experiments, then the amount of red staining will decrease, suggesting DNA replication has been inhibited, even if it is not inhibited. As several researchers previously used this wrong solution, we can conclude that these experiments are flawed, and do not reflect what is actually happening.

Which of the following best illustrates a flaw in this argument?
A. From the fact that the compound inhibits DNA replication, it cannot be concluded that it has potential as an anticancer drug.
B. From the fact that the wrong solutions were used, it cannot be concluded that the experiments may produce misleading results.
C. From the fact that the experiments are old, it cannot be concluded that the wrong solutions were used.
D. From the fact that the compound is old, it cannot be concluded that it is safe.

Question 64:
Rotherham football club are currently top of the league, with 90 points. Their closest competitors are South Shields football club, with 84 points. Next week, the teams will play each other, and after this, they each have 2 games left before the end of the season. Each win is worth 3 points, a draw is worth 1 point, and a loss is worth 0 points. Thus, if Rotherham beat South Shields, they will win the league (as they will then be 9 points clear, and South Shields would only be able to earn 6 more points).

In the match of Rotherham vs. South Shields, Rotherham are winning until the 85th minute, when Alberto Simeone scores an equaliser for South Shields, and South Shields then go on to win the match. Thus, Rotherham will not win the league.

Which of the following best illustrates a flaw in this passage's reasoning?
A. It has assumed that Alberto Simeone scored the winning goal for South Shields.
B. It has assumed that beating South Shields was necessary for Rotherham to win the league, when in fact it was only sufficient.
C. Rotherham may have scored an equaliser later in the game, and not lost the match.
D. It has failed to consider what other teams might win the league.

Question 65:
Oakville Supermarkets is looking to build a new superstore, and a meeting of its directors has been convened to decide where the best place to build the supermarket would be. The Chairperson of the Board suggests that the best place would be Warrington, a town that does not currently have a large supermarket, and would thus give them an excellent share of the shopping market.

However, the CEO notes that the population of Warrington has been steadily declining for several years, whilst Middlesbrough has recently been experiencing high population growth. The CEO therefore argues that they should build the new supermarket in Middlesbrough, as they would then be within range of more people, and so of more potential customers.

Which of the following best illustrates a flaw in the CEO's reasoning?
A. Middlesbrough may already have other supermarkets, so the new superstore may get a lower share of the town's shoppers.
B. Despite the recent population changes, Warrington may still have a larger population than Middlesbrough.
C. Middlesbrough's population is projected to continue growing, whilst Warrington's is projected to keep falling.
D. Many people in Warrington travel to Liverpool or Manchester, 2 nearby major cities, in order to do their shopping.

Question 66:
Global warming is a key challenge facing the world today, and the changes in weather patterns caused by this phenomenon have led to the destruction of many natural habitats, causing many species to become extinct. Recent data has shown that extinctions have been occurring at a faster rate over the last 40 years than at any other point in the earth's history, exceeding the great Permian mass extinction, which wiped out 96% of life on earth. If this rate continues, over 50% of species on earth will be extinct by 2100. It is clear that in the face of this huge challenge, conservation programmes will require significantly increased levels of funding in order to prevent most of the species on earth from becoming extinct.

Which of the following are assumptions in this argument?
1. The rate of extinctions seen in the last 40 years will continue to occur without a step-up in conservation efforts.
2. Conservation programmes cannot prevent further extinctions without increased funding.
3. Global warming has caused many extinction events, directly or indirectly.

A. 1 only
B. 2 only
C. 3 only
D. 1 and 2
E. 1 and 3
F. 2 and 3
G. 1, 2 and 3

SECTION 1A: CRITICAL THINKING — QUESTIONS

Question 67:
After an election in Britain, the new government is debating what policy to adopt on the railway system, and whether it should be entirely privatised, or whether public subsidies should be used to supplement costs and ensure that sufficient services are run. Studies in Austria, which has high public funding for railways, have shown that the rail service is used by many people, and is highly thought of by the population. However, this is clearly down to the fact that Austria has many mountainous and high-altitude areas, which experience significant amounts of snow and ice. This makes many roads impassable, and travelling by road difficult. Thus, rail is often the only way to travel, explaining the high passenger numbers and approval ratings. Thus, the high public subsidies clearly have no effect.

Which of the following, if true, would weaken this argument?

1. France also has high public subsidy of railways, but does not have large areas where travel by road is difficult. The French railway also has high passenger numbers and approval ratings.
2. Italy also has high public subsidy of railways, but the local population dislike using the rail service, and it has poor passenger numbers.
3. There are many reasons affecting the passenger numbers and approval ratings of a given country's rail serviced.

A. 1 only
B. 2 only
C. 3 only
D. 1 and 2
E. 1 and 3
F. 2 and 3

Question 68:
In 2001-2002, 1,019 patients were admitted to hospital due to obesity. This figure was more than 11 times higher by 2011-12 when there were 11,736 patients admitted to hospital with the primary reason for admission being obesity. Data has shown higher percentages of both men and women were either obese or overweight in 2011 compared to 1993, with male obesity climbing from 58% to 65%, and female from 49% to 58%. Rates of adult obesity have increased even more steeply within this period – 13% to 24% for men and 16% to 26% for women.

Studies in 2011 found that nearly a third of children between 2 – 15 years were either overweight or obese, however this was not significantly different from 2010. Lifestyles are also becoming less healthy, with a decline in both children and adults eating the recommended number of fruit and vegetables each day and taking the recommended amount of exercise each week. The ease of availability of fast-food outlets may be partly to blame for the rising number of obese people. Education is required to teach people the importance of a healthy lifestyle, however people must take some personal responsibility for their health.

Using only information from the passage, which of the following statements is correct?

A. In 2011, there was a higher proportion of obese men than women.
B. Obesity rates are rising steeply for both males and females of all age groups.
C. Responsibility needs to be taken by both individuals and local authorities to effectively tackle the epidemic.
D. The main reason people eat fast food is because it's cheaper in times of reducing income.

Question 69:
Tobacco companies sell cigarettes despite being fully aware that cigarettes cause significant harm to the wellbeing of those that smoke them. Diseases caused or aggravated by smoking cost billions of pounds for the NHS to treat each year. This is extremely irresponsible behaviour from the tobacco companies. Tobacco companies should be taxed, and the money raised put towards funding the NHS.

Which of the following conclusions **CANNOT** be drawn from the above?
A. There is a connection between lung cancer and smoking.
B. There is a connection between liver disease and smoking.
C. There is a connection between oral cancer and smoking.
D. All smokers drink excessively.
E. All of the above.

Question 70:
Investigations in the origins of species suggest that humans and the great apes have the same ancestors. This is suggested by the high degree of genetic similarity between humans and chimpanzees (estimated at 99%). At the same time there is an 84% homology between the human genome and that of pigs. This raises the interesting question of whether it would be possible to use pig or chimpanzee organs for the treatment of human disease.

Which conclusion can be reasonably drawn from the above article?
A. Pigs and chimpanzees have a common ancestor.
B. Pigs and humans have a common ancestor.
C. It can be assumed that chimpanzees will develop into humans if given enough time.
D. There seems to be great genetic homology across a variety of species.
E. Organs from pigs or chimpanzees present a good alternative for human organ donation.

Question 71:
Poor blood supply to a part of the body can cause damage of the affected tissue - i.e. lead to an infarction. There are a variety of known risk factors for vascular disease. Diabetes is a major risk factor. Other risk factors are more dependent on the individual as they represent individual choices such as smoking, poor dietary habits as well as little to no exercise. In some cases infarction of the limbs and in particular the feet can become very bad and extensive with patches of tissue dying. This is known as necrosis and is marked by affected area of the body turning black. Necrotic tissue is usually removed in surgery.

Which of the following statements **CANNOT** be concluded from the information in the above passage?
A. Smoking causes vascular disease.
B. Diabetes causes vascular disease.
C. Vascular disease always leads to infarctions.
D. Necrotic tissue must be removed surgically.
E. Necrotic tissue only occurs following severe infarction.
F. All of the above.

Question 72:
People who can afford to pay for private education should not have access to the state school system. This would allow more funding for students from lower income backgrounds. More funding will provide better resources for students from lower income backgrounds, and will help to bridge the gap in educational attainment between students from higher income and lower income backgrounds.

Which of the following statements, if true, would most strengthen the above argument?
A. Educational attainment is a significant factor in determining future prospects.
B. Providing better resources for students has been demonstrated to lead to an increase in educational attainment.
C. Most people who can afford to do so choose to purchase private education for their children.
D. A significant gap exists in educational attainment between students from high income and low-income backgrounds.
E. Most schools currently receive a similar amount of funding relative to the number of students in the school.

Question 73:
Increasing numbers of people are choosing to watch films on DVD in recent years. In the past few years, cinemas have lost customers, causing them to close down. Many cinemas have recently closed, removing an important focal point for many local communities and causing damage to those communities. Therefore, we should ban DVDs in order to help local communities.

Which of the following best states an assumption made in this argument?
A. The cinemas that have recently closed have done so because of reduced profits due to people choosing to watch DVDs instead.
B. Cinemas being forced to close causes damage to local communities.
C. DVDs are improving local communities by allowing people to meet up and watch films together.
D. Sales of DVDs have increased due to economic growth.
E. Local communities have called for DVDs to be banned.

Question 74:
Aeroplanes are the fastest form of transport available. An aeroplane can travel a given distance in less time than a train or a car. John needs to travel from Glasgow to Birmingham. If he wants to arrive as soon as possible, he should travel by aeroplane.

Which of the following best illustrates a flaw in this argument?
A. One day, there could be faster cars built that could travel as fast as aeroplanes.
B. Travelling by air is often more expensive.
C. It ignores the time taken to travel to an airport and check in to a flight, which may mean he will arrive later if travelling by aeroplane.
D. John may not own a car, and thus may not have any option.
E. John may not be legally allowed to make the journey.

Question 75:
During autumn, spiders frequently enter people's homes to escape the cold weather. Many people dislike spiders and seek ways to prevent them from entering properties, leading to spider populations falling as they struggle to cope with the cold weather. Studies have demonstrated that when spider populations fall, the population of flies rises. Higher numbers of flies are associated with an increase in food poisoning cases. Therefore, people must not seek to prevent spiders from entering their homes.

Which of the following best illustrates the main conclusion of this argument?
A. People should not dislike spiders being present in their homes.
B. People should seek methods to prevent flies from entering their homes.
C. People should actively encourage spiders to occupy their homes to increase biodiversity.
D. People should accept the presence of spiders in their homes to reduce the incidence of food poisoning.
E. Spiders should be cultivated and used as a biological pest control to combat flies.

Question 76:
Each year, thousands of people acquire infections during prolonged stays at hospital. Concurrently, bacteria are becoming resistant to antibiotics at an ever-increasing rate. In spite of this, progressively less pharmaceutical companies are investing in research into new antibiotics, and the number of antibiotics coming onto the market is decreasing. As a result, the number of antibiotics that can be used to treat infections is falling. If pharmaceutical companies were pressured into investing in new antibiotic research, many lives could be saved.

Which of the following best illustrates a flaw in this argument?
A. It assumes the infections acquired during stays at hospital are resulting in deaths.
B. It ignores the fact that many people never have to stay in hospital.
C. It does not take into account the fact that antibiotics do not produce much profit for pharmaceutical companies.
D. It ignores the fact that some hospital-acquired infections are caused by organisms that cannot be treated by antibiotics, such as viruses.
E. It assumes that bacterial resistance to antibiotics has not been happening for some time.

Question 77:
Katherine has shaved her armpits most of her adult life, but has now decided to stop. She explains her reasons for this to John, saying she does not like the pressures society puts on women to be shaven in this area. John listens to her reasons, but ultimately responds 'just because you explain why I should find your hairiness attractive, it does not mean I will. I find you unattractive, as I do not like girls with hair on their arm pits.'

What assumption has John made?
A. That just because he finds Katherine unattractive, he would find other girls with unshaven arm pits unattractive.
B. That Katherine is trying to make John find her armpit hair attractive.
C. That Katherine will never conceal her armpit hair.
D. Katherine must be wrong, because she is a woman.
E. That Katherine thinks women should stop shaving.

Question 78:
Medicine has improved significantly over the last century. Better medicine causes a reduction in the death rate from all causes. However, as people get older, they suffer from infectious disease more readily.

Many third world countries have a high rate of deaths from infectious disease. Sunita argues that this high death rate is caused by better medicine, which has given an ageing population, thus giving a high rate of deaths from infectious disease as elderly people suffer from infectious disease more readily. Sunita believes that better medicine is thus indirectly responsible for this high death rate from infectious disease.

However, this cannot be the case. In third world countries, most people do not live to old age, often dying from infectious disease at a young age. Therefore, an ageing population cannot be the reason behind the high rate of death from infectious disease. As better medicine causes a reduction in the death rate from all causes, it is clear that better medicine will lead to a reduction in the death rate from infectious disease in third world countries.

Which of the following best states the main conclusion of this argument?
A. We can expect that improvements in medicine seen over the last century will improve.
B. Better medicine is not responsible for the increased prevalence of infectious disease in third world countries.
C. Better medicine has caused the overall death rate of third world countries to increase.
D. Better medicine will cause a decrease in the rate of death from infectious disease in third world countries.
E. As people get older, they suffer from infectious disease more readily.

Question 79:
Bristol and Cardiff are 2 cities with similar demographics, and located in a roughly similar area of the country. Bristol has higher demand for housing than Cardiff. Therefore, a house in Bristol will cost more than a similar house in Cardiff.

Which of the following best illustrates an assumption in the statement above?
A. House prices will be higher if demand for housing is higher.
B. People can commute from Cardiff to Bristol.
C. Supply of housing in Cardiff will not be lower than in Bristol.
D. Bristol is a better place to live.
E. Cardiff has sufficient housing to provide for the needs of its communities.

Question 80:
Jellicoe Motors is a small motor company in Sheffield, employing 3 people. The company is hiring a new mechanic and interviews several candidates. New research into production lines has indicated that having employees with a good ability to work as part of a team boosts a company's productivity and profits. Therefore, Jellicoe motors should hire a candidate with good team-working skills.

Which of the following best illustrates the main conclusion of this argument?
A. Jellicoe Motors should not hire a new mechanic.
B. Jellicoe motors should hire a candidate with good team-working skills in order to boost their productivity and profits.
C. Jellicoe motors should hire several new candidates in order to form a good team, and boost their productivity.
D. If Jellicoe motors does not hire a candidate with good team-working skills, they may struggle to be profitable.
E. Jellicoe motors should not listen to the new research.

Question 81:
Research into new antibiotics does not normally hold much profit for pharmaceutical firms. As a consequence many firms are not investing in antibiotic research, and very few new antibiotics are being produced. However, with bacteria becoming increasingly resistant to current antibiotics, new ones are desperately needed to avoid running the risk of thousands of deaths from bacterial infections. Therefore, the UK government must provide financial incentives for pharmaceutical companies to invest in research into new antibiotics.

Which of the following best expresses the main conclusion of this argument?
A. If bacteria continue to become resistant to antibiotics, there could be thousands of deaths from bacterial infections.
B. Pharmaceutical firms are not investing in new antibiotic research due to a lack of potential profit.
C. If the UK government invests in research into new antibiotics, thousands of lives will be saved.
D. The pharmaceutical firms should invest in areas of research that are profitable, and ignore antibiotic research.
E. The UK government must provide financial incentives for pharmaceutical firms to invest into antibiotic research if it wishes to avoid risking thousands of deaths from bacterial infections.

Question 82:
People in developing countries use far less water per person than those in developed countries. It is estimated that at present, people in the developing world use an average of 30 litres of water per person per day, whilst those in developed countries use on average 70 litres of water per person per day. It is estimated that for the current world population, an average water usage of 60 litres per person per day would be sustainable, but any higher than this would be unsustainable.

The UN has set development targets such that in 20 years, people living in developing countries will be using the same amount of water per person per day as those living in developed countries. Assuming the world population stays constant for the next 20 years, if these targets are met the world's population will be using water at an unsustainable rate.

Which of the following, if true, would most weaken the argument above?
A. The prices of water bills are dropping in developed countries like the UK.
B. The level of water usage in developed countries is falling, and may be below 60 litres per person per day in 20 years.
C. The population of all developing countries is less than the population of all developed countries.
D. Climate change is likely to decrease the amount of water available for human use over the next 20 years.
E. The UN's development targets are unlikely to be met.

SECTION 1A: CRITICAL THINKING — QUESTIONS

Question 83:
In this Senior Management post we need someone who can keep a cool head in a crisis and react quickly to events. The applicant says he suffers from a phobia about flying, and panics especially when an aircraft is landing and that therefore he would prefer not to travel abroad on business if it could be avoided. He is obviously a very nervous type of person who would clearly go to pieces and panic in an emergency and fail to provide the leadership qualities necessary for the job. Therefore this person is not a suitable candidate for the post.

Which of the following highlights the biggest flaw in the argument above?
A. It falsely assumes that phobias are untreatable or capable of being eliminated.
B. It falsely assumes that the person appointed to the job will need to travel abroad.
C. It falsely assumes that a specific phobia indicates a general tendency to panic.
D. It falsely assumes that people who stay cool in a crisis will be good leaders.
E. It fails to take into account other qualities the person might have for the post.

Question 84:
There are significant numbers of people attending university every year, as many as 45% of 18 year olds. As a result, there are many more graduates entering the workforce with better skills and better earning potential. Going to university makes economic sense and we should encourage as many people to go there as possible.

Which of the following highlights the biggest flaw in the argument above?
A. There are no more university places left.
B. Students can succeed without going to university.
C. Not all degrees equip students with the skills needed to earn higher salaries.
D. Some universities are better than others.

Question 85:
Young people spend too much time watching television, which is bad for them. Watching excessive amounts of TV is linked to obesity, social exclusion and can cause eye damage. If young people were to spend just one evening a week playing sport or going for a walk the benefits would be manifold. They would lose weight, feel better about themselves and it would be a sociable activity. Exercise is also linked to strong performance at school and so young people would be more likely to perform well in their exams.

Which of the following highlights the biggest flaw in the argument above?
A. Young people can watch sport on television.
B. There are many factors that affect exam performance.
C. Television does not necessarily have any damaging effect.
D. Television and sport are not linked.

Question 86:
Campaigners pushing for legalisation of cannabis have many arguments for their cause. Most claim there is little evidence of any adverse affects to health caused by cannabis usage, that many otherwise law-abiding people are users of cannabis and that in any case, prohibition of drugs does not reduce their usage. Legalising cannabis would also reduce crime associated with drug trafficking and would provide an additional revenue stream for the government.

Which of the following best represents the conclusion of the passage?
A. Regular cannabis users are unlikely to have health problems.
B. Legalising cannabis would be good for cannabis users.
C. There are multiple reasons to legalise cannabis.
D. Prohibition is an effective measure to reduce drugs usage.
E. Drug associated crime would reduce if cannabis was legal.

Question 87:
Mohan has been offered a new job in Birmingham, starting in several months with a fixed salary. In order to ensure he can afford to live in Birmingham on his new salary, Mohan compares the prices of some houses in Birmingham. He finds that a 2 bedroomed house will cost £200,000. A 3 bedroomed house will cost £250,000. A 4 bedroomed house with a garden will cost £300,000.

Mohan's bank tells him that if he is earning the salary of the job he has been offered, they will grant him a mortgage for a house costing up to £275,000. After a month of deliberation, Mohan accepts the job and decides to move to Wolverhampton. He begins searching for a house to buy. He reasons that he will not be able to purchase a 4-bedroomed house.

Which of the following is NOT an assumption that Mohan has made?
A. A house in Wolverhampton will cost the same as a similar house in Birmingham.
B. A different bank will not offer him a mortgage for a more expensive house on the same salary.
C. The salary for the job could increase, allowing him to purchase a more expensive house.
D. A 4-bedroomed house without a garden will not cost less than a 4-bedroomed house with a garden.
E. House prices in Birmingham will not have fall in the time between now and Mohan purchasing a house.

Question 88:
We should teach the Holocaust in schools. It is important that young people see what it was like for Jewish people under Nazi rule. If we expose the harsh realities to impressionable people then this will help improve tolerance of other races. It will also prevent other such terrible events happening again.

Which is the best conclusion?
A. We should teach about the Holocaust in schools.
B. The Holocaust was a tragedy.
C. The Nazis were evil.
D. We should not let terrible events happen again.
E. Educating people is the best solution to the world's problems.

Question 89:
The popular series 'Game of Thrones' should not be allowed on television because it shows scenes of a disturbing nature, in particular scenes of rape. Children may find themselves watching the programme on TV, and then going on to commit the terrible crime of rape, mimicking what they have watched.

Which of the following best illustrates a flaw in this argument?
A. Children may also watch the show on DVD.
B. Adults may watch the show on television.
C. Watching an action does not necessarily lead to recreating the action yourself.
D. There are lots of non-violent scenes in the show.

Question 90:
The TV series 'House of Cards' teaches us all a valuable lesson: the world is not a place that rewards kind behaviour. The protagonist of the series, Frank Underwood, uses intrigue and guile to achieve his goals, and through clever political tactics he is able to climb in rank. If he were to be kinder to people, he would not be able to be so successful. Success is predicated on his refusal to conform to conventional morality. The TV series should be shown to small children in schools, as it could teach them how to achieve their dreams.

Which of the following is an assumption made in the argument?
A. Children pay attention to school lessons.
B. The TV series is sufficiently entertaining.
C. One cannot both obey a moral code and succeed.
D. Frank Underwood is a likable character.

Question 91:
Freddy makes lewd comments on a female passer-by's body to his friend, Neil, loud enough for the woman in question to hear. Neil is uncomfortable with this, and states that it is inappropriate for Freddy to do so, and that Freddy is being sexist. Freddy refutes this, and Neil retorts that Freddy would not make these comments about a man's body. Freddy replies by saying 'it is not sexist, I am a feminist, I believe in equality for men and women.'

Which of the following describes a flaw made in Freddy's logic?
A. A self-proclaimed feminist could still say a sexist thing.
B. The female passer-by in question felt uncomfortable.
C. Neil, too, considers himself a feminist.
D. It would still not be OK to make lewd comments at male passers-by.
E. Lewd comments are always inappropriate.

Question 92:
The release of CO_2 from consumption of fossil fuels is the main reason behind global warming, which is causing significant damage to many natural environments throughout the world. One significant source of CO_2 emissions is cars, which release CO_2 as they use up petrol. In order to tackle this problem, many car companies have begun to design cars with engines that do not use as much petrol. However, engines which use less petrol are not as powerful, and less powerful cars are not attractive to the public. If a car company produces cars which are not attractive to the public, they will not be profitable.

Which of the following best illustrates the main conclusion of this argument?
A. Car companies which produce cars that use less petrol will not be profitable.
B. The public prefer more powerful cars.
C. Car companies should prioritise profits over helping the environment.
D. Car companies should seek to produce engines that use less petrol but are still just as powerful.
E. The public are not interested in helping the environment.

SECTION 1A: Problem Solving

Section 1A problem solving questions are arguably the hardest to prepare for. However, there are some useful techniques you can employ to solve some types of questions much more quickly:

Construct Equations

Some of the problems in Section 1 are quite complex and you'll need to be comfortable with turning prose into equations and manipulating them. For example, when you read "Mark is twice as old as Jon" – this should immediately register as $M = 2J$. Once you get comfortable forming equations, you can start to approach some of the harder questions in this book (and past papers) which may require you to form and solve simultaneous equations. Consider the example:

Nick has a sleigh that contains toy horses and clowns and counts 44 heads and 132 legs in his sleigh. Given that horses have one head and four legs, and clowns have one head and two legs, calculate the difference between the number of horses and clowns.

A. 0
B. 5
C. 22
D. 28
E. 132
F. More information needed

To start with, let C= Clowns and H= Horses.
For Heads: $C + H = 44$; For Legs: $2C + 4H = 132$

This now sets up your two equations that you can solve simultaneously.
$C = 44 - H$ so $2(44 - H) + 4H = 132$

Thus, $88 - 2H + 4H = 132$;
Therefore, $2H = 44; H = 22$

Substitute back in to give $C = 44 - H = 44 - 22 = 22$
Thus the difference between horses and clowns $= C - H = 22 - 22 = 0$

It's important you are able to do these types of questions quickly (and **without resorting to trial & error** as they are commonplace in section 1.

Diagrams

When a question asks about timetables, orders or sequences, draw out diagrams. By doing this, you can organise your thoughts and help make sense of the question.

"Mordor is West of Gondor but East of Rivendale. Lorien is midway between Gondor and Mordor. Erebus is West of Mordor. Eden is not East of Gondor."

*Which of the following **cannot** be concluded?*

A. Lorien is East of Erebus and Mordor.
B. Mordor is West of Gondor and East of Erebus.
C. Rivendale is west of Lorien and Gondor.
D. Gondor is East of Mordor and East of Lorien
E. Erebus is West of Mordor and West of Rivendale.

Whilst it is possible to solve this in your head, it becomes much more manageable if you draw a quick diagram and plot the positions of each town:

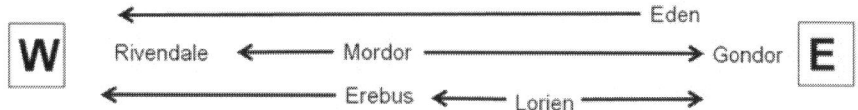

Now, it's a simple case of going through each option and seeing if it is correct according to the diagram. You can now easily see that Option E- Erebus cannot be west of Rivendale.

Don't feel that you have to restrict yourself to linear diagrams like this either – for some questions you may need to draw tables or even Venn diagrams. Consider the example:

Slifers and Osiris are not legendary. Krakens and Minotaurs are legendary. Minotaurs and Lords are both divine. Humans are neither legendary nor divine.

A. Krakens may be only legendary or legendary and divine.
B. Humans are not divine.
C. Slifers are only divine.
D. Osiris may be divine.
E. Humans and Slifers are the same in terms of both qualities.

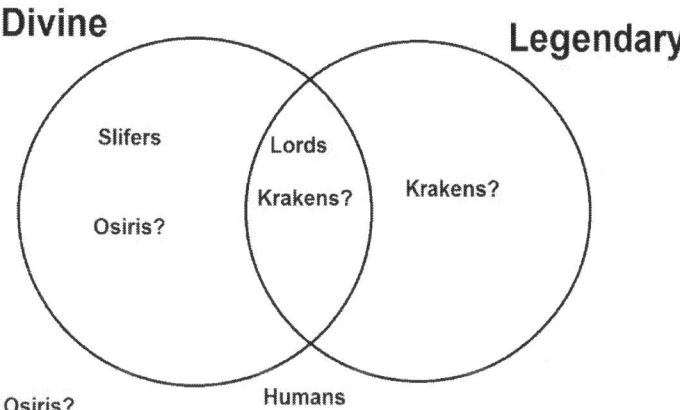

Constructing a Venn diagram allows us to quickly see that the position of Osiris and Krakens aren't certain. Thus, A and D must be true. Humans are neither so B is true. Krakens may be divine so A is true. E cannot be concluded as Slifers are divine but are humans are not. Thus, E is False.

Spatial Reasoning

There are usually 1-2 spatial reasoning questions every year. They usually give nets for a shape or a patterned cuboid and ask which options are possible rotations. Unfortunately, they are extremely difficult to prepare for because the skills necessary to solve these types of questions can take a very long time to improve. The best thing you can do to prepare is to familiarise yourself with the basics of how cube nets work and what the effect of transformations are e.g. what happens if a shape is reflected in a mirror etc.

It is also a good idea to try to learn to draw basic shapes like cubes from multiple angles if you can't do so already. Finally, remember that if the shape is straightforward like a cube, it might be easier for you to draw a net, cut it out and fold it yourself to see which of the options are possible.

Problem Solving Questions

Question 93:

Pilbury is south of Westside, which is south of Harrington. Twotown is north of Pilbury and Crewville but not further north than Westside. Crewville is:

A. South of Westside, Pilbury and Harrington but not necessarily Twotown.
B. North of Pilbury, and Westside.
C. South of Westside and Twotown, but north of Pilbury.
D. South of Westside, Harrington and Twotown but not necessarily Pilbury.
E. South of Harrington, Westside, Twotown and Pilbury.

Question 94:

The hospital coordinator is making the rota for the ward for next week; two of Drs Evans, James and Luca must be working on weekdays, none of them on Sundays and all of them on Saturdays. Dr Evans works 4 days a week including Mondays and Fridays. Dr Luca cannot work Monday or Thursday. Only Dr James can work 4 days consecutively, but he cannot do 5.

What days does Dr James work?

A. Saturday, Sunday and Monday.
B. Monday, Tuesday, Wednesday, Thursday and Saturday.
C. Monday, Thursday Friday and Saturday.
D. Tuesday, Wednesday, Friday and Saturday.
E. Monday, Tuesday, Wednesday, Thursday and Friday.

Question 95:

Michael, a taxi driver, charges a call out rate and a rate per mile for taxi rides. For a 4 mile ride he charges £11, and for a 5 mile ride, £13.

How much does he charge for a 9-mile ride?

A. £15   B. £17   C. £19   D. £20   E. £21

Question 96:

Goblins and trolls are not magical. Fairies and goblins are both mythical. Elves and fairies are magical. Gnomes are neither mythical nor magical.

Which of the following is **FALSE**?

A. Elves may be only magical or magical and mythical.
B. Gnomes are not mythical.
C. Goblins are only mythical.
D. Trolls may be mythical.
E. Gnomes and goblins are the same in terms of both qualities.

Question 97:

Jessica runs a small business making bespoke wall tiles. She has just had a rush order for 100 tiles placed that must be ready for today at 7pm. The client wants the tiles packed all together, a process which will take 15 minutes. Only 50 tiles can go in the kiln at any point and they must be put in the kiln to heat for 45 minutes. The tiles then sit in the kiln to cool before they can be packed, a process which takes 20 minutes. While tiles are in the kiln Jessica is able to decorate more tiles at a rate of 1 tile per minute.

What is the latest time Jessica can start making the tiles?

A. 2:55pm   B. 3:15pm   C. 3:30pm   D. 3:45pm

SECTION 1A: PROBLEM SOLVING — QUESTIONS

Question 98:
Pain nerve impulses are twice as fast as normal touch impulses. If Yun touches a boiling hot pan this message reaches her brain, 1 metre away, in 1 millisecond.

What is the speed of a normal touch impulse?
A. 5 m/s   B. 20 m/s   C. 50 m/s   D. 200m/s   E. 500 m/s

Question 99:
A woman has two children Melissa and Jack, yearly, their birthdays are 3 months apart, both being on the 22nd. The woman wishes to continue the trend of her children's names beginning with the same letter as the month they were born. If her next child, Alina is born on the 22nd 2 months after Jack's birthday, how many months after Alina is born will Melissa have her next birthday?
A. 2 months   B. 4 months   C. 5 months   D. 6 months   E. 7 months

Question 100:
Policemen work in pairs. PC Carter, PC Dirk, PC Adams and PC Bryan must work together but not for more than seven days in a row, which PC Adams and PC Bryan now have. PC Dirk has worked with PC Carter for 3 days in a row. PC Carter does not want to work with PC Adams if it can be avoided.

Who should work with PC Bryan?
A. PC Carter
B. PC Dirk
C. PC Adams
D. Nobody is available under the guidelines above.

Question 101:
My hair-dressers charges £30 for a haircut, £50 for a cut and blow-dry, and £60 for a full hair dye. They also do manicures, of which the first costs £15, and includes a bottle of nail polish, but are subsequently reduced by £5 if I bring my bottle of polish. The price is reduced by 10% if I book and pay for the next 5 appointments in advance and by 15% if I book at least the next 10.

I want to pay for my next 5 cut and blow-dry appointments, as well as for my next 3 manicures. How much will it cost?
A. £170   B. £255   C. £260   D. £285   E. £305

Question 102:
Alex, Bertha, David, Gemma, Charlie, Elena and Frankie are all members of the same family consisting of three children, two of whom, Frankie and Gemma are girls. No other assumption of gender based on name can be established. There are also four adults. Alex is a doctor and is David's brother. One of them is married to Elena, and they have two children. Bertha is married to David; Gemma is their child.
Who is Charlie?

A. Alex's daughter
B. Frankie's father
C. Gemma's brother
D. Elena's son
E. Gemma's sister

SECTION 1A: PROBLEM SOLVING — **QUESTIONS**

Question 103:
At 14:30 three medical students were asked to examine a patient's heart. Having already watched their colleague, the second two students were twice as fast as the first to examine. During the 8 minutes break after the final student had finished, they were told by their consultant that they had taken too long and so should go back and do the examinations again. The second time all the students took half as long as they had taken the first time with the exception of the first student who, instead took the same time as his two colleagues' second attempt. Assuming there was a one minute change over time between each student and they were finished by 15:15, how long did the second student take to examine the first time?

A. 3 minutes B. 4 minutes C. 6 minutes D. 7 minutes E. 8 minutes

Question 104:
I pay for 2 chocolate bars that cost £1.65 each with a £5 note. I receive 8 coins change, only 3 of which are the same.

Which **TWO** coins do I not receive in my change?
A. 1p
B. 2p
C. 5p
D. 10p
E. 20p
F. £2
G. £1

Question 105:
Two 140m long trains are running at the same speed in opposite directions. If they cross each other in 14 seconds then what is speed of each train?
A. 10 km/hr B. 18 km/hr C. 32 km/hr D. 36 km/hr E. 42 km/hr

Question 106:
Anil has to refill his home's swimming pool. He has four hoses which all run at different speeds. Alone, the first would completely fill the pool with water in 6 hours, the second in two days, the third in three days and the fourth in four days.

Using all the hoses together, how long will it take to fill the pool to the nearest quarter of an hour?
A. 4 hours 15 minutes
B. 4 hours 30 minutes
C. 4 hours 45 minutes
D. 5 hours
E. 5 hours 15 minutes

Question 107:
An ant is stuck in a 30 cm deep ditch. When the ant reaches the top of the ditch he will be able to climb out straight away. The ant is able to climb 3 cm upwards during the day, but falls back 2 cm at night.

How many days does it take for the ant to climb out of the ditch?
A. 27 B. 28 C. 29 D. 30 E. 31

Question 108:
When buying his ingredients a chef gets a discount of 10% when he buys 10 or more of each item, and 20% discount when he buys 20 or more. On one order he bought 5 sausages and 10 Oranges and paid £8.50. On another, he bought 10 sausages and 10 apples and paid £9, on a third he bought 30 oranges and paid £12.

How much would an order of 2 oranges, 13 sausages and 12 apples cost?
A. £12.52 B. £12.76 C. £13.52 D. £13.76 E. £13.80

Question 109:
My hairdressers encourage all of its clients to become members. By paying an annual member fee, the cost of haircuts decreases. VIP membership costs £125 annually with a £10 reduction on haircuts. Executive VIP membership costs £200 for the year with a £15 reduction per haircut. At the moment I am not a member and pay £60 per haircut. I know how many haircuts I have a year, and I work out that by becoming a member on either programme it would work out cheaper, and I would save the same amount of money per year on either programme.

How much will I save this year by buying membership?

A. £10   B. £15   C. £25   D. £30   E. £50

Question 110:
If criminals, thieves and judges are represented below:

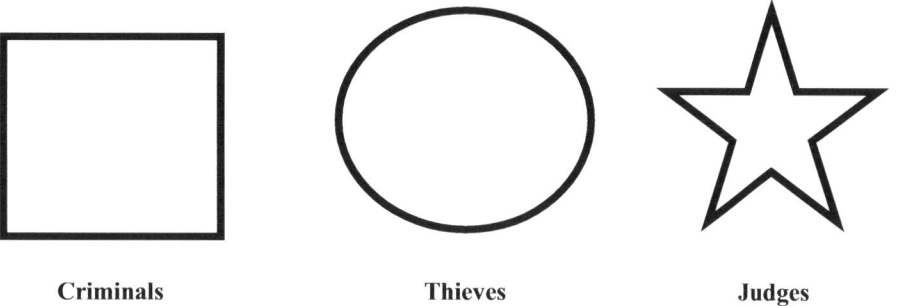

Criminals   Thieves   Judges

Assuming that judges must have clean record, all thieves are criminals and all those who are guilty are convicted of their crimes, which of one of the following best represents their interaction?

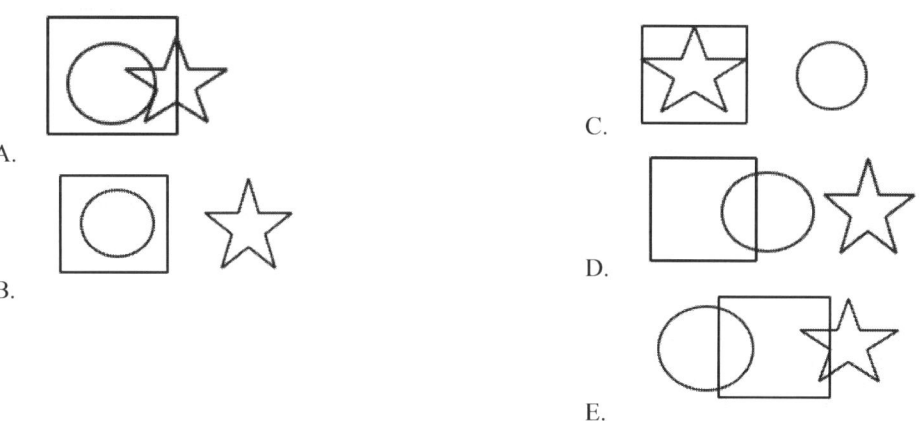

SECTION 1A: PROBLEM SOLVING QUESTIONS

Question 111:
The months of the year have been made into number codes. The code is comprised of three factors, including two of these being related the letters that make up the name of the month. No two months would have the same first number. But some such as March, which has the code 3513, have the same last number as others, such as May, which has the code 5313. October would be coded as 10715 while February is 286.

What would be the code for April?
A. 154   B. 441   C. 451   D. 514   E. 541

Question 112:
A mother gives yearly birthday presents of money to her children based on the age and their exam results. She gives them £5 each plus £3 for every year they are older than 5, and a further £10 for every A* they achieved in their results. Josie is 16 and gained 9 A*s in her results. Although Josie's brother Carson is 2 years older he receives £44 less a year for his birthday.

How many more A*s did Josie get than Carson?
A. 2   B. 3   C. 4   D. 5   E. 10

Question 113:
Apples are more expensive than pears, which are more expensive than oranges. Peaches are more expensive than oranges. Apples are less expensive than grapes.

Which two of the following must be true?
A. Grapes are less expensive than oranges.
B. Peaches may be less expensive than pears.
C. Grapes are more expensive than pears.
D. Pears and peaches are the same price.
E. Apples and peaches are the same price.

Question 114:
What is the minimum number of straight cutting motions needed to slice a cylindrical cake into 8 equally sized pieces?
A. 2   B. 3   C. 4   D. 5   E. 6   F. 8

Question 115
Three friends, Mark, Russell and Tom had agreed to meet for lunch at 12 PM on Sunday. Daylight saving time (GMT+1) had started at 2 AM the same day, where clocks should be put forward by one hour. Mark's phone automatically changes the time but he does not realise this so when he wakes up he puts his phone forward an hour and uses his phone to time his arrival to lunch. Tom puts all of his clocks forward one hour at 7 AM. Russell forgets that the clocks should go forward, wakes at 10 AM doesn't change his clocks. All of the friends arrive on time as far as they are concerned.

Assuming that none of the friends realise any errors before arriving, which **TWO** of the following statements are **FALSE**?
A. Tom arrives at 12 PM (GMT +1).
B. All three friends arrive at the same time.
C. There is a 2 hour difference between when the first and last friend arrive.
D. Mark arrives late.
E. Mark arrives at 1 PM (GMT+3).
F. Russell arrives at 12 PM (GMT+0).

SECTION 1A: PROBLEM SOLVING QUESTIONS

Question 116:
A class of young students has a pet spider. Deciding to play a practical joke on their teacher, one day during morning break one of the students put the spider in their teachers' desk. When first questioned by the head teacher, Mr Jones, the five students who were in the classroom during morning break all lied about what they saw. Realising that the students were all lying, Mr Jones called all 5 students back individually and, threatened with suspension, all the students told the truth. Unfortunately Mr Jones only wrote down the student's statements not whether they had been told in the truthful or lying questioning.

The students' two statements appear below:

Archie: "It wasn't Edward. "
   "It was Bella."

Charlotte: "It was Edward."
   "It wasn't Archie"

Darcy: "It was Charlotte"
   "It was Bella"

Bella: "It wasn't Charlotte."
   "It wasn't Edward."

Edward: "It was Darcy"
   "It wasn't Archie"

Who put the spider in the teacher's desk?

A. Edward
B. Bella
C. Darcy
D. Charlotte
E. More information needed.

Question 117:
Dr Massey wants to measure out 0.1 litres of solution. Unfortunately the lab assistant dropped the 200 ml measuring cylinder, and so the scientist only has a 300 ml and a half litre-measuring beaker. Assuming he cannot accurately use the beakers to measure anything less than their full capacity, what is the minimum volume he will have to use to be able to ensure he measures the right amount?

A. 100 ml
B. 200 ml
C. 300 ml
D. 400 ml
E. 500 ml
F. 600 ml

Question 118:
Francis lives on a street with houses all consecutively numbered evenly. When one adds up the value of all the house numbers it totals 870.

In order to determine Francis' house number:
1. The relative position of Francis' house must be known.
2. The number of houses in the street must be known.
3. At least three of the house numbers must be known.

A. 1 only
B. 2 only
C. 3 only
D. 1 and 2
E. 2 and 3

Question 119:
There were 20 people exercising in the cardio room of a gym. Four people were about to leave when suddenly a man collapsed on one of the machines. Fortunately a doctor was on the machine beside him. Emerging from his office, one of the personal trainers called an ambulance. In the 5 minutes that followed before the two paramedics arrived, half of the people who were leaving, left upon hearing the commotion, and eight people came in from the changing rooms to hear the paramedics pronouncing the man dead.

How many living people were left in the room?

A. 25   B. 26   C. 27   D. 28   E. 29   F. 30

SECTION 1A: PROBLEM SOLVING QUESTIONS

Question 120:
A man and woman are in an accident. They both suffer the same trauma, which causes both of them to lose blood at a rate of 0.2 Litres/minute. At normal blood volume the man has 8 litres and the woman 7 litres, and people collapse when they lose 40% of their normal blood volume.

Which **TWO** of the following are true?

A. The man will collapse 2 minutes before the woman.
B. The woman collapses 2 minutes before the man.
C. The total blood loss is 5 litres.
D. The woman has 4.2 litres of blood in her body when she collapses.
E. The man's blood loss is 4.8 litres when he collapses.
F. Blood loss is at a rate of 2 litres every 12 minutes.

Question 121:
Jenny, Helen and Rachel have to run a distance of 13 km. Jenny runs at a pace of 8 kmph, Helen at a pace of 10 kmph, and Rachel 11 kmph.

If Jenny sets off 15 minutes before Helen, and 25 minutes before Rachel, what order will they arrive at the destination?

A. Jenny, Helen, Rachel.
B. Helen, Rachel, Jenny.
C. Helen, Jenny, Rachel.
D. Rachel, Helen, Jenny.
E. Jenny, Rachel, Helen.
F. None of the above.

Question 122:
On a specific day at a GP surgery 150 people visited the surgery and common complaints were recorded as a percentage of total patients. Each patient could use their appointment to discuss up to 2 complaints. 56% flu-like symptoms, 48% pain, 20% diabetes, 40% asthma or COPD, 30% high blood pressure.

Which statement must be true?
A. A minimum of 8 patients complained of pain and flu-like symptoms.
B. No more than 45 patients complained of high blood pressure and diabetes.
C. There were a minimum of 21 patients who did not complain about flu-like symptoms or high blood pressure.
D. There were actually 291 patients who visited the surgery.
E. None of the above.

Question 123:
All products in a store were marked up by 15%. They were subsequently reduced in a sale with quoted saving of 25% from the higher price. What is the true reduction from the original price?
A. 5%
B. 10%
C. 13.75%
D. 18.25%
E. 20%
F. None of the above.

SECTION 1A: PROBLEM SOLVING — QUESTIONS

Question 124:

A recipe states it makes 12 pancakes and requires the following ingredients: 2 eggs, 100g plain flour, and 300ml milk. Steve is cooking pancakes for 15 people and wants to have sufficient mixture for 3 pancakes each.

What quantities should Steve use to ensure this whilst using whole eggs?
A. 2½ eggs, 125g plain flour, 375ml milk
B. 3 eggs, 150g plain flour, 450 ml milk
C. 7½ eggs, 375g plain flour, 1125 ml milk
D. 8 eggs, 400g plain flour, 1200 ml milk
E. 12 eggs, 600g plain flour, 1800 ml milk
F. None of the above.

Question 125:

Spring Cleaning cleaners buy industrial bleach from a warehouse and dilute it twice before using it domestically. The first dilution is by 9:1 and then the second, 4:1.

If the cleaners require 6 litres of diluted bleach, how much warehouse bleach do they require?
A. 30 ml
B. 120 ml
C. 166 ml
D. 666 ml
E. 1,200 ml
F. None of the above

Question 126:

During a GP consultation in 2015, Ms Smith tells the GP about her grandchildren. Ms Smith states that Charles is the middle grandchild and was born in 2002. In 2010, Bertie was twice the age of Adam and that in 2015 there are 5 years between Bertie and Adam. Charles and Adam are separated by 3 years.

How old are the 3 grandchildren in 2015?
A. Adam = 16, Bertie = 11, Charles = 13
B. Adam = 5, Bertie = 10, Charles = 8
C. Adam = 10, Bertie = 15, Charles = 13
D. Adam = 10, Bertie = 20, Charles = 13
E. Adam = 11, Bertie = 10, Charles = 8
F. More information needed.

Question 127:

Kayak Hire charges a fixed flat rate and then an additional half-hourly rate. Peter hires the kayak for 3 hours and pays £14.50, and his friend Kevin hires 2 kayaks for 4hrs30mins each and pays £41. How much would

Tom pay to hire one kayak for 2 hours?
A. £8
B. £10.50
C. £15
D. £33.20
E. £35.70
F. None of the above.

Question 128:

A ticketing system uses a common digital display of numbers 0 – 9. The number 7 is showing. However, a number of the light elements are not currently working.

Which set of the following digits is possible?
A. 3, 4, 7
B. 0, 1, 9
C. 2, 7, 8
D. 0, 5, 9
E. 3, 8, 9
F. 3, 4, 9

SECTION 1A: PROBLEM SOLVING — QUESTIONS

Question 129:

A team of 4 builders take 12 days of 7 hours work to complete a house. The company decides to recruit 3 extra builders.

How many 8 hour days will it take the new workforce to build a house?

A. 2 days
B. 6 days
C. 7 days
D. 10 days
E. 12 days
F. More information needed

Question 130:

All astragalus are fabacaea as are all gummifer. Acacia are not astragalus. Which of the following statements is true?

A. Acacia are not fabacaea.
B. No astragalus are also gummifer.
C. All fabacae are astragalus or gummifer.
D. Some acacia may be fabacaea.
E. Gummifer are all acacia.
F. None of the above.

Question 131:

The Smiths want to reupholster both sides of their seating cushions (dimensions shown on diagram). The fabric they are using costs £10/m, can only be bought in whole metre lengths and has a standard width of 1m. Each side of a cushion must be made from a single peice of fabric. The seamstress changes a flat rate of £25 per cushion. How much will it cost them to reupholster 4 cushions?

A. £ 20
B. £ 80
C. £ 110
D. £ 130
E. £ 150
F. £ 200

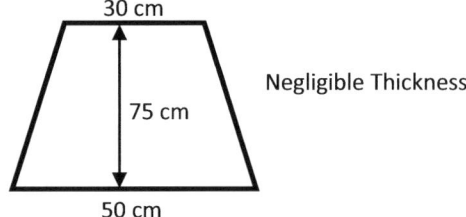

Question 132:

Lisa buys a cappuccino from either Milk or Beans Coffee shops each day. The quality of the coffee is the same but she wishes to work out the relative costs once the loyalty scheme has been taken into account. In Milk, a regular cappuccino is £2.40, and in Beans, £2.15. However, the loyalty scheme in Milk gives Lisa a free cappuccino for every 9 she buys, whereas Beans use a points system of 10 points per full pound spent (each point is worth 1p) which can be used to cover the cost of a full cappuccino.

If Lisa buys a cappuccino each day of September, which coffee shop would work out cheaper, and by how much?

A. Milk, by £4.60
B. Beans by £6.30
C. Beans, by £4.60
D. Beans, by £2.45
E. Milk, by £2.45
F. Milk, by £6.25

Question 133:

Paula needs to be at a meeting in Notting Hill at 11am. The route requires her to walk 5 minutes to the 283 bus which takes 25 minutes, and then change to the 220 bus which takes 14 minutes. Finally she walks for 3 minutes to her meeting. If the 283 bus comes every 10 minutes, and the 220 bus at 0 minutes, 20 minutes and 40 minutes past the hour, what is the latest time she can leave and still be at her meeting on time?

| A. 09.45 | B. 09.58 | C. 10.01 | D. 10.05 | E. 10.10 | F. 10.15 |

Question 134:

Two trains, a high speed train A and a slower local train B, travel from Manchester to London. Train A travels the first 20 km at 100 km/hr and then at an average speed of 150km/hr. Train B travels at a constant average speed of 90 km/hr. If train B leaves 20 minutes before train A, at what distance will train A pass train B?

| A. 75 km | B. 90 km | C. 100 km | D. 120 km | E. 150 km |

Question 135:

The university gym has an upfront cost of £35 with no contract fee, but classes are charged at £3 each. The local gym has no joining fee and is £15 per month. What is the minimum number of classes I need to attend in a 12 month period to make the local gym cheaper than the university gym?

| A. 40 | B. 48 | C. 49 | D. 50 | E. 55 | F. 60 |

Question 136:

"All medicines are drugs, but not all drugs are medicines", goes a well-known saying. If we accept this statement as true, and consider that all antibiotics are medicines, but no herbal drugs are medicines, then which of the following is definitely **FALSE**?

A. Some herbal drugs are not medicines.
B. All antibiotics are drugs.
C. Some herbal drugs are antibiotics.
D. Some medicines are antibiotics

Question 137:

Sonia has been studying the paths taken by various trains travelling between London and Edinburgh on the East coast. Trains can stop at the following stations: Newark, Peterborough, Doncaster, York, Northallerton, Darlington, Durham and Newcastle.

She notes the following:

- All trains stop at Peterborough, York, Darlington and Newcastle.
- All trains which stop at Northallerton also stop at Durham.
- Each day, 50% of the trains stop at both Newark *and* Northallerton.
- All designated "Fast" trains make less than 5 stops. All other trains make 5 stops or more.
- On average, 16 trains run each day.

Which of the following can be reliably concluded from these observations?
A. All trains, which are not designated "fast" trains, must stop at Durham.
B. No more than 8 trains on any 1 day will stop at Northallerton.
C. No designated "Fast" trains will stop at Durham.
D. It is possible for a train to make 5 stops, including Northallerton.
E. A train which stops at Newark will also stop at Durham.

Question 138:

Rakton is 5 miles directly north of Blueville. Gallford is 8 miles directly south of Haston. Lepstone is situated 5 miles directly east of Blueville, and 5 miles directly west of Gallford.

Which of the following **CANNOT** be reliably concluded from this information?
A. Lepstone is South of Rakton
B. Haston is North of Rakton
C. Gallford is East of Rakton
D. Blueville is East of Haston

E. Haston is North of Lepstone

Question 139

The Eastminster Parliament is undergoing a new set of elections. There are 600 seats up for election, each of which will be elected separately by the people living in that constituency. 6 parties win at least 1 seat in the election, the Blue Party, the Red party, the Orange party, the Yellow party, the Green party and the Purple party. In order to form a government, a party (or coalition) must hold *over* 50% of the seats. After the election, a political analysis committee produces the following report:

- No party has gained more than 45% of the seats, so nobody is able to form a government by themselves.
- The red and the blue party each gained over 40% of the seats.
- No other party gained more than 4% of the seats.
- The green party gained the 4th highest number of seats.

The red party work out that if they collaborate with the green party and the orange party, between the 3 of them, they will have enough seats to form a coalition government.

What is the minimum number of seats that the green party could have?

A. 5   C. 7   E. 9
B. 6   D. 8   F. 10

Questions 140-144 are based on the following information:

A grandmother wants to give her 5 grandchildren £100 between them for Christmas this year. She wants to grade the money she gives to each grandchild exactly so that the older children receive more than the younger ones. She wants share the money such that she will give the 2nd youngest child as much more than the youngest, as the 3rd youngest gets than the 2nd youngest, as the 4th youngest gets from the 3rd youngest and so on. The result will be that the two youngest children together will get seven times as less money than the three oldest.

M is the amount of money the youngest child receives, and D the difference between the amount the youngest and 2nd youngest children receive.

Question 140:

What is the expression for the amount the oldest child receives?

A. M C. $2M$ E. $M + 4D$
B. $M + D$ D. $4M^2$ F. None of the above.

Question 141:

What is the correct expression for the total money received?

A. $5M = £100$
B. $5D + 10M = £100$
C. $D = \dfrac{M}{100}$
D. $5M + 10D = £100$
E. $M = \dfrac{2D}{11}$

Question 142:

"The two youngest children together will get seven times less money than the three oldest."
Which one of the following best expresses the above statement?

A. $7(3M + 9D) = 2M + D$ C. $7(2M + D) = 3M + 9D$
B. $7D = M$ D. $2(7M + D) = 3M + 9D$

Question 143

Using the statement in the previous question, what is the correct expression for M?

A. $\dfrac{2D}{11}$ B. $\dfrac{2}{11}$ C. $\dfrac{10D}{11}$ D. $\dfrac{120}{11}$

Question 144:

Express £100 in terms of D.

A. $£100 = \dfrac{120D}{11}$

B. $£100 = \dfrac{120D}{10}$

C. $£100 = \dfrac{120}{11D}$

D. $£100 = 21D$

E. $£100 = 5M + 10D$

Question 145:

Four young girls entered a local baking competition. Though a bit burnt, Ellen's carrot cake did not come last. The girl who baked a Madeira sponge had practiced a lot, and so came first, while Jaya came third with her entry. Aleena did better than the girl who made the Tiramisu, and the girl who made the Victoria sponge did better than Veronica.

Which **TWO** of the following were **NOT** results of the competition?

A. Veronica made a tiramisu
B. Ellen came second
C. Aleena made a Victoria sponge
D. The Victoria sponge came in 3rd place
E. The carrot cake came 3rd

Question 146:

In a young children's football league of 5 teams were; Celtic Changers, Eire Lions, Nordic Nesters, Sorten Swipers and the Whistling Winners. One of the boys playing in the league, after being asked by his parents, said that while he could remember the other teams' total points he could not remember his own, the Eire Lions, score. He said that all the teams played each other and when teams lost they were given 0 points, when they drew, 1 point, and 3 for a win. He remembered that the Celtic Changers had a total of 2 points; the Sorten Swipers had 5; the Nordic Nesters had 8, and the Whistling Winners 1.

How many did the boy's team score?

A. 1
B. 4
C. 8
D. 10
E. 11
F. None of the above.

Question 147:

T is the son of Z, Z and J are sisters, R is the mother of J and S is the son of R.

Which one of the following statements is correct?

A. T and J are cousins
B. S and J are sisters
C. J is the maternal uncle of T
D. S is the maternal uncle of T
E. R is the grandmother of Z.

Question 148:

John likes to shoot bottles off a shelf. In the first round he places 16 bottles on the shelf and knocks off 8 bottles. 3 of the knocked off bottles are damaged and can no longer be used, whilst 1 bottle is lost. He puts the undamaged bottles back on the shelf before continuing. In the second round he shoots six times and misses 50% of these shots. He damages two bottles with every shot which does not miss. 2 bottles also fall off the shelf at the end. He puts up 2 new bottles before continuing. In the final round, John misses all his shots and in frustration, knocks over gets angry and knocks over 50% of the remaining bottles.

How many bottles were left on the wall after the final round?

A. 2
B. 3
C. 4
D. 5
E. 6
F. More information needed.

SECTION 1A: PROBLEM SOLVING | **QUESTIONS**

Questions 149 - 155 are based on the information below:

All lines are named after a station they serve, apart from the Oval and Rectangle lines, which are named for their recognisable shapes. Trains run in both directions.
- There are express trains that run from end to end of the St Mark's and Straightly lines in 5 and 6 minutes respectively.
- It takes 2 minutes to change between St Mark's and both Oval and Rectangle lines, 1 minute between Rectangle and Oval.
- It takes 3 minutes to change between the Straightly and all other lines, except with the St Mark's line which only takes 30 seconds
- The Straightly line is a fast line and takes only 2 minutes between stops apart from to and from Keyton, which only takes 1 minute, and to and from Lime St which takes 3 minutes.
- The Oval line is much slower and takes 4 minutes between stops, apart from between Baxton and Marven, and also Archite and West Quays, which takes 5 minutes.
- The Rectangle line a reliable line; never running late but as a consequence is much slower taking 6 minutes between stops.
- The St Mark's line is fast and takes 2 and half minutes between stations.
- If a passenger reaches the end of the line, it takes three minutes to change onto a train travelling back in the opposite direction.

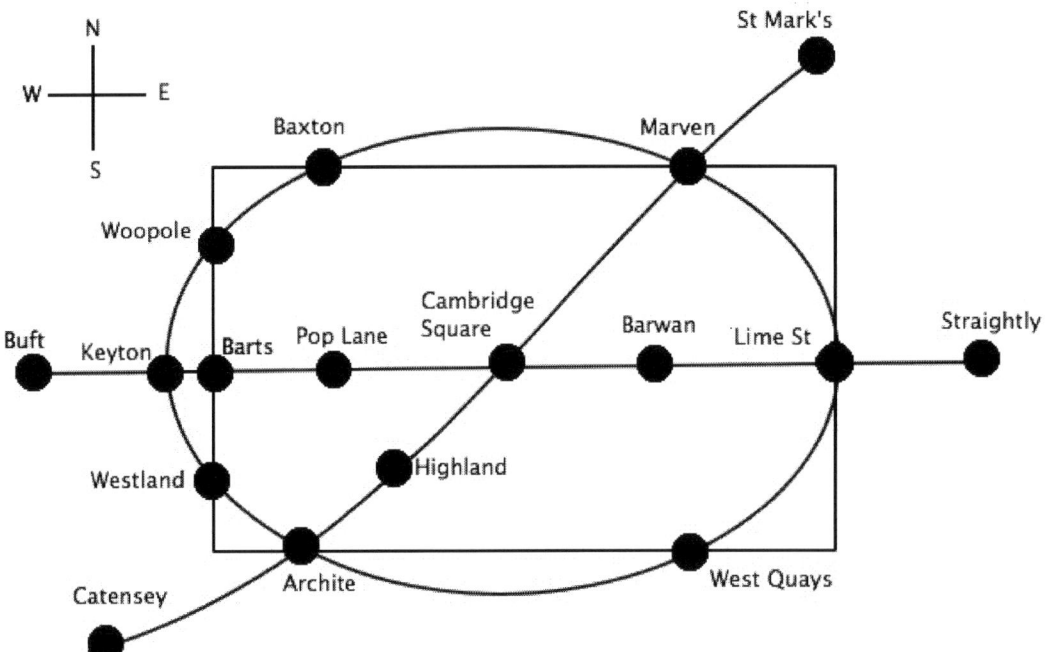

Question 149:
Assuming all lines are running on time, how long does it take to go from St Mark's to Archite on the St Mark's line?

A. 5 minutes
B. 6 minutes
C. 7.5 minutes
D. 10 minutes
E. 12.5 minutes

SECTION 1A: PROBLEM SOLVING QUESTIONS

Question 150:
Assuming all lines are running on time, what's the shortest time it will take to go from Buft to Straightly?

A. 6 minutes
B. 10 minutes
C. 12 minutes
D. 14 minutes
E. 16 minutes

Question 151:
What is the shortest time it will take to go from Baxton to Pop Lane?

A. 11 minutes
B. 12 minutes
C. 13 minutes
D. 14 minutes
E. 15 minutes

Question 152
Which station, even at the quickest journey time, is furthest in terms of time from Cambridge Square?
A. Catensey
B. Buft
C. Woopole
D. Westland

Questions 153-155 use this additional information:
On a difficult day there are signal problems whereby all lines except the reliable line are delayed, such that train travel times between stations are doubled. These delays have caused overcrowding at the platforms which means that while changeover times between lines are still the same, passengers always have to wait an extra 5 minutes on all of the platforms before catching the next train.

Question 153
At best, how long will it now take to go from Westland to Marven?

A. 25 minutes
B. 29 minutes
C. 30 minutes
D. 33 minutes
E. 35 minutes

Question 154:
There is a bus that goes from Baxton to Archite and takes 27-31 minutes. Susan lives in Baxton and needs to get to her office in Archite as quickly as possible. With all the delays and lines out of service,

How should you advise Susan best to get to work?

A. Baxton to Archite via Barts using the Rectangle line.
B. Baxton to Woopole on the Rectangle line, then Oval to Archite via Keyton.
C. It is not possible to tell between the fastest two options.
D. Baxton to Woopole on the Rectangle line, then Oval to Archite via Keyton.
E. Baxton to Archite on the Oval line.
F. Baxton to Archite using the bus.

Question 155:
In addition to the delays the Oval line signals fail completely, so the line falls out of service. How long will it now take to go from St Mark's to West Quays as quickly as possible?

A. 35 minutes
B. 30 minutes
C. 33 minutes
D. 29 minutes
E. 30.5 minutes
F. None of the above.

SECTION 1A: PROBLEM SOLVING — QUESTIONS

Question 156:

In an unusual horserace, only 4 horses, each with different racing colours and numbers competed. Simon's horse wore number 1. Lila's horse wasn't painted yellow nor blue, and the horse that wore 3, which was wearing red, beat the horse that came in third. Only one horse wore the same number as the position it finished in. Arthur's horse beat Simon's horse, whereas Celia's horse beat the horse that wore number 1. The horse wearing green, Celia's, came second, and the horse wearing blue wore number 4. Which one of the following must be true?

A. Simon's horse was yellow and placed 3rd.
B. Celia's horse was red.
C. Celia's horse was in third place.
D. Arthur's horse was blue.
E. Lila's horse wore number 4.

Question 157:

Jessie plants a tree with a height of 40 cm. The information leaflet states that the plant should grow by 20% each year for the first 2 years, and then 10% each year thereafter.

What is the expected height at 4 years?

A. 58.08 cm
B. 64.89 cm
C. 69.696 cm
D. 89.696 cm
E. 82.944 cm
F. None of the above

Question 158

A company is required to pay each employee 10% of their wage into a pension fund if their annual total wage bill is above £200,000. However, there is a legal loophole that if the company splits over two sites, the £200,000 bill is per site. The company therefore decides to have an east site, and a west site.

Name	Annual Salary (£)
Luke	47,000
John	78,400
Emma	68,250
Nicola	88,500
Victoria	52,500
Daniel	63,000

Which employees should be grouped at the same site to minimise the cost to the company?

A. John, Nicola, Luke
B. Nicola, Victoria, Daniel
C. Nicola, Daniel, Luke
D. John, Daniel, Emma
E. Luke, Victoria, Emma

Question 159:

A bus takes 24 minutes to travel from White City to Hammersmith with no stops. Each time the bus stops to pick up and/or drop off passengers, it takes approximately 90 seconds. This morning, the bus picked up passengers from 5 stops, and dropped off passengers at 7 stops.

What is the minimum journey time from White City to Hammersmith this morning?

A. 28 minutes
B. 34 minutes
C. 34.5 minutes
D. 36 minutes
E. 37.5 minutes
F. 42 minutes

Question 160:
Sally is making a Sunday roast for her family and is planning her schedule regarding cooking times. The chicken takes 15 minutes to prepare, 75 minutes to cook, and needs to stand for exactly 5 minutes after cooking. The potatoes take 18 minutes to prepare, 5 minutes to boil, then 50 minutes to roast, and must be roasted immediately after boiling, and then served immediately. The vegetables require only 5 minutes preparation time and 8 minutes boiling time before serving, and can be kept warm to be served at any time after cooking. Given that the cooker can only be cooking two items at any given time and Sally can prepare only one item at a time, what should Sally's schedule be if she wishes to serve dinner at 4pm and wants to start cooking each item as late as possible?

A. Chicken 2.25, potatoes 2.47, vegetables 2.42
B. Chicken 2.25, potatoes 2.47, vegetables 3.47
C. Chicken 2.35, potatoes 3.47, vegetables 2.47
D. Chicken 2.35, potatoes 2.47, vegetables 3.47
E. Chicken 2.45, potatoes 3.47, vegetables 2.47
F. Chicken 2.45, potatoes 2.47, vegetables 3.47

Question 161:
The Smiths have 4 children whose total age is 80. Paul is double the age of Jeremy. Annie is exactly half way between the ages of Jeremy and Paul, and Rebecca is 2 years older than Paul. How old are each of the children?

A. Paul 23, Jeremy 12, Rebecca 26, Annie 19.
B. Paul 22, Jeremy, 11, Rebecca 24, Annie 16.
C. Paul 24, Jeremy 12, Rebecca 26, Annie 18.
D. Paul 28, Jeremy 14, Rebecca 30, Annie 21.
E. More information needed.

Question 162:
Sarah has a jar of spare buttons that are a mix of colours and sizes. The jar contains the following assortment of buttons:

	10mm	25mm	40mm
Cream	15	22	13
Red	6	15	7
Green	9	19	8
Blue	20	6	15
Yellow	4	8	26
Black	17	16	14
Total	**71**	**86**	**83**

Sarah wants to use a 25mm diameter button, but doesn't mind if it is cream or yellow. What is the maximum number of buttons she will have to remove in order to guarantee to pick a suitable button on the next attempt?

A. 210
B. 218
C. 219
D. 239
E. None of the above

SECTION 1A: PROBLEM SOLVING QUESTIONS

Question 163:
Ben wants to optimise his score with one throw of a dart. 50% of the time he hits a segment to either side of the one he is aiming at. With this in mind, which segment should he aim for?
[Ignore all double/triple modifiers]

A. 15
B. 16
C. 17
D. 18
E. 19
F. 20

Question 164:
Victoria is completing her weekly shop, and the total cost of the items is £8.65. She looks in her purse and sees that she has a £5 note, and a large amount of change, including all types of coins. She uses the £5 note, and pays the remainder using the maximum number of coins possible in order to remove some weight from the purse. However, the store has certain rules she has to follow when paying:

- No more than 20p can be paid in "bronze" change (the name given to any combination of 1p pieces and 2p pieces)
- No more than 50p can be paid using any combination of 5p pieces and 10p pieces.
- No more than £1.50 can be paid using any combination of 20p pieces and 50p pieces.

Victoria pays the exact amount, and does not receive any change. Under these rules, what is the *maximum* number of coins that Victoria can have paid with?

A. 30   B. 31   C. 36   D. 41   E. 46

Question 165:
I look at the clock on my bedside table, and I see the following digits:

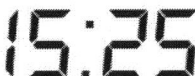

However, I also see that there is a glass of water between me and the clock, which is in front of 2 adjacent figures. I know that this means these 2 figures will appear reversed. For example, 10 would appear as 01, and 20 would appear as 05 (as 5 on a digital clock is a reversed image of a 2). Some numbers, such as 3, cannot appear reversed because there are no numbers which look like the reverse of 3.

Which of the following could be the actual time?

A. 15:52   B. 21:25   C. 12:55   D. 12:22   E. 21:52

Question 166:
Slavica has invaded Worsid, whilst Nordic has invaded Lorkdon. Worsid, spotting an opportunity to bolster its amount of land and natural resources, invades Nordic. Each of these countries is either a dictatorship or a democracy. Slavica is a dictatorship, but Lorkdon is a democracy. 10 years ago, a treaty was signed which guaranteed that no democracy would invade another democracy. No dictatorship has both invaded another dictatorship *and* been invaded by another dictatorship.

Assuming the aforementioned treaty has been upheld, what style of government is practiced in Worsid?

A. Worsid is a Dictatorship.
B. Worsid is a Democracy.
C. Worsid does not practice either of these forms of government.
D. It is impossible to tell.

SECTION 1A: PROBLEM SOLVING — QUESTIONS

Question 167:
Sheila is on a shift at the local supermarket. Unfortunately, the till has developed a fault, meaning it cannot tell her how much change to give each customer. A customer is purchasing the following items, at the following costs:
- A packet of grated cheese priced at £3.25
- A whole cucumber, priced at 75p
- A fish pie mix, priced at £4.00
- 3 DVDs, each priced at £3.00

Sheila knows there is an offer on DVDs in the store at present, in which 3 DVDs bought together will only cost £8.00. The customer pays with a £50 note.

How much change will Sheila need to give the customer?
A. £4   B. £33   C. £34   D. £36   E. £38

Question 168:
Ryan is cooking breakfast for several guests at his hotel. He is frying most of the items using the same large frying pan, to get as much food prepared in as little time as possible. Ryan is cooking Bacon, Sausages, and eggs in this pan. He calculates how much room is taken up in the pan by each item. He calculates the following:
- Each rasher of bacon takes up 7% of the available space in the pan
- Each sausage takes up 3% of the available space in the pan.
- Each egg takes up 12% of the available space in the pan.

Ryan is cooking 2 rashers of bacon, 4 sausages and 1 egg for each guest. He decides to cook all the food for each guest at the same time, rather than cooking all of each item at once.

How many guests can he cook for at once?
A. 1   B. 2   C. 3   D. 4   E. 5

Question 169:
SafeEat Inc. is a national food development testing agency. The Manchester-based laboratory has a system for recording all the laboratory employees' birthdays, and presenting them with cake on their birthday, in order to keep staff morale high. Certain amounts of petty cash are set aside each month in order to fund this. 40% of the staff have their birthday in March, and the secretary works out that £60 is required to fund the birthday cake scheme during this month.

If all birthdays cost £2 to provide a cake for, how many people work at the laboratory?
A. 45   B. 60   C. 75   D. 100   E. 150

Question 170:
Many diseases, such as cancer, require specialist treatment, and thus cannot be treated by a general practitioner. Instead, these diseases must be *referred* to a specialist after an initial, more generalised, medical assessment. Bob has had a biopsy on the 1st of August on a lump found in his abdomen. The results show that it is a tumour, with a slight chance of becoming metastatic, so he is referred to a waiting list for specialist radiotherapy and chemotherapy. The average waiting time in the UK for such treatment is 3 weeks, but in Bob's local district, high demand means that it takes 50% longer for each patient to receive treatment. As he is a lower risk case, with a low risk of metastasis, his waiting time is extended by another 20%.

How many weeks will it be before Bob receives specialist treatment?
A. 4.5   B. 4.6   C. 5.0   D. 5.1   E. 5.4   F. 5.6

SECTION 1A: PROBLEM SOLVING — QUESTIONS

Question 171:

In a class of 30 seventeen year old students, 40% drink alcohol at least once a month. Of those who drink alcohol at least once a month, 75% drink alcohol at least once a week. 1 in 3 of the students who drink alcohol at least once a week also smoke marijuana. 1 in 3 of the students who drink alcohol less than once a month also smoke marijuana.

How many of the students in total smoke marijuana?

A. 3 B. 4 C. 6 D. 9 E. 10 F. 15

Question 172:

Complete the following sequence of numbers: 1, 4, 10, 22, 46, ...

A. 84 B. 92 C. 94 D. 96 E. 100

Question 173:

If the mean of 5 numbers is 7, the median is 8 and the mode is 3, what must the two largest numbers in the set of numbers add up to?

A. 14
B. 21
C. 24
D. 26
E. 35
F. More information needed.

Question 174:

Ahmed buys 1kg bags of potatoes from the supermarket. 1kg bags have to weigh between 900 and 1100 grams. In the first week, there are 10 potatoes in the bag. The next week, there are only 5. Assuming that the potatoes in the bag in week 1 are all the same weight as each other, and the potatoes in the bag in week 2 are all the same weight as each other, what is the maximum possible difference between the heaviest and lightest potato in the two bags?

A. 50g B. 70g C. 90g D. 110g E. 130g

Question 175:

A football tournament involves a group stage, then a knockout stage. In the group stage, groups of four teams play in a round robin format (i.e. each team plays every other team once) and the team that wins the most matches in each group proceeds through to a knockout stage. In addition, the single best performing second place team across all the groups gains a place in the knockout stage. In the knockout stage, sets of two teams play each other and the one that wins proceeds to the next round until there are two teams left, who play the final.

If we start with 60 teams, how many matches are played altogether?

A. 75 B. 90 C. 100 D. 105 E. 165

Question 176:

The last 4 digits of my card number are 2 times my PIN number, plus 200. The last 4 digits of my husband's card number are the last four digits of my card number doubled, plus 200. My husband's PIN number is 2 times the last 4 digits of his card number, plus 200. Given that all these numbers are 4 digits long, whole numbers, and cannot begin with 0, what is the largest number my PIN number can be?

A. 1,074
B. 1,174
C. 2,348
D. 4,096
E. 9,999
F. More information needed.

SECTION 1A: PROBLEM SOLVING — QUESTIONS

Question 177:
All women between 50 and 70 in the UK are invited for breast cancer screening every 3 years. Patients at Doddinghurst Surgery are invited for screening for the first time at any point between their 50th and 53rd birthday. If they ignore an invitation, they are sent reminders every 5 months. We can assume that a woman is screened exactly 1 month after she is sent the invitation or reminder that she accepts. The next invitation for screening is sent exactly 3 years after the previous screening.

If a woman accepts the screening on the second reminder each time, what is the youngest she can be when she has her 4th screening?
A. 60   B. 61   C. 62   D. 63   E. 64   F. 65

Question 178:
Ellie gets a pay rise of k thousand pounds on every anniversary of joining the company, where k is the number of years she has been at the company. She currently earns £40,000, and she has been at the company for 5.5 years. What was her salary when she started at the company?
A. £25,000   C. £28,000   E. £31,000
B. £27,000   D. £30,000   F. £32,000

Question 179:
Northern Line trains arrive into Kings Cross station every 8 minutes, Piccadilly Line trains every 5 minutes and Victoria Line trains every 2 minutes. If trains from all 3 lines arrived into the station exactly 15 minutes ago, how long will it be before they do so again?

A. 24 minutes   C. 40 minutes   E. 65 minutes
B. 25 minutes   D. 60 minutes   F. 80 minutes

Question 180:
If you do not smoke or drink alcohol, your risk of getting Disease X is 1 in 12. If you smoke, you are half as likely to get Disease X as someone who does not smoke. If you drink alcohol, you are twice as likely to get Disease X. A new drug is released that halves anyone's total risk of getting Disease X for each tablet taken. How many tablets of the drug would someone who drinks alcohol have to take to reduce their risk to the same level as someone who smoked but did not take the drug?
A. 0   B. 1   C. 2   D. 3   E. 4   F. 5

Questions 181 – 183 refer to the following information:
There are 20 balls in a bag. 1/2 are red. 1/10 of those that are not red are yellow. The rest are green except 1, which is blue.

Question 181:
If I draw 2 balls from the bag (without replacement), what is the most likely combination to draw?
A. Red and green   C. Red and red
B. Red and yellow   D. Blue and yellow

Question 182:
If I draw 2 balls from the bag (without replacement), what is the least likely (without being impossible) combination to draw?
A. Blue and green   C. Yellow and yellow
B. Blue and yellow   D. Yellow and green

Question 183:
How many balls do you have to draw (without replacement) to guarantee getting at least one of at least three different colours?
A. 5   B. 12   C. 13   D. 17   E. 18   F. 19

SECTION 1A: PROBLEM SOLVING | QUESTIONS

Question 184:

A general election in the UK resulted in a hung parliament, with no single party gaining more than 50% of the seats. Thus, the main political parties are engaged in discussion over the formation of a coalition government. The results of this election are shown below:

Political Party	Seats won
Conservatives	260
Labour	270
Liberal Democrats	50
UKIP	35
Green Party	20
Scottish National Party	17
Plaid Cymru	13
Sinn Fein	9
Democratic Unionist Party (DUP)	11
Other	14 (14 other parties won 1 seat each)

There are a total of 699 seats, meaning that in order to form a government, any coalition must have at least 350 seats between them. Several of the party leaders have released statements about who they are and are not willing to form a coalition with, which are summarised as follows:

- The Conservative party and Labour are not willing to take part in a coalition together.
- The Liberal Democrats refuse to take part in any coalition which also involves UKIP.
- The Labour party will only form a coalition with UKIP if the Green party are also part of this coalition.
- The Conservative party are not willing to take part in any coalition with UKIP unless the Liberal Democrats are also involved.

Considering this information, what is the minimum number of parties required to form a coalition government?

A) 2　　　　B) 3　　　　C) 4　　　　D) 5　　　　E) 6

Question 185:

On Tuesday, 360 patients attend appointments at Doddinghurst Surgery. Of the appointments that are booked in, only 90% are attended. Of the appointments that are booked in, 1 in 2 are for male patients, the remaining appointments are for female patients. Male patients are three times as likely to miss their booked appointment as female patients.

How many male patients attend appointments at Doddinghurst Surgery on Tuesday?

A. 30　　　　B. 60　　　　C. 130　　　　D. 150　　　　E. 170

Question 186:

Every A Level student at Greentown Sixth Form studies Maths. Additionally, 60% study Biology, 50% study Economics and 50% study Chemistry. The other subject on offer at Greentown Sixth Form is Physics. Assuming every student studies 3 subjects and that there are 60 students altogether, how many students study Physics?

A. 15	C. 30	E. 60
B. 24	D. 40	F. More information needed

Question 187:

100,000 people are diagnosed with chlamydia each year in the UK. An average of 0.6 sexual partners are informed per diagnosis. Of these, 80% have tests for chlamydia themselves. Half of these tests come back positive.

Assuming that each of the people diagnosed has had an average of 3 sexual partners (none of them share sexual partners or have sex with each other) and that the likelihood of having chlamydia is the same for those partners who are tested and those who are not, how many of the sexual partners who were not tested (whether they were informed or not) have chlamydia?

A. 120,000	C. 136,000	E. 240,000
B. 126,000	D. 150,000	F. 252,000

Question 188:

In how many different positions can you place an additional tile to make a straight line of 3 tiles?

A. 6
B. 7
C. 8
D. 9
E. 10
F. 11
G. 12

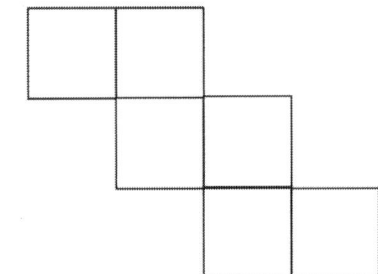

Question 189:

Harry is making orange squash for his daughter's birthday party. He wants to have a 200ml glass of squash for each of the 20 children attending and a 300ml glass of squash for him and each of 3 parents who are helping him out. He has 1,040ml of the concentrated squash.

What ratio of water:concentrated squash should he use in the dilution to ensure he has the right amount to go around?

A. 2:1	C. 4:1	E. 6:1
B. 3:1	D. 5:1	F. 5:2

Question 190:

4 children, Alex, Beth, Cathy and Daniel are each sitting on one of the 4 swings in the park. The swings are in a straight line. One possible arrangement of the children is, left to right, Alex, Beth, Cathy, Daniel.

How many other possible arrangements are there?

A. 5	C. 23	E. 64
B. 12	D. 24	F. 256

Question 191:

A delivery driver is looking to make deliveries in several towns. He is given the following map of the various towns in the area. The lines indicate roads between the towns, along with the lengths of these roads.

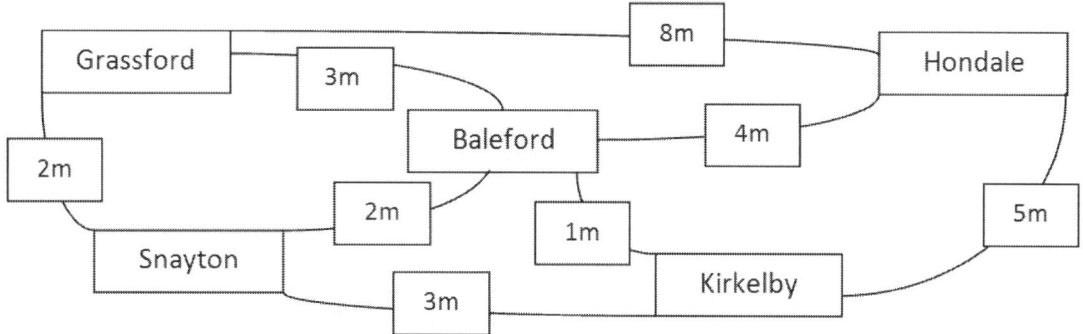

The delivery driver's vehicle has a black box which records the distance travelled and locations visited. At the end of the day, the black box recording shows that he has travelled a total of 14 miles. It also shows that he has visited one town twice, but has not visited any other town more than once. Which of the following is a possible route the driver could have taken?

A. Snayton → Baleford→ Grassford → Snayton→ Kirkelby
B. Baleford → Kirkelby→ Hondale → Grassford→ Baleford→ Snayton
C. Kirkelby → Hondale→ Baleford →Grassford→ Snayton
D. Baleford → Hondale→ Grassford → Baleford→ Hondale→ Kirkelby
E. Snayton → Baleford→ Kirkelby → Hondale→ Grassford
F. None of the above.

Question 192:

Ellie, her brother Tom, her sister Georgia, her mum and her dad line up in height order from shortest to tallest for a family photograph. Ellie is shorter than her dad but taller than her mum. Georgia is shorter than both her parents. Tom is taller than both his parents.

If 1 is shortest and 5 is tallest, what position is Ellie in the line?
A. 1   B. 2   C. 3   D. 4   E. 5

Question 193:

Miss Briggs is trying to arrange the 5 students in her class into a seating plan. Ashley must sit on the front row because she has poor eyesight. Danielle disrupts anyone she sits next to apart from Caitlin, so she must sit next to Caitlin and no-one else. Bella needs to have a teaching assistant sat next to her. The teaching assistant must be sat on the left hand side of the row, near to the teacher. Emily does not get on with Bella, so they need to be sat apart from one another. The teacher has 2 tables which each sit 3 people, which are arranged 1 behind the other.

Who is sitting in the front right seat?
A. Ashley   B. Bella   C. Caitlin   D. Danielle   E. Emily

Question 194:

My aunt runs the dishwasher twice a week, plus an extra time for each person who is living in the house that week. When her son is away at university, she buys a new pack of dishwasher tablets every 6 weeks, but when her son is home she has to buy a new one every 5 weeks. How many people are living in the house when her son is home?

A. 2   C. 4   E. 6
B. 3   D. 5   F. 7

SECTION 1A: PROBLEM SOLVING QUESTIONS

Question 195:
Dates can be written in an 8 digit form, for example 26-12-2014. How many days after 26-12-2014 would be the next time that the 8 digits were made up of exactly 4 different integers?

A. 6
B. 8
C. 10
D. 16
E. 24
F. 30

Question 196:
Redtown is 4 miles east of Greentown. Bluetown is 5 miles north of Greentown. If every town is due North, South, East or West of at least two other towns, and the only other town is Yellowtown, how many miles away from Yellowtown is Redtown, and in what direction?

A. 4 miles east of Yellowtown.
B. 5 miles south of Yellowtown.
C. 5 miles north of Yellowtown.
D. 4 miles west of Yellowtown.
E. 5 miles west of Yellowtown.
F. None of the above.

Question 197:
Jenna pours wine from two 750ml bottles into glasses. The glasses hold 250ml, but she only fills them to 4/5 of capacity, except the last glass, where she puts whatever she has left. How full is the last glass compared to its capacity?

A. 1/5
B. 2/5
C. 3/5
D. 4/5
E. 5/5

Question 198:
There are 30 children in Miss Ellis's class. Two thirds of the girls in Miss Ellis's class have brown eyes, and two thirds of the class as a whole have brown hair. Given that the class is half boys and half girls, what is the difference between the minimum and maximum number of girls that could have brown eyes and brown hair?

A. 0
B. 2
C. 5
D. 7
E. 10
F. More information needed.

Question 199:
A biased die with the numbers 1 to 6 on it is rolled twice. The resulting numbers are multiplied together, and then their sum subtracted from this result to get the 'score' of the dice roll. If the probability of getting a negative (non-zero) score is 0.75, what is the probability of rolling a 1 on a third throw of the die?

A. 0.1
B. 0.2
C. 0.3
D. 0.4
E. 0.5
F. More information needed.

SECTION 1A: PROBLEM SOLVING — QUESTIONS

Questions 200 - 202 are based on the following information:

Fares on the number 11 bus are charged at a number of pence per stop that you travel, plus a flat rate. Emma, who is 21, travels 15 stops and pays £1.70. Charlie, who is 43, travels 8 stops and pays £1.14. Children (under 16) pay half the adult flat rate plus a quarter of the adult charge "per stop".

Question 200:

How much does 17 year old Megan pay to travel 30 stops to college?

A. £0.85
B. £2.40
C. £2.90
D. £3.40
E. More information needed.

Question 201:

How much does 14 year old Alice pay to travel 25 stops to school?

A. £0.50
B. £0.75
C. £1.25
D. £2.50
E. More information needed.

Question 202:

James, who is 24, wants to get the bus into town. The town stop is the 25th stop along a straight road from his house, but he only has £2.

Assuming he has to walk past the stop nearest his house, how many stops will he need to walk past before he gets to the stop he can afford to catch the bus from?

A. 4
B. 6
C. 7
D. 8
E. 9
F. 10

Questions 203 -205 are based on the following information:

Emma mounts and frames paintings. Each painting needs a mount which is 2 inches bigger in each dimension than the painting, and a wooden frame which is 1 inch bigger in each dimension than the mount. Mounts are priced by multiplying 50p by the largest dimension of the mount, so a mount which is 8 inches in one direction and 6 in the other would be £4. Frames are priced by multiplying £2 by the smallest dimension of the frame, so a frame which is 8 inches in one direction and 6 in the other would be £12.

Question 203:

How much would mounting and framing a painting that is 10 x 14 inches cost?

A. £8   B. £26   C. £27   D. £34   E. £42

Question 204:

How much more would mounting and framing a 10 x 10 inch painting cost than mounting and framing an 8 x 8 inch painting?

A. £3.00   B. £4.00   C. £5.00   D. £6.00   E. £7.00

Question 205:

What is the largest square painting that can be framed for £40?

A. 12 inches
B. 13 inches
C. 14 inches
D. 15 inches
E. 16 inches

SECTION 1A: PROBLEM SOLVING — QUESTIONS

Question 206:

If the word 'CREATURES' is coded as 'FTEAWUTEV', which itself would be coded as 'HWEAYUWEX'. What would be the second coding of the word 'MAGICAL'?

A. QCKIGAN
B. OCIIEAN
C. PAJIFAN
D. RALIHAQ
E. RCIMGEP

Question 207:

Jane's mum has asked Jane to go to the shops to get some items that they need. She tells Jane that she will pay her per kilometre that she cycles on her bike to get to the shop, plus a flat rate payment for each place she goes to. Jane receives £6 to go to the grocers, a distance of 5 km, and £4.20 to go the supermarket, a distance of 3 km.

How much would she earn if she then cycles to the library to change some books, a distance of 7 km?

A. £7.50
B. £7.70
C. £7.80
D. £8.00
E. £8.10
F. £8.20

Question 208:

In 2001-2002, 1,019 patients were admitted to hospital due to obesity. This figure was more than 11 times higher by 2011-12 when there were 11,736 patients admitted to hospital with the primary reason for admission being obesity.

If the rate of admissions due to obesity continues to increase at the same linear rate as it has from 2001/2 to 2011/12, how many admissions would you expect in 2031/32?

A. 22,453
B. 23,437
C. 33,170
D. 134,964
E. 269,928
F. 300,000

Question 209:

A shop puts its dresses on sale at 20% off the normal selling price. During the sale, the shop makes a 25% profit over the price at which they bought the dresses. What is the percentage profit when the dresses are sold at full price?

A. 36%
B. 42.5%
C. 56.25%
D. 64%
E. 77%
F. 80%

Question 210:

The 'Keys MedSoc committee' is made up of 20 students from each of the 6 years at the university. However, the president and vice-president are sabbatical roles (students take a year out from studying). There must be at least two general committee students from each year, as well as the specialist roles. Additionally, the social and welfare officers must be pre-clinical students (years 1-3) but not first years, and the treasurer must be a clinical student (years 4-6).

Which **TWO** of the following statements must be true?

1. There can be a maximum of 13 preclinical (years 1-3) students on the committee.
2. There must be a minimum of 6 2nd and 3rd years.
3. There is an unequal distribution of committee members over the different year groups.
4. There can be a maximum of 10 clinical (years 4-6) students on the committee.
5. There can be a maximum of 2 first year students on the committee.
6. General committee members are equally spread across the 6 years.

A. 1 and 4
B. 2 and 3
C. 2 and 4
D. 3 and 6
E. 4 and 5
F. 4 and 6

SECTION 1A: PROBLEM SOLVING QUESTIONS

Question 211:
Friday the 13th is superstitiously considered an 'unlucky' day. If 13th January 2012 was a Friday, when would the next Friday the 13th be?
A. March 2012
B. April 2012
C. May 2012
D. June 2012
E. July 2012
F. August 2012
G. September 2012
H. January has the only Friday 13th in 2012.

Question 212:
A farmer has 18 sheep, 8 of which are male. Unfortunately, 9 sheep die, of which 5 were female. The farmer decides to breed his remaining sheep in order to increase the size of his herd. Assuming every female gives birth to two lambs, how many sheep does the farmer have after all the females have given birth once?
A. 10   B. 14   C. 15   D. 16   E. 19

Question 213:
Piyanga writes a coded message for Nishita. Each letter of the original message is coded as a letter a specific number of characters further on in the alphabet (the specific number is the same for all letters). Piyanga's coded message includes the word "PJVN". What could the original word say?
A. CAME   B. DAME   C. FAME   D. GAME   E. LAME

Question 214:
A number of people get on the bus at the station, which is considered the first stop. At each subsequent stop, 1/2 of the people on the bus get off and then 2 people get on. Between the 4th and 5th stop after the station, there are 5 people on the bus.

How many people got on at the station?
A. 4   B. 6   C. 20   D. 24   E. 30

Question 215:
I have recently moved into a new house, and I am looking to repaint my new living room. The price of several different colours of paint is displayed in the table below. A small can contains enough to paint 10 m² of wall. A large can contains enough to paint 25 m² of wall.

Colour	Cost for a Small Can	Cost for a Large Can
Red	£4	£12
Blue	£8	£15
Black	£3	£9
White	£2	£13
Green	£7	£15
Orange	£5	£20
Yellow	£10	£12

I decide to paint my room a mixture of blue and white, and I purchase some small cans of blue paint and white paint. The cost of blue paint accounts for 50% of the total cost. I paint a total of 100 m² of wall space. I use up all the paint. How many m² of wall space have I painted blue?

A. 10 m²   B. 20 m²   C. 40 m²   D. 50 m²   E. 80 m²

Question 216:
Cakes usually cost 42p at the bakers. The bakers want to introduce a new offer where the amount in pence you pay for each cake is discounted by the square of the number of cakes you buy. For example, buying 3 cakes would mean each cake costs 33p. Isobel says that this is not a good offer from the baker's perspective as it would be cheaper to buy several cakes than just 1. How many cakes would you have to buy for the total cost to fall below 40p?

A. 2   B. 3   C. 4   D. 5   E. 6

Question 217:
The table below shows the percentages of students in two different universities who take various courses. There are 800 students in University A and 1200 students in University B. Biology, Chemistry and Physics are counted as "Sciences".

	University A	University B
Biology	23.50	13.25
Economics	10.25	14.5
Physics	6.25	14.75
Mathematics	11.50	17.25
Chemistry	30.25	7.00
Psychology	18.25	33.25

Assuming each student only takes one course, how many more students in University A than University B study a "Science"?

A. 10   B. 25   C. 60   D. 250   E. 600

Question 218:
Traveleasy Coaches charge passengers at a rate of 50p per mile travelled, plus an additional charge of £5.00 for each international border crossed during the journey. Europremier Coaches charge £15 for every journey, plus 10p per mile travelled, with no charge for crossing international borders. Sonia is travelling from France to Germany, crossing 1 international border. She finds that both companies will charge the same price for this journey.

How many miles is Sonia travelling?

A. 10   B. 20   C. 25   D. 35   E. 40

Question 219:
Lauren, Amy and Chloe live in different cities across England. They decide to meet up together in London and have a meal together. Lauren departs from Southampton at 2:30pm, and arrives in London at 4pm. Amy's journey lasts twice as long as Lauren's journey and she arrives in London at 4:15pm. Chloe departs from Sheffield at 1:30pm, and her journey lasts an hour longer than Lauren's journey.

Which of the following statements is definitely true?
A. Chloe's journey took the longest time.
B. Amy departed after Lauren.

C. Chloe arrived last.
D. Everybody travelled by train.
E. Amy departed before Chloe.

SECTION 1A: PROBLEM SOLVING QUESTIONS

Question 220:
Emma is packing to go on holiday by aeroplane. On the aeroplane, she can take a case of dimension 50cm by 50cm by 20cm, which, when fully packed, can weigh up to 20kg. The empty suitcase weighs 2kg. In her suitcase, she needs to take 3 books, each of which is 0.2m by 0.1m by 0.05m in size, and weighs 1000g. She would also like to take as many items of clothing as possible. Each item of clothing has volume 1500cm^3 and weighs 400 g.

Assuming each item of clothing can be squashed so as to fill any shape gap, how many items of clothing can she take in her case?
A. 28 B. 31 C. 34 D. 37 E. 40

Question 221:
Alex is buying a new bed and mattress. There are 5 bed shops Alex can buy the bed and mattress he wants from, each of which sells the bed and mattress for a different price as follows:
➢ **Bed Shop A:** Bed £120, Mattress £70
➢ **Bed Shop B:** All beds and mattresses £90 each
➢ **Bed Shop C:** Bed £140, Mattress £60. Mattress half price when you buy a bed and mattress together.
➢ **Bed Shop D:** Bed £140, Mattress £100. Get 33% off when you buy a bed and mattress together.
➢ **Bed Shop E:** Bed £175. All beds come with a free mattress.

Which is the cheapest place for Alex to buy the bed and mattress from?
A. Bed Shop A C. Bed Shop C E. Bed Shop E
B. Bed Shop B D. Bed Shop D

Question 222:
In Joseph's sock drawer, there are 21 socks. 4 are blue, 5 are red, 6 are green and the rest are black. How many socks does he need to take from the drawer in order to guarantee he has a matching pair?
A. 3 B. 4 C. 5 D. 6 E. 7

Question 223:
Printing a magazine uses 1 sheet of card and 25 sheets of paper. It also uses ink. Paper comes in packs of 500 and card comes in packs of 60 which are twice the price of a pack of paper. Each ink cartridge prints 130 sheets of either paper or card. A pack of paper costs £3. Ink cartridges cost £5 each.

How many complete magazines can be printed with a budget of £300?
A. 210 B. 220 C. 230 D. 240 E. 250

Question 224:
Rebecca went swimming yesterday. After a while she had covered one fifth of her intended distance. After swimming six more lengths of the pool, she had covered one quarter of her intended distance. How many lengths of the pool did she intend to complete?
A. 40 B. 72 C. 80 D. 100 E. 120

Question 225:
As a special treat, Sammy is allowed to eat five sweets from his very large jar which contains many sweets of each of three flavours – Lemon, Orange and Strawberry. He wants to eat his five sweets in such a way that no two consecutive sweets have the same flavour.

In how many ways can he do this?
A. 32 B. 48 C. 72 D. 108 E. 162

SECTION 1A: PROBLEM SOLVING — QUESTIONS

Question 226:
Granny and her granddaughter Gill both had their birthday yesterday. Today, Granny's age in years is an even number and 15 times that of Gill. In 4 years' time Granny's age in years will be the square of Gill's age in years.

How many years older than Gill is Granny today?
A. 42   B. 49   C. 56   D. 60   E. 64

Question 227:
Pierre said, "Just one of us is telling the truth". Qadr said, "What Pierre says is not true". Ratna said, "What Qadr says is not true". Sven said, "What Ratna says is not true". Tanya said, "What Sven says is not true".

How many of them were telling the truth?
A. 0   B. 1   C. 2   D. 3   E. 4

Question 228:
Two entrants in a school's sponsored run adopt different tactics. Angus walks for half the time and runs for the other half, whilst Bruce walks for half the distance and runs for the other half. Both competitors walk at 3 mph and run at 6 mph. Angus takes 40 minutes to complete the course.

How many minutes does Bruce take?
A. 30   B. 35   C. 40   D. 45   E. 50

Question 229:
Dr Song discovers two new alien life forms on Mars. Species 8472 have one head and two legs. Species 24601 have four legs and one head. Dr Song counts a total of 73 heads and 290 legs in the area. How many members of Species 8472 are present?

A. 0   C. 72   E. 145
B. 1   D. 73   F. More information needed.

Question 230:
A restaurant menu states that:
"All chicken dishes are creamy and all vegetable dishes are spicy. No creamy dishes contain vegetables."

Which of the following **must** be true?

A. Some chicken dishes are spicy.
B. All spicy dishes contain vegetables.
C. Some creamy dishes are spicy.
D. Some vegetable dishes contain tomatoes.
E. None of the above

Question 231:
Simon and his sister Lucy both cycle home from school. One day, Simon is kept back in detention so Lucy sets off for home first. Lucy cycles the 8 miles home at 10 mph. Simon leaves school 20 minutes later than Lucy. How fast must he cycle in order to arrive home at the same time as Lucy?

A. 10 mph   B. 14 mph   C. 17 mph   D. 21 mph   E. 24 mph

Question 232:
Dr. Whu buys 2000 shares in a company at a rate of 50p per share. He then sells the shares for 58p per share. Subsequently he buys 1000 shares at 55p per share then sells them for 61p per share. There is a charge of £20 for each transaction of buying or selling shares. What is Dr. Whu's total profit?

A. £140 B. £160 C. £180 D. £200 E. £220

Question 233:
Jina is playing darts. A dartboard is composed of equal segments, numbered from 1 to 20. She takes three throws, and each of the darts lands in a numbered segment. None land in the centre or in double or triple sections. What is the probability that her total score with the three darts is odd?

A. $1/4$ B. $1/3$ C. $1/2$ D. $3/5$ E. $2/3$

Question 234:
John Morgan invests £5,000 in a savings bond paying 5% interest per annum. What is the value of the investment in 5 years' time?

A. £6,250 B. £6,315 C. £6,381 D. £6,442 E. £6,570

Question 235:
Joe is 12 years younger than Michael. In 5 years the sum of their ages will be 62. How old was Michael two years ago?

A. 20 B. 24 C. 26 D. 30 E. 32

Question 236:
A book has 500 pages. Vicky tears every page out that is a multiple of 3. She then tears out every remaining page that is a multiple of 6. Finally, she tears out half of the remaining pages. If the book measures 15 cm x 30cm and is made from paper of weight 110 gm^{-2}, how much lighter is the book now than at the start?

A. 1,648 g B. 1,698 g C. 1,722 g D. 1,790 g E. 1,848 g

Question 237:
A farmer is fertilising his crops. The more fertiliser is used, the more the crops grow. Fertiliser costs 80p per kilo. Fertilising at a rate of 0.2 kgm^{-2} increases the crop yield by £1.30 m^{-2}. For each additional 100g of fertiliser above 200g, the extra yield is 30% lower than the linear projection of the stated rate. At what rate of fertiliser application is it no longer cost effective to increase the dose

A. 0.5 kgm^{-2} B. 0.6 kgm^{-2} C. 0.7 kgm^{-2} D. 0.8 kgm^{-2} E. 0.9 kgm^{-2}

SECTION 1A: PROBLEM SOLVING — QUESTIONS

Question 238:

Pet-Star, Furry Friends and Creature Cuddles are three pet shops, which each sell food for various types of pets.

Type of pet food	Amount of food required per week	Price per Kg in:		
		Pet-star	Furry Friends	Creature Cuddles
Guinea Pig	3 Kg	£2	£1	£1.50
Cat	6 Kg	£4	£6	£5
Rabbit	4 Kg	£3	£1	£2.50
Dog	8 Kg	£5	£8	£6
Chinchilla	2 Kg	£1.50	£0.50	£1

Given the information above, which of the following statements can we state is definitely *not* true?

A. Regardless of which of these shops you use, the most expensive animal to provide food for will be a dog.
B. If I own a mixture of cats and rabbits, it will be cheaper for me to shop at Pet-star.
C. If I own 3 cats and a dog, the cheapest place for me to shop is at Pet-star
D. Furry Friends sells the cheapest food for the type of pet requiring the most food
E. If I only have one pet, Creature Cuddles will not be the cheapest place to shop regardless of which type of pet I have.

Question 239:

I record my bank balance at the start of each month for six months to help me see how much I am spending each month. My salary is paid on the 10th of each month. At the start of the year, I earn £1000 a month but from March inclusive I receive a pay rise of 10%.

Date	Bank balance
January 1st	1,200
February 1st	1,029
March 1st	1,189
April 1st	1,050
May 1st	925
June 1st	1,025

In which month did I spend the most money?

A. January
B. February
C. March
D. April
E. May

SECTION 1A: PROBLEM SOLVING — QUESTIONS

Question 240:

Amy needs to travel from Southtown station to Northtown station, which are 100 miles apart. She can travel by 3 different methods: train, aeroplane or taxi. The tables below show the different times for these 3 methods. The taxi takes 1 minute to cover a distance of 1 mile. Aeroplane passengers must be at the airport 30 minutes before their flight. Southtown airport is 10 minutes travelling time from Southtown station and Northtown airport is 30 minutes travelling time from Northtown station.

If Amy wants to arrive by 1700 and wants to set off as late as possible, what method of travel should she choose and what time will she leave Southtown station?

Train	Departs Southtown station	1400	1500	1600
	Arrives Northtown station	1615	1650	1715
Flights	Departs Southtown airport	1610		
	Arrives Northtown airport	1645		

A. Flight, 1530
B. Train, 1600
C. Taxi, 1520
D. Train, 1500
E. Flight, 1610

Question 241:

In the multiplication grid below, a, b, c and d are all integers. What does d equal?

A. 18
B. 24
C. 30
D. 40
E. 45

	c	d
a	168	720
b	119	510

Question 242:

A sixth form college has 1,500 students. 48% are girls. 80 of the girls are mixed race.

If an equal proportion of boys and girls are mixed race, how many mixed race boys are there in the college to the nearest 10?

A. 50
B. 60
C. 70
D. 80
E. 90

Question 243:

Christine is a control engineer at the Browdon Nuclear Power Plant. On Wednesday, she is invited to a party on the Friday, and asks her manager if she can take the Friday off. She acknowledged that this will mean she will have worked less than the required number of hours this week, and offers to make this up by working extra hours next week. Her manager suggests that instead, she works 5 hours this Sunday, and 3 extra hours next Thursday to make up the required hours. Christine accepts this proposal. Christine's amended schedule for the week is shown below:

Day	Monday	Tuesday	Wednesday	Thursday	Friday	Saturday	Sunday
Hours worked	8	7	9	6	0	0	5

How many hours was Christine supposed to have worked this week, if she had completed her usual Friday shift?

A. 34
B. 35
C. 36
D. 38
E. 40
F. 42

Question 244:

Leonidas notes that the time on a normal analogue clock is 0340. What is the smaller angle between the hands on the clock?

A. 110°
B. 120°
C. 130°
D. 140°
E. 150°

Question 245:

Sheila is on a shift at the local supermarket. Unfortunately, the till has developed a fault, meaning it cannot tell her how much change to give each customer. A customer is purchasing the following items, at the following costs:

- A packet of grated cheese priced at £3.25
- A whole cucumber, priced at 75p
- A fish pie mix, priced at £4.00
- 3 DVDs, each priced at £3.00

Sheila knows there is an offer on DVDs in the store at present, in which 3 DVDs bought together will only cost £8.00. The customer pays with a £50 note. How much change will Sheila need to give the customer?

A. £33
B. £34
C. £35
D. £36
E. £37

A.

SECTION 1B

Section 1B tests GCSE level Maths + Biology ; it's the most time-pressured section of the PBSAA. You have to answer 30 questions in 40 minutes. The questions can be quite difficult and it's easy to get bogged down. However, it's also the section in which you can improve the most quickly in so it's well worth spending time on it.

Although the vast majority of questions in section 1B aren't particularly difficult, the intense time pressure of having to do one question every minute makes this section the hardest in the PBSAA. As with section 1A, the trick is to identify and do the easy questions whilst leaving the hard ones for the end.

In general, the biology questions in the PBSAA require the least amount of time per question whilst the maths questions are more time-draining as they frequently consist of multi-step calculations.

Gaps in Knowledge

The PBSAA only tests GCSE level knowledge. However, there is a large variation in content between the GCSE exam boards meaning that you may not have covered some topics that are examinable. This is more likely if you didn't carry on with Biology to AS level (e.g. hormones and stem cells). If you fall into this category, you are highly advised to go through the PBSAA Specification and ensure that you have covered all examinable topics. An electronic copy of this can be obtained from **www.uniadmissions.co.uk/PBSAA**.

The questions in this book will help highlight any particular areas of weakness or gaps in your knowledge that you may have. Upon discovering these, make sure you take some time to revise these topics before carrying on – there is little to be gained by attempting section 2 questions with huge gaps in your knowledge.

Maths

Being confident with maths is extremely important for section 1B. Many students find that improving their numerical and algebraic skills usually results in big improvements in both their section 1A and 1B scores. So if you find yourself consistently running out of time in this section, spending a few hours on brushing up your basic maths skills may do wonders for you.

SECTION 1B: Biology

Thankfully, the biology questions tend to be fairly straightforward and require the least amount of time. You should be able to do the majority of these within the 60 second limit (often far less). This means that you should be aiming to make up time in these questions. In the majority of cases – you'll either know the answer or not i.e. they test advanced recall so the trick is to ensure that there are no obvious gaps in your knowledge.

Before going onto to do the practice questions in this book, ensure you are comfortable with the following commonly tested topics:

- Structure of animal, plant and bacterial cells
- Osmosis, Diffusion and Active Transport
- Cell Division (mitosis + meiosis)
- Family pedigrees and Inheritance
- DNA structure and replication
- Gene Technology & Stem Cells
- Enzymes – Function, mechanism and examples of digestive enzymes
- Aerobic and Anaerobic Respiration
- The central vs. peripheral nervous system
- The respiratory cycle including movement of ribs and diaphragm
- The Cardiac Cycle
- Hormones
- Basic immunology
- Food chains and food webs
- The carbon and nitrogen cycles

Top tip! If you find yourself getting less than 50% of biology questions correct in this book, make sure you revisit the syllabus before attempting more questions as this is the best way to maximise your efficiency. In general, there is no reason why you shouldn't be able to get the vast majority of biology questions correct (and in well under 60 seconds) with sufficient practice.

Biology Questions

Question 246:
In relation to the human genome, which of the following are correct?

1. The DNA genome is coded by 4 different bases.
2. The sugar backbone of the DNA strand is formed of glucose.
3. DNA is found in the nucleus of bacteria.

A. 1 only
B. 2 only
C. 3 only
D. 1 and 2
E. 1 and 3
F. 2 and 3
G. 1, 2 and 3

Question 247:
Animal cells contain organelles that take part in vital processes. Which of the following is true?

1. The majority of energy production by animal cells occurs in the mitochondria.
2. The cell wall protects the animal cell membrane from outside pressure differences.
3. The endoplasmic reticulum plays a role in protein synthesis.

A. 1 only
B. 2 only
C. 3 only
D. 1 and 2
E. 2 and 3
F. 1 and 3
G. 1, 2 and 3

Question 248:
With regards to animal mitochondria, which of the following is correct?

A. Mitochondria are not necessary for aerobic respiration.
B. Mitochondria are the sole cause of sperm cell movement.
C. The majority of DNA replication happens inside mitochondria.
D. Mitochondria are more abundant in fat cells than in skeletal muscle.
E. The majority of protein synthesis occurs in mitochondria.
F. Mitochondria are enveloped by a double membrane.

Question 249:
In relation to bacteria, which of the following is **FALSE**?

A. Bacteria always lead to disease.
B. Bacteria contain plasmid DNA.
C. Bacteria do not contain mitochondria.
D. Bacteria have a cell wall and a plasma membrane.
E. Some bacteria are susceptible to antibiotics.

Question 250:
In relation to bacterial replication, which of the following is correct?

A. Bacteria undergo sexual reproduction.
B. Bacteria have a nucleus.
C. Bacteria carry genetic information on circular plasmids.
D. Bacterial genomes are formed of RNA instead of DNA.
E. Bacteria require gametes to replicate.

SECTION 1B: BIOLOGY QUESTIONS

Question 251:
Which of the following are correct regarding active transport?

A. ATP is necessary and sufficient for active transport.
B. ATP is not necessary but sufficient for active transport.
C. The relative concentrations of the material being transported have little impact on the rate of active transport.
D. Transport proteins are necessary and sufficient for active transport.
E. Active transport relies on transport proteins that are powered by an electrochemical gradient.

Question 252:
Concerning mammalian reproduction, which of the following is **FALSE**?

A. Fertilisation involves the fusion of two gametes.
B. Reproduction is sexual and the offspring display genetic variation.
C. Reproduction relies upon the exchange of genetic material.
D. Mammalian gametes are diploid cells produced via meiosis.
E. Embryonic growth requires carefully controlled mitosis.

Question 253:
Which of the following apply to Mendelian inheritance?

1. It only applies to plants.
2. It treats different traits as either dominant or recessive.
3. Heterozygotes have a 25% chance of expressing a recessive trait.

A. 1 only
B. 2 only
C. 3 only
D. 1 and 2
E. 1 and 3
F. 2 and 3
G. All of the above

Question 254:
Which of the following statements are correct?

A. Hormones are secreted into the blood stream and act over long distances at specific target organs.
B. Hormones are substances that almost always cause muscles to contract.
C. Hormones have no impact on the nervous or enteric systems.
D. Hormones are always derived from food and never synthesised.
E. Hormones act rapidly to restore homeostasis.

Question 255:
With regard to neuronal signalling in the body, which of the following are true?

1. Neuronal transmission can be caused by both electrical and chemical stimulation.
2. Synapses ultimately result in the production of an electrical current for signal transduction.
3. All synapses in humans are electrical and unidirectional.

A. 1 only
B. 2 only
C. 3 only
D. 1 and 2
E. 1 and 3
F. 2 and 3
G. 1, 2 and 3

SECTION 1B: BIOLOGY — QUESTIONS

Question 256:
What is the **primary** reason that pH is controlled so tightly in humans?

A. To allow rapid protein synthesis.
B. To allow for effective digestion throughout the GI tract.
C. To ensure ions can function properly in neural signalling.
D. To prevent changes in electrical charge in polypeptide chains.
E. To prevent changes in core body temperature.

Question 257:
Which of the following statements are correct regarding cell walls?

1. The cell wall confers protection against external environmental stimuli.
2. The cell wall is an evolutionary remnant and now has little functional significance in most bacteria.
3. The cell wall is made up primarily of glucose.

A. Only 1   C. Only 3   E. 2 and 3   G. 1, 2 and 3
B. Only 2   D. 1 and 2   F. 1 and 3

Question 258:
Which of the following statements are correct regarding mitosis?

1. It is important in sexual reproduction.
2. A single round of mitosis results in the formation of 2 genetically distinct daughter cells.
3. Mitosis is vital for tissue growth, as it is the basis for cell multiplication.

A. Only 1   C. Only 3   E. 2 and 3   G. 1, 2 and 3
B. Only 2   D. 1 and 2   F. 1 and 3

Question 259:
Which of the following is the best definition of a mutation?

A. A mutation is a permanent change in DNA.
B. A mutation is a permanent change in DNA that is harmful to an organism.
C. A mutation is a permanent change in the structure of intra-cellular organelles caused by changes in DNA/RNA.
D. A mutation is a permanent change in chromosomal structure caused by DNA/RNA changes.

Question 260:
In relation to mutations, which of the following are correct?

1. Mutations always lead to discernible changes in the phenotype of an organism.
2. Mutations are central to natural processes such as evolution.
3. Mutations play a role in cancer.

A. Only 1   C. Only 3   E. 2 and 3   G. 1, 2 and 3
B. Only 2   D. 1 and 2   F. 1 and 3

Question 261:
Which of the following is the most accurate definition of an antibody?

A. An antibody is a molecule that protects red blood cells from changes in pH.
B. An antibody is a molecule produced only by humans and has a pivotal role in the immune system.
C. An antibody is a toxin produced by a pathogen to damage the host organism.
D. An antibody is a molecule that is used by the immune system to identify and neutralize foreign objects and molecules.
E. Antibodies are small proteins found in red blood cells that help increase oxygen carriage.

Question 262:
Which of the following statements about the kidney are correct?

1. The kidneys filter the blood and remove waste products from the body.
2. The kidneys are involved in the digestion of food.
3. In a healthy individual, the kidneys produce urine that contains high levels of glucose.

A. Only 1
B. Only 2
C. Only 3
D. 1 and 2
E. 2 and 3
F. 1 and 3
G. 1, 2 and 3

Question 263:
Which of the following statements are correct?
1. Hormones are slower acting than nerves.
2. Hormones act for a very short time.
3. Hormones act more generally than nerves.
4. Hormones are released when you get a scare.

A. 1 only
B. 1 and 3 only
C. 2 and 4 only
D. 1, 3 and 4 only
E. 1, 2, 3 and 4

Question 264:
Which statements about homeostasis are correct?

1. Homeostasis is about ensuring the inputs within your body exceed the outputs to maintain a constant internal environment.
2. Homeostasis is about ensuring the inputs within your body are less than the outputs to maintain a constant internal environment.
3. Homeostasis is about balancing the inputs within your body with the outputs to ensure your body fluctuates with the needs of the external environment.
4. Homeostasis is about balancing the inputs within your body with the outputs to maintain a constant internal environment.

A. 1 only
B. 2 only
C. 3 only
D. 4 only
E. 1 and 3 only
F. 2 and 4 only
G. 2 and 3 only

Question 265:
Which of the following statement is true?

A. There is more energy and biomass each time you move up a trophic level.
B. There is less energy and biomass each time you move up a trophic level.
C. There is more energy but less biomass each time you move up a trophic level.
D. There is less energy but more biomass each time you move up a trophic level.
E. There is no difference in the energy or biomass when you move up a trophic level.

SECTION 1B: BIOLOGY QUESTIONS

Question 266:
Which of the following statements are true about asexual reproduction?

1. There is no fusion of gametes.
2. There are two parents.
3. There is no mixing of chromosomes.
4. There is genetic variation.

A. 1 and 3 only
B. 1 and 4 only
C. 2 and 3 only
D. 3 and 4 only
E. 2 and 4 only
F. 1, 2, 3 and 4

Question 267:
Put the following in the order which they occur when Jonas sees a bowl of chicken and moves towards it.

1. Retina
2. Motor neuron
3. Sensory neuron
4. Brain
5. Muscle

A. 1 - 3 - 4 - 5 - 2
B. 1 - 2 - 3 - 4 - 5
C. 5 - 1 - 3 - 2 - 4
D. 1 - 3 - 2 - 4 - 5
E. 1 - 3 - 4 - 2 - 5
F. 4 - 1 - 3 - 2 - 5

Question 268:
What path does blood take from the kidney to the liver?

1. Pulmonary artery
2. Inferior vena cava
3. Hepatic artery
4. Aorta
5. Pulmonary vein
6. Renal vein

A. 2 - 1 - 4 - 3 - 5 - 6
B. 1 - 2 - 3 - 4 - 5 - 6
C. 6 - 2 - 5 - 1 - 4 - 3
D. 6 - 2 - 1 - 5 - 4 - 3
E. 3 - 2 - 1 - 4 - 6 - 5
F. 3 - 6 - 2 - 4 - 1 - 5

Question 269:
Which of the following statements are true about animal cloning?

1. Animals cloned from embryo transplants are genetically identical.
2. The genetic material is removed from an unfertilised egg during adult cell cloning.
3. Cloning can cause a reduced gene pool.
4. Cloning is only possible with mammals.

A. 1 only
B. 2 only
C. 3 only
D. 4 only
E. 1 and 2 only
F. 1, 2 and 3 only
G. 1, 2, 3 and 4

Question 270:
Which of the following statements are true with regard to evolution?

1. Individuals within a species show variation because of differences in their genes.
2. Beneficial mutations will accumulate within a population.
3. Gene differences are caused by sexual reproduction and mutations.
4. Species with similar characteristics never have similar genes.

A. 1 only
B. 1 and 4 only
C. 2 and 3 only
D. 2 and 4 only
E. 3 and 4 only
F. 1, 2 and 3 only

Question 271:
Which of the following genetic statements are correct?

1. Alleles are a similar version of different cells.
2. If you are homozygous for a trait, you have three alleles the same for that particular gene.
3. If you are heterozygous for a trait, you have two different alleles for that particular gene.
4. To show the characteristic that is caused by a recessive allele, both carried alleles for the gene have to be recessive.

A. 1 only
B. 2 only
C. 3 only
D. 4 only
E. 1 and 2 only
F. 3 and 4 only
G. 1, 2, and 3 only

Question 272:
Which of the following statements are correct about meiosis?

1. The DNA content of a gamete is half that of a human red blood cell.
2. Meiosis requires ATP.
3. Meiosis only takes place in reproductive tissue.
4. In meiosis, a diploid cell divides in such a way so as to produce two haploid cells.

A. 1 only
B. 3 only
C. 1 and 2 only
D. 2 and 3 only
E. 2 and 4 only
F. 1, 2, 3 and 4

Question 273:
Put the following statements in the correct order of events for when there is too little water in the blood.

1. Urine is more concentrated
2. Pituary gland releases ADH
3. Blood water level returns to normal
4. Hypothalamus detects too little water in blood
5. Kidney affects water level

A. 1 - 2 - 3 - 4 - 5
B. 5 - 4 - 3 - 2 - 1
C. 4 - 2 - 5 - 1 - 3
D. 3 - 2 - 4 - 1 - 5
E. 5 - 2 - 3 - 4 - 1
F. 4 - 2 – 1- 5 - 3

Question 274:
The pH of venous blood is 7.35. Which of the following is the likely pH of arterial blood?

A. 4.4
B. 5.2
C. 6.5
D. 7.0
E. 7.4
F. 7.95

Question 275:
Which of the following are true of the cytoplasm?

1. The vast majority of the cytoplasm is made up of water.
2. All contents of animal cells are contained in the cytoplasm.
3. The cytoplasm contains electrolytes and proteins.

A. 1 only
B. 2 only
C. 3 only
D. 1 and 2 only
E. 1 and 3 only
F. 1, 2 and 3

Question 276:
ATP is produced in which of the following organelles?

1. The golgi apparatus
2. The rough endoplasmic reticulum
3. The mitochondria
4. The nucleus

A. 1 only
B. 2 only
C. 3 only
D. 4 only
E. 1 and 2
F. 2 and 3 only
G. 3 and 4 only
H. 1, 2, 3 and 4

Question 277:
The cell membrane:
A. Is made up of a phospholipid bilayer which only allows active transport across it.
B. Is not found in bacteria.
C. Is a semi-permeable barrier to ions and organic molecules.
D. Consists purely of enzymes.

Question 278:
Cells of the *Polyommatus atlantica* butterfly of the Lycaenidae family have 446 chromosomes. Which of the following statements about a *P. atlantica* butterfly are correct?

1. Mitosis will produce 2 daughter cells each with 223 pairs of chromosomes
2. Meiosis will produce 4 daughter cells each with 223 chromosomes
3. Mitosis will produce 4 daughter cells each with 446 chromosomes
4. Meiosis will produce 2 daughter cells each with 223 pairs of chromosomes

A. 1 and 2 only
B. 1 and 3 only
C. 2 and 3 only
D. 3 and 4 only
E. 1, 2 and 3 only
F. 1, 2, 3 and 4

SECTION 1B: BIOLOGY QUESTIONS

Questions 279-281 are based on the following information:
Assume that hair colour is determined by a single allele. The R allele is dominant and results in black hair. The r allele is recessive for red hair. Mary (red hair) and Bob (black hair) are having a baby girl.

Question 279:
What is the probability that she will have red hair?

A. 0% only
B. 25% only
C. 50% only
D. 0% or 25%
E. 0% or 50%
F. 25% or 50%

Question 280:
Mary and Bob have a second child, Tim, who is born with red hair. What does this confirm about Bob?

A. Bob is heterozygous for the hair allele.
B. Bob is homozygous dominant for the hair allele.
C. Bob is homozygous recessive for the hair allele.
D. Bob does not have the hair allele.

Question 281:
Mary and Bob go on to have a third child. What are the chances that this child will be born homozygous for black hair?

A. 0%
B. 25%
C. 50%
D. 75%
E. 100%

Question 282:
Why does air flow into the chest on inspiration?

1. Atmospheric pressure is smaller than intra-thoracic pressure during inspiration.
2. Atmospheric pressure is greater than intra-thoracic pressure during inspiration.
3. Anterior and lateral chest expansion decreases absolute intra-thoracic pressure.
4. Anterior and lateral chest expansion increases absolute intra-thoracic pressure.

A. 1 only
B. 2 only
C. 2 and 3
D. 1 and 4
E. 1 and 3
F. 2 and 4

Question 283:
Which of the following components of a food chain represent the largest biomass?

A. Producers
B. Decomposers
C. Primary consumers
D. Secondary consumers
E. Tertiary consumers

Question 284:
Concerning the nitrogen cycle, which of the following are true?

1. The majority of the Earth's atmosphere is nitrogen.
2. Most of the nitrogen in the Earth's atmosphere is inert.
3. Bacteria are essential for nitrogen fixation.
4. Nitrogen fixation occurs during lightning strikes.

A. 1 and 2
B. 1 and 3
C. 2 and 3
D. 2 and 4
E. 3 and 4
F. 1, 2, 3 and 4

Question 285:
Which of the following statement are correct regarding mutations?

1. Mutations always cause proteins to lose their function.
2. Mutations always change the structure of the protein encoded by the affected gene.
3. Mutations always result in cancer.

A. Only 1
B. Only 2
C. Only 3
D. 1 and 2
E. 2 and 3
F. 1 and 3
G. 1, 2 and 3
H. None are correct

Question 286:
Which of the following is not a function of the central nervous system?

A. Coordination of movement
B. Decision making and executive functions
C. Control of heart rate
D. Cognition
E. Memory

Question 287:
Which of the following control mechanisms are involved in modulating cardiac output?

1. Voluntary control.
2. Sympathetic control to decrease heart rate.
3. Parasympathetic control to increase heart rate.

A. Only 1
B. Only 2
C. Only 3
D. 1 and 2
E. 2 and 3
F. 1 and 3
G. 1, 2 and 3
H. None are correct.

Question 288:
Vijay goes to see his GP with fatty, smelly stools that float on water. Which of the following enzymes is most likely to be malfunctioning?

A. Amylase
B. Lipase
C. Protease
D. Sucrase
E. Lactase

Question 289:
Which of the following statements concerning the cardiovascular system is correct?

A. Oxygenated blood from the lungs flows to the heart via the pulmonary artery.
B. All arteries carry oxygenated blood.
C. All animals have a double circulatory system.
D. The superior vena cava contains oxygenated blood
E. All veins have valves.
F. None of the above.

Question 290:
Which part of the GI tract has the least amount of enzymatic digestion occurring?

A. Mouth
B. Stomach
C. Small intestine
D. Large intestine
E. Rectum

SECTION 1B: BIOLOGY QUESTIONS

Question 291:
Oge touches a hot stove and immediately moves her hand away. Which of the following components are **NOT** involved in this reaction?

1. Thermo-receptor
2. Brain
3. Spinal Cord
4. Sensory nerve
5. Motor nerve
6. Muscle

A. 1 only
B. 2 only
C. 3 only
D. 1 and 2 only
E. 1, 2 and 3 only
F. 3, 4, 5 and 6

Question 292:
Which of the following represents a scenario with an appropriate description of the mode of transport?

1. Water moving from a hypotonic solution outside of a potato cell, across the cell wall and cell membrane and into the hypertonic cytoplasm of the potato cell → Osmosis.
2. Carbon dioxide moving across a respiring cell's membrane and dissolving in blood plasma → Active transport.
3. Reabsorption of amino acids against a concentration gradient in the glomeruluar apparatus → Diffusion.

A. 1 only
B. 2 only
C. 3 only
D. 1 and 2 only
E. 2 and 3 only
F. 1 and 3 only
G. 1, 2 and 3

Question 293:
Which of the following equations represents anaerobic respiration?

1. Carbohydrate + Oxygen → Energy + Carbon Dioxide + Water
2. Carbohydrate → Energy + Lactic Acid + Carbon dioxide
3. Carbohydrate → Energy + Lactic Acid
4. Carbohydrate → Energy + Ethanol + Carbon dioxide

A. 1 only
B. 2 only
C. 3 only
D. 4 only
E. 1 and 2
F. 1 and 3
G. 1 and 4
H. 2 and 4 only
I. 3 and 4 only

Question 294:
Which of the following statements regarding respiration are correct?

1. The mitochondria are the centres for both aerobic and anaerobic respiration.
2. The cytoplasm is the main site of anaerobic respiration.
3. For every two moles of glucose that is respired aerobically, 12 moles of CO_2 are liberated.
4. Anaerobic respiration is more efficient than aerobic respiration.

A. 1 and 2
B. 1 and 4
C. 2 and 3
D. 2 and 4
E. 3 and 4

Question 295:
Which of the following statements are true?

1. The nucleus contains the cell's chromosomes.
2. The cytoplasm consists purely of water.
3. The plasma membrane is a single phospholipid layer.
4. The cell wall prevents plants cells from lysing due to osmotic pressure.

A. 1 and 2
B. 1 and 4
C. 1, 3 and 4
D. 1, 2 and 3
E. 1, 2 and 4
F. 2, 3 and 4

SECTION 1B: BIOLOGY — **QUESTIONS**

Question 296:
Which of the following statements are true about osmosis?

1. If a medium is hypertonic relative to the cell cytoplasm, the cell will gain water through osmosis.
2. If a medium is hypotonic relative to the cell cytoplasm, the cell will gain water through osmosis.
3. If a medium is hypotonic relative to the cell cytoplasm, the cell will lose water through osmosis.
4. If a medium is hypertonic relative to the cell cytoplasm, the cell will lose water through osmosis.
5. The medium's tonicity has no impact on the movement of water.

A. 1 only   B. 2 only   C. 1 and 3   D. 2 and 4   E. 5 only

Question 297:
Which of the following statements are true about stem cells?

1. Stem cells have the ability to differentiate into other mature types of cells.
2. Stem cells are unable to maintain their undifferentiated state.
3. Stem cells can be classified as embryonic stem cells or adult stem cells.
4. Stem cells are only found in embryos.

A. 1 and 3   B. 3 and 4   C. 2 and 3   D. 1 and 2   E. 2 and 4

Question 298:
Which of the following are **NOT** examples of natural selection?

1. Giraffes growing longer necks to eat taller plants.
2. Antibiotic resistance developed by certain strains of bacteria.
3. Pesticide resistance among locusts in farms.
4. Breeding of horses to make them run faster.

A. 1 only   B. 4 only   C. 1 and 3   D. 1 and 4   E. 2 and 4

Question 299:
Which of the following statements are true?

1. Enzymes stabilise the transition state and therefore lower the activation energy.
2. Enzymes distort substrates in order to lower activation energy.
3. Enzymes decrease temperature to slow down reactions and lower the activation energy.
4. Enzymes provide alternative pathways for reactions to occur.

A. 1 only   B. 1 and 2   C. 1 and 4   D. 2 and 4   E. 3 and 4

Question 300:
Which of the following are examples of negative feedback?

1. Salivating whilst waiting for a meal.
2. Throwing a dart.
3. The regulation of blood pH.
4. The regulation of blood pressure.

A. 1 only
B. 1 and 2
C. 3 and 4
D. 2, 3, and 4
E. 1, 2, 3 and 4

SECTION 1B: BIOLOGY QUESTIONS

Question 301:
Which of the following statements about the immune system are true?

1. White blood cells defend against bacterial and fungal infections.
2. White blood cells can temporarily disable but not kill pathogens.
3. White blood cells use antibodies to fight pathogens.
4. Antibodies are produced by bone marrow stem cells.

A. 1 and 3
B. 1 and 4
C. 2 and 3
D. 2 and 4
E. 1, 2, and 3
F. 1, 3, and 4

Question 302:
The cardiovascular system does **NOT**:

A. Deliver vital nutrients to peripheral cells.
B. Oxygenate blood and transports it to peripheral cells.
C. Act as a mode of transportation for hormones to reach their target organ.
D. Facilitate thermoregulation.
E. Respond to exercise by increasing cardiac output to exercising muscles.

Question 303:
Which of the following statements is correct?

A. Adrenaline can sometimes decrease heart rate.
B. Adrenaline is rarely released during flight or fight responses.
C. Adrenaline causes peripheral vasoconstriction.
D. Adrenaline only affects the cardiovascular system.
E. Adrenaline travels primarily in lymphatic vessels.
F. None of the above.

Question 304:
Which of the following statements is true?

A. Protein synthesis occurs solely in the nucleus.
B. Each amino acid is coded for by three DNA bases.
C. Each protein is coded for by three amino acids.
D. Red blood cells can create new proteins to prolong their lifespan.
E. Protein synthesis isn't necessary for mitosis to take place.
F. None of the above.

Question 305:
A solution of amylase and carbohydrate is present in a beaker, where the pH of the contents is 6.3. Assuming amylase is saturated, which of the following will increase the rate of production of the product?

1. Add sodium bicarbonate
2. Add carbohydrate
3. Add amylase
4. Increase the temperature to 100° C

A. 1 only
B. 2 only
C. 3 only
D. 4 only
E. 1 and 2
F. 1 and 3
G. 1, 2 and 3
H. 1, 3 and 4

SECTION 1B: BIOLOGY — QUESTIONS

Question 306:
Celestial Necrosis is a newly discovered autosomal recessive disorder. A female carrier and a male with the disease produce two boys. What is the probability that neither boy's genotype contains the celestial necrosis allele?

A. 100%   B. 75%   C. 50%   D. 25%   E. 0%

Question 307:
Which among the following has no endocrine function?

A. The thyroid
B. The ovary
C. The pancreas
D. The adrenal gland
E. The testes
F. None of the above.

Question 308:
Which of the following statements are true?

1. Increasing levels of insulin cause a decrease in blood glucose levels.
2. Increasing levels of glycogen cause an increase in blood glucose levels.
3. Increasing levels of adrenaline decrease the heart rate.

A. 1 only
B. 2 only
C. 3 only
D. 1 and 2
E. 2 and 3
F. 1 and 3
G. 1, 2 and 3

Question 309:
Which of the following rows is correct?

	Oxygenated Blood		Deoxygenated Blood	
A.	Left atrium	Left ventricle	Right atrium	Right ventricle
B.	Left atrium	Right atrium	Left ventricle	Right ventricle
C.	Left atrium	Right ventricle	Right atrium	Right ventricle
D.	Right atrium	Right ventricle	Left atrium	Left ventricle
E.	Left ventricle	Right atrium	Left atrium	Right ventricle

Questions 310-312 are based on the following information:
The pedigree below shows the inheritance of a newly discovered disease that affects connective tissue called Nafram syndrome. Individual 1 is a normal homozygote.

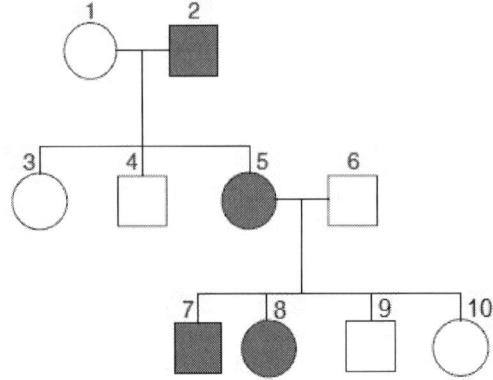

Question 310:
What is the inheritance of Nafram syndrome?

A. Autosomal dominant
B. Autosomal recessive
C. X-linked dominant
D. X-linked recessive
E. Co-dominant

Question 311:
Which individuals must be heterozygous for Nafram syndrome?

A. 1 and 2
B. 8 and 9
C. 2 and 5
D. 5 and 6
E. 6 and 8
F. 6 and 10

Question 312:
Taking N to denote a diseased allele and n to denote a normal allele, which of the following are **NOT** possible genotypes for 6's parents?

1. NN x NN
2. NN x Nn
3. Nn x nn
4. Nn x Nn
5. nn x nn

A. 1 and 2
B. 1 and 3
C. 2 and 3
D. 2 and 5
E. 3 and 4
F. 4 and 5

Question 313:
Which of the following correctly describes the passage of urine through the body?

	1st	2nd	3rd	4th
A	Kidney	Ureter	Bladder	Urethra
B	Kidney	Urethra	Bladder	Ureter
C	Urethra	Bladder	Ureter	Kidney
D	Ureter	Kidney	Bladder	Urethra

SECTION 1B: BIOLOGY — QUESTIONS

Question 314:
Which of the following best describes the passage of blood from the body, through the heart, back to the body?

A. Aorta → Left Ventricle → Left Atrium → Inferior Vena Cava → Right Atrium → Right Ventricle → Lungs → Aorta
B. Inferior vena cava → Left Atrium → Left Ventricle → Lungs → Right Atrium → Right Ventricle → Aorta
C. Inferior vena cava → Right Ventricle → Right Atrium → Lungs → Left Atrium → Left Ventricle → Aorta
D. Aorta → Left Atrium → Left Ventricle → Lungs → Right Atrium → Right Ventricle → Inferior Vena Cava
E. Right Atrium → Left Atrium → Inferior vena cava → Lungs → Left Atrium → Right Ventricle → Aorta
F. None of the above.

Question 315:
Which of the following best describes the events during inspiration?

	Intrathoracic Pressure	Intercostal Muscles	Diaphragm
A	Increases	Contract	Contracts
B	Increases	Relax	Contracts
C	Increases	Contract	Relaxes
D	Increases	Relax	Relaxes
E	Decreases	Contract	Contracts
F	Decreases	Relax	Contracts
G	Decreases	Contract	Relaxes
H	Decreases	Relax	Relaxes

Questions 316- 317 are based on the following information:
DNA is made up of the four nucleotide bases: adenine, cytosine, guanine and thymine. A triplet repeat or codon is a sequence of three nucleotides which code for an amino acid. While there are only 20 amino acids there are 64 different combinations of the four DNA nucleotide bases. This means that more than one combination of 3 DNA nucleotides sequences code for the same amino acid.

Question 316:
Which property of the DNA code is described above?

A. The code is unambiguous.
B. The code is universal.
C. The code is non-overlapping.
D. The code is degenerate.
E. The code is preserved.
F. The code has no punctuation.

Question 317:
Which type of mutation does the described property protect against the most?
A. An insertion - where a single nucleotide is inserted.
B. A point mutation - where a single nucleotide is replaced for another.
C. A deletion - where a single nucleotide is deleted.
D. A repeat expansion - where a repeated trinucleotide sequence is added.
E. A duplication - where a piece of DNA is abnormally copied.

Question 318:
Which row of the table below describes what happens when external temperature decreases?

	Temperature Change Detected by	Sweat Gland Secretion	Cutaneous Blood Flow
A	Hypothalamus	Increases	Increases
B	Hypothalamus	Increases	Decreases
C	Hypothalamus	Decreases	Increases
D	Hypothalamus	Decreases	Decreases
E	Cerebral Cortex	Increases	Increases
F	Cerebral Cortex	Increases	Decreases
G	Cerebral Cortex	Decreases	Increases
H	Cerebral Cortex	Decreases	Decreases

Question 319:
Which of the following processes involve active transport?

1. Reabsorption of glucose in the kidney.
2. Movement of carbon dioxide into the alveoli in the lungs.
3. Movement of chemicals in a neural synapse.

A. 1 only
B. 2 only
C. 3 only
D. 1 and 2
E. 1 and 3
F. 2 and 3
G. 1, 2 and 3

Question 320:
Which of the following statements is correct about enzymes?

A. All enzymes are made up of amino acids only.
B. Enzymes can sometimes slow the rate of reactions.
C. Enzymes have no impact on reaction temperatures.
D. Enzymes are heat sensitive but resistant to changes in pH.
E. Enzymes are unspecific in their substrate use.
F. None of the above.

SECTION 1B: Maths

PBSAA Maths questions are designed to be time draining- if you find yourself consistently not finishing, consider prioritising the biology questions. If you find yourself really struggling as it's been sometime since you've formally studied maths, consider doing section 1C instead.

Good students sometimes have a habit of making easy questions difficult; remember that the PBSAA only tests GCSE level knowledge so you are not expected to know or use calculus or trigonometry in the exam.

Formulas you MUST know:

2D Shapes		3D Shapes		
	Area		Surface Area	Volume
Circle	πr^2	**Cuboid**	Sum of all 6 faces	Length x width x height
Parallelogram	Base x Vertical height	**Cylinder**	$2\pi r^2 + 2\pi r l$	$\pi r^2 \times l$
Trapezium	0.5 x h x (a+b)	**Cone**	$\pi r^2 + \pi r l$	$\pi r^2 \times (h/3)$
Triangle	0.5 x base x height	**Sphere**	$4\pi r^2$	$(4/3)\pi r^3$

Even good students who are studying maths at A2 can struggle with certain PBSAA maths topics because they're usually glossed over at school. These include:

Quadratic Formula

The solutions for a quadratic equation in the form $ax^2 + bx + c = 0$ are given by: $x = \dfrac{-b \pm \sqrt{b^2 - 4ac}}{2a}$

Remember that you can also use the discriminant to quickly see if a quadratic equation has any solutions:

If $b^2 - 4ac < 0$: No solutions   If $b^2 - 4ac = 0$: One solution   If $b^2 - 4ac > 2$: Two solutions

Completing the Square

If a quadratic equation cannot be factorised easily and is in the format $ax^2 + bx + c = 0$ then you can rearrange it into the form $a\left(x + \dfrac{b}{2a}\right)^2 + \left[c - \dfrac{b^2}{4a}\right] = 0$

This looks more complicated than it is – remember that in the PBSAA, you're extremely unlikely to get quadratic equations where $a > 1$ and the equation doesn't have any easy factors. This gives you an easier equation: $\left(x + \dfrac{b}{2}\right)^2 + \left[c - \dfrac{b^2}{4}\right] = 0$ and is best understood with an example.

Consider: $x^2 + 6x + 10 = 0$

This equation cannot be factorised easily but note that: $x^2 + 6x - 10 = (x+3)^2 - 19 = 0$

Therefore, $x = -3 \pm \sqrt{19}$. Completing the square is an important skill – make sure you're comfortable with it.

Difference between 2 Squares

If you are asked to simplify expressions and find that there are no common factors but it involves square numbers – you might be able to factorise by using the 'difference between two squares'.

For example, $x^2 - 25$ can also be expressed as $(x + 5)(x - 5)$.

SECTION 1B: MATHS QUESTIONS

Maths Questions

Question 321:

Robert has a box of building blocks. The box contains 8 yellow blocks and 12 red blocks. He picks three blocks from the box and stacks them up high. Calculate the probability that he stacks two red building blocks and one yellow building block, in **any** order.

A. $\dfrac{8}{20}$ B. $\dfrac{44}{95}$ C. $\dfrac{11}{18}$ D. $\dfrac{8}{19}$ E. $\dfrac{12}{20}$ F. $\dfrac{35}{60}$

Question 322:

Solve $\dfrac{3x+5}{5} + \dfrac{2x-2}{3} = 18$

A. 12.11   B. 13.49   C. 13.95   D. 14.2   E. 19   F. 265

Question 323:

Solve $3x^2 + 11x - 20 = 0$

A. 0.75 and $-\dfrac{4}{3}$ C. -5 and $\dfrac{4}{3}$ E. 12 only

B. -0.75 and $\dfrac{4}{3}$ D. 5 and $\dfrac{4}{3}$ F. -12 only

Question 324:

Express $\dfrac{5}{x+2} + \dfrac{3}{x-4}$ as a single fraction.

A. $\dfrac{15x-120}{(x+2)(x-4)}$ C. $\dfrac{8x-14}{(x+2)(x-4)}$ E. 24

B. $\dfrac{8x-26}{(x+2)(x-4)}$ D. $\dfrac{15}{8x}$ F. $\dfrac{8x-14}{x^2-8}$

Question 325:

The value of p is directly proportional to the cube root of q. When p = 12, q = 27. Find the value of q when p = 24.

A. 32   B. 64   C. 124   D. 128   E. 216   F. 1728

Question 326:

Write 72^2 as a product of its prime factors.

A. $2^6 \times 3^4$ B. $2^6 \times 3^5$ C. $2^4 \times 3^4$

D. 2×3^3 E. $2^6 \times 3$ F. $2^3 \times 3^2$

SECTION 1B: MATHS QUESTIONS

Question 327:

Calculate: $\dfrac{2.302 \times 10^5 + 2.302 \times 10^2}{1.151 \times 10^{10}}$

A. 0.0000202
B. 0.00020002
C. 0.00002002
D. 0.00000002
E. 0.000002002
F. 0.000002002

Question 328:

Given that $y^2 + ay + b = (y + 2)^2 - 5$, find the values of **a** and **b**.

	a	b
A	-1	4
B	1	9
C	-1	-9
D	-9	1
E	4	-1
F	4	1

Question 329:

Express $\dfrac{4}{5} + \dfrac{m-2n}{m+4n}$ as a single fraction in its simplest form:

A. $\dfrac{6m+6n}{5(m+4n)}$
B. $\dfrac{9m+26n}{5(m+4n)}$
C. $\dfrac{20m+6n}{5(m+4n)}$
D. $\dfrac{3m+9n}{5(m+4n)}$
E. $\dfrac{3(3m+2n)}{5(m+4n)}$
F. $\dfrac{6m+6n}{3(m+4n)}$

Question 330:

A is inversely proportional to the square root of B. When A = 4, B = 25.
Calculate the value of A when B = 16.

A. 0.8   B. 4   C. 5   D. 6   E. 10   F. 20

Question 331:

S, T, U and V are points on the circumference of a circle, and O is the centre of the circle.

Given that angle SVU = 89°, calculate the size of the smaller angle SOU.

A. 89°   B. 91°   C. 102°   D. 178°   E. 182°   F. 212°

Question 332:

Open cylinder A has a surface area of 8π cm² and a volume of 2π cm³. Open cylinder B is an enlargement of A and has a surface area of 32π cm². Calculate the volume of cylinder B.

~ 107 ~

A. 2π cm³
B. 8π cm³
C. 10π cm³
D. 14π cm³
E. 16π cm³
F. 32π cm³

Question 333:

Express $\dfrac{8}{x(3-x)} - \dfrac{6}{x}$ in its simplest form.

A. $\dfrac{3x-10}{x(3-x)}$
B. $\dfrac{3x+10}{x(3-x)}$
C. $\dfrac{6x-10}{x(3-2x)}$
D. $\dfrac{6x-10}{x(3+2x)}$
E. $\dfrac{6x-10}{x(3-x)}$
F. $\dfrac{6x+10}{x(3-x)}$

Question 334:

A bag contains 10 balls. 9 of those are white and 1 is black. What is the probability that the black ball is drawn in the tenth and final draw if the drawn balls are not replaced?

A. 0
B. $\dfrac{1}{10}$
C. $\dfrac{1}{100}$
D. $\dfrac{1}{10^{10}}$
E. $\dfrac{1}{362,880}$

Question 335:

Gambit has an ordinary deck of 52 cards. What is the probability of Gambit drawing 2 Kings (without replacement)?

A. 0
B. $\dfrac{1}{169}$
C. $\dfrac{1}{221}$
D. $\dfrac{4}{663}$
E. None of the above

Question 336:

I have two identical unfair dice, where the probability that the dice get a 6 is twice as high as the probability of any other outcome, which are all equally likely. What is the probability that when I roll both dice the total will be 12?

A. 0
B. $\dfrac{4}{49}$
C. $\dfrac{1}{9}$
D. $\dfrac{2}{7}$
E. None of the above

Question 337:

A roulette wheel consists of 36 numbered spots and 1 zero spot (i.e. 37 spots in total).
What is the probability that the ball will stop in a spot either divisible by 3 or 2?

A. 0
B. $\dfrac{25}{37}$
C. $\dfrac{25}{36}$
D. $\dfrac{18}{37}$
E. $\dfrac{24}{37}$

Question 338:

I have a fair coin that I flip 4 times. What is the probability I get 2 heads and 2 tails?

A. $\dfrac{1}{16}$
B. $\dfrac{3}{16}$

C. $\dfrac{3}{8}$

D. $\dfrac{9}{16}$

E. None of the above

SECTION 1B: MATHS QUESTIONS

Question 339:

Shivun rolls two fair dice. What is the probability that he gets a total of 5, 6 or 7?

A. $\frac{9}{36}$

B. $\frac{7}{12}$

C. $\frac{1}{6}$

D. $\frac{5}{12}$

E. None of the above

Question 340:

Dr Savary has a bag that contains x red balls, y blue balls and z green balls (and no others). He pulls out a ball, replaces it, and then pulls out another. What is the probability that he picks one red ball and one green ball?

A. $\frac{2(x+y)}{x+y+z}$

B. $\frac{xz}{(x+y+z)^2}$

C. $\frac{2xz}{(x+y+z)^2}$

D. $\frac{(x+z)}{(x+y+z)^2}$

E. $\frac{4xz}{(x+y+z)^4}$

F. More information necessary

Question 341:

Mr Kilbane has a bag that contains x red balls, y blue balls and z green balls (and no others). He pulls out a ball, does **NOT** replace it, and then pulls out another. What is the probability that he picks one red ball and one blue ball?

A. $\frac{2xy}{(x+y+z)^2}$

B. $\frac{2xy}{(x+y+z)(x+y+z-1)}$

C. $\frac{2xy}{(x+y+z)^2}$

D. $\frac{2xy}{(x+y+z)(x+y+z-1)}$

E. $\frac{4xy}{(x+y+z-1)^2}$

F. More information needed

Question 342:

There are two tennis players. The first player wins the point with probability p, and the second player wins the point with probability 1-p. The rules of tennis say that the first player to score four points wins the game, unless the score is 4-3. At this point the first player to get two points ahead wins.

What is the probability that the first player wins in exactly 5 rounds?

A. 4p⁴(1-p)

B. p⁴(1-p)

C. 4p(1-p)

D. 4p(1-p)⁴

E. 4p⁵(1-p)

F. More information needed.

Question 343:

Solve the equation $\frac{4x+7}{2} + 9x + 10 = 7$

A. $\frac{22}{13}$ B. $-\frac{22}{13}$ C. $\frac{10}{13}$ D. $-\frac{10}{13}$ E. $\frac{13}{22}$ F. $-\frac{13}{22}$

Question 344:

The volume of a sphere is $V = \frac{4}{3}\pi r^3$, and the surface area of a sphere is $S = 4\pi r^2$. Express S in terms of V

A. $S = (4\pi)^{2/3}(3V)^{2/3}$
B. $S = (8\pi)^{1/3}(3V)^{2/3}$
C. $S = (4\pi)^{1/3}(9V)^{2/3}$
D. $S = (4\pi)^{1/3}(3V)^{2/3}$
E. $S = (16\pi)^{1/3}(9V)^{2/3}$

Question 345:

Express the volume of a cube, V, in terms of its surface area, S.

A. $V = (S/6)^{3/2}$
B. $V = S^{3/2}$
C. $V = (6/S)^{3/2}$
D. $V = (S/6)^{1/2}$
E. $V = (S/36)^{1/2}$
F. $V = (S/36)^{3/2}$

Question 346:

Solve the equations $4x + 3y = 7$ and $2x + 8y = 12$

A. $(x,y) = \left(\frac{17}{13}, \frac{10}{13}\right)$
B. $(x,y) = \left(\frac{10}{13}, \frac{17}{13}\right)$
C. $(x,y) = (1, 2)$
D. $(x,y) = (2, 1)$
E. $(x,y) = (6, 3)$
F. $(x,y) = (3, 6)$
G. No solutions possible.

Question 347:

Rearrange $\frac{(7x + 10)}{(9x + 5)} = 3y^2 + 2$, to make x the subject.

A. $\frac{15 y^2}{7 - 9(3y^2 + 2)}$
B. $\frac{15 y^2}{7 + 9(3y^2 + 2)}$
C. $-\frac{15 y^2}{7 - 9(3y^2 + 2)}$
D. $-\frac{15 y^2}{7 + 9(3y^2 + 2)}$
E. $-\frac{5 y^2}{7 + 9(3y^2 + 2)}$
F. $\frac{5 y^2}{7 + 9(3y^2 + 2)}$

Question 348:

Simplify $3x\left(\frac{3x^7}{x^{\frac{1}{3}}}\right)^3$

A. $9x^{20}$ B. $27x^{20}$ C. $87x^{20}$ D. $9x^{21}$ E. $27x^{21}$ F. $81x^{21}$

Question 349:

Simplify $2x[(2x)^7]^{\frac{1}{14}}$

A. $2x\sqrt{2x^4}$
B. $2x\sqrt{2x^3}$
C. $2\sqrt{2x^4}$
D. $2\sqrt{2x^3}$
E. $8x^3$
F. $8x$

Question 350:

What is the circumference of a circle with an area of 10π?

A. $2\pi\sqrt{10}$
B. $\pi\sqrt{10}$
C. 10π
D. 20π
E. $\sqrt{10}$
F. More information needed.

Question 351:

If $a.b = (ab) + (a+b)$, then calculate the value of $(3.4).5$

A. 19
B. 54
C. 100
D. 119
E. 132

Question 352:

If $a.b = \dfrac{a^b}{a}$, calculate $(2.3).2$

A. $\dfrac{16}{3}$
B. 1
C. 2
D. 4
E. 8

Question 353:

Solve $x^2 + 3x - 5 = 0$

A. $x = -\dfrac{3}{2} \pm \dfrac{\sqrt{11}}{2}$
B. $x = \dfrac{3}{2} \pm \dfrac{\sqrt{11}}{2}$
C. $x = -\dfrac{3}{2} \pm \dfrac{\sqrt{11}}{4}$
D. $x = \dfrac{3}{2} \pm \dfrac{\sqrt{11}}{4}$
E. $x = \dfrac{3}{2} \pm \dfrac{\sqrt{29}}{2}$
F. $x = -\dfrac{3}{2} \pm \dfrac{\sqrt{29}}{2}$

Question 354:

How many times do the curves $y = x^3$ and $y = x^2 + 4x + 14$ intersect?

A. 0
B. 1
C. 2
D. 3
E. 4

Question 355:

Which of the following graphs **do not** intersect?

1. $y = x$
2. $y = x^2$
3. $y = 1-x^2$
4. $y = 2$

A. 1 and 2
B. 2 and 3
C. 3 and 4
D. 1 and 3
E. 1 and 4
F. 2 and 4

Question 356:

Calculate the product of 897,653 and 0.009764.

A. 87646.8
B. 8764.68
C. 876.468
D. 87.6468

E. 8.76468   F. 0.876468

Question 357:

Solve for x: $\dfrac{7x+3}{10} + \dfrac{3x+1}{7} = 14$

A. $\dfrac{929}{51}$ B. $\dfrac{949}{47}$ C. $\dfrac{949}{79}$ D. $\dfrac{980}{79}$

Question 358:

What is the area of an equilateral triangle with side length x.

A. $\dfrac{x^2\sqrt{3}}{4}$ B. $\dfrac{x\sqrt{3}}{4}$ C. $\dfrac{x^2}{2}$ D. $\dfrac{x}{2}$ E. x^2 F. x

Question 359:

Simplify $3 - \dfrac{7x(25x^2 - 1)}{49x^2(5x+1)}$

A. $3 - \dfrac{5x-1}{7x}$
B. $3 - \dfrac{5x+1}{7x}$
C. $3 + \dfrac{5x-1}{7x}$
D. $3 + \dfrac{5x+1}{7x}$
E. $3 - \dfrac{5x^2}{49}$
F. $3 + \dfrac{5x^2}{49}$

Question 360:

Solve the equation $x^2 - 10x - 100 = 0$

A. $-5 \pm 5\sqrt{5}$
B. $-5 \pm \sqrt{5}$
C. $5 \pm 5\sqrt{5}$
D. $5 \pm \sqrt{5}$
E. $5 \pm 5\sqrt{125}$
F. $-5 \pm \sqrt{125}$

Question 361:

Rearrange $x^2 - 4x + 7 = y^3 + 2$ to make x the subject.

A. $x = 2 \pm \sqrt{y^3 + 1}$
B. $x = 2 \pm \sqrt{y^3 - 1}$
C. $x = -2 \pm \sqrt{y^3 - 1}$
D. $x = -2 \pm \sqrt{y^3 + 1}$
E. x cannot be made the subject for this equation.

Question 362:

Rearrange $3x + 2 = \sqrt{7x^2 + 2x + y}$ to make y the subject.

A. $y = 4x^2 + 8x + 2$
B. $y = 4x^2 + 8x + 4$
C. $y = 2x^2 + 10x + 2$
D. $y = 2x^2 + 10x + 4$
E. $y = x^2 + 10x + 2$
F. $y = x^2 + 10x + 4$

SECTION 1B: MATHS — QUESTIONS

Question 363:

Rearrange $y^4 - 4y^3 + 6y^2 - 4y + 2 = x^5 + 7$ to make y the subject.

A. $y = 1 + (x^5 + 7)^{1/4}$
B. $y = -1 + (x^5 + 7)^{1/4}$
C. $y = 1 + (x^5 + 6)^{1/4}$
D. $y = -1 + (x^5 + 6)^{1/4}$

Question 364:

The aspect ratio of my television screen is 4:3 and the diagonal is 50 inches. What is the area of my television screen?

A. 1,200 inches²
B. 1,000 inches²
C. 120 inches²
D. 100 inches²
E. More information needed.

Question 365:

Rearrange the equation $\sqrt{1 + 3x^{-2}} = y^5 + 1$ to make x the subject.

A. $x = \dfrac{(y^{10} + 2y^5)}{3}$
B. $x = \dfrac{3}{(y^{10} + 2y^5)}$
C. $x = \sqrt{\dfrac{3}{y^{10} + 2y^5}}$
D. $x = \sqrt{\dfrac{y^{10} + 2y^5}{3}}$
E. $x = \sqrt{\dfrac{y^{10} + 2y^5 + 2}{3}}$
F. $x = \sqrt{\dfrac{3}{y^{10} + 2y^5 + 2}}$

Question 366:

Solve $3x - 5y = 10$ and $2x + 2y = 13$.

A. $(x,y) = (\dfrac{19}{16}, \dfrac{85}{16})$
B. $(x,y) = (\dfrac{85}{16}, -\dfrac{19}{16})$
C. $(x,y) = (\dfrac{85}{16}, \dfrac{19}{16})$
D. $(x,y) = (-\dfrac{85}{16}, -\dfrac{19}{16})$
E. No solutions possible.

Question 367:

The two inequalities $x + y \leq 3$ and $x^3 - y^2 < 3$ define a region on a plane. Which of the following points is inside the region?

A. (2, 1)
B. (2.5, 1)
C. (1, 2)
D. (3, 5)
E. (1, 2.5)
F. None of the above.

Question 368:

How many times do $y = x + 4$ and $y = 4x^2 + 5x + 5$ intersect?

A. 0
B. 1
C. 2
D. 3
E. 4

Question 369:

How many times do $y = x^3$ and $y = x$ intersect?

A. 0   B. 1   C. 2   D. 3   E. 4

Question 370:

A cube has unit length sides. What is the length of a line joining a vertex to the midpoint of the opposite side?

A. $\sqrt{2}$

B. $\sqrt{\frac{3}{2}}$

C. $\sqrt{3}$

D. $\sqrt{5}$

E. $\frac{\sqrt{5}}{2}$

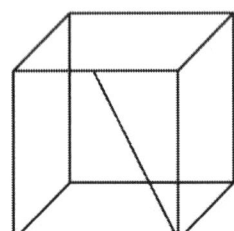

Question 371:

Solve for x, y, and z.

1. $x + y - z = -1$
2. $2x - 2y + 3z = 8$
3. $2x - y + 2z = 9$

	x	y	z
A	2	-15	-14
B	15	2	14
C	14	15	-2
D	-2	15	14
E	2	-15	14
F	No solutions possible		

Question 372:

Fully factorise: $3a^3 - 30a^2 + 75a$

A. $3a(a-3)^3$

B. $a(3a-5)^2$

C. $3a(a^2 - 10a + 25)$

D. $3a(a-5)^2$

E. $3a(a+5)^2$

SECTION 1B: MATHS QUESTIONS

Question 373:

Solve for x and y:

$4x + 3y = 48$

$3x + 2y = 34$

	x	y
A	8	6
B	6	8
C	3	4
D	4	3
E	30	12
F	12	30
G	No solutions possible	

Question 374:

Evaluate: $\dfrac{-(5^2 - 4 \times 7)^2}{-6^2 + 2 \times 7}$

A. $-\dfrac{3}{50}$
B. $\dfrac{11}{22}$
C. $-\dfrac{3}{22}$
D. $\dfrac{9}{50}$
E. $\dfrac{9}{22}$
F. 0

Question 375:

All license plates are 6 characters long. The first 3 characters consist of letters and the next 3 characters of numbers. How many unique license plates are possible?

A. 676,000
B. 6,760,000
C. 67,600,000
D. 1,757,600
E. 17,576,000
F. 175,760,000

Question 376:

How many solutions are there for: $2(2(x^2 - 3x)) = -9$

A. 0
B. 1
C. 2
D. 3
E. Infinite solutions.

Question 377:

Evaluate: $\left(x^{\frac{1}{2}} y^{-3}\right)^{\frac{1}{2}}$

A. $\dfrac{x^{\frac{1}{2}}}{y}$
B. $\dfrac{x}{y^{\frac{3}{2}}}$
C. $\dfrac{x^{\frac{1}{4}}}{y^{\frac{3}{2}}}$
D. $\dfrac{y^{\frac{1}{4}}}{x^{\frac{3}{2}}}$

SECTION 1B: MATHS QUESTIONS

Question 378:

Bryan earned a total of £ 1,240 last week from renting out three flats. From this, he had to pay 10% of the rent from the 1-bedroom flat for repairs, 20% of the rent from the 2-bedroom flat for repairs, and 30% from the 3-bedroom flat for repairs. The 3-bedroom flat costs twice as much as the 1-bedroom flat. Given that the total repair bill was £ 276 calculate the rent for each apartment.

	1 Bedroom	2 Bedrooms	3 Bedrooms
A	280	400	560
B	140	200	280
C	420	600	840
D	250	300	500
E	500	600	1,000

Question 379:

Evaluate: $5[5(6^2 - 5 \times 3) + 400^{\frac{1}{2}}]^{1/3} + 7$

A. 0
B. 25
C. 32
D. 49
E. 56
F. 200

Question 380:

What is the area of a regular hexagon with side length 1?

A. $3\sqrt{3}$
B. $\dfrac{3\sqrt{3}}{2}$
C. $\sqrt{3}$
D. $\dfrac{\sqrt{3}}{2}$
E. 6
F. More information needed

Question 381:

Dexter moves into a new rectangular room that is 19 metres longer than it is wide, and its total area is 780 square metres. What are the room's dimensions?

A. Width = 20 m; Length = -39 m
B. Width = 20 m; Length = 39 m
C. Width = 39 m; Length = 20 m
D. Width = -39 m; Length = 20 m
E. Width = -20 m; Length = 39 m

Question 382:

Tom uses 34 meters of fencing to enclose his rectangular lot. He measured the diagonals to 13 metres long. What is the length and width of the lot?

A. 3 m by 4 m
B. 5 m by 12 m
C. 6 m by 12 m
D. 8 m by 15 m
E. 9 m by 15 m
F. 10 m by 10 m

Question 383:

Solve $\dfrac{3x-5}{2} + \dfrac{x+5}{4} = x+1$

A. 1
B. 1.5
C. 3
D. 3.5
E. 4.5
F. None of the above

Question 384:

Calculate: $\dfrac{5.226 \times 10^6 + 5.226 \times 10^5}{1.742 \times 10^{10}}$

A. 0.033
B. 0.0033
C. 0.00033
D. 0.000033
E. 0.0000033

Question 385:

Calculate the area of the triangle shown to the right:

A. $\dfrac{3+\sqrt{2}}{2}$
B. $\dfrac{2+2\sqrt{2}}{2}$
C. $2+5\sqrt{2}$
D. $3-\sqrt{2}$
E. 3
F. 6

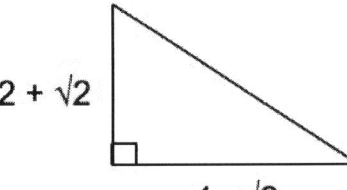

Question 386:

Rearrange $\sqrt{\dfrac{4}{x}+9} = y-2$ to make x the subject.

A. $x = \dfrac{11}{(y-2)^2}$
B. $x = \dfrac{9}{(y-2)^2}$
C. $x = \dfrac{4}{(y+1)(y-5)}$
D. $x = \dfrac{4}{(y-1)(y+5)}$
E. $x = \dfrac{4}{(y+1)(y+5)}$
F. $x = \dfrac{4}{(y-1)(y-5)}$

Question 387:

When 5 is subtracted from 5x the result is half the sum of 2 and 6x. What is the value of x?

A. 0
B. 1
C. 2
D. 3
E. 4
F. 6

Question 388:

Estimate $\dfrac{54.98 + 2.25^2}{\sqrt{905}}$

A. 0
B. 1
C. 2
D. 3
E. 4
F. 5

Question 389:

At a Pizza Parlour, you can order single, double or triple cheese in the crust. You also have the option to include ham, olives, pepperoni, bell pepper, meat balls, tomato slices, and pineapples. How many different types of pizza are available at the Pizza Parlour?

A. 10
B. 96
C. 192
D. 384
E. 768
F. None of the above

Question 390:

Solve the simultaneous equations $x^2 + y^2 = 1 \text{ and } x + y = \sqrt{2}$, for x, y > 0

A. $(x,y) = (\frac{\sqrt{2}}{2}, \frac{\sqrt{2}}{2})$

B. $(x,y) = (½, \frac{\sqrt{3}}{2})$

C. $(x,y) = (\sqrt{2} - 1, 1)$

D. $(x,y) = (\sqrt{2}, ½)$

Question 391:

Which of the following statements is **FALSE**?

A. Congruent objects always have the same dimensions and shape.
B. Congruent objects can be mirror images of each other.
C. Congruent objects do not always have the same angles.
D. Congruent objects can be rotations of each other.
E. Two triangles are congruent if they have two sides and one angle of the same magnitude.

Question 392:

Solve the inequality $x^2 \geq 6 - x$

A. $x \leq -3$ and $x \leq 2$
B. $x \leq -3$ and $x \geq 2$
C. $x \geq -3$ and $x \leq 2$
D. $x \geq -3$ and $x \geq 2$
E. $x \geq 2$ only
F. $x \geq -3$ only

Question 393:

The hypotenuse of an equilateral right-angled triangle is x cm. What is the area of the triangle in terms of x?

A. $\frac{\sqrt{x}}{2}$
B. $\frac{x^2}{4}$
C. $\frac{x}{4}$
D. $\frac{3x^2}{4}$
E. $\frac{x^2}{10}$

Question 394:

Mr Heard derives a formula: $Q = \frac{(X+Y)^2 A}{3B}$. He doubles the values of X and Y, halves the value of A and triples the value of B. What happens to value of Q?

A. Decreases by $\frac{1}{3}$
B. Increases by $\frac{1}{3}$
C. Decreases by $\frac{2}{3}$
D. Increases by $\frac{2}{3}$
E. Increases by $\frac{4}{3}$
F. Decreases by $\frac{4}{3}$

Question 395:

Consider the graphs $y = x^2 - 2x + 3$, and $y = x^2 - 6x - 10$. Which of the following is true?

A. Both equations intersect the x-axis.
B. Neither equation intersects the x-axis.
C. The first equation does not intersect the x-axis; the second equation intersects the x-axis.

D. The first equation intersects the x-axis; the second equation does not intersect the x-axis.

SECTION 1C: Reading Comprehension

Section 1C consists of 24 multiple choice questions on several short passages. You will be provided with a separate text booklet which contains passages needed for the questions. There is a total of 80 minutes for Sections 1A and 1C and you're advised to split your time evenly between the sections.

The aim of this section is to test your comprehension, interprepation and deduction skills. Therefore, it's important to revise the principles of what constitutes a good argument:
1. **Evidence:** Arguments which are heavily based on value judgements and subjective statements tend to be weaker than those based on facts, statistics and the available evidence.
2. **Logic**: A good argument should flow and the constituent parts should fit well into an overriding view or belief.
3. **Balance:** A good argument must concede that there are other views or beliefs (counter-argument). The key is to carefully dismantle these ideas and explain why they are wrong.

Sometimes, the question requires you to consider whether an argument is 'strong' or 'weak'. All arguments include reasons (premises) which aim to support a conclusion. Here, we are considering whether the reasons provide weak or strong support.

The parts of an argument:
An argument is an untimely attempt to persuade with the use of reasons. This can be distinguished from an assertion, which is simply a statement of fact or belief.

Assertion: It is raining outside.
Argument: I can hear the continuous sound of water splashing on the roof. Therefore, it must be raining outside.

The argument involves an attempt to persuade another that it is raining and it includes a reason as to why the speaker thinks it is raining, which is the splashing on the roof. The assertion, on the other hand, is not backed up with a reason – it is simply a statement.

An argument involves a premise and a conclusion.
A premise is simply a statement from which another can be inferred or follows as a conclusion.
A conclusion though is a summary of the arguments made.

For example:
Premise 1: All dogs bark.
Premise 2: My pet is a dog.
Conclusion: My pet barks.
The conclusion here follows from both of the premises.

Explanation
Sometimes, it will be necessary to distinguish an argument from an explanation and you will need to be careful here as it can be difficult to distinguish sometimes. In essence, an argument will always involve an attempt to persuade the reader as to a point of view. Explanations, on the other hand, do not. Explanations may describe why something is the way it is or account for how something has occurred.

For example:
1. **Explanation:** We can hear the sound of water drops because the tap is leaking.
2. **Argument:** We can hear the sound of water drops. Therefore, we need to call the plumber.

Example 1 just accounts for *why* water drops can be heard – there is no attempt to persuade the reader that there are either water drops or that the tap is leaking. The tap leaking is just asserted as an explanation for the sound of the water drops.

In example 2, the author is advancing an argument as the author is making the case to call the plumber. The premise being the sound of water drops.

Premise vs. Conclusion

- A **Conclusion** is a summary of the arguments being made and is usually explicitly stated or heavily implied.
- A **Premise** is a statement from which another statement can be inferred or follows as a conclusion.

Hence, a conclusion is shown/implied/proven by a premise. Similarly, a premise shows/indicates/establishes a conclusion. Consider for example: *My mom, being a woman, is clever as all women are clever.*

Premise 1: My mom is a woman + **Premise 2:** Women are clever = **Conclusion:** My mom is clever.

This is fairly straightforward as it's a very short passage and the conclusion is explicitly stated. Sometimes the latter may not happen. Consider: *My mom is a woman and all women are clever.*

Here, whilst the conclusion is not explicitly being stated, both premises still stand and can be used to reach the same conclusion.

You may sometimes be asked to identify if any of the options cannot be "reliably concluded". This is effectively asking you to identify why an option **cannot** be the conclusion. There are many reasons why but the most common ones are:

1. Over-generalising: *My mom is clever therefore all women are clever.*
2. Being too specific: *All kids like candy thus my son also likes candy.*
3. Confusing Correlation vs. Causation: *Lung cancer is much more likely in patients who drink water. Hence, water causes lung cancer.*
4. Confusing Cause and Effect: *Lung cancer patients tend to smoke so it follows that having lung cancer must make people want to smoke.*

Note how conjunctives like hence, thus, therefore, and it follows, give you a clue as to when a conclusion is being stated. More examples of these include: "it follows that, implies that, whence, entails that".

Similarly, words like "because, as indicated by, in that, given that, due to the fact that" usually identify premises.

Assumptions

It is important to be able to identify assumptions in a passage as questions frequently ask to identify these. **An assumption is a reasonable assertion that can be made based on the available evidence.**

A crucial difference between an assumption and a premise is that a premise is normally mentioned in the passage, whereas an assumption is not. A useful way to consider whether there is a particular assumption in the passage is to consider whether the conclusion relies on it to work – i.e. if the assumption is taken away, does that affect the conclusion? If it does, then it's an assumption.

Fact vs. Opinion

Sometimes you will be required to distinguish between a fact and an opinion. A fact is something that can be tested to be true or false. An opinion, on the other hand, cannot be tested to be true or false – it is someone's view on something and is a value judgement.

For example: "Tuition fees were reduced by the Welsh government in 2012. Many viewed this as a fair outcome."

Fact: Tuition fees were reduced by the Welsh government.
Opinion: It is a fair outcome.

What one person sees as being 'fair' may not be 'fair' to another person – even if many people see a particular policy as fair. It is a normative statement that cannot be tested as true or false.

> *Top tip!* Don't get confused between premises and assumptions. A **premise** is a statement that is explicitly stated in the passage. An **assumption** is an inference that is made from the passage.

Correlation vs. Causation

Just because two incidents or events have occurred does not mean that one has caused the other. For example: "French people are known for having a glass of wine with dinner and they have a larger life expectancy than we do. Therefore, we should consume wine to be healthier."

This argument is flawed. There are 2 events: (i) French people known for having wine and (ii) French people having a larger life expectancy. There is no suggestion in the extract that (i) wine is causally related to (ii) or that having wine actually leads to a longer life. Accordingly, in itself, the premises do not adequately support the conclusion – there could be other reasons such as diet or exercise.

Responses

For each question, there are 5 options to choose from. Only one can be correct. Therefore, if you cannot find the correct one initially, you can use the process of elimination to find the correct one.

If you are stuck on a particular passage or question, do not spend too long on it as this can take time away from your other questions. It would be best to leave it until the end if you have time left.

The Passage

Take every fact in the passage as true and your answer must be based on the information in the passage only – so do not use your own knowledge, even if you feel that you personally know the topic. For example, if the question asks who the first person was to walk on the moon, then states "the three crew members of the first lunar mission were Edwin Aldrin, Neil Armstrong, and Michael Collins". The correct answer is "cannot tell" – even though you know it was Neil Armstrong and see his name, the passage itself does not tell you who left the landing craft first. Likewise, if there is a quotation or an extract from a book which is factually inaccurate, you should answer based on the information available to you rather than what you know to be true.

Read the Questions First

Different strategies work well for different people but indeed, having a look at the questions before going through the passage can help you focus on the important details in the passage in the first reading of it, thereby saving you time. It would be best to try this strategy with some of the passages in this book to see if it works for you.

Common Types of Questions

- What unstated assumption is being made?
- Which of the following is an assertion?
- What is the main idea in the passage?
- What is the main argument in the passage?
- Which of the following is an argument in favour of…?
- What is meant by?
- What conclusion is reached by the author?
- Which of the following weakens or strengthens the writer's argument?
- Which of the following is an assertion of fact?

> *Top tip!* Though it might initially sound counter-intuitive, it is often best to read the question *before* reading the passage. Then you'll have a much better idea of what you're looking for and are therefore more likely to find it quicker.

Reading Non-Fiction

As well as critically analysing the passages in the book, a great way to prepare for the PBSAA is to engage in further non-fiction reading and to consider some of the following questions:

- What issues are being raised?
- What assumptions are made?
- What is the conclusion?
- Is there adequate support for the conclusion?
- Whose perspective is it coming from?
- How would you create a counter-argument?

Critically reading non-fiction, such as in a quality newspaper, will not only help improve your Section A performance but would also improve your knowledge bank for the Section B essay.

Reading Comprehension Questions

Passage 1 – Controlled Drugs

There is a consensus among Parliamentarians that the current drug policy is simply not working. Approximately 1 in 12 adults in the UK have taken an illicit drug in the last year (amounting to 2.8 million people) and 1 in 5 young adults have taken an illicit drug. It is thus clear that the Government needs to do more. However, while it is clear that there needs to be a shift in policy, politicians cannot agree on what changes are needed.

Possessing a banned drug is a criminal offence but how can it be that all these individuals are potentially criminals? Is it moral to label these individuals as criminals? Around the world, there have been growing calls for the legalisation of drugs. In 2001, Portugal legislated to decriminalise the use of small amounts of drugs. Since then, drug consumption in Portugal has been below the European average and the percentage of young people aged 15-24 consuming drugs in Portugal has decreased. It is clear that the legalisation of drugs has not had the effect that opponents of the policy claimed it would have. Accordingly, decriminalising drugs may be a pointer in the right direction for the UK.

A key justification for criminalising the possession of drugs is that it would reduce the propensity of drug consumption (or deter people from consuming drugs). However, there is no strong evidence to support this notion. Once a person is in possession of a controlled drug, they have committed a criminal offence, yet this has not deterred the 2.8 million users. Further, a study by the European Union's Drugs Monitoring Agency found no correlation between harsher punishments for drug offences and lower drug consumption. This makes the argument for legalisation much more compelling.

Moreover, drug consumption in itself is a victimless crime in that it doesn't harm anyone apart from the drug user. Furthermore, the majority of users only consume drugs in small amounts which are unlikely to harm themselves. Any negative health effects that can be incurred are limited to the individual. This is in contrast to smoking, where 'passive smoking' can have a serious impact on others.

Opponents of legalisation have suggested that a drug addiction can lead to other crimes, such as theft and robbery, as the individual resorts to secondary crimes to fund their expensive addiction. Accordingly, they argue that taking controlled drugs can be criminogenic. However, this misses the point. The underlying reason for which individuals participate in such secondary crimes (e.g. robbery or theft) is the very high prices of controlled drugs, which are, in turn, a consequence of their prohibition. The very fact that they are illegal means that only criminal gangs end up supplying the controlled drugs, leading to the high prices. If the prohibition is removed, the increase in supply would reduce the price of the drugs and thus, reduce the 'need' to resort to crimes such as theft or robbery.

Legalisation is preferable to criminalisation but that is not to say that legalisation alone would suffice. Excess drug use should be seen as a public health issue, rather than a problem for the criminal law. While a drug addiction can lead to medical issues, so too can excess alcohol. Is it not incoherent for a society to allow any amount of alcohol consumption and yet totally prohibit the smallest consumption of controlled drugs? Accordingly, the freedom that individuals have to choose whether to consume alcohol should be accorded to them in regard to drugs.

SECTION 1C: READING COMPREHENSION — QUESTIONS

Question 396:

What is the meaning of **criminogenic** in its context in this passage?
- A. That consuming a controlled drug is a crime
- B. That taking controlled drugs can lead to other crimes being committed
- C. That taking controlled drugs is a victimless crime
- D. That criminalisation is not the best response to reduce the consumption of drugs
- E. Crimes such as theft or robbery

Question 397:

Which of the following is presented as being *paradoxical* by the author?
- A. That smoking is not prohibited and yet drugs are prohibited
- B. That alcohol is not prohibited and yet drugs are prohibited
- C. That drug consumption is a victimless crime
- D. That it is not drugs per se that lead to robbery or theft but the high prices of the drugs
- E. That a justification for criminalising drugs is to reduce the consumption of drugs but there is no strong evidence to support that point

Question 398:

What is the main argument in the passage?
- A. Drug use is a public health issue, rather than a problem for the criminal law
- B. Drug consumption is victimless
- C. Drug consumption is not criminogenic
- D. That controlled drugs should be regulated
- E. That controlled drugs should be legalised

Question 399:

What practical effect does the author believe would come about if the consumption of drugs were legalised?
- A. Drug consumption would fall
- B. Drug consumption would increase
- C. Drug users would take part in fewer secondary crimes (such as robbery and theft)
- D. It makes society fairer
- E. Drug use would be seen as a public health issue

Question 400:

Which of the following would most weaken the author's main argument?
- A. Drug consumption has a tendency to increase one's propensity for violence
- B. Criminalisation is moral
- C. Drugs have more negative health effects than alcohol
- D. Drug dealers could turn to other crimes – such as people trafficking
- E. It is not clear that there isn't a deterrent effect of criminalisation

Passage 2 – Sweeney Todd

Despite the fact that some associate musicals with cheesy joy, the genre is not limited to gleeful stories, as can be demonstrated by the macabre musical, 'Sweeney Todd'. The original story of the murderous barber appears in a Victorian penny dreadful, 'The String of Pearls: A Romance'. The penny dreadful material was adapted for the 19th century stage, and in the 20th century was adapted into two separate melodramas, before the story was taken up by Stephen Sondheim and Hugh Wheeler. The pair turned it into a new musical, which has since been performed across the globe and been adapted into a film starring Johnny Depp.

Sondheim and Wheeler's drama tells a disturbing narrative: the protagonist, falsely accused of a crime by a crooked judge, escapes from Australia to be told that his wife was raped by that same man of the court. In response, she has committed suicide, and her daughter - Todd's daughter - has been made the ward of the judge. The eponymous figure ultimately goes on a killing spree, vowing vengeance against the people who have wronged him but also declaring 'we all deserve to die', and acting on this belief by killing many of his clients; men who come to his barbershop. His new partner in crime, Mrs Lovett, comes up with the idea of turning the bodies of his victims into the filling of pies, as a way of sourcing affordable meat - after all, she claims, 'times is hard'.

Cannibalism, vengeance, murder, and corruption - these are all themes that demonstrate that this show does not conform to a happy-clappy preconception of its genre.

Sondheim and Wheeler's musical has been adapted into a number of formats over the years, including the film 'Sweeney Todd: The Demon Barber of Fleet Street' directed by Tim Burton. The nature of a film production necessitated a number of changes to the musical. Burton even acknowledged that while it was based on the musical, they were out to make a film and not a Broadway show. Accordingly, a three-hour musical was cut into a two-hour film, which brought a number of challenges: some of the songs and the romance between Todd's daughter and Anthony (a sailor) had to be removed.

There was initially concern though as the film actors, while critically acclaimed in their profession, were not professional singers. However, that turned out to be a non-issue as the film's soundtrack received glowing reviews, in particular, Depp's voice which received positive critical appraisals.

SECTION 1C: READING COMPREHENSION QUESTIONS

Question 401:

Which of the following statements are best supported by the above passage?
- A. Sondheim is a brilliant musician and lyricist
- B. Most musicals deal with morbid themes
- C. Wheeler is an avid penny dreadful fan
- D. Generalisations can be misleading
- E. Film adaptations lead to fundamental changes in the storyline

Question 402:

All the adjectives below are explicitly supported by the passage as ways of describing the crimes described within it, except:
- A. Comic
- B. Culinary
- C. Vengeful
- D. Sexual
- E. Disturbing

Question 403:

Which of the following statements best sums up Todd's belief?
- A. Bad people should die so good can live and prosper
- B. Good people should die because the bad have basically taken over
- C. All men should die
- D. All humans merit death
- E. Death is unavoidable

Question 404:

Which of the following statements is best supported in the above passage?
- A. There are four themes in 'Sweeney Todd'
- B. Legal corruption is the predominate theme of 'Sweeney Todd'
- C. Several 'Sweeney Todd' themes are morbid
- D. There is nothing positive in 'Sweeney Todd'
- E. Sadness is the focus of Sweeny Todd

Question 405:

Which of the following is true?
- A. Mrs Lovett and Sweeney Todd are in a romantic relationship
- B. All of the songs from the musical were removed or adjusted
- C. The storyline of the film adaptation was fundamentally different to the musical
- D. The film did not receive positive critical acclaim
- E. The film actors did not have professional musical experience

Passage 3 – Youth Unemployment

Youth Unemployment -that is: those young people who are in search of work but are unable to get into work -is disturbingly high. The current youth unemployment figure for the UK is at an unsettling 12%. This is much higher than that of other developed countries such as Germany and Switzerland and the societal implications of this are greater than what the politicians acknowledge. The longer a young person is unemployed, the less likely they are to find a job at all. This has destructive effects on the country: it increases the government's spending on welfare pay-outs, reduces the economy's capacity and increases the likelihood of crime. The personal impact of youth unemployment is equally devastating; lower quality of life, low self-esteem, and lack of confidence and even depression, which can lead to a never-ending cycle of unemployment. It is, thus, clear that youth unemployment is a dangerous virus that demands immediate government attention.

There are a number of reasons for the high youth unemployment rate, such as the sluggish state of the economy and the global financial crash in 2007/08. When the economy is not doing well, businesses tend to lay off workers in response to a lack of sales. This happened in 2008 when the economy slumped and unemployment drastically increased. Since then, the economy has only recovered lethargically.

However, this alone does not account for the entirety of the youth unemployment rate. Since the economic slump of 2008, total unemployment has reduced to 5.4%, while youth unemployment is at a much higher 12%. Why is there such a big difference? Is it just an inherent feature of society? Do businesses not want young people? A number of young people report that there aren't enough jobs for them. Yet at the same time, businesses say they are desperate to find skilled young people. They just can't find young people with the right skills to suit their needs. For example, Dulux, the paint manufacturer, has pointed out that there simply aren't enough skilled painters and decorators. In London, two-thirds of construction firms have had to turn down work as they don't have enough practical and skilled workers. And herein lies the problem – many young people do not have the skills that businesses are looking for.

That is not to say that it is the fault of those who are unemployed. The root of the problem is the lack of courses that are geared to the kind of skills that businesses want and the existing structural inadequacies within our education system. The head of Ofsted recently pointed out that the lack of high-quality vocational courses in England is a concern. Vocational courses have traditionally been seen as a 'second-rate' option in the country, with the academic A Levels being the 'gold' standard. This view must change – not everyone is destined for academia and vocationally trained individuals have an important role in our society. Would you rather have a well-read English graduate or a vocationally trained engineer fix your central heating? Thus, the government must make high-quality vocational provision a priority. Vocational education tends to be incorrectly seen as second-rate by students and this must change. Putting an emphasis on vocational courses will address the skills shortage in the UK, make the UK more productive, and crucially improve the prospects of our young generation. In addition, the education sector and businesses should engage with each other more closely to ensure that skill deficits are addressed in the national curriculum.

A report from the Institute for Public Policy Research (IPPR) suggests that youth unemployment tends to be lower in countries where there is a vocational route into employment and not just an academic one. This shines a lot of light on the situation in the UK.

Question 406:

Which of the following is **not** a potential personal impact of youth unemployment?

    A. Lower quality of life
    B. Increases the government's spending on welfare pay-outs
    C. Lack of confidence
    D. Low self-esteem
    E. Depression

Question 407:

Which of the following is the underlying reason for the high youth unemployment rate?

    A. The global financial crash of 2007/08
    B. Not enough jobs for young people
    C. Lack of skills
    D. The head of Ofsted
    E. The lack of high-quality vocational courses

Question 408:

Which of the following is implied but **not** stated in the passage?

    A. There is a mismatch between the skills that young people have and the skills that employers are looking for
    B. Young people don't have the skills that businesses are looking for
    C. Teachers should encourage young people to undertake vocational courses
    D. Businesses should provide training to improve the skills of young people
    E. Unemployment is bad

Question 409:

Which of the following is the author's main argument in the passage?

    A. An increased emphasis should be placed on vocational courses
    B. An increase in the skills of young people needs to be brought about
    C. Better jobs for young people are needed
    D. That unemployment has caused a lack of skills
    E. That there aren't enough skilled young people

Question 410:

According to the author, what can businesses do to reduce youth unemployment?

    A. Create more jobs
    B. Increase young people's skills
    C. Engage with the education sector
    D. Train more young people
    E. Create vocational courses

Passage 4 – The English Reformation

In the early 1500s, King Henry VIII set the English Church on a different course forever. Henry was undoubtedly a devout catholic when he took the throne. Indeed, he was a staunch defender of Catholicism in the face of threats from religious reformers, such as Luther. Impressed by Henry VIII's defence, the Pope gave him the title 'Defender of the Faith'. So how did Henry come to separate from the Roman Church?

Although historians are not universally in agreement, many put Henry VIII as the key driver behind separating the Church of England from Rome. Henry was disappointed in his marriage with Catherine of Aragon as, in spite of multiple pregnancies, they only had one daughter together. Henry though was desperate to conceive a son. He had a monumental ego and was, thus, concerned about his legacy. In order to secure his dynasty and ensure that the Tudor reign remained strong, he needed a legitimate son. Accordingly, he was eager to secure a divorce with his current wife and marry Anne Boleyn with the aim of having a legitimate son with her. The English church was under the authority of the Roman Catholic Church (of whom the Pope was the leader) and in order to separate from Catherine, Henry needed to obtain an annulment from the Pope. Despite the mammoth efforts of Henry's right-hand man, he was unable to secure an annulment of the marriage from Rome, which would have been the straightforward option. It became clear that Rome was not going to budge on this and from then, Henry began to pursue a separation from the Roman Church.

Historians also point to another reason for Henry's desire to break away from Rome. He liked the idea of being the only head of the church and the supreme leader. His ego influenced many of his key decisions, such as engaging in wars abroad, and this decision was no different.

A number of historians suggest that Thomas Cromwell was the man behind the separation. Indeed, Cromwell played a significant role in engineering it. With control of the King's parliamentary affairs, he persuaded Parliament to enact a supplication pronouncing Henry as 'the only head' of the church, establishing the doctrine of royal supremacy. This was in clear conflict with Papal authority and began the process of breaking away from the Roman Church. But while it is clear that Cromwell had a vital role in the break from Rome, the obvious must still be repeated – were it not for Henry's desire of a break, there would not have been such a break.

Through a series of Acts of Parliament over two years, the break from Rome was secured and ties between the English church and Rome were severed. One such Act of Parliament in 1934, the Act of Supremacy, declared the King as 'the only Supreme head in earth of the Church of England.' This drastic change put the English church on a new course and while there were no major day-to-day changes initially, it planted the seed for the differences we see today between the Roman Catholic Church and the Church of England.

SECTION 1C: READING COMPREHENSION QUESTIONS

Question 411:

What was the ultimate cause of the Church of England's breakaway from Rome?
- A. Henry VIII's ego
- B. Rome wouldn't grant him a divorce
- C. Henry wanted a son
- D. Royal Supremacy
- E. Religious reasons

Question 412:

What does 'dynasty' mean in the Passage?
- A. Family
- B. Henry's control of the Kingdom
- C. Succession of people from Henry's family to the throne
- D. Exertion of dominion by the Tudors
- E. The power of Henry VIII

Question 413:

Why did Henry want a son?
- A. To secure Royal Supremacy
- B. He wanted to divorce Catherine
- C. To secure the Tudor reign
- D. Males were preferred in the 16th Century
- E. None of the above

Question 414:

Which of the following is an unstated assumption?
- A. Henry had an ego
- B. There was no opposition to the reformation
- C. The public was supportive of the break from Rome
- D. Henry needed Cromwell to make the break from Rome
- E. Henry believed that he couldn't get a divorce through Rome

Question 415:

What is the Royal Supremacy?
- A. The breaking away from Rome
- B. The idea of the King being the supreme authority
- C. The King becoming the leader of the church
- D. The authority of the Pope over the Church
- E. The Act of Supremacy 1934

Passage 5 – Charities and Public Schools

What constitutes a charity is a matter of public significance, but also an important issue in determining the taxable income a charity receives. In the popular sense, charities are seen as institutions which primarily help the poor, however, a question has been raised as to why public schools should be considered as charities considering the fees required to attend them.

In order to be classified and registered as a charity, it is necessary for an institution to demonstrate that its purposes are for the public benefit. Once accorded charity status, the institution gains a number of fiscal benefits from the government. For example, no corporation tax is paid on most types of income. In contrast, corporation tax, which currently stands at 20% of all profits, is paid by all other private businesses. The law should not allow a 'free-for-all' where any profit-making company can be a charity by just doing a minuscule charitable act, as this would have a negative impact on the public purse. Nonetheless, charitable status is highly sought out by many organisations for these reasons and has become highly controversial in the case of public schools.

Public schools charge a fee for admission, in contrast with state schools, which are funded by the Government. Accordingly, as public schools are private institutions, becoming charitable will help their finances. Whether this should be possible hinges on what acting for the public benefit means and requires in the context of education.

In 2011, the Independent Schools Council (ISC), representing public schools, sought a judicial review of the Charity Commission's guidance on what is required for a public school to demonstrate a 'public benefit'. The ISC argued that they did provide a public benefit, but they did face opposition. The Education Review Group, who helped draft the Commission's disputed guidance, also intervened in the case, advancing arguments in the trial. Ultimately, the tribunal held that the Commission's guidance was wrong as a matter of law and required them to change it. The trial judge decided that in order to operate for the public benefit, a sufficient section of society must directly benefit from the education provided, which he said must include children whose parents would be unable to afford the fees without assistance.

In the trial, a number of arguments were advanced on either side of the issue. One such argument was that independent schools are a net cost to society as they remove able pupils from state schools and present barriers to social mobility. However, the tribunal did not consider such an argument as it related to a 'political' issue, rather than a judicial one.

Further, private education provision can provide a multitude of benefits to society. Indeed, it educates the children whose parents pay for the provision. While this may not seem inherently charitable because parents are paying for the education, there are public benefits too. Firstly, the provision of education in itself is a benefit – having an educated population benefits not only the individuals through enabling them to enjoy a higher living standard, but also the general economy. More taxes will be paid and there will be less crime. That is not to say that we should ignore the gap between public schools and state schools. Indeed, state schools that are struggling should be willing to receive help from public schools and public schools should, in accordance with their public duty, offer such help.

SECTION 1C: READING COMPREHENSION — QUESTIONS

Question 416:

Which of the following is definitely true based on the passage?

- A. Any institution that provides a public benefit gains fiscal benefits from the government
- B. Every organisation would rather be a charity than a private company
- C. If an organisation is not a charity, it does not provide a public benefit
- D. Charities may not have to pay corporation tax
- E. The law should not allow a free-for-all

Question 417:

Which of the following is required if an organisation is to become a charity?

- A. To help the poor
- B. Nothing
- C. To exist for the public good
- D. To demonstrate that the fiscal benefits gained would be for the public benefit
- E. To not make private profits

Question 418:

Who is most likely to have advanced the argument that public schools are a net cost to society based on the passage?

- A. The Independent Schools Council
- B. The tribunal judges
- C. State schools
- D. The Education Review Group
- E. The government

Question 419:

Which of the following is an opinion as opposed to a fact?

- A. The tribunal did not consider the argument that there was a net cost to society
- B. No corporation tax is paid on most types of income
- C. Public schools charge a fee for admission
- D. The law should not allow a free-for-all
- E. A charity has to demonstrate that it operates for the public benefit

Question 420:

Which of the following would have adequately supported the argument that there is a public benefit from public schools before the tribunal?

- A. Public schools educate the children whose parents pay for it
- B. Public schools provide scholarships to others who can't afford the fees
- C. Public schools can make better use of money, as opposed to it being paid through tax
- D. Public schools are better than state schools
- E. State schools can learn from public schools

Passage 6 – Amazon vs. Hachette

The public does not normally witness corporate trade negotiations or disputes. They are generally held behind closed doors and in private for the mutual benefit of the companies in the dispute. However, there was an exception in the dispute between the international publisher, Hachette, and Amazon in 2014. Both of them are powerful organisations with market power, however, this episode has shown that one is more powerful than the other.

It is first necessary to go into the background of this dispute. The sale of a book involves three main protagonists. Arguably the most important, the author writes the book. The publisher prints and distributes the book. The retailers then act as the point of sale to consumers. In the US, there are five very large publishers who have enjoyed significant market dominance. When distributing their books, publishers want them in the biggest retailers and crucially, the biggest of them all by far is Amazon. It is estimated by some that 50% of all book sales (both printed and electronic) across the US go through Amazon. It is the most dominant bookseller and, therefore, it is imperative for publishers to get their books on Amazon. In order to do this though, each publisher needs to enter into a legal contract with Amazon, which is normally a private arrangement.

In 2014, Hachette and Amazon were in negotiations to renew their contract for the pricing and distribution of Hachette's books. While the exact issues in the negotiations remain private, it became clear that the negotiations weren't going well. Amazon stopped selling a number of Hachette's books and delayed deliveries of many by weeks. Famous books such as those by *JK Rowling* were delayed. Was this just business? Or did Amazon go too far? It infuriated both Hachette and the authors of the books that Hachette publish. It showed the length that Amazon would go to in order to get what they want. Hachette's authors, who normally stayed out of publisher-retailer contracts, weighed in and criticised Amazon. Amazon had used their enormous market power to restrict the sales of the books from Hachette to try to get their way and many authors argued that Amazon had abused their market power. However, it was only a minority of authors (and mainly the successful ones) that spoke out.

In reality, Hachette and their authors are not the innocent victims in all of this. Hachette, with their market power in publishing, conspired with the other major US publishers and Apple to fix the prices of eBooks (i.e. to keep them artificially high) in 2012. When the US Department of Justice sued, the publishers (including Hachette) made a settlement for $164m. So it's a bit rich for Hachette to complain about Amazon's aggressive price strategy.

In regard to individual authors, the major publishers haven't always been friendly either. It is a monstrous task for an up and coming author to get even a small book deal with a publisher. Publishers generally have a narrow view as to what a suitable book is and are primarily focused on what they think the monetary returns will be. Amazon, though, has taken a new step. They have introduced a suite of services that allows authors to self-publish their work through Amazon. It allows individuals to publish both an eBook and a print book. Amazon, with their vast resources, are also able to offer a 'print-on-demand' service whereby Amazon prints each book to order. This bypasses the need for traditional publishers or any need for a large pot of cash to fund a print run. Surely, this genius innovation should be applauded. It allows many more small-time authors to self-publish their works and disrupts the unfairness that the big publishers created. Yes, Amazon has excessive market power, but at least they're using it to the benefit of small authors, unlike the traditional publishers. So let them engage in whatever tactics they want to with Hachette.

SECTION 1C: READING COMPREHENSION QUESTIONS

Question 421:

What is the author's view as to the balance of power between Amazon and Hachette?
- A. Hachette is more powerful than Amazon
- B. Amazon is more powerful than Hachette
- C. They are both powerful
- D. The author doesn't have a view as to which
- E. They have both exerted market power

Question 422:

The author stated that it is 'a bit rich for Hachette to complain about Amazon's aggressive strategy'. What is he suggesting about Hachette's complaint?
- A. It attacks Amazon's views
- B. It's ironic
- C. It's unfair
- D. It's sarcastic
- E. It's awkward

Question 423:

What is the main conclusion of the author's article?
- A. That Amazon has a lot of market power
- B. That Hachette has a lot of market power
- C. Amazon are disruptive
- D. Amazon has done more for small-time authors than Hachette has done
- E. Amazon's actions against Hachette are just business

Question 424:

What did the author imply by the use of the word 'monstrous' in the passage?
- A. That the publishers are monsters
- B. That it's a big task to get a book deal
- C. That it is unacceptably too tough to get a book deal
- D. That authors have to work hard
- E. That authors have to act like monsters

Question 425:

Which of the following would, if true, most undermine the author's argument in the final paragraph?
- A. Amazon charge high fees to authors for their 'self-publishing' services
- B. Amazon is not the first company to offer services in self-publishing
- C. Hachette offers the same 'self-publishing' services
- D. Amazon has caused a loss to some authors from their aggressive negotiations with Hachette
- E. Amazon are taking away business from the publishers

Question 426:

Which of the following would the author most likely disagree with?
- A. It would be easier for authors to use Amazon's services than that of a traditional publisher
- B. Hachette and Amazon have a lot of market power
- C. Amazon has abused their market position
- D. Hachette has abused their market position
- E. Authors have been given a hard deal by the main publishers

Passage 7 – Online Courts

There are two main ways to resolve a private dispute concerning a question of law. Firstly, you can come to a private settlement with the person you disagree with – this can either (i) just be between the two sides of the case or (ii) involve a third party as a mediator. Alternatively, if that doesn't work, you can sue the other person and seek redress from the courts. It is well known, though, that the court system in the UK is expensive, inefficient, and not suited to the needs of the ordinary person.

Let's say, for example, that you are having an electrician complete some wiring in your house at a price of £300. You pay the electrician and he leaves, but it then transpires that he completed the task erroneously and you want your money back. How do you go about getting it back? Would you go to court? The court fee alone is £35 for each side in the case though and any legal advice from a solicitor would cost approximately £200 per hour. It must be noted that there is a well-established principle that the losing side in a civil case pays the winning side's legal costs. However, in the event that you don't win the case, you could potentially lose even more money from having to pay the winning side's (the electrician's) legal costs.

The cost is disproportionately high here in relation to the value of the claim and herein lies a flaw in the justice system. The high cost limits access to justice. The existing court process takes too long, involves too much paperwork and unnecessarily involves the use of expensive lawyers. Lord Dyson, a leading judge in the Court of Appeal (the second highest court in the UK), echoed these comments. Crucially, there are ways to make the system more efficient and the best way is to introduce an online court.

Firstly, we must accept the truth: lawyers aren't always needed for small-time disputes. We can look to eBay for inspiration. eBay is a well-renowned online auction site where private individuals can sell goods to other individuals. It is not always smooth sailing, however, and frequently disputes arise (for example, when a damaged defective item is sold). When disagreements arise, the seller and buyer are encouraged to negotiate online. If negotiation fails, eBay offers an online resolution service whereby an eBay official decides on the case and makes a binding decision. No lawyers and not even any face-to-face interaction with the eBay official. For simple matters, it would be unnecessary and inefficient to hire a lawyer to complete the task. Crucially, this means much lower costs than in a courtroom.

This system should be used by the justice system for small claims. There should be an online mediation system to allow each side to negotiate in an online discussion area.

Anyone watching the ITV hit television show, 'Judge Rinder', would realise that small-time claims don't require a lawyer. The setting for the show resembles a courtroom where small-time disputes are heard before a 'judge' who mediates between each side. The 'judge' then makes a decision that binds each side. There are no lawyers and each person represents him or herself. While there are a wealth of differences between the TV show and actual court proceedings, it does show that lawyers are not always needed to resolve disputes.

Accordingly, the Government should go one step further and establish an online court to resolve small-time legal disputes. This would involve real judges from the judiciary deciding cases online. They would review the documentary evidence submitted online by the parties and, if necessary, conduct a hearing via video link. While it would cost a lot to set up the online system, it would, in the long run, result in significant cost efficiencies both to the government and to the users of the online court.

SECTION 1C: READING COMPREHENSION QUESTIONS

Question 427:

Which of the following most undermines the author's argument in the second and third paragraphs?
- A. For small claims, people don't need to go to court to resolve disputes – there are alternative methods (such as private mediators)
- B. Such small cases are normally successfully settled outside of court
- C. The UK's justice system is cheaper than that of many other countries in the world
- D. The losing party pays the winning party's legal costs
- E. Solicitors fees for court cases are greater than their fees for out-of-court settlement

Question 428:

Assume that you and the plumber go to court. You each take 1 hour of legal advice from a solicitor. How much are the total legal fees for the losing side in the case?
- A. £35
- B. £200
- C. £235
- D. £300
- E. £470

Question 429:

Which of the following is an assertion of opinion?
- A. '60 million disagreements between traders and buyers are settled online'
- B. 'the seller and buyer are encouraged to negotiate online'
- C. 'this means much lower costs than in a courtroom'
- D. 'This system should be applied by the justice system'
- E. None of the above

Question 430:

Which of the following is implied but not stated about the TV show 'Judge Rinder'?
- A. Judge Rinder decides real cases
- B. The two sides are not represented by lawyers
- C. It is fake
- D. The TV show is not set in a real courtroom
- E. It is innovative

Question 431:

Which of the following was not argued by the author?
- A. That an online court should be introduced
- B. The online court should be modelled on the 'Judge Rinder' TV Show
- C. The online court should be modelled on eBay's dispute resolution system
- D. That existing legal costs are too high
- E. Lawyers are not always needed for legal disputes

Question 432:

The author argues that the justice system is inefficient. Which of the following best describes why his argument is weak?
- A. It involves a generalisation – the author only referred to small claims but this does not necessarily mean that the whole justice system is inefficient
- B. People don't have to use the justice system to reach a settlement
- C. Only one judge's approval was cited
- D. The author did not say how much the online court would cost
- E. eBay and the justice system are not comparable

Passage 8 – Cars

We live in a world of technological change and it seems that nothing is immune from it. Our phones, computers, kitchens, gardens and cars are all undergoing significant change. If businesses want to keep the custom of consumers, they must engage in technological change and find new, innovative ways to improve their products.

Ever since the introduction of the car over 100 years ago, one thing has remained constant: a human being has always driven the car. While the look, feel, and efficiencies of cars have improved enormously, cars have always required a human being to drive them. Indeed, the law requires human beings to be in control of cars. However, all of this is going to change.

Car companies – and some traditionally non-car companies – have been developing 'driverless cars' at a monumental rate. Famously, TopGear presenter Jeremy Clarkson tried an autonomous BMW around their race track in 2011. While driving on a race track is not comparable to driving on busy roads, there have been significant developments since. Google, for instance, have been testing autonomous cars on open roads in California. A key feature of autonomous vehicles is that they are capable of sensing their environment without human input.

Driverless cars are expected by industry experts to be the norm within 20 years. According to the Society of Motor Manufacturers and Traders, the market for autonomous car technology is expected to contribute £51 billion to the UK economy and over 300,000 jobs. A lot needs to happen in the meantime, though. Car companies need to rigorously test their cars on open roads and the public need to be convinced of their utility. Testing on open roads will allow companies to develop the accuracy and safety of the technology used. Indeed, such testing is essential to develop autonomous cars – how else can we be sure that they will be safe in the real world?

The current law requires a human being to be in control of a car. However, governments have issued special dispensations to car companies wanting to test autonomous cars on public roads. The UK government allow autonomous vehicles to be tested as long as a driver is ready to take over in the case of a system fault. The government has also announced that 40 miles of road in Coventry is to be equipped with technology to aid autonomous vehicles. The significance of the government's support is that it will accelerate the development of autonomous cars and will encourage worldwide car companies to set up permanent research facilities in the UK to test autonomous cars. If the UK can become a world leader in autonomous vehicles, the industry may well contribute a lot more than the expected £50 billion to the UK economy.

However, not everyone is convinced of the success of the driverless car. The CEO of Porsche, a luxury car company, recently dismissed the use of driverless cars, saying that his cars are meant to be driven. That may well be correct for the luxury car market – people want to drive the cars they spend £100,000+ on. However, it does not follow that it's the same for the rest of the car market. People will see that the benefits of autonomous cars outweigh the use of traditional cars. Firstly, autonomous cars are expected to be safer than traditional cars. For instance, a computer system can react much faster than a human to a dangerous situation. Secondly, the driver becomes a passenger and can do something else with his time – the age old saying that time is money still rings true today. This alone will encourage drivers to buy driverless cars. While people may find driverless cars strange initially, they will get used to them. The first desktop computer seemed strange but it is now virtually ubiquitous. So peculiarity should actually be an incentive to development.

Question 433:

What is the **main** point the author is making by using the first desktop computer analogy [final paragraph]?
- A. Desktop computers are strange
- B. The public should adapt to the driverless car
- C. People find new things strange
- D. People eventually adapt to new things
- E. The public will adapt to the driverless car

Question 434:

What is the underlying **assumption** that the author made in using the first desktop computer analogy?
- A. That people will adapt to new things
- B. People find new things strange
- C. Desktop computers are strange
- D. The public should adapt to the driverless car
- E. Peculiarity should actually be an incentive to development

Question 435:

What does the Top Gear autonomous BMW test suggest about the potential for autonomous cars on roads?
- A. It shows that autonomous cars can work on public roads
- B. There would not be accidents from the use of autonomous cars
- C. Autonomous cars will be well received by the public
- D. It would appeal to celebrities, such as Jeremy Clarkson
- E. None of the above

Question 436:

What is an underlying theme of the article?
- A. To describe the advent of the driverless car
- B. The autonomous car industry will contribute £50 billion to the UK economy
- C. The public will want to drive an autonomous car
- D. Development of driverless cars has been at a fast rate
- E. There are arguments for and against the adoption of driverless cars

Question 437:

Which of the following most undermines the author's argument in the final paragraph?
- A. The fact that driverless cars will be expensive
- B. Cars are meant to be driven
- C. The public would not be convinced by the safety of it
- D. A survey showed that many people are doubtful of the uptake of the autonomous car
- E. The CEO of Porsche is correct

Passage 9 – Beauchamp and Childress

Euthanasia, derived from the Greek word for 'easy death', involves the purposeful killing of a sick patient where the actual death is caused by a third party. Assisted suicide is the purposeful killing of one's self, made possible with the support of another person. So the individual takes the final action to end their life (e.g. injecting lethal drugs) but there is assistance from another person (e.g. a doctor providing the lethal drugs). Both assisted suicide and euthanasia involve at least a second person in the death whereas suicide just involves the deceased person. For this reason, assisted suicide and euthanasia are more controversial.

Beauchamp and Childress highlight four principles (Autonomy, Beneficence, Non-maleficence and Justice) that they believe should have a role in the decision-making process of medical ethics. These can conflict with one another and also, each principle can potentially conflict with itself.

Autonomy is the ability to self-govern one's own actions. The obvious point is that in order to respect autonomy, people should have the right to decide for themselves if they would like to die, for whatever reason. Otherwise, it would not accord sufficient respect to their position as autonomous human beings capable of reason.

However, when a person is mentally ill to the extent that their capacity to understand their own situation and determine their own actions is diminished, the ability to be autonomous is effectively lost. Therefore, no decisions relating to their own death should be taken by them. But still, this view is only relevant if the person is suffering from some form of mental incapacity.

However, the Society for the Protection of the Unborn Children suggests that a "patient's freedom entails a responsibility to act ethically" thereby implying a condition (or a limit) is attached to a person's autonomous abilities. Thus, they believe that refusing a patient's request for assisted suicide or euthanasia would not restrict the person's autonomy as, in making such a request, the person is not adhering to their responsibility.

However, this definition of autonomy is not universally accepted and incorporates an artificial condition. Further, it follows from the Society's argument that they would argue that suicide should become illegal.

The overruling idea is that patients should be able to make decisions regarding assisted suicide and euthanasia for themselves.

On the other hand, the principle of **non-maleficence** is that there is a commitment by medical professionals to do no harm. This may be seen as a very clear reason not to cause or assist in a death and militates against allowing euthanasia and assisted suicide. However, the principle should also be interpreted to mean: do not cause pain. Not yielding to a patient's own wish of death may prolong their suffering and, thus, result in further pain. Hence, "harm" can be interpreted in two different ways here to support opposing views.

These principles can be useful in deciding whether to allow an assisted suicide. When deciding on particular cases, certain arguments can be ruled out or be more relevant and thus, have more weight placed on them to come to an overall conclusion.

For example, the court in the case involving Diane Pretty in 2002 did not allow her husband to assist in her death. The court arguably gave priority to the principle of non-maleficence over personal autonomy. Yet still, in the case of Miss B, she won the case for her treatment to be withdrawn (a ventilator to be turned off) with the intention of letting her die without it - this is because it was different from Pretty's case. Here, the second person would not actually be 'acting' or causing harm. The hospital simply didn't act (in not providing treatment). Hence, it appears that the principle of non-maleficence had a significant weighting in both these cases as a dangerous precedent might have been set if a second party was allowed to participate in a killing because of the consequences for the exploitation of the vulnerable.

Question 438:

What does the Society for the Protection of Unborn Children assume about an intentional killing?
- A. It is not a function of autonomy
- B. It is unethical
- C. It is a crime
- D. It goes against autonomy
- E. It involves harm to the patient

Question 439:

Which of the following constitutes an explanation of why there is a gap in the author's argument that it follows from the Society's argument that suicide should become illegal?
- A. Suicide is not necessarily unethical
- B. Assisted suicide and euthanasia can't be assimilated with suicide
- C. Suicide is not illegal
- D. The Society did not argue that suicide should be illegal
- E. Suicide is not wrong

Question 440:

According to the passage, what is the implicit argument that the Society is making?
- A. Assisted suicide and euthanasia should not be allowed
- B. Assisted suicide and euthanasia are unethical
- C. Assisted suicide and euthanasia are illegal
- D. Suicide is illegal
- E. Suicide should be illegal

Question 441:

Which principle has priority according to the author?
- A. Autonomy
- B. Non-maleficence
- C. Euthanasia
- D. Assisted Suicide
- E. No principle has priority over another

Question 442:

According to the author, why did the court allow treatment to be withdrawn in the case of Miss B?
- A. The principle of non-maleficence was satisfied
- B. In order to respect the patient's autonomy
- C. It was not euthanasia
- D. The patient was not vulnerable
- E. The patient made the choice out of her own free will

Passage 10 – The IMF

The International Monetary Fund (IMF) is an international organisation, with 188 member countries whose main goal is to encourage monetary cooperation and secure financial stability across the world. It was formed in 1944 in response to the issues raised by the Great Depression in 1930. The IMF's most well-known feature is the ability to make loans to countries in need. All the member countries contribute money to a pool of funds, which can be distributed to any country experiencing difficulties. Indeed, this has saved many countries from financial ruin but the IMF's policy of attaching conditions has been severely criticised by many economists.

The IMF, among other things, operates a formal policy known as 'Surveillance', which involves reviewing each member's economy and their economic policies. The organisation then provides an assessment of each government's policies and gives suggestions as to what policies governments should take. Surveillance is also designed to warn countries of risks to their economies. In spite of this, no one at the IMF predicted the global financial crash which affected the entire world in 2007. What this made clear is that the IMF is unable to determine what the true risks in the world are. This surely would have dented confidence in the IMF and given their incompetence on this front, it would be unsurprising if countries don't rely so heavily on their advice.

When countries have financial difficulties – for example, when they have run out of money or have run up huge debts to international creditors – the IMF can step in and provide a loan. These are not the run-of-the-mill bank loans which consumers get from banks. Crucially, the IMF is the last port of call and can prevent a country from going into bankruptcy. For instance, Ireland was hit very badly by the recession, unemployment dramatically increased, the government ran out of money and they had difficulty in borrowing money. The IMF stepped in (with others) and provided a bailout loan to Ireland. This proved to be what Ireland needed and they have since made a solid economic recovery, which just shows what the IMF can do.

However, it has not always been plain sailing. Another debt crisis unfolded in Greece in 2010, where the Greek government also ran out of money. The situation was more serious than in Ireland though, as the Greek government had spent even more money than what they had, borrowed a lot of money and then they couldn't afford to meet the repayments on their loans. The IMF (and the EU) did come along to bail them out with a loan but they imposed strict conditions, such as a requirement that the Greek government reduced spending significantly. These conditions differentiate an IMF loan from an ordinary bank loan. Banks don't dictate what borrowers can spend in their lives but the IMF dictates what proportion of a loan countries can spend. Many economists criticised the IMF for requiring this as it meant that the Greek government could not stimulate their flailing economy. Indeed, the economy did get worse and the IMF must take some responsibility for it.

While the IMF has an important role to play in the world, they must not attach such strict conditions to the loans they give. Doing so can potentially make a bad situation even worse, as it did in Greece.

Question 443:

The Passage does not suggest:
- A. That the IMF could have done better
- B. That the IMF has caused some problems for countries
- C. The IMF should be replaced
- D. The IMF should be improved
- E. The IMF has been incompetent

Question 444:

Which of the following does the author portray as a positive intervention by the IMF?
- A. Giving a loan to Greece
- B. Giving advice to countries
- C. Making loans to countries in need
- D. Attaching conditions to loans
- E. Giving a loan to Ireland

Question 445:

According to the Passage, what was the root cause of the Greek debt crisis?
- A. The IMF's strict conditions on its loan to Greece
- B. The global financial crisis
- C. The government spent more money than what it had
- D. The IMF requiring the Greek government to reduce spending significantly
- E. The IMF's loan

Question 446:

Which of the following would the author be least likely to agree with?
- A. The IMF needs to change its procedures
- B. The IMF has only been beneficial in the world
- C. The IMF should have a replacement
- D. The IMF made a positive difference in Ireland
- E. The IMF made a negative difference in Greece

Question 447:

Which of the following is implicit in the author's assertion that the IMF is incompetent?
- A. The IMF should have been able to give a warning about the financial crisis
- B. The IMF should be replaced
- C. The IMF is useless
- D. The IMF failed to warn countries about the global financial crisis
- E. The IMF did not help in the Greek debt crisis

Passage 11 – The European Convention

The Human Rights Act in the UK has caused significant controversy and there have been calls from figures within the government to scrap it. While it has accorded many basic rights and freedoms to individuals, there have been instances where it has led to controversy. This has dented public confidence in it.

To understand the position, it is necessary to look at the background story. After the atrocities of World War II, European countries got together and signed the European Convention on Human Rights (ECHR) in 1950 and it came into force in 1953. There are 46 signatories to the Convention. This is an international treaty which contains a number of rights and freedoms which every person is entitled to in their countries (these rights are colloquially known as the 'Convention rights'). It included articles guaranteeing liberties such as the right to a fair trial, right to life and a prohibition on discrimination. From then on, all the States that signed up to the treaty were bound to uphold the rights of their citizens. The treaty also established a Court based in Strasbourg, known as the 'European Court of Human Rights', which can determine whether a State has breached a person's human rights and can hear cases from aggrieved citizens. If they find that a State has breached a person's human rights, they can award compensation (an award which the particular government must satisfy). So since 1953, if the UK government made a law that infringed a person's human rights, that person could take the UK government to the European Court and seek redress. However, international law operates differently to national law and UK citizens could not make a claim in the UK courts for a breach of the ECHR. They could only make a claim against the government in the European Court. This meant that people had to incur significant and unnecessary expenses if they were to vindicate their human rights. This changed at the beginning of the millennium, though.

In 1998, the UK Parliament passed the Human Rights Act, which came into force in 2000. This incorporated the Convention rights into domestic law. Crucially, this means that where the government breached the European Convention on Human Rights, UK citizens could sue in domestic courts (rather than just the European Court in Strasbourg). The domestic courts can quash government decisions and instruments that are inconsistent with the Convention rights and the Act it makes human rights a part of the law of our country.

There have been concerns though that the European Court has given too much protection to dangerous individuals. In the case of Abu Qatada, the UK government wanted to deport a terrorist suspect to Jordan to face criminal prosecution for terrorism offences. However, the European Court of Human Rights had a different say on the matter and effectively blocked the move, saying that it would be a breach of his right to a fair trial. It determined that there was a real risk of evidence obtained from torture being used in Qatada's trial in Jordan. The UK wanted to deport him nonetheless and appealed the ruling. It ended up taking over 10 years, numerous appeals, and a treaty between Jordan and the UK, by which it was agreed that evidence from torture would not be used, to send Qatada back to Jordan. In another instance, the European Court held that prisoners in the UK, who are currently not allowed to vote, should get the right to vote. Both these matters were given enormous press coverage, compared to other cases involving human rights. In particular, newspapers focused on the fact that most of the judges in the European court are 'foreign' and 'unelected'. The fact that Abu Qatada claimed £700,000 in legal aid from the government to pay for his numerous appeals further infuriated the public, but arguably that was an issue relating to the domestic government and not the Convention.

These are just two isolated cases, though. In the vast majority of instances, there have been more positive cases, which have not been reported as widely. For example, the Court has held that the security services can't shoot to kill without good reason. After 9/11, it was held that it is inconsistent with human rights to imprison a terror suspect (or, indeed, any suspect) indefinitely without a criminal charge. In 2015, the Court of Appeal held that the Convention requires the police to investigate rape allegations. Can anyone disagree with these judgements? They are just a few examples of the numerous instances in which the European Convention on Human Rights has helped give rights to the ordinary person in the UK while balancing concerns for national security. Indeed, the European Court may not be perfect – but what system (or person) is perfect?

SECTION 1C: READING COMPREHENSION — QUESTIONS

Question 448:

Which of the following is an unstated assumption in the second paragraph?
- A. European countries were disgusted at World War II
- B. That the UK was a participant to the European Convention on Human Rights
- C. That the UK introduced the Human Rights Act
- D. A person whose human rights were infringed could sue to the government abroad
- E. The European Court of Human Rights can award compensation

Question 449:

Since which year could UK citizens seek protection of their Convention rights through domestic law?
- A. 1950
- B. 1953
- C. 1998
- D. 2000
- E. The year in which the Human Rights Act was introduced

Question 450:

Which of the following is an argument made by the author?
- A. The European Court of Human Rights were wrong in the Abu Qatada case
- B. The European Convention on Human Rights has caused endless problems for the UK
- C. The European Convention on Human Rights is not beneficial to the UK
- D. The European Convention on Human Rights has benefited UK citizens
- E. If a State breaches the Convention, they can be sued

Question 451:

According to the author, why did the UK not deport Qatada back to Jordan for over 10 years?
- A. The European Court of Human Rights didn't allow it
- B. They were unsure as to whether the European Convention on Human Rights prevented it
- C. The possibility of torture in Jordan
- D. There was a risk that evidence from torture would be used against Abu Qatada in a trial in Jordan
- E. The UK did not want to give Abu Qatada a fair trial

Question 452:

What is the author's main point about the 'more positive' cases in the final paragraph?
- A. Positive cases do not receive as much attention as the negative cases
- B. The Human Rights Act does not lead to bad outcomes
- C. The European Convention is not perfect
- D. The benefits of the European Convention outweigh the negatives
- E. The European Court is unelected

Question 453:

Which of the following would be a suitable main conclusion to the article?
- A. The UK should keep the European Convention on Human Rights
- B. The UK should not keep the European Convention on Human Rights
- C. The European Convention on Human Rights should be altered
- D. The European Court of Human Rights needs to be improved
- E. There are drawbacks to the European Convention on Human Rights

Passage 12 – Business Objectives

Most institutions in the country are businesses – shops, factories, energy companies, airlines, and train companies, to name a few types. They are the bedrock of society, employ most people in it and it is, thus, crucial that we examine their values.

The overriding objective of businesses is to make the most profit (i.e. maximise on revenue and minimise on costs). The notion was first popularly expounded by Adam Smith in his book, 'The Wealth of Nations' in 1776. Furthermore, his view was that if an individual considers merely their own interests to create and sell goods or services for the most profit, the invisible hand of the market will lead that activity to maximise the welfare of society. For example, in order to maximise profits, sellers will only produce and sell goods that society wants. If they try to sell things people don't want, no one would buy it. This is how the free market works. Indeed, the focus on profit is the basis on which companies operate and encourages them to innovate and produce goods that consumers want, such as iPhones and computers. So there are clear benefits to the profit maximisation theory.

This is a more effective society than, for example, a communist society where the government decides what to produce – as the government has no accurate way of deciding what consumers need and want. Arguably, the poverty that communist regimes such as the Soviet Union created have instilled this notion further.

However, were companies left to their own devices to engage in profit maximisation, what would stop them from exploiting workers? What would stop them from dumping toxic chemicals into public rivers? Engaging in such practices would reduce their costs of production, which would increase their profits. However, this would be very damaging to the environment. Accordingly, other objectives should be relevant. Businesses can also do other bad things to make a profit as well. For example, selling products to people who don't want or need them.

Corporate social responsibility entails other possible objectives for businesses, such as a consideration of the interests of stakeholders. A stakeholder is, in essence, anyone who is significantly affected by a company decision, such as employees or the local community. One business decision can have huge impacts on stakeholders. For example, a decision to transfer a call centre from the UK to India would likely increase profits, as wage costs for Indian workers can be much lower than that of British workers. This increase in profits would benefit the shareholders, however, it negatively harms other stakeholders. It would make many employees redundant. Here, there is arguably a direct conflict between profit maximisation and employees' interest. Nonetheless, moving call centres abroad does not always work. Given the different cultures and accents, companies have received complaints from frustrated customers. This, in fact, led BT to bring back a number of call centres to the UK.

However, the objective of profit maximisation has not always led to maximum welfare for society. Arguably, as banks sought to maximise their profits, they lent money to individuals who could not afford to pay it back. Eventually, many borrowers stopped meeting their repayments and lost banks enormous amounts. This led to a need for banks to be bailed out by the government and Lehman Brothers; one of the largest US banks that collapsed. Arguably, though, this was more due to idiocy rather than profit maximisation alone – in the end, the banks lost billions.

Question 454:

What literary technique did the author use by referring to an 'invisible hand'?
- A. A simile
- B. A metaphor
- C. An organisation that ensures that welfare for society is maximised
- D. Irony
- E. Analogy

Question 455:

Which of the following groups is a stakeholder in a business that was implicitly mentioned in the passage?
- A. Employees
- B. People
- C. Shareholders
- D. Pressure Groups
- E. Business rivals

Question 456:

Why does the author discuss the example of call centres?
- A. To argue that businesses are bad
- B. To show that call centres should not be moved abroad
- C. To show that moving call centres abroad can harm UK jobs
- D. To show the consequences of profit maximisation
- E. Because the author is against call centres moving abroad

Question 457:

Which of the following best encapsulates the author's position?
- A. Profit maximisation should be abandoned
- B. Adam Smith is wrong
- C. Profit maximisation works
- D. Profit maximisation should not be the only business objective
- E. Employees should have a greater role in businesses

Question 458:

What is Adam Smith's view according to the Passage?
- A. Profit maximisation arose because of the invisible hand
- B. The invisible hand had an important role in establishing profit maximisation
- C. Profit maximisation leads to the invisible hand
- D. Profit maximisation maximises welfare for society
- E. Profit maximisation is the best option for society

Passage 13

Global oil prices have fallen over the past year to rock bottom – from over $100 per barrel in 2013 to $30 at the dawn of 2016. At the possible peril of oil producers, there appears to be no let-up in the oil price. The ultimate reason for this is a simple matter of demand and supply. The so-called 'shale boom' in the US, where fracking was used to extract oil in an alternative way, meant that there was a lot more oil in the world – i.e. the supply of oil was boosted. This reduced the need to import oil into the US and other sellers (like Saudi Arabia and Nigeria) had to sell their oil elsewhere. However, there was no one else to sell it to and thus, to get rid of it, the price had to be reduced.

A major problem for oil companies is that the oil price reduction has drastically reduced their revenues by over 70%. Crucially, the revenue reduction has harmed the profitability of many oil companies. BP have even run a loss of £4.5 billion in 2015 – a dangerously high figure which has led them to cut 7,000 jobs. Indeed, job cuts are the staple response to low profits. In particular, many skilled North Sea oil workers have been made redundant, thereby increasing unemployment in Northern Scotland (particularly in Aberdeen). This has had devastating impacts on families, some of whom may require state benefits until new work is found. There would also be knock-on effects in the local community. As significantly fewer people have an income from work, much less money will be spent in local shops. Instead, 7,000 people paying taxes to the government will end up seeking unemployment benefits from the government. Unfortunately, there seems to be little other option for businesses like BP where their woes were brought on by the oil price. They're losing money and must cut costs, including employees, in order to survive. Otherwise, the loss-making Oil Company will eventually go bust. What now needs to happen is that the government must provide adequate support to those made redundant and sponsor retraining schemes where required.

The low oil price has caused other problems as well. Many oil businesses are highly 'leveraged'. In other words, they have borrowed significant amounts of money from banks. Such money was borrowed in order to fund new projects and new oil rigs, but they are less likely to be profitable now. If, as is the case with many at the moment, an oil company is making a loss, they will no longer be able to pay back their loans to the banks. Given this new likelihood, many loans previously seen as 'safe' are seen as significantly risky and could cause monumental losses for banks exposed to oil companies. This requires incredibly careful attention from financial regulators as this may have wider effects on the economy.

It doesn't stop there. Oil companies engage many other businesses (or contractors) to build projects or to help with maintenance. Unlike consumer businesses (like Tesco or Sainsbury) who deal with millions of customers, these contractors only deal with a few customers (such as oil companies). Accordingly, those contractors who only supplied the oil industry will find lower business and might potentially end up bust themselves (which means that they will have to make their employees redundant too).

All this will involve work for law firms. While they may get less work from advising on exploration projects and on buying oil rigs, they will, at least, get more work from administrators advising on insolvency, from banks for the restructuring of debts, and from oil companies looking to merge with one another to save on costs.

The low oil price has already had immediate impacts on consumers. Fuel (both diesel and petrol) comes from oil. Therefore, the lower oil price should influence the fuel prices as it will cost much less to produce the fuel. This would benefit consumers. Again, fuel is a significant factor in airline ticket prices so there should be a corresponding impact there too. Finally, as fuel gets cheaper, transportation costs will fall. As such costs have a significant impact on imported goods (such as electronics and computers from China), there should be price drops there too.

SECTION 1C: READING COMPREHENSION — QUESTIONS

Question 459:

According to the author, who has the most to gain from the low oil prices?
- A. Oil contractors
- B. Business rivals
- C. The government
- D. Law firms
- E. Consumers

Question 460:

What is the immediate reason given in the passage for the unemployment resulting from the cuts made by BP?
- A. Low oil prices
- B. Demand and supply
- C. Many workers have been made redundant
- D. A loss of £4.5 biilion
- E. Low revenues

Question 461:

What unstated assumption is made when the author states that the 7,000 unemployed individuals will end up 'seeking unemployment benefits' from the government?
- A. Those individuals have become unemployed
- B. The government has unemployed benefits to give
- C. Those individuals will not find work elsewhere initially
- D. That the low oil price has caused the unemployment
- E. That the low profits has caused the unemployment

Question 462:

What was the main reason for the reduction in the price of oil?
- A. Lack of demand
- B. People aren't interested in buying as much oil anymore
- C. The 'shale boom' in the US
- D. Saudi Arabia couldn't sell their oil in the US, but couldn't sell it elsewhere either
- E. The peril of oil producers

Question 463:

According to the author, why do some oil companies have little option but to make the redundancies that they have made?
- A. Low oil prices
- B. Workers are no longer useful
- C. Redundancies are necessary to boost profits
- D. US fracking
- E. Survival

Passage 14 – Nuclear Energy

Energy is ubiquitous in all of our lives, such that life without it would be very different. Where our energy comes from and the consequences of using it has come centre stage in the last half century. Non-renewable energy comes from energy sources that will run out in our lifetimes. Examples include fossil fuels: such as coal, oil, and natural gas. Accordingly, the current over-reliance on these sources is not ideal as they will run out, maybe not in our lives, but certainly in our children's and grandchildren's lives. Therefore, we must take action to develop renewable energies in order to give future generations a sustainable future.

A further and more significant consequence of fossil fuels is that they pollute the atmosphere. Their use involves the emission of carbon into the atmosphere, which most scientists believe contributes to global warming over time. Many also believe that upsetting the carbon balance in the atmosphere will lead to more unforeseen weather patterns. Given that 80% of the UK's energy came from fossil fuels in 2013, it is necessary to further develop cleaner alternatives.

Nuclear power, already an important source of energy, has been a government priority recently. In fact, in 2015, the government have even offered very significant subsidies for nuclear power with ministers proclaiming that nuclear power is the future for the UK's energy needs, being the most beneficial source of energy. The big attraction of nuclear power is that it is a clean form of energy – it does not emit carbon into the atmosphere. It just emits harmless water vapour. Crucially, the increased use of nuclear power can help the UK meet its obligations under international treaties to reduce carbon emissions. However, the use of nuclear power raises some significant concerns.

Harnessing nuclear energy involves a complex process and numerous steps to ensure that it is done in a safe manner. Nuclear materials emit dangerous radioactive material, which has the potential to kill or cause serious injury. The danger of radiation can be seen from the disaster at Chernobyl, where an explosion took place at a nuclear power plant. This led to 31 immediate deaths and an estimated 4,000 deaths due to cancer, resulting from the radiation. The surrounding area, of approximately 1,600 square miles, has been declared uninhabitable for 20,000 years. While there are significant safeguards to prevent such an accident happening again, such that we can consider nuclear power effectively safe for the most part, the risk of an accident cannot be ruled out. In 2011, another serious radiation release occurred in Japan.

Producing nuclear energy leads to 'nuclear' waste which is officially separated into three categories: low-level waste, medium-level waste, and high-level waste. High-level waste includes the by-products of the reactions inside the nuclear reactor and this stays highly radioactive, and, thus, dangerous, for many thousands of years. Accordingly, safe disposal is critical. Suitable storage is at an enormous cost and requires effective government planning. Yet it does not seem that the government always consider the long term implications of nuclear waste. In 2007, for example, the High Court quashed the government's decision to build new nuclear power stations because of inadequate and misleading consideration given to waste disposal. This is worrying. If the government were to account for the implications and the true cost of dealing with nuclear waste, they would see that it's not necessarily the 'economical' future for the UK's energy needs.

Question 464:

Which of the following is not true based on the passage?
- A. All the non-renewable energy sources emit carbon into the atmosphere
- B. Carbon emissions are harmful to the atmosphere
- C. There is currently an over-reliance on fossil fuels
- D. The UK is under an obligation to reduce carbon emissions
- E. Nuclear waste can be dangerous

Question 465:

Which of the following does the author argue the passage?
- A. Nuclear power has been a government priority recently
- B. Nuclear power stations will kill or cause serious injury
- C. Nuclear power should be made into a clean form of energy
- D. Society should develop clean renewable energies
- E. Nuclear power is economical

Question 466:

Which of the following would the author most likely agree with?
- A. Nuclear power is worse than fossil fuels
- B. Nuclear power is the most beneficial to society
- C. There should be greater focus on renewable energy sources (such as solar and tidal power) that do not create dangerous waste
- D. The government should consider the cost of nuclear waste
- E. Nuclear power is unsafe

Question 467:

What did the author refer to as 'worrying'?
- A. That the High Court quashed a government decision
- B. That the government wanted to build new nuclear power stations
- C. The high cost of dealing with nuclear waste
- D. The fact of the government giving inadequate consideration to nuclear waste disposal
- E. Nuclear waste disposal

Question 468:

Which of the following most weakens the government's argument that nuclear power is most beneficial to society?
- A. Other forms of energy are cheaper
- B. Other types of energy are important
- C. There are cheaper and cleaner alternatives
- D. The disaster in Chernobyl caused mass damage
- E. The High Court's decision

Passage 15 – Equal Pay

Figures from the Office for National Statistics show that there is a 14% difference in average pay between men and women in full-time jobs. Yet since the Equal Pay Act in 1970, it has been unlawful for an employer to pay differential wages to men and women doing the same work. So why, 45 years since then, are women earning less than men?

Essentially, it is against the law for an employer to directly discriminate on the grounds of gender. If a woman can show that they're being paid less than a man for doing exactly the same value of work for the same employer, they can sue their employer in an employment tribunal. However, the effectiveness of this has been inhibited by high tribunal fees, which act as a disincentive to women to bring forward their claims. Some have also reported fears of career progression being hindered by bringing a claim. Accordingly, it would be more effective for a governmental body to identify and bring prosecutions against employers who discriminate, rather than leaving it to individuals.

Nonetheless, direct wage discrimination does not entirely account for the gender gap in average pay in the whole of the UK. The average salary for a male in an executive role is £40,625 whereas the average for a female in an executive role is £30,125. It does not conclusively follow that there is direct discrimination by individual employers on wages – executive roles differ from organisation to organisation and so do their pay structures.

A particular issue highlighted by the Fawcett Society is that 47% of women are in low paid jobs whereas the figure for men is just 17%. A reason for this is that women tend to be in lower paid sectors – for example, 80% of care and leisure workers are women while only 10% of those in better paid skilled trades are women. This cannot necessarily be attributed to discrimination. The reasons for entering lower paid professions are multi-factorial, and can include discrimination in recruitment, especially in traditionally male-dominated sectors. Indeed, traditional stereotypes may well permeate the career decisions of both girls and boys – traditionally, boys have tended to take up STEM subjects, particularly Physics, whereas girls have tended to take more of the Arts and Humanities subjects.

Even within sectors, women tend to occupy lower positions than men, which inevitably leads to lower salaries. Out of all the FTSE 250 directors, only 19.6% are female. Figures from HMRC further highlight that women are underrepresented in the top jobs as only 27% of women are higher rate tax payers. It is, thus, clear that women do not get as far in the world of work as men do, which is deeply concerning. Whatever the reason for the pay differential is, it needs to change as women are equally as talented as men.

While current laws may well be making a difference, they can't, in their current form, change attitudes. What can the government do about all of this? Some have suggested a mandatory minimum of women in certain roles. While this will undoubtedly help the figures, it may just be sticking a plaster on the wound. Yes, companies will improve the number of women represented in the workforce but it may not lead to the culture change that is required. It may further cause resentment and doubt as to whether those who reached those positions did so on merit.

The government has, alternatively, proposed to require any organisation with more than 250 employees to report the pay gap between men and women in their workforce. They will be legally required to show the number of men and women in each pay range, which will highlight the pay gaps within the organisation. The government then propose to create a league table of the best and worst employers. This would likely lead to significant public pressure on employers to improve the pay gaps within their organisation. Crucially, this would be more likely to stimulate the culture change required – from recruitment to promotions - while also helping the enforcement of existing laws by notifying employees of when there may be potential discrimination. If companies do not address the issue after this, it may, in fact, become necessary for the government to impose a mandatory minimum number of women in higher positions.

SECTION 1C: READING COMPREHENSION QUESTIONS

Question 469:

What is the author's preferred option for tackling the gender pay gap?
- A. Strengthen discrimination law
- B. Implement a reporting obligation
- C. A mandatory minimum number of women in higher positions
- D. Reduce tribunal fees
- E. The government should bring prosecutions against discriminatory employers

Question 470:

Which of the following is an argument made by the author?
- A. Women are equally talented as men
- B. Lower tribunal fees are necessary
- C. Current laws are not making a difference
- D. Maternity leave should be increased
- E. The government should prosecute employers who directly discriminate

Question 471:

Why does the author prefer a reporting obligation as opposed to a mandatory minimum?
- A. A reporting obligation will help change the culture
- B. A reporting obligation may be more effective
- C. It will reduce the gender pay gap
- D. It does not require people to pay high tribunal fees
- E. It allows the companies to take action themselves first

Question 472:

Which of the following are reasons for the differential in *average* pay between genders?
- A. Discrimination
- B. There are more women in lower paid sectors
- C. Men occupy higher positions in the same sector
- D. A, B, and C
- E. Resentment

Question 473:

What is the author's concern with the current discrimination laws?
- A. They do not make a difference
- B. The government needs to enforce it better
- C. Direct discrimination is only one part of the problem
- D. They only work in cases of discrimination by one employer
- E. The high costs of bringing a claim (high tribunal fees) under current discrimination laws

Passage 16 – Trade

We enjoy TVs, phones, computers, electronics, and clothes, but we do so at our eventual risk.

International trade is an enormous advantage to the entire world – it allows people in the world to enjoy goods made in other countries. However, it does benefit some countries more than others. The UK has for some time been a net importer of products from the rest of the world. Importing involves buying goods from abroad, whereas exporting involves selling goods abroad. Put simply, we buy more from other countries than we sell to them.

For consumers in the UK, importing may seem beneficial – we can benefit from televisions, phones, computers, food, and other cheaper goods from other countries. In particular, the development of low-cost manufacturing in China and India in the last 30 years has meant that it's much cheaper to produce goods there rather in the UK. It's not so much an innovation but more an expansion, due to the ability to pay workers much lower wages. While the UK is a net exporter of services (in particular financial services), it is a net importer of physical goods and when considering both goods and services together, the UK is a net importer.

Importing goods mean that British money is going abroad to foreign companies as opposed to British companies, but this is not a problem in itself. As long as Britain exports to the rest of the world as much as it imports, which economists call a 'trade balance', the position is satisfactory.

Oddly, even in spite of a weakening currency, the country is nowhere near to having a trade balance. In 2014, we imported £34bn more than what we exported. This means that £34bn leaves the UK each year. If that was instead spent on UK goods (rather than foreign goods), it would boost British businesses, British jobs, and reduce our reliance on debt.

Indeed, debt is a direct consequence of being a net importer. How do we, as a country, fund these extra £34bn purchases from abroad? Debt. The UK borrows a lot of money and these debts are held by foreign investors, which is fine in the short run but eventually, that money will have to be paid back and with interest.

Being a net importer (which is the same as not exporting enough) is also a symptom of a wider problem in the UK. Due to the process of de-industrialisation in the 1980s, the UK has produced significantly fewer manufactured and semi-manufactured goods. Given the lack of investment in those industries, it costs a lot more to manufacture those goods in the UK when compared to, for example, Germany. It is also a symptom of a poorer skills base among UK workers. Simply, when we are not as skilled as those in other countries, it costs more to produce things here and, thus, we have to sell our products at higher prices. In this global marketplace, people can simply get products more cheaply from other countries. This, in turn, reduces our exports.

SECTION 1C: READING COMPREHENSION — QUESTIONS

Question 474:

What should a weakening currency ordinarily achieve according to the author?
- A. Lead to more imports
- B. Not lead to a trade balance between imports and exports
- C. Lead to a trade balance between imports and exports
- D. More trade
- E. £34bn of net imports

Question 475:

Which of the following best explains what a 'trade balance' is?
- A. When there is a balance in trade
- B. When there are no imports
- C. When exports are greater than imports
- D. When the level of exports is the same as the level of imports
- E. When there is a satisfactory level of trade

Question 476:

Why does the UK not have a trade balance?
- A. Foreign debt from abroad coming into the UK
- B. The UK's imports are much greater than their exports
- C. Cheap Chinese goods
- D. International trade
- E. De-industrialisation and a poor skills base among UK workers

Question 477:

Which of the following is the author's purpose in writing the article?
- A. To explain the UK's import and export levels
- B. To argue that the UK should not import as much
- C. To argue that the Chinese low-cost goods are bad for the UK
- D. To show that the UK have net imports of £34bn
- E. To show that the UK owes money to foreigners

Question 478:

Based on the last paragraph, why would an overseas individual buy a manufactured good from Germany as opposed to the UK?
- A. A preference for German goods
- B. Germany produces more goods than the UK
- C. The individual is German
- D. There is a lack of investment in the UK manufacturing sector
- E. The prices of German goods are cheaper than UK goods

Passage 17 – Star Wars

Star Wars has stormed back onto the box office, just 10 years after the last one. In 2012, Disney famously bought the rights to the Star Wars franchise from the original founder, George Lucas. With the intention of producing another trilogy, Disney released the first film, "Star Wars: The Force Awakens" in December 2015 to the delight of fans.

A few suggested that the film was based too much on the old style, but they were few and far between. The majority of cinema goers pronounced the film a success on social media and it immediately received positive critical acclaim. You know you've created a successful film when hard-to-please and meticulous critics give it a good rating. The actors themselves received heaps of praise as two up and coming British actors came into stardom.

The film didn't just achieve success on this front. As a result of being a box office hit, it has reached $2 billion in box office sales, one of only three films to have ever done so. According to analysts, the success doesn't stop there, though. Some suggest that merchandise sales will outstrip the takings from box office sales.

An important part of most successful films is the consumer products that go with them and Star Wars is no exception. Disney exploited the pre-existing goodwill that the first six Star Wars films built up and licensed and created a vast array of products – from toy action figures of the film's characters to remote controlled droids. Significantly, Disney did not create all of these products themselves. They have licensed the Star Wars brand to other companies, who are allowed to use the Star Wars brand on their own goods. This has meant that other companies can use their expertise to produce Star Wars related goods which Disney could not produce. Significantly, in return for using the Star Wars brand, such companies pay Disney a license fee. For example, Electronic Arts, the game software developer was granted a license to produce Star Wars video games. In return, they gave Disney $225 million.

Disney picked an unorthodox time of year to release the Star Wars film but this was another inspired decision, both in terms of film screenings and consumer products. Given the Christmas period, where parents would have been wondering what gifts to buy their children, Disney gave them a clear answer. In releasing the Star Wars products a month before the film, Disney gave fans and, crucially, parents the opportunity to consider buying them for Christmas. Unlike most children's films, many of today's parents were teenagers at the time of the original Star Wars trilogy (in 1977 to 1983) and, thus, would have had a greater inclination towards purchasing the Star Wars goods. It's clear that this merchandising strategy played out well as Star Wars merchandise sales boosted profits in their consumer products section by 23%.

Paradoxically, it seems, Disney's share price has gone down since the release of the film. It appears though that this is due to concerns about a different part of the Disney Company, such as its ESPN network.

Question 479:

Why did Disney's share price go down after the release of the latest Star Wars film?
- A. Some people did not like the film
- B. The film did not get as much revenue as expected by investors
- C. Concerns about the next Star Wars film
- D. Investors are concerned about other areas of the Disney company
- E. Disney's performance has been poor

Question 480:

Which of the following is an opinion rather than an assertion of fact?
- A. The film received positive critical acclaim
- B. Disney mobilised a commercial enterprise
- C. Many of today's parents were teenagers at the time of the first trilogy
- D. The new Star Wars trilogy is a resounding success
- E. Parents were wondering what gifts to buy their children

Question 481:

What prediction does the author specifically make about Star Wars merchandise?
- A. Other companies will produce Star Wars branded products
- B. That merchandise revenues will exceed box office revenues
- C. Parents will be interested in buying Star Wars merchandise
- D. It will make the Star Wars film a success
- E. The Star Wars merchandise will get good reviews

Question 482:

Which of the following would be a view held by the author?
- A. The Star Wars film was based too much on the old films
- B. Disney's share price should not have gone down
- C. Any successful film would have significant merchandising from toys
- D. The success of the merchandising contributed to the success of the Star Wars film
- E. The success of the Star Wars products created by other companies should not be credited to Disney

Question 483:

Which of the following is definitely false based on the passage?
- A. Disney licensed all their merchandise to other companies
- B. The film was successful
- C. The founder of Star Wars played a role in the new film
- D. The film was not a British film
- E. The film was not a success in the eyes of a few people

Passage 18 – Marriage

In 2014, the Marriage (Same Sex Couples) Act 2013 brought a revolution in society where, for the first time, individuals of the same sex could enter into a marriage. Previously, marriage was only exclusively available for opposite-sex couples (a man and a woman), a fundamental part of marriage for hundreds of years. In 2004, same-sex couples were allowed to enter into a civil partnership, being a marriage in all but name. Some see this as insignificant. Others argue that, by giving same-sex couples a different label, their relationship would be seen as different. Whether this is a legitimate difference was and is a matter of debate. In any event, Parliament took the bold step in 2013 by legislating to allow same-sex marriage. The institution of marriage has now evolved to allow both opposite-sex and same-sex couples to marry.

Some opponents of same-sex marriage argue though that marriage is, by definition, a relationship between a man and a woman. Therefore, it should remain as just between a man and woman. However, this reasoning is circular. Such reasoning follows as such: a marriage is between a man and woman, therefore, it's between a man and woman. It adds nothing to the argument at stake and does not address the question of what a marriage should be. It is an extraordinarily shallow argument.

In considering what marriage is, many opponents base their view on marriage being a religious construct. Marriage ceremonies frequently, but not exclusively, take place in churches and other places of worship. In Christianity, the institution of marriage is a sacrament. Crucially, the main denominations of Christianity do not recognise same-sex marriage. Accordingly, on religious grounds, it is opposed.

Significantly, the Marriage (Same Sex Couples) Act guarantees the availability of a civil (non-religious) marriage and allows a religious marriage if the particular place of worship wishes to allow it.

Some opponents take the position that marriage can only be between a man and a woman because of biological or 'natural' reasons. This is because, in order to procreate (i.e. to produce a child) naturally, there must be a man and a woman. However, as the courts have highlighted in a different context, the essential feature of being in an opposite-sex relationship does not necessarily involve children – a number of opposite-sex couples are married but without children. Same-sex relationships can have exactly the same qualities of intimacy, stability, and interdependence that opposite-sex couples can have. Further, a marriage cannot be nullified by a lack of children.

Proponents of same-sex marriage indeed base their argument on the view that marriage is a social construct. Accordingly, as society evolves to accept that there is not a relevant distinction between opposite-sex and same-sex couples, same-sex couples should be accorded the same rights as opposite-sex couples – i.e. to marry should they so wish.

Whether the modern institution of marriage is a religious construct or a social construct is a matter of debate. Some proponents of same-sex marriage have pointed out that marriage is no longer a religious construct, but a matter for society as a whole. Opponents though insist on the continuing significance of religion. These two views are not as inconsistent as they first seem. It is indeed true that marriage started out as solely a religious construct, with its origins being in the 12th Century.

Marriage was still a social construct though – the vast majority of society was religious and religion had a ubiquitous role in daily life. On this basis, it had significant social relevance. That's not to say that religion is not important today – it certainly still is. That said, it is not as universal now and ever since 1837, marriages need not have taken place through a religious ceremony.

What has been a constant though since the 12th Century and now is that the institution of marriage has reflected society and has continued to evolve in order to do so.

SECTION 1C: READING COMPREHENSION — QUESTIONS

Question 484:

What is the author's belief as to the availability of same-sex marriage?
- A. It should be allowed
- B. It should not be allowed
- C. The concerns raised of same-sex marriage are valid
- D. That same-sex marriage is a religious construct
- E. None of the above

Question 485:

What is the author's concern in the second paragraph?
- A. Marriage is not just between a man and woman
- B. Marriage should not just be between a man and a woman
- C. It is illogical to suggest that marriage is just between a man and a woman
- D. The reasoning employed by the opponents' argument here was circular
- E. Marriage should be open to same-sex and opposite-sex couples

Question 486:

Which of the following best encapsulates the author's view as to marriage?
- A. It is not a religious concept
- B. Religion should not be relevant in marriage
- C. Marriage has always been a social construct
- D. Religion should not inform marriage
- E. Not as many people are religious in the 21st Century

Question 487:

What did the author imply about the state of marriage before 1837?
- A. Society was entirely religious
- B. It was only possible to get a marriage through a religious ceremony
- C. Marriage started out as a religious construct since the 12th Century
- D. It was different
- E. More individuals took it seriously

Question 488:

Based on the whole passage, what does the author imply about marriage today in the final sentence?
- A. Marriage is a social construct
- B. The acceptance of same-sex marriage is a reflection of society
- C. Religion is not relevant anymore
- D. Marriage has evolved to reduce the relevance of religion
- E. Same-sex marriage should be allowed

Passage 19 - Sugar Tax

According to an analysis in the Global Burden of Disease Study, 67% of men and 57% of women are obese or overweight. According to the study, the UK has one of the highest levels of obesity in Western Europe, which carries severe consequences for the population, health services, and the economy.

One proposal under consideration by the government is to impose a tax on sugary products, in proportion to the amount of added sugar in a particular beverage. This is particularly relevant as most adults and children consume too much sugar.

The government currently recommends that sugars should be limited to 5% of the total energy an individual consumes in a given day. This means a recommended maximum of 30g of sugar per day. Significantly, anyone who consumes a full can of ordinary coke is instantly above the recommended maximum. The government hope that their recommendations influence people's behaviour but given the high obesity rates in the UK, it is clear that it has not solved the problem. Accordingly, stronger action is clearly required but a sugar tax has led to controversy.

Being overweight and obese causes significant health issues such as diabetes, heart disease, and cancer. It not only reduces the quality of life but also one's life expectancy. It, thus, has major implications. Even though there are labels on products displaying the amount of sugar, people tend not to look at them and even when people do, they're not aware of the significance of it. Arguably, as individuals do appreciate an immediate or short-term negative health consequence of sugary food and drinks, many may not see it as a serious issue until they actually develop health problems. Not only are there serious personal consequences but the total social cost of obesity is at a mammoth £47 billion.

Imposing a sugar tax should both dis-incentivise excessive sugar consumption and make sure that those who are likely to add to the social cost of obesity contribute more to society.

It is sometimes attested that a sugar tax or any limit on sugar infringes on people's freedom, as the government is intervening in people's lives to reduce what they can consume. If an individual wants to consume sugar, they should be free to do so, with an absence of government interference. However, this argument can be countered by the fact that consumers can still consume sugary foods should they wish, they will just pay an extra tax which reflects the costs to society of obesity. Surely it is better that they pay for the health costs they cause than for the whole of society to pay, which is what currently happens. Accordingly, it would be fair to impose the sugar tax.

It is, finally, arguable whether a choice to consume sugary drinks involves the exercise of free will. Our decisions to consume say, a can of fizzy pop, are heavily influenced by advertising campaigns and the social acceptance of it. However, this does not necessarily lead to informed consent to the consequences of obesity and being overweight. A large swathe of society is ignorant of the health consequences so it appears that the public does not truly understands the risks of consuming too much sugar.

However, imposing a tax is not the end of the government's problems and as the chief nutritionist at Public Health England pointed out: obesity does not have a 'single bullet solution'. Other actions such as education are vitally important but whatever the cost of these policies, their benefits must surely outweigh the cost of picking up the pieces. It's better to put up a fence at the top of the cliff rather than an ambulance at the bottom.

SECTION 1C: READING COMPREHENSION QUESTIONS

Question 489:

Which of the following best accords with the main idea in the article?
- A. Obese individuals are to blame for their health consequences
- B. Sugar should be taxed
- C. Sugar should not be taxed
- D. There are other policies which should be done
- E. To consider the pros and cons of a sugar tax

Question 490:

Which of the following would, if true, most weaken the author's argument?
- A. A sugar tax is immoral
- B. A sugar tax affects the poor
- C. A sugar tax would lead to public protest
- D. A sugar tax would increase prices
- E. People would not reduce consumption in response to an increase in prices in sugary products

Question 491:

Which of the following would undermine the 'fairness' argument made by the author [sixth paragraph]?
- A. Some people would disagree with the sugar tax
- B. The sugar tax would not reduce the consumption of sugary products
- C. People are unaware of the health consequences of sugary products
- D. Sugar doesn't necessarily cause health problems in people, particularly when they consume small quantities
- E. Not everyone is ignorant of the health consequences

Question 492:

Which of the following is not true based on the passage?
- A. Around the world, more men are obese than women
- B. Social cost of obesity is estimated at £47 billion
- C. Being overweight causes health problems
- D. All cases of obesity can be blamed on excess sugar consumption
- E. Many individuals are ignorant of the health consequences of obesity

Question 493:

Which of the following is an <u>unstated</u> assumption in the passage?
- A. Sugar consumption is a cause of obesity and heart disease
- B. The social cost of obesity is £47 billion
- C. A full can of coke exceeds government sugar recommendations
- D. The government proposed the sugar tax
- E. A sugar tax will not solve all of the problems

Question 494:

Which of the following best illustrates the final sentence of the passage:
- A. The government should not provide health assistance to those who suffer from obesity
- B. The government should focus entirely on stopping people from consuming sugar
- C. Preventing a high consumption of sugar is more effective than trying to cure the health consequences of it
- D. Education is better than taxes
- E. Someone is falling off a cliff

Passage 20 – Tour de France

The Tour de France was established in 1903 to increase sales of the newspaper L'Auto, yet it went on to become the world's biggest cycle race and arguably the toughest sporting challenge on the planet. The modern version is a 23-day event, consisting of 21 days of racing where the competitors cycle at least 100 miles on each day. On half of the stages, the cyclists go up a number of mountains, including those in the Alps. Such a feat is absolutely astonishing both for seasoned fans and particularly for the uninitiated. It is, thus, easy to forget that the competitors themselves are human. Crowds line the streets in support of their favourite cyclists or just to see the spectacle. It is something that the whole of France and the world of cycling gets behind. So its humble beginnings would naturally surprise most people.

While the exact route of the Tour de France changes from year to year, the finish line is always at the heart of Paris on the world famous Champs-Elysees. The person with the fastest time wins the competition and is awarded the coveted Yellow Jersey.

What makes this sport even more intriguing is its structure. Approximately 200 cyclists take part and each rider is part of a team. In each team, there are nine riders. The team provides mechanical support, race support, medical assistance, massages after the race, and food specifically prepared for the demands of the race. The team's race director determines the strategy for each day of racing and for the competition as a whole. Gaining a place on a team is, some say, even harder than actually doing the race itself. The team must be convinced that you will be able to complete the course, that you're dedicated to the success of the team and if you're not going to be the team leader, that you'll sacrifice yourself for the leader.

It is not the organisers nor an official qualification round that determines who enters the competition; it is the teams. The teams have the freedom to choose who races for them. Cycling looks like a deceptively easy sport to understand – after all, what is there to a bunch of men racing around France for 3 weeks?

On flat stages, most of the cyclists tend to stay together in a group (or 'peleton' in French) for most of the day, which has a major influence on the team's racing strategy. Further, each team of cyclists has one individual designated as the team leader, which the others must support.

A significant factor in cycling is the slipstreaming effect. This effect is not just in cycling – it occurs whenever two objects move in space with one closely followed by the other. It applies to motor racing as well. It also explains why birds fly in a V-formation. When one cyclist follows another very closely, the cyclist behind saves a significant amount of energy. Conversely, that means that the cyclist in front uses up more energy. For these reasons, the cyclists tend to stay together in the races – each cyclist can take it lighter by being behind someone.

That leads on to a crucial point. The team chooses one rider to be the leader – it is simply determined on who, in their opinion, is the best cyclist at the time of choosing. The rest of the riders in the team are expected to support the lead cyclist in the race. They do this by, among other things, making sure the leader is behind them. As this happens with all teams, it is, in essence, each 'lead' rider against each other, each of whom is supported by their teammates. While this is the convention, it isn't always crystal clear how the best is chosen.

For example, when Team Sky had two very strong cyclists in 2012, a supporting rider demonstrated superior vigour on many of the stages. The leader of the team won the whole race but it was not without its controversy.

Given the extra amount of energy used up by the supporting cyclist in order to help his team leader, if they were going head-to-head, it would not be possible to say that the result would have been the same. That would have also led to a far more exciting spectacle as well. Interestingly enough, while the team leader won the race, in the end, the 'supporting rider' came 2nd, beating all the other team's lead cyclists – something unheard of in the historic sport. And yet, unlike every team leader (including his own), he didn't have the support that team leaders have.

Question 495:

Which of the following is an opinion?
- A. [The Tour de France] 'has become the world's biggest cycle race'
- B. It is the 'toughest sporting challenge on the planet'
- C. The competitors are human
- D. The route is 3000km
- E. A condition for becoming part of the team is that one would be willing to make sacrifices

Question 496:

Why does the lead rider in a team benefit from being the lead rider?
- A. The leader has the support of the team management
- B. The leader can beat the riders from the other teams
- C. The leader is the best of the rest in his team
- D. He is more likely to win the race
- E. He is dominant over his teammates

Question 497:

Why do the cyclists stay in a group in the races on flat stages?
- A. It is the best team strategy
- B. The slipstreaming effect
- C. It is the team's racing strategy
- D. To support the team leaders
- E. They are supported by riders at the front

Question 498:

Which of the following is implied but not stated by the author in the final paragraph?
- A. The correct result was reached in the 2012 race
- B. Team Sky's choice of leader was not correct for them
- C. A different result may have been reached in an equal race
- D. The slipstreaming effect meant that the supporting rider was a better rider
- E. The supporting cyclist may have been stronger in the 2012 race

Question 499:

Based on the passage, why would the supporting cyclist in the 2012 Tour de France have used extra energy?
- A. He was inefficient
- B. He was a better cyclist
- C. He was helping the team leader win, with the slipstreaming effect
- D. He was not as good a cyclist
- E. He was racing against the team leader

Passage 21 – Criminal Justice

The principle of equality before the law is a fundamental part of our justice system and the rule of law. While this has many facets, one is that people should not be treated more severely on account of their race or colour. Yet the treatment of ethnic minority individuals has been a never-ending concern due to the disproportionate numbers of ethnic minorities in prison. It has now reached the top of government and the Prime Minister has ordered a government review into discrimination against black and ethnic minority people in the criminal justice system.

Statistics from the Home Office indeed show that 25% of the prison population are ethnic minorities, and yet they only account for 14% of the UK population. Ethnic groups also receive longer custodial sentences than for white offenders. These are troubling statistics. It is, therefore, imperative to find out what the root cause of this is, and the government's review will hopefully go in depth enough to shed more light onto the matter.

Once a person is found guilty of a criminal offence, the courts then consider what their 'sentence' or punishment should be. Judges have discretion in choosing what sentences to give to offenders, even among those convicted of the same offence, and are required by law to consider a number of factors in making up their minds. For example, aggravating factors such as violence, previous offences, and pre-meditation, can increase the sentence the judge gives. Likewise, cooperation with the police may reduce the sentence. A guilty plea at the start of the trial leads to an automatic reduction of a third of the sentence. These factors explain why those convicted of the same offence can receive different sentences.

However, a study in 1992 by Roger Hood found that 7% of the over-representation of ethnic minorities in prison came from a higher use of custody than would have been predicted from legally relevant factors, which indicates discrimination in the exercise of judicial discretion. Indeed, other possible reasons also abound.

Cultural differences play a significant role. For example, admitting guilt in a criminal case (officially termed a 'guilty plea') can lead to a significant reduction in the sentence given (up to a third in some cases). Ethnic minority offenders, though, are significantly less likely to plead guilty than white offenders and are less likely to opt for legal advice. This may be a significant reason for the longer sentences. On the face of it, this does not appear to be discrimination. Given that judges are legally required to give the sentencing 'discount' for a guilty plea, it may be necessary to consider whether this discount should remain.

Finally, a black individual is six times more likely to be stopped and searched by police than a white person. The racial disparity in stop and searches are particularly disturbing given that the chances of arrest are not different for a black or white person. This may be for a number of reasons. It could be due to a police force's priority in high-crime rate neighbourhoods. However, a number of researchers have found that racial stereotypes exist, consciously and subconsciously, among police officers which could lead to a greater targeting of ethnic communities. Increased targeting, whether subconscious or conscious, would naturally lead to an increase in the numbers of ethnic minority offenders arrested. Accordingly, the significance of the disparity in stop and searches among racial groups requires urgent attention in the government's review. The government have already been encouraging police forces to reduce the disparity but it appears that more needs to be done. These figures in themselves do not conclusively demonstrate discrimination but may be indicative of it.

SECTION 1C: READING COMPREHENSION QUESTIONS

Question 500:

Which of the following is an opinion as opposed to an assertion of fact?
- A. The disparity requires urgent attention
- B. There is an over-representation of ethnic minorities in prisons
- C. Ethnic minority offenders are less likely to plead guilty
- D. Judges are required to give a sentencing discount for a guilty plea
- E. A black person is more likely to be stopped and searched than a white person

Question 501:

What is the implication of the second paragraph?
- A. More ethnic minorities are criminals
- B. There are a disproportionate number of ethnic minorities in prisons
- C. The government needs to find out the cause of it
- D. The statistics are not ideal
- E. There is racism in the criminal justice system

Question 502:

Which of the following is true, based on the passage?
- A. The higher sentences given to ethnic minorities is a breach of the rule of law
- B. Judges have a discretion to giving a guilty plea discount
- C. Ethnic minorities are more likely to have longer sentences than white individuals
- D. Judges consciously discriminate against ethnic minority defendants
- E. Socio-economic factors are not related to the longer sentences of ethnic minorities

Question 503:

What is the main reason for those convicted of the same offence being given different sentences?
- A. Discrimination
- B. Judicial discretion
- C. A different level of harm is caused
- D. More stop and searches of ethnic minorities
- E. The legal requirement to consider aggravating factors

Question 504:

How could the final paragraph explain the disproportionate number of ethnic minorities in the prison population?
- A. More ethnic minorities commit crimes
- B. The police are discriminating against ethnic minorities
- C. The increased targeting means that ethnic minority offenders are more likely to be caught than white offenders
- D. The chances of arrest do not differ between white and black individuals
- E. The government should act to reduce the number of ethnic minorities in prison

Question 505:

What is implied by the author in the final paragraph?
- A. There may be discrimination in the police
- B. The government needs to take further action
- C. There needs to be further investigation into the reasons for the disparity
- D. The reason for the disparity is multi-factorial
- E. Judicial discretion is not a factor for the disproportionately high % of ethnic minorities in prison

Passage 22 – Tax Incentives

Tax inversions have been on a trend throughout 2015. A well-known instance is when Pfizer, a large pharmaceutical company, made a deal to buy Allergan, a much smaller drug company which produces Botox. A tax inversion is where a company purchases a smaller company in a different jurisdiction so that it can relocate its headquarters to benefit from a lower corporate tax rate. A number of American companies have taken this route, to the annoyance of the US Government.

This also leads to another issue. A number of countries have offered competitive tax regimes or tax incentives to encourage foreign companies to set up there. A tax incentive involves the reduction or exemption of a tax liability. In particular, it appears that the UK are taking this approach in their tax policy – in 2015, the UK government announced a reduction in the corporate tax rate from 20% to 18% by 2020.

In the US in contrast, the corporate tax rate is at 35% for most companies and uniquely, it is on both the profits earned in the US and abroad. Both these features make the US rate one of the highest in the world.

Concerns have been raised about companies moving around to take advantage of competitive taxes in other countries. Such moves may well improve the profitability of companies and their returns to shareholders. However, the tax inverters still maintain their activities in the country that they left. Lower contributions from corporations mean that individual citizens have to pick up the tab and that the government has to reduce spending in society.

A further issue is that it may lead to unfairness to smaller companies, who have a limited ability to do a tax inversion, which in turn gives them a competitive disadvantage. On the other hand, though, supporters of tax inversions argue that the benefit of tax competition means that multinational companies can pass savings on to customers and invest more. The CEO of Pfizer claimed that their merger with Allergen will allow them to invest more in the US.

Proponents of low tax rates argue that regardless of geography, complex and high taxes are inefficient and stifle investment. Accordingly, taxes should be lowered and simplified in order to stimulate business activity and growth. When businesses grow, so too can jobs, wages, and prosperity generally. An incidental point is that the drive to attract business can encourage more efficient tax regimes. These can apply to both large and small business, and take forms such as the UK's wholesale reduction of corporation tax to 18%.

Famous businessman, Warren Buffett, has pointed out that on the contrary, investors want good roads, an educated and healthy workforce, and the rule of law - all of which help prosperity, but inextricably mean tax is needed.

SECTION 1C: READING COMPREHENSION QUESTIONS

Question 506:

Which of the following is true based on the passage?
- A. There were no tax inversions before 2015
- B. Tax inversions are bad
- C. Tax inversions always lead to more investment
- D. The Pfizer-Allergen deal will benefit society
- E. Allergen is in a different country to Pfizer

Question 507:

Which of the following is a defining feature of a tax inversion?
- A. A company buying another company
- B. Moving to another country
- C. A company making more profit
- D. A company moving its headquarters to a lower-tax regime
- E. A company evading tax

Question 508:

What is the main motivation for American companies buying companies in other countries?
- A. To expand reach to other countries
- B. To benefit customers
- C. To have lower taxes
- D. To leave America
- E. To benefit from simpler tax regimes

Question 509:

Which of the following is stated as a benefit to society of a company doing a tax inversion?
- A. Lower tax rate
- B. An efficient tax system and lower tax rate
- C. More jobs
- D. Lower taxes to both big and small businesses
- E. More businesses being attracted to the society

Question 510:

Which of the following is an argument that is implied but not stated in Warren Buffett's statement?
- A. The US should keep increasing its tax rate
- B. The UK's tax rate is too low
- C. Taxes are good for businesses
- D. Taxes should be raised
- E. Businesses should pay their taxes

Passage 23 – Black Death

In the Middle Ages, most people tended to form small communities on a feudal manor, which consisted of a village, church, and a castle presided over by a lord. Peasants typically held some land in the manor and in return, had to provide some services to the lord. While they could occupy a property, they were not allowed to leave the manor without permission.

The high mortality of the Black Death shocked medieval British society in more ways than could have been predicted at the time. Although historians disagree on the precise mortality rate, a number of estimates put the decline in population size at 50%. Perversely, this might have actually been to the benefit of the peasants that remained.

The decrease in population reduced the supply of labour and, thus, wages rose and peasants were able to demand higher wages. This allowed them to enjoy a higher standard of living. Due to the massive death rate, many vacant land holdings became available when people died without an heir. This transformed the position of peasants, as they could now move to different manors. Due to the labour shortage, the lords wanted the peasants to stay and were willing to increase wages and improve conditions. For example, some labourers were given a hot meal as opposed to a cold one. However, this increase in wage costs meant that lords could not farm as much of their demesne and had to change the way in which it was used.

This change in bargaining position shifted the economic balance of power and marked the breakdown of the feudal system. An example can be shown in Great Waltham and High Ester, where 7 in 51 marriages before the Black Death took place without merchet being paid. After the Black Death, though, this increased to 20 out of 46. Accordingly, it is clear that the power of the lords in the manorial system had weakened and they no longer held ultimate control over their peasants.

Peasants at the bottom of the social hierarchy were marked by a greater individualism. Their labour to the lord was no longer determined by their ties to the land or by custom but by market forces – i.e. which lord was offering the best pay. Given the greater availability of land, those who were doing well, such as merchants and clothiers, could also buy it and improve their status. This is remarkably reminiscent of a capitalist society as opposed to a feudal one.

Interestingly, women were valued a lot more and their wages increased. The Black Death's high mortality meant that much of the workforce was dead and needed to be replaced. However, there was not much of a transformation in society as the general attitudes towards women remained.

It is not a ubiquitous view though that the Black Death caused this change in the balance of power between peasants and the lords.

The Great Famine had already started the reduction of the population that led to increasing wages. Accordingly, some see the Black Death as an accelerator of social change, rather than an initial cause. Others also question the very basis of the view that the Black Death 'caused' the increase in entrepreneurialism among the lower orders in society. In order for a move from feudalism to capitalism to occur, there must surely be a change in attitudes (such as an increase in risk taking) – otherwise, even the death of half the population would not change things. Accordingly, some view the Black Death as merely giving an opportunity for the shift in the balance of power.

Question 511:

Which of the following fits in logically with the third paragraph?
- A. Peasants were previously tied to their manor
- B. Peasants transformed society
- C. Peasants were poor
- D. The power of the lords increased
- E. Peasants became more powerful than the lords

Question 512:

Why did women get higher wages?
- A. Women were valued a lot more
- B. Attitudes in society changed
- C. There were more women than men
- D. There was a shortage of labour
- E. The end of feudalism and a move to a capitalist society

Question 513:

Which of the following is true based on the passage?
- A. Peasants had permission to move to different manors
- B. The lords were happy for peasants to leave
- C. The Black Death caused the social change that was described
- D. The Black Death triggered the end of the manorial system
- E. Peasants were able to demand higher wages

Question 514:

Which of the following is an assumption made about the Great Famine?
- A. It reduced the population
- B. It had an impact on wages
- C. It occurred before the Black Death
- D. It was more severe than the Black Death
- E. It was a bigger cause of the shift in the balance of power

Question 515:

What is a common feature among the views in the final paragraph?
- A. The Great Famine had a role in shifting the balance of power
- B. The Black Death had a role in the shift of the balance of power
- C. The Black Death did not impact the shift in the balance of power
- D. Black Death was just an accelerator of social change
- E. Society was going to change even without the Black Death

Question 516:

Which of the following, if true, most weakens the author's argument in the fourth paragraph?
- A. In most manors, there was not a reduction in the number those paying merchet
- B. Most peasants were still paying merchet
- C. The lords still owned the land which was being used
- D. The lords still decided the wages to pay peasants
- E. The shift in the balance of power was small

Passage 24 – Cohabitation

Out of the 18.6 million families in the UK, 12.5m consist of married couples, and this has traditionally been the most common family type in the UK. However, cohabitation is on the rise, with statistics displaying an increase of 30% in cohabitation since 2004, thereby making cohabitation the fastest growing type of family in the UK. Accordingly, this should raise concerns as to whether the current legal regime for families is still suitable for society.

A difference between marriage and cohabitation is that, as a legal construct, many legal rights and responsibilities flow from the fact of being married. No additional legal rights flow from the fact of being a cohabitant.

In essence, a cohabitation is where two adults live together as a couple in an intimate and committed relationship. Strictly speaking, there is no legal definition of cohabitation – it is simply whenever people are living together in a relationship but are not married. It's more a descriptor denoting a relationship, which may be like a marriage, but is not formally one.

For example, a key difference is when one partner dies without creating a will. In the instance of a married couple, most of the property would pass to the spouse. Alternatively, the partner in a cohabitation would not automatically receive such property, unless it was stated in the will. Indeed, it is easy for a cohabiting couple to get round this by simply creating a will but thinking about the consequences of death is not particularly common among couples.

Furthermore, the process of separating is markedly different for a married couple compared to a cohabiting couple. An unmarried couple can just go their own ways and separate informally. On the other hand, separation from a marriage requires the consent of the court (although that is a mere formality) but crucially, the courts can, and frequently do, transfer property between spouses on divorce. For example, in the high-profile divorce between Heather Mills and Paul McCartney, Mills was awarded £24.3 million out of McCartney's estate. No such award would have been made had they been cohabitants.

While some have argued for such legal rights, both on death and separation, to be accorded to cohabitants, there are serious issues with such assertions. The most serious issue is that of consent. In regard to cohabitation, it is not possible to say that the parties consented to giving each other additional rights and responsibilities in respect of the other. Accordingly, it would infringe the parties' freedom and autonomy. Or would it? Campaigners retort that 58% of cohabiting couples believe their rights are the same as that of married couples anyway.

However, given that the rest of the couples surveyed do not consent to having new legal duties, surely the law should not impose that on them against their wishes. The law also becomes significantly more uncertain in giving rights and responsibilities to cohabitants: at what point do people living together become cohabitants? A legal definition would be required, which would descend into arbitrariness. In particular, it must be decided how long it would take for a couple to legally become a cohabitee. Further, to determine whether one is a cohabitee, it would likely be necessary to undertake an inquiry of a couple's relationship, which would hardly be an easy and inexpensive task.

While the status quo may not entirely reflect the public's understanding, improving the latter as opposed to forcing individuals to undertake greater legal duties and responsibilities would surely be the ideal solution.

Question 517:

How does a marriage and cohabitation differ?

- A The individuals in cohabitation are not committed to each other for life
- B The legal rights and obligations are lower for a cohabitation than a marriage
- C The courts have given more rights to cohabitees recently as opposed to married couples
- D In cohabitation, the partners can separate
- E Married couples tend to have children

Question 518:

How can a cohabiting couple put themselves on the same legal basis as a married couple in the event of a death of one of the parties?

- A They cannot under the current law
- B They need to get married
- C They need to separate
- D Write a will
- E Write a contractual agreement

Question 519:

What would the argument of the 'Campaigners' in the [final] paragraph most likely be?

- A For cohabitants to get all the same legal rights and responsibilities as married couples
- B Having legal rights and responsibilities would infringe the cohabiting couple's freedom
- C Having legal rights and responsibilities would not infringe the cohabiting couple's freedom
- D That 58% of cohabiting couples believe their rights and responsibilities are the same as married couples
- E The parties' freedoms should not be infringed

Question 520:

Which of the following policies would the author most likely agree with?

- A Making cohabitation a legal concept
- B Give cohabiting couples rights and responsibilities in regard to each other
- C Banning cohabitation
- D Require cohabiting couples to enter into a marriage
- E A campaign to raise awareness of the differences between cohabitation and marriage

Question 521:

Which of the following does the author disagree with?

- A Cohabitation
- B Legal rights and responsibilities
- C That 58% of cohabiting couples consent to the same rights as in marriage
- D Imposing additional legal rights and responsibilities on cohabiting couples
- E The £24.3 million settlement for Heather Mills

Passage 25 – F1

Formula 1, the pinnacle of motorsport, should epitomise the best racing the world has to offer and yet television viewing figures are decreasing and the outcomes of races are more predictable than ever. Worryingly, a survey in 2015 of over 200,000 fans highlighted significant disquiet over the way the sport is going. One of the top three descriptors of the sport was 'boring' and 89% of fans said that F1 needs to be more competitive. This should not be a surprise given that one team has dominated since 2014 but hopefully, this will be a wakeup call. At the same time, costs in F1 are spiralling out of control, which make it difficult for smaller teams to catch up.

F1 has tried to project an image of being environmentally friendly by requiring all teams' engines to have a capacity of 1.6 litres, much smaller than in previous regulations, and electrical and kinetic energy recovery systems in order to harvest energy that would have otherwise been wasted. Indeed, an object of this was to attract more commercial partners. In particular, if F1 regulations are more relevant to road cars, manufacturers would be more likely to enter, or remain in, Formula 1 as it would have a greater relevance to their commercial operations. A corollary of this is that costs of engines have doubled, coming into the region of £18 million for a year's supply. This is double that of the previous engines and is the biggest single expense for the teams. Such costs are significantly inhibiting for smaller teams.

It is not just the cost of engines that is large – the entire budgets of teams stretch to 100s of millions. Red Bull is estimated to have the largest budget at over €460 million with Mercedes close behind. While these large operations can add to the prestige of the teams, it doesn't necessarily add to the excitement of the sport. Arguably the latter is more important and serious issues in F1 remain.

Since the new regulations were introduced, one team, in particular, the Mercedes F1 team have by all accounts dominated the sport with very few drivers from other teams winning. While Mercedes have undoubtedly produced the best car and thus, are deserving of their success, it has led to accusations that the spectacle has become boring. It is mostly clear which team is going to win before the race has even started. This issue always abounds when one team dominates and may make a Grand Prix more of a procession than a race.

Mercedes have received criticism for their continued winning streak. Indeed, a famous driver from a rival team, Sebastian Vettel, has suggested that this is why the sport is boring. However, dominance is not a new phenomenon in F1 though, it has happened before – Vettel himself enjoyed a number of years in a dominant Red Bull with little competition from the other drivers. In 2000-2004, Ferrari dominated F1. It is thus clear that dominance is a key feature in Formula 1.

Accordingly, Mercedes should not be criticised for doing what every other team is doing, which is building the best F1 car they can. Mercedes built the best of the rest which is why they're winners. However, the tendency of F1 to produce a dominating team should not be attributed to the Mercedes car, but to the nature of some of the rules and regulations of the sport. The rules must be created in such a way as to promote competition. While the drive for environmentally friendly engines did not aim to achieve this, it did not help and may have even hampered competition.

Rule changes should include making it easier for cars to overtake, reducing engine costs and even reducing the total costs of teams. Such changes would reduce the large disparity between teams and make for closer racing. Whether the F1 rulers can make such changes depends on their will but it is in their interest too. Ultimately, change is required as should television numbers continue to drop, F1 will no longer be a draw on sponsors' and TV companies' money. In the long run, at least, F1's success is inextricably linked to the fans and the powers that be in F1 should recognise that.

Question 522:

What does the word 'corollary' mean in the context in which it is used?
- A. A benefit
- B. A consequence
- C. An incidence
- D. Cost
- E. Price

Question 523:

Which of the following is an opinion as opposed to a fact?
- A. The entire budgets of teams stretch to 100s of millions
- B. One of the top three descriptors of the sport by fans was 'boring'
- C. Engine costs have doubled
- D. F1 is the pinnacle of motorsport
- E. Mercedes should not be criticised

Question 524:

Based on the whole passage, how might the drive for environmentally friendly cars have hampered competition?
- A. It caused the dominance of Mercedes
- B. It led to slower engines
- C. It increased engine costs, which hit smaller teams harder
- D. It reduced the excitement of racing
- E. It has led to a procession rather than a race

Question 525:

To what does the author attribute the success of Mercedes?
- A. Mercedes building the best car
- B. The rules and regulations of F1
- C. The engine changes
- D. The drive for environmentally friendly engines
- E. Spending the most money

Question 526:

Why is there dominance in F1 according to the author?
- A. The racing is not close enough
- B. Mercedes' winning streak
- C. The new environmentally friendly engines
- D. Large spending
- E. The rules and regulations of F1

Passage 26 – Reparations

The transatlantic slave trade lasted approximately four centuries, and Britain played a well-known role in it. Over this period, English ships made slaving voyages to Africa, where Africans were captured and transported to the Americas to be sold as goods. David Richardson, a prominent historian, has calculated that over 3 million enslaved Africans were transported to the Americas. The Royal African Company gave the slave trade a formal royal charter and it has been argued that the slave trade was the richest part of Britain's trade in the 18th century. Karl Marx has argued that the slave trade created the financial conditions for Britain's industrial revolution but the extent of economic benefit to Britain has been heavily disputed. Slavery was formally abolished through The Slavery Abolition Act 1833 across the British Empire.

Recently there have been calls for the UK to pay reparations to compensate for the atrocity of the slave trade centuries ago. On Prime Minister David Cameron's first state visit to Jamaica in 2015, he faced calls from politicians (including the Jamaican leader) for Britain to pay reparations for its involvement in the slave trade. According to calculations by researchers, total reparations could be between $5.9 trillion and $14 trillion.

It is a fundamental moral right of anyone to seek redress for damage caused to them. However, the damage was done centuries ago so many question whether modern Brits should be subject to reparations when no actual damage was done by them. They committed no wrong.

Indeed, one line of argument is that we embrace our history in other aspects, such as the success of Britain in World War II. The British government has also apologised for tragic events such as the Hillsborough tragedy. Accordingly, when embracing our history, we should surely embrace our full history. Indeed, Germany has paid over €89 billion in reparations to compensate Jewish victims of Nazi war crimes in World War II in the 60 years after it. However, opponents of reparations suggest that this is not analogous to giving reparations for the slave trade.

If it was decided that Britain should pay reparations, critics argue that it is not clear who should be paid. Did countries such as Jamaica suffer the entirety of the damage? From another perspective, the damage was done to individuals specifically as opposed to just the countries as a whole.

In a further argument outlined by Julia Hartley-Brewer, she points out that the majority of slaves were, in fact, sold by African rulers to Europeans in exchange for goods, such as weapons. Accordingly, should the current ruling classes of Africa benefit from reparations? However, even though others had a role in the slave trade, it should not displace any responsibility of one of the main antagonists.

Some argue that it's clear that given Britain's involvement, they owe a clear and substantial debt to the descendants of slaves who were harmed. However, opponents of reparations dispute the idea that the damage of slavery continues to the present day.

Question 527:

Why might the German reparations not be analogous to reparations for the slave trade?
- A. The Nazi war crimes were more recent
- B. The Nazi war crimes were worse
- C. Victims of the Nazi war crimes themselves were being paid
- D. More died from Nazi war crimes than through the slave trade
- E. Modern Brits are not at fault for the slave trade

Question 528:

Which of the following best *illustrates* the implicit argument made when considering who Britain should pay reparations to [5th paragraph]?
- A. A company should not claim damages when its employee is injured by another person
- B. When an employee is injured, its descendants should be able to claim damages
- C. When an employee is injured, the community should benefit
- D. When a company suffers damage, its employees should benefit
- E. When an employee suffers harm, they should be compensated by the community

Question 529:

What was the author's purpose in writing this article?
- A. To argue for reparations for the slave trade
- B. To argue against reparations for the slave trade
- C. To point out and consider arguments for and against giving reparations for the slave trade
- D. To argue for the position of modern British people
- E. To argue that Britain was not wholly responsible for the slave trade

Question 530:

What is the author's view as to Julia Hartley-Brewer's point [penultimate paragraph]?
- A. African rulers were to blame for the slave trade and not Britain
- B. The slave trade was wrong
- C. It should not affect the UK's responsibility
- D. The UK was the main antagonist
- E. That it is incorrect

SECTION 1C: READING COMPREHENSION QUESTIONS

Passage 27 - Animal Experimentation

Animal experimentation has become significantly controversial in recent years. With the advocacy of groups such as the National Anti-Vivisection Society, public discourse on animal testing has taken on a new light. Extremist animal rights groups have taken to violent demonstrations and the harassment of employees engaged in animal testing. Indeed, the arguments for animal rights are important but extremist actions tend to shut off the oxygn for such debate. Many animal rights groups tend to believe that any animal testing is unacceptable and cruel, without being willing to consider a balanced view, though. That's not to say that their arguments are not useful, but that there must be consideration of the benefits of animal testing.

Reasonable scientists do not aim to make animals suffer if unnecessary. In fact, the law does not allow that. The current legal position, as laid out in the Animals (Scientific Procedures) Act, is more restrictive than one may first envisage. Firstly, animal testing is not allowed unless a license is granted by the government to the researcher carrying out the testing, to the particular project as a whole and for the place at which the work is carried out. When deciding whether to grant a license, there must be a clear potential benefit to either people, animals or the environment. In essence, the potential costs and benefits are weighed up. Animal rights groups even disagree with this, though. Ultimately, animal testing is not undertaken unless necessary and harm is minimised at all points in the process. Crucially, the legal position makes sure that there is a net benefit to society from the use of animals in research. Furthermore, strides in technology reduce the need to use animal experimentation.

The benefits of using animal testing cannot be understated – there are approximately 120,000 sufferers of dementia in the UK, to which animal testing is being used in the development of treatments to mitigate against the symptoms of it.

Of course, that's not to say that a blanket allowance should be given – licenses should only be given where there are no other possible treatments. Developments in technology and computer modelling have meant that the need to engage in animal testing may well reduce.

Public opinion also appears to be on the side of animal researchers -a 2005 poll by MORI showed that 89% of the public accept the need to use animals, so long as animals do not suffer unnecessarily.

In the instance of tinnitus, which affects approximately 10% of the UK population, the use of animals in research has the potential to improve the quality of lives of millions of people. Testing has involved a wire being inserted into the brains of mice and sounds being played to gauge their neurological response to sound. The mice are sedated with anaesthetic and given pain killers. Crucially, animal research does not always necessarily involve harm to animals, which makes the uncompromising position of animal rights groups untenable.

SECTION 1C: READING COMPREHENSION QUESTIONS

Question 531:

Which of the following is true based on the passage?
- A. Reasonable scientists do not make animals suffer
- B. Animal testing is always necessary
- C. The government considers the costs and benefits of engaging in animal testing
- D. Not enough animal testing is done
- E. Scientists are reasonable

Question 532:

What is the author's view as to the use of animal testing?
- A. Animal testing should be allowed
- B. Animal testing should not be allowed
- C. Cannot tell
- D. Animal testing is not necessary for society
- E. Animal rights groups should be banned

Question 533:

Which of the following is an opinion?
- A. Reasonable scientists do not aim to make animals suffer unnecessarily
- B. Animal testing is not allowed unless a license is granted
- C. Tinnitus affects 10% of the UK population
- D. 89% of the public agree with the need to use animals in testing
- E. There are 120,000 sufferers of dementia in the UK

Question 534:

What is the author's objection to animal rights groups?
- A. They advocate against animal testing, which is beneficial
- B. They take an absolutist position
- C. They do not understand the benefits of animal testing
- D. They are out of step with public opinion
- E. They do not help those with serious diseases, such as Parkinson's

Question 535:

Which of the following most undermines the author's viewpoint?
- A. The estimated benefit of animal research is far higher than the actual benefit derived
- B. Animals can feel harm
- C. The public is misinformed as to the ability of animals to suffer harm
- D. There are other methods of research that could be usefully used
- E. Patients may not know that they're being treated with animal-tested products

Passage 28 – Copyright

Copyright is a significant form of intellectual property right. It is a legal right that is accorded to the creator of, among other things, films, soundtracks, and original literary, artistic, dramatic and musical works. It lasts for 70 years after the death of the author and any person who copies, sells or distributes a copyrighted work without authorisation can be sued by the author. The author can claim damages for a loss of earnings and seek a court injunction to stop the individual infringing the author's rights. Breach of this would be a contempt of court, which carries, even more, consequences for the individual.

However, the relevance of copyright in the modern world has been questioned more than ever. It is meant to protect song artists, but illegal downloading is all too prevalent in the world. Indeed, within a day of Kanye West's latest album release, there were reports of over 500,000 unlawful downloads, with an estimated cost of $10 million to West. A particular concern is whether the law is now out of touch, particularly when improvements in technology have meant that enforcement of copyright is significantly more arduous. For example, it is harder to close down websites, and this allows them to operate above the law. In the meantime, record labels have been developing technology to help inhibit infringement. However, the very nature of digital products, such as songs, means that preventing the illegal use of them will continue to be laborious.

Accordingly, copyright is now more relevant than ever. Removing copyright protection would leave artists' incomes even more in peril of the morals of the population. It would legalise an immoral act and mean an even greater amount of free downloading. The fact of copyright protection indicates to society that it is wrong to download music without paying for it, or without authorisation. Removing that protection will increase unauthorised use.

Indeed, a prime justification of copyright protection is the natural rights theory, first advanced by Locke. The premise here is that every person 'has property in his own person'. Accordingly, when using your labour with things from nature, those things become yours. Using labour confers natural rights over the resultant output of that labour. Therefore, allowing copyright protection is vital to recognising those rights.

Locke's approach though is only superficially satisfying in regard to copyright protection. Many critics point out that copyrighted works, such as books and songs are not the complete creation of the author. The author's work may well have been influenced by other creators and works that had an impact on the author. Further, academics Alpin and Davies suggest that 'labour' alone is too imprecise to determine the boundaries of intangible goods.

Nonetheless, an alternate theory put forward by Hettinger may provide the answer. Based on the utilitarian theory, as founded by Bentham, Hettinger suggests that laws should promote the creation of valuable intellectual works, such as music, books, and films. Accordingly, this requires artists to be granted copyright protection in what they produce in order to incentivise the production of such works. The provision of copyright allows authors greater control over what they can do with their work – they can decide on its sale and distribution and at a price of their choosing. If anyone tries to sell their work without their consent, that person can be taken to court. However, a concern with Hettinger's view is that it is not clear whether empirical evidence exists to back this up or even whether it would be possible to acquire such legitimate evidence.

SECTION 1C: READING COMPREHENSION — QUESTIONS

Question 536:

What have improvements in technology done?
- A. Allowed illegal downloading to be stopped
- B. Discouraged illegal downloading
- C. Made illegal downloading free
- D. Made illegal downloading unfair
- E. Allowed illegal websites to evade authorities

Question 537:

What effect does the writer believe that removing copyright protection will have?
- A. Artists' incomes would be at the peril of the morals of the population
- B. Legalise an immoral act
- C. Legalise the free downloading of music
- D. Increase the number of free downloads
- E. Hamper efforts of record labels to increase protection

Question 538:

Which of the following is a conclusion which can be derived from Locke's theory of natural rights?
- A. Every person has natural rights
- B. Every person has a right to the things that they create
- C. It would not be right to give one's own creation for free
- D. Copyright protection should be increased
- E. People's creations should not be used without their consent

Question 539:

According to Hettinger, why should copyright exist?
- A. To allow authors a fair price for their work
- B. To ensure that a person's creation receives a just reward
- C. To accord with utilitarianism
- D. To incentivise the production of intellectual works
- E. To stop people free-riding

Question 540:

Which of the following is implied but not stated in Hettinger's argument?
- A. Having control over one's intellectual creation encourages creation
- B. Author's getting paid for their works encourages creation of their works
- C. There is no evidence backing it up
- D. There is evidence backing it up
- E. Locke's justification should not apply at all

Question 541:

Which of the following is common among Locke and Hettinger's justifications?
- A. They both critique the status quo
- B. They both advocate against the use of the law to provide copyright
- C. They both suggest that there should be copyright protection
- D. Authors always want to get paid
- E. Not paying an author for their work is always wrong

Passage 29 – Tax Avoidance

The tax affairs of large corporations have taken centre stage over the last few years, and mostly, but not wholly, through their own fault. While tax is a controversial matter in itself, for corporations, it has become even more significant. Tax reduces a business's paper profits and so businesses indeed have an incentive to pursue lower taxes. There are two main ways to do this directly: tax evasion and tax avoidance. Tax evasion is the illegal reduction of one's tax liability – this can be through misreporting a company's sales or simply not paying the correct liability. Tax avoidance, on the other hand, is the legal reduction of one's tax liability and is basically where a company's tax liability is lower than it should be – sometimes this is quite subjective but it can be obvious at other times. Tax avoidance can occur through setting up offshore subsidiaries, transfer pricing and benefiting from vague tax laws.

Tax rates are deceptively clear. Each company has to pay 20% of all UK profits as corporation tax to HM Revenue & Customs. If a company does not pay the 20% tax on its declared profits, it is breaking the law. Crucially, if no UK profits are made, the company is liable for no tax. However, this is an issue given that the profits that a company can legally declare may not be a sign of their true profits. This is where tax avoidance occurs.

However, Starbucks took headlines in 2012 when Reuters pointed out that since setting up in the UK in 1998, they had paid a meagre £8.6 million corporation tax on £3 billion of sales. In a number of years, they paid zero tax. This revelation led to boycotts and protests at Starbucks stores. Indeed, they were acting within the law, but as one protester pointed out: "They've shown utter contempt for our tax system."

It is unacceptable for such companies to be paying such little tax. In particular, companies that benefit from public infrastructure, such as roads and railway, and from public services, all of which require tax. It's, thus, quite ironic that Starbucks relied on the police to protect their stores from protests and yet they contributed a pittance to the public purse.

However, a significant issue is where the responsibility for such an unacceptable situation lies. Such companies are already acting lawfully and abiding by the rules. Some even question whether companies such as Starbucks are acting immorally, given that they're 'just' following the rules. The government do indeed have responsibility for implementing rules. While it may be quite difficult in this globalised world to establish laws to reduce tax avoidance, it is still the responsibility of world governments to coordinate efficient tax policies and prevent or reduce tax avoidance.

That's not to say that multi-national companies are absolved from responsibility, though. They have benefited enormously from basing their operations in the UK – with £3 billion of revenue in the example of Starbucks. It allowed shareholders to gain wealth while not contributing to society. It is quite simply unfair. Small businesses are less able to avoid tax because they can't shift their profits to subsidiaries abroad or hire expert tax lawyers. Individual citizens also can't avoid tax. So it is quite clear that politicians and companies need to restore balance in the tax system, however hard it may be.

Question 542:

What is the difference between tax evasion and tax avoidance?
- A. The public only condemns tax avoidance
- B. Google and Starbucks have only committed tax avoidance
- C. Tax evasion is morally bad
- D. Tax avoidance is moral
- E. Avoidance is legal but evasion is illegal

SECTION 1C: READING COMPREHENSION QUESTIONS

Question 543:

How much profit did Starbucks declare in the years when it paid zero tax?
- A. £8.6 million
- B. £3 billion
- C. 20%
- D. Zero
- E. Cannot tell

Question 544:

Why was there a boycott of Starbucks stores in 2012?
- A. Starbucks engaged in tax evasion
- B. Starbucks engaged in tax avoidance
- C. Consumers did not like Starbucks
- D. Too many companies were acting in defiance of the tax rules
- E. Starbucks paid the wrong form of tax

Question 545:

What is the implied argument in the fourth paragraph?
- A. Companies should not prioritise profit over tax
- B. Companies should pay for the infrastructure and police
- C. Companies should pay tax
- D. The police should not have protected Starbucks stores
- E. The tax rate should reduce

Question 546:

Which of the following is a matter of opinion?
- A. The tax rate
- B. Tax evasion
- C. Tax avoidance
- D. The amount of profit declared
- E. Starbucks had £3 billion of sales in the UK

Question 547:

Who holds responsibility, according to the author, for the tax avoidance in the UK?
- A. The tax system
- B. Small businesses
- C. Tax avoiding companies
- D. Government
- E. The government and tax avoiding companies

Question 548:

Why is there unfairness in the tax system generally according to the author?
- A. Tax avoidance
- B. Globalisation
- C. Starbucks avoiding tax
- D. Multinational companies avoiding tax while individuals have to pay their way
- E. The corporation tax rate is only 20%

Passage 30 – Susan B. Anthony

At the election of President and Vice President of the United States, and members of Congress in November 1872, Susan B. Anthony, and several other women, offered their votes to the inspectors of election, claiming the right to vote, as among the privileges and immunities secured to them as citizens by the fourteenth amendment to the Constitution of the United States. The inspectors, Jones, Hall, and Marsh, by a majority, decided in favour of receiving the offered votes, against the dissent of Hall, and they were received and deposited in the ballot box. For this act, the women, fourteen in number, were arrested and held on bail and indictments were found against them under the 19th Section of the Act of Congress of May 30th, 1870, (16 St. at L. 144.), independently charging them with the offense of knowingly voting without having a lawful right to vote. The three inspectors were also arrested, but only two of them were held to bail, Hall having been discharged by the Commissioner on whose warrant they were arrested. All three, however, were jointly indicted under the same statute—for having knowingly and wilfully received the votes of persons not entitled to vote.

Of the women voters, the case of Miss Anthony alone was brought to trial, a nolle prosequi having been entered upon the other indictments. Before the trial, Miss Anthony gave lectures in all of the twenty-nine districts in Monroe County, the location of the trial, where she argued that she had a lawful right to vote. US Supreme Justice, Judge Ward Hunt, was persuaded that Miss Anthony might have prejudiced potential jurors and moved the trial to Canandaigua, Ontario County. Miss Anthony continued to give lectures in Ontario County, but the trial was not altered again and set to go ahead.

Upon the trial of Miss Anthony before the U.S. Circuit Court for the Northern District of New York, at Canandaigua, in June, 1873, it was proved that before offering her vote she was advised by her counsel that she had a right to vote; and that she entertained no doubt, at the time of voting, that she was entitled to vote.

Question 549:

According to the above passage, how many people in total were arrested due to the group of women voting?
- A. Fourteen
- B. Three
- C. Seventeen
- D. Sixteen
- E. Fifteen

Question 550:

Based on the passage only, who was definitely brought to trial over the incident?
- A. Susan B. Anthony
- B. Susan B. Anthony and the inspectors
- C. Susan B. Anthony, Jones, and Marsh
- D. Jones, Marsh, and Hall
- E. None of the above

Question 551:

Which of the following best describes initial opinions of the election officers?
- A. United by each member's personal support of the women's votes
- B. Divided in response to the women's actions
- C. Apathetic about the women's actions
- D. United by general disapproval of the women's actions
- E. Unequivocal about the legality of the women's actions

Question 552:

Which defence for Susan B. Anthony is mentioned above?
- A. She did not realise she was not allowed to vote
- B. That all people born in the USA should be able to vote for their president
- C. That gender should not prevent her vote
- D. The election officers accepted her vote, showing that the responsibility did not lie with her
- E. The previous law was wrong

Question 553:

Why did Judge Ward move the case to Ontario County?
- A. The judge was against Anthony's case
- B. The judge believed that the jury could have been prejudiced in Monroe County
- C. The judge believed that the jury was biased
- D. The judge disagreed with the content of Anthony's lectures
- E. The judge was based in the Ontario County

SECTION 2: Writing Task

The ultimate goal of any essay is to convey an argument to the reader. In order to do that, the essay needs to be as clear as possible, follow a logical structure, and develop a coherent argument. In section 2, you have 40 minutes to write the essay.

The key to creating a solid essay in the exam is to develop a good, persuasive argument in clear written English. It is **not** about writing as much as you can – indeed, some of the best essays are the shortest; and a rambling essay can attract low marks.

Ultimately, the examiners are testing your **ability to argue** and **not** particularly on your knowledge. That being said, having a good general knowledge will help you create good arguments and will stand you well for the exam. Crucially, it means that you'll be comfortable answering the questions in the exam.

Structuring your Essay

The structure of an essay consists of 3 parts:

1. Introduction
2. Main Body
3. Conclusion

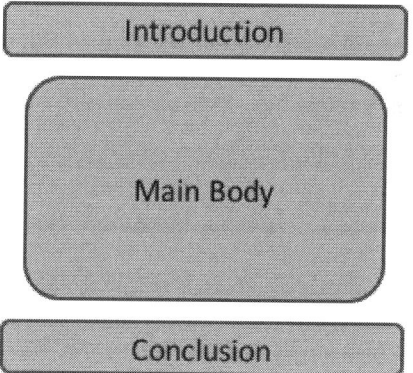

This is a well-known structure and while it is not necessary to give headings or to say that you're writing your introduction, keeping your essay in this format will be more clear and understandable.

A well-known saying is that: In your introduction, say what you're going to say; in the main body, you say it and in your conclusion, say what you've already said by bringing it all together.

The Exam Approach

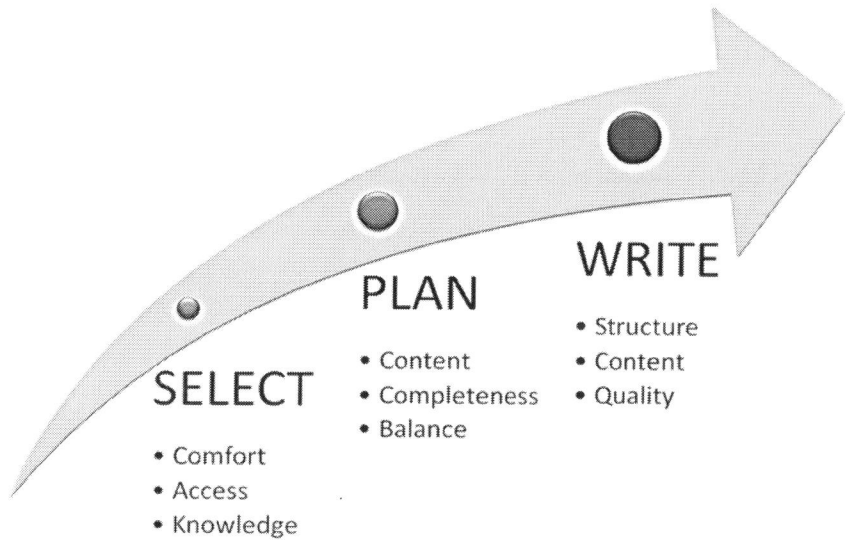

Most students think that the "writing" component is most important. This is simply not true.

The vast **majority of problems are caused by a lack of planning and essay selection** – usually, because students just want to get writing as they are worried about finishing on time. 45 minutes is long enough to be able to plan your essay well and *still* have time to write it, so don't feel pressured to immediately start writing.

Step 1: Selecting

You will be given a choice of 4 essays to choose from and crucially, you will have no idea of what it could be beforehand. Selecting your essay is crucial- make sure you're comfortable with the topic and ensure you understand the actual question- it sounds silly but about 25% of essays that we mark score poorly because they don't actually answer the question!

Take two minutes to read all the questions. Whilst one essay might originally seem the easiest, if you haven't thought through it, you might quickly find yourself running out of ideas. Likewise, a seemingly difficult essay might actually offer you a good opportunity to make interesting points.

Use this time to carefully select which question you will answer by gauging how accessible and comfortable you are with it given your background knowledge.

It's surprisingly easy to change a question into something similar, but with a different meaning. Thus, you may end up answering a completely different essay title. Once you've decided which question you're going to do, read it very carefully a few times to make sure you fully understand it. Answer all aspects of the question. Keep reading it as you answer to ensure you stay on track!

Step 2: Planning

Why should I plan my essay?
There are multiple reasons you should plan your essay for the first 5 minutes of Section B:

- As you don't have much space to write, make the most of it by writing a very well-organised essay.
- It allows you to get all your thoughts ready before you put pen to paper.
- You'll write faster once you have a plan.
- You run the risk of missing the point of the essay or only answering part of it if you don't plan adequately.

How much time should I plan for?
There is no set period of time that should be dedicated to planning, and everyone will dedicate a different length of time to the planning process. You should spend as long planning your essay as you require, but it is essential that you leave enough time to write the essay. As a rough guide, it is **worth spending about 5-10 minutes to plan** and the remaining time on writing the essay. However, this is not a strict rule, and you are advised to tailor your time management to suit your individual style.

How should I go about the planning process?
There are a variety of methods that can be employed in order to plan essays (e.g. bullet-points, mind-maps etc). If you don't already know what works best, it's a good idea to experiment with different methods.

Generally, the first step is to gather ideas relevant to the question, which will form the basic arguments around which the essay is to be built. You can then begin to structure your essay, including the way that points will be linked. At this stage, it is worth considering the balance of your argument, and confirming that you have considered arguments from both sides of the debate. Once this general structure has been established, it is useful to consider any examples or real world information that may help to support your arguments. Finally, you can begin to assess the plan as a whole and establish what your conclusion will be based on your arguments.

How do I plan my essay?
Different methods work best for different students, but some are as follows:

➢ A mind-map
➢ Bullet-points
➢ A side by side list of PROS and CONS

Step 3: Writing

Introduction

The introduction should explain the statement and define any key terms. Here, you can say what you're going to say and suggest (either affirmatively or tentatively) a response or answer to the question.

It is important not to spend too long on an introduction as that would use up too much time unnecessarily, which could be better spent on other parts of the essay.

Main Body

The main body is where you discuss your arguments, consider counter arguments or consider the pros and cons of a particular statement or policy position.

In particular, while you may have numerous ideas, it is generally better to spend more time developing and evaluating fewer points, rather than listing as many points as possible and not going into much depth on each point.

Just like in GCSE English, using the Point-Evidence-Evaluation technique can help ensure you develop and deploy your ideas more fully.

In particular, using relevant examples where you can will help bolster your argument and provide for a more persuasive essay. However, it is crucial that real world examples are only used if they fit in with your argument – otherwise, it adds nothing and will not gain you marks.

How do I go about making a convincing point?
Each idea that you propose should be supported and justified in order to build a convincing overall argument. A point can be solidified through a basic Point → Evidence → Evaluation process. By following this process, you can be assured each sentence within a paragraph builds upon the last and that all the ideas presented are well solidified.

How do I achieve a logical flow between ideas?
One of the most effective ways of displaying a good understanding of the question is to keep a logical flow throughout your essay. This means linking points effectively between paragraphs and creating a congruent train of thought for the examiner as the argument develops. A good way to generate this flow of ideas is to provide ongoing comparisons of arguments and discussing whether points support or dispute one another.

Conclusion

The conclusion provides an opportunity to emphasise the **overall sentiment of your essay** which readers can then take away. It should summarise what has been discussed during the main body and give a definitive answer to the question. It's not necessary to restate your points but this is where you can weigh up the advantages and disadvantages and explain why you've attached more weight to an advantage or disadvantage.

Some students use the conclusion to **introduce a new idea that hasn't been discussed**. This can be an interesting addition to an essay and can help make you stand out. However, it is by no means, a necessity. In fact, a well-organised, 'standard' conclusion is likely to be more effective than an adventurous but poorly executed one.

Crucially, it is important to give a judgement in the conclusion, or a decisive response to the question posed, based on the arguments you've advanced in the main body. For example, do you agree with the statement?

Worked Example

"Abortion should only be permitted in certain circumstances" Discuss.

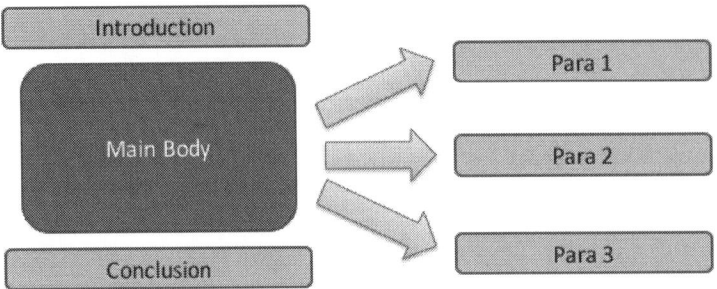

Introduction
In the introduction, it would be useful to present a brief outline of what you're going to discuss. After planning the essay (discussed below), you will know what you're going to talk about in the main body and can give a <u>very brief</u> outline in the introduction.

It is also important to define any key terms in the question here. It is quite clear that 'abortion' could be usefully defined ('the termination of a pregnancy').

If you wish, you can also highlight the key themes that will run through the essay.

Main Body
A key issue is what you write in the main body.

In the planning stage, jot down the ideas that first come to your head. For this question, you should think of possible circumstances where abortion should be permitted and possible circumstances in which it shouldn't be permitted.

Possible circumstances to consider abortion:
➤ *When the mother just wants to give up the foetus*
➤ *In the event of a medical issue*
➤ *Disability of the child*
➤ *Sexual Assault*
➤ *When the mother is too young*

Five possible lines of inquiry are listed here but there won't be time in 40 minutes to consider all of them in enough detail. In the exam, it's much better to focus on <u>quality</u> rather than quantity. Accordingly, choose the areas where you have the most knowledge or where you feel like you can make an original contribution and shine.

It is then necessary to choose a structure, and one possible structure is to devote each paragraph to a 'circumstance' and in order to cover fewer points, but in more detail, three circumstances will be considered. In each paragraph, the pros and cons should be considered to produce a balanced essay.

Structure of Main Body:
Paragraph 1: Abortion when the mother wants to give up foetus
Paragraph 2: Disability of the child
Paragraph 3: Medical issue

Detailed plan of Main Body
- *Abortion when the mother wants to give up foetus*
    1. **For Allowing Abortion**
        a. Some may argue that the mother should be able to give up the foetus should she want to.
        b. This is based on her freedom to plan her life as she chooses.
        c. Forcing the mother to have a child may not be in the child's best interests – would the child be cared for?
    2. **Against Allowing Abortion**
        a. The foetus has a right to life.
        b. The mother already made her choice during consummation and exercised her freedom to choose then.
    3. Therefore, abortion should not be permitted in this circumstance as the right to life should take greater precedence. The mother should be encouraged to think carefully about having a child before consummation.

Disability of the child
4. **For Allowing Abortion**
    a. The child would have a poor quality of life.
    b. Would be more expensive to bring up a child with a disability.
5. **Against Allowing Abortion**
    a. Again, against the child's right to life.
    b. Hard to tell what the child's quality of life would be if there's a known disability.
    c. Even if the child will be disabled, disabled people play an important role in society.
    d. The rights of a foetus shouldn't be different depending on a disability.
6. Arguably, the right to life of the foetus should prevail here. It would, in any case, be discriminatory to lower the rights of an abnormal foetus when compared to that of a healthy foetus. It's against the law to discriminate against disabled humans and surely the same should be the case for a disabled foetus.

Medical Issue
7. **For Allowing Abortion**
    a. Health risk to the mother.
8. **Against Allowing Abortion**
    a. Right to life of the foetus.
9. On balance, the right to life of a living person should take precedence in this circumstance.

This is a detailed plan and your plan in the exam does not need to be this detailed, but it should still cover the main points. Once a plan is written, you can get straight into writing the essay.

Note carefully how alternative points of view are <u>always</u> considered in the detailed plan above. Ultimately, your goal is to write a persuasive and balanced essay. When you consider alternative points of view, it strengthens your main argument. This is because it shows that you have thought about the different sides of the issue.

In the detailed plan above, point (c) is an intermediate (or interim) conclusion at the end of each paragraph. This is simply a statement which concludes a *paragraph*. It is generally desirable to include tentative conclusions where possible here as it makes it easier for the reader to understand your essay.

Conclusion
In the conclusion, the arguments advanced in the main body are brought together. In this question, the interim conclusions on each circumstance went into a lot of depth, so just a basic summary suffices for the main conclusion. An example could be as follows:

"On balance, abortion should only be permitted in certain circumstances. The right to life of the foetus demands that abortion is not allowed at the behest of the mother alone. However, there are certain situations when abortion should be permitted, such as when there is a health risk to the mother as her rights must be considered alongside that of the foetus."

Common Mistakes

1) Ignoring the other side of the argument
Although you're normally required to support one side of the debate, it is important to **consider arguments against your judgement** in order to get the higher marks. A good way to do this is to propose an argument that might be used against you, and then to argue why it doesn't hold true or seem relevant. You may use the format: *"some may say that...but this doesn't seem to be important because..."* in order to dispel opposition arguments whilst still displaying that you have considered them. For example, *"some may say that fox hunting shouldn't be banned because it is a tradition. However, witch hunting was also once a tradition – we must move on with the times"*.

2) Answering the topic/Answering only part of the question
One of the most common mistakes is to only answer a part of the question whilst ignoring the rest of it as it's inaccessible.

3) Long Introductions
Some students can start rambling and make introductions too long and unfocused. Although background information about the topic can be useful, it is normally not necessary. Instead, the **emphasis should be placed on responding to the question**. Some students also just **rephrase the question** rather than actually explaining it. The examiner knows what the question is, and repeating it in the introduction is simply a waste of space.

4) Not including a Conclusion
An essay that lacks a conclusion is incomplete and can signal that the answer has not been considered carefully or that your organisation skills are lacking. **The conclusion should be a distinct paragraph** in its own right and not just a couple of rushed lines at the end of the essay.

5) Sitting on the Fence
Students sometimes don't reach a clear conclusion. You need to **ensure that you give a decisive answer to the question** and clearly explain how you've reached this judgement. Essays that do not come to a clear conclusion generally have a smaller impact and score lower.

General Advice

- ✓ Always answer the question clearly – this is the key thing examiners look for in an essay.
- ✓ Analyse each argument made, justifying or dismissing with logical reasoning.
- ✓ Keep an eye on the time/space available – an incomplete essay may be taken as a sign of a candidate with poor organisational skills.
- ✓ Use pre-existing knowledge when possible – examples and real world data can be a great way to strengthen an argument- but don't make up statistics!
- ✓ Present ideas in a neat, logical fashion (easier for an examiner to absorb).
- ✓ Complete some practice papers in advance in order to best establish your personal approach to the paper (particularly timings, how you plan etc.).
- ✗ Attempt to answer a question that you don't fully understand, or ignore part of a question.
- ✗ Rush or attempt to use too many arguments – it is much better to have fewer, more substantial points.
- ✗ Attempt to be too clever or present false knowledge to support an argument – a tutor may call out incorrect facts etc.
- ✗ Panic if you don't know the answer the examiner wants – there is no right answer, the essay is not a test of knowledge but a chance to display reasoning skill.
- ✗ Leave an essay unfinished – if time/space is short, wrap up the essay early in order to provide a conclusive response to the question.

Annotated Essays

Example Essay 1

"There is a time and place for censorship of the internet" Discuss with particular reference to the right of freedom of expression.

Internet is the main source of connection for people all around the world. It's where we get the latest news and information worldwide effectively and effortlessly. The lack of barrier in this internet world gives easy access to information that we might not want to see and might cause us offence. This essay is about the act of censorship, which filters offensive information of the internet, given there's a time and a place we can do so in this modern era. There's "a place" suggests there's enough room which needs to be censored and there's "a time" suggest it's the time to act on censorship.

Firstly, censorship is necessary to a certain extent as due to freedom of expression, we might be access to information that we found offended by, such as pornography. These might affect viewers mentally and easily cause depression, and affect minds especially the early teens.

However, an age limit could be set on a pornography website and refuse access to such images. It's taking an active role, to click into those websites. Setting age limits can prevent youngsters receiving non-educational information and affect their youth development. Freedom of expression is also offended as some might treat pornography as a form of art. It's very difficult to monitor whether the viewer is really above the age limit.

Also, definition of Art is very blurry, which as an excuse for people to share it through the internet. Parental education is also a key. Instead of setting limits to the children, we should given them advice on what they should go on, and guide them to make the right decision on choosing suitable materials. In this way, not only the children's development is protected, it also trains them to give the right judgements and develop logical thinking.

Another place for censorship is political/religious offensive comments and materials. Religious behaviours should be protected due to the freedom of expression in society and political views in order to keep harmony.

However, in order to achieve this, censorship is not necessary, as it would block the minds and thoughts and might be a chance for the government to brain-wash the citizens with the 'right kind' of political behaviour, which might ironically break harmony in society, and slow down its development.

Examiner's Comments:

Introduction: The introduction rambles on too long – it could have been much shorter and concise. It was also not clear. It's not necessary to say "This essay is about the act of censorship" – this is obvious. It was good to define censorship in the introduction (when the student said 'filters offensive information') although the rest of the introduction was not clear and did not make sense. Accordingly, the student would have lost marks here and wasted time. The student did not address the entire question either – it would have been good to point out how freedom of expression will come into play as well. The introduction only really needs to be 3 or 4 lines.

Main Body: In the main body, the student makes some wild assertions, such as the point regarding depression. The first sentence in the main body doesn't make much sense either. The main issue with the essay is that the student's points are not linked together logically: the essay consists of a large number of separate assertions. The point made about 'art' is not very clear either.

Conclusion: Lastly, the candidate finishes with no conclusion. The final paragraph did not draw together all the relevant information, which is bad practice. Even if a candidate is running out of time, writing a solid conclusion will gain many more marks than not writing one. Indeed, a lack of conclusion would likely lose marks.

Example Essay 2

"There is a time and place for censorship of the internet" **Discuss with particular reference to the right of freedom of expression.**

Censorship of the internet is not a new concept, nor does it seem like one that will ever cease. I believe that there are a multitude of reasons for its presence and hence in this essay I will argue for the statement provided.

Firstly, censorship of the internet has the capability to protect certain groups. For example, a widely accepted and often promoted form of this is the blocking of certain websites by parents and schools. In this case, the group being protected are children. We accept the fact that children should not be exposed to 'mature' content such as violence and sexual activity and by blocking certain sites, children are free to surf the internet safely. This seemingly innocent form of censorship hardly poses much threat to the right to freedom of expression as no party is being prevented from having their views heard. If this form of censorship was deemed illegal, it may paradoxically push such parties to tone down their content by pressures from parental organisations and child safety bodies in order to create a child friendly internet, which ultimately would be restrictive to free expression.

Secondly, the restriction of content that is deemed extremist or might incite acts of terrorism, whilst going against the right to freedom of expression, could be necessary to uphold the security of a nation. Thus, taking a utilitarian perspective to this issue, as the safety of the nation takes on a greater value than the right to freedom of expression. Although it may seem like a cold approach, it is justified for the well-being of a greater number of individuals and thus, society generally. Truly, the recruitment of ISIS supports is a disturbing example of the necessity of censorship of extremist views and preventative measures must be taken to ensure that the young and susceptible are not taken in by the terrorist propaganda. Accordingly, there must be a point where we deem the safety of a nation as more imperative than the freedom of expression of certain individuals.

Lastly, the freedom of expression is easily abused in the cyber world. The animosity that the internet provides gives the users a sense of invisibility where they see themselves as above the law. Abusive remarks are made without consideration of their consequence or lack of this providing an environment for cyber bullying to grow.

Censorship is not necessarily tyrannical but is a practice that must co-exist with any form of content creation and like all else, there is a time and place for it.

Examiner's Comments:

Introduction: The introduction is very concise, which is good. However, it would have been even better if the student considered freedom of expression in the introduction.

Main Body: This is a good attempt at the question and relates directly to the question. The candidate refers to the relationship between censorship and freedom of expression throughout the main body. She points out when freedom of expression is hindered by censorship and when censorship is justified. Given that it relates to the question throughout, it would yield many more marks than Example 1 (even though both are of a similar length).

However, the candidate did not consider whether censorship might be bad in the first place: why can't the government just censor what they want to? The essay would have been stronger if this were considered (even briefly). It would have been worthwhile to bring in the countervailing principle of 'freedom of expression' at some point in the essay. This would be a reason why the government should *not* be able to censor any information. The penultimate paragraph doesn't add much to the essay though – is censorship acceptable in this situation? Is this the place for censorship? Or should people be expected to put up with other people's views? Other than this paragraph, the rest of the essay is very good.

Conclusion: The conclusion is quite short. While there is nothing inherently wrong with the conclusion being concise, it must answer the question. The candidate's conclusion did not refer to freedom of expression and so she has not fully addressed the question.

Example Essay 3

"There is a time and place for censorship of the internet" Discuss with particular reference to the right of freedom of expression".

In today's day and age it's extremely easy for anyone to access explicit or dangerous content on the internet. There have been talks of censorship on the internet, but is it necessary? One would argue that the censorship of the internet is against our freedom of expression, which is why in this essay I will come with an answer in response to the statement 'There is a time and place for censorship of the internet'.

In our current education system there is a heavy emphasis put on the usage of the internet to aid our learning. However, once children learn how to use the internet, the whole world is just one click away. Children could be easily exposed to indecent images, which is why some say the government should censor the internet for the safety of children. Possible solutions could be only allowing websites with adult material to be accessible at late-night, reducing the chances of indecent exposure to children. Accordingly, in this instance, censorship is justified.

Similarly, one could easily research the internet to find information about illegal activities such as drug or bomb making. This means that the internet could be used as a tool to threaten national security, hence why the internet should have tough censorship in order to prevent criminals from accessing dangerous material, for the benefit of everyone's safety.

On the other hand, blocking certain websites strictly goes against our right of freedom of expression and instead of blocking certain dangerous websites, the government should have a more efficient surveillance strategy in order to track people who are accessing such dangerous websites. This would ensure that our right of freedom of expression isn't breached and at the same time, criminal activity would be prevented.

Furthermore, with regards to the access of sexually explicit websites, more work should be some in order to educate children not to access such websites. Good parent is a better alternative to preventing children accessing such websites, rather than blocking sites which goes against our right of freedom of expression.

In conclusion, there is no time and place for censorship as it goes against our right to freedom of expression. Other alternatives such as internet surveillance would be more effective as it ensures the safety of the general public and at the same time our freedom of expression is not breached.

Examiner's Comments:

Introduction: This is a very good introduction. It highlights the conflict between censorship and freedom of expression, which is a good place to point it out. In the final sentence, though, the student wastes time in saying "which is why in this essay I will come with an answer in response to the statement...." – this is obvious and there's little point in saying it. It just wastes time and prevents one using the time for writing something more useful. Other than this, the introduction is very good and concise.

Main Body: The student considers two main instances of censorship in the main body (indecent images and dangerous websites) and suggests that censorship could be used, but suggests alternatives would be more effective. This is quite a persuasive essay because the student has considered alternative points of view, which makes the essay balanced.

Conclusion: The conclusion is very clear and brings the arguments advanced in the essay to a final judgement. The candidate directly addresses the question and refers to the whole part of the question by considering freedom of expression (unlike in Example Essay 2). On the whole, this is a very impressive essay.

Example Essay 4

"Developed countries have a higher obligation to tackle climate change than developing countries"
Discuss the extent to which you agree with this statement

Developed countries, such as the UK, Dubai and Japan have economies and political standings which are considered fairly stable. Developing countries strive to achieve the stable GDP, inflation and political welfare of developed countries. Climate change occurs due to excess emission of gas pollutants, melting of ice caps, global warming and in the case of such serious disasters, is it fair to place greater responsibility towards the more developed first and then the second world countries?

Statistically, it is shown that developed countries have been the main pollutants and indirectly, cause global warming. Due to its higher living standards, citizens of these countries have a higher propensity to consume, thus contributing to greater factory industries. As they would also have the best resources and research and development facilities, these countries would be more capable of producing greater findings to tackle climate change. This can also avoid conflicting interests among developing countries whose main focus would still be on growing. The countries may still be facing radical political changes which could affect their views and focus on the country's wellbeing. The Kyoto protocol, a Japanese originated project to reduce air pollution mainly forced on the more developed countries, as knowing it might create economical downfall as many of these countries on oil refinement and exporting of cheap factory produced goods. Under these circumstances, having more developed and stable countries to hold higher obligations towards issues of climate change would not be too wrong.

However, looking at this from a different perspective, climate change issues should not be delegated only to a few countries, but everyone altogether. It should be notably, responsibility of all, as it would require effort and contribution, as well as a mutual understanding form every country. It would also be considered unfair, as some may take this for granted. Countries at war, Iran and Syria, should be held dully responsible for the countless bombing and air strikes which has greatly contributed to global warming. This should be an issue for all. Other than that, developed countries would be blamed for any mistake or distasteful occurrences, which would have been inevitable, by countries where the cause originated from. Therefore, it should be recognised that combating climate change should be the responsibility of all.

Why should these countries make sacrifices to their economical welfare for others? World organisations like NATO, combinations of many different countries, work as a whole, with more developed countries contributing resources and research equipment required. Tackling of climate change should be the responsibility of all, and every country should feel obligated to it.

Examiner's Comments:

Introduction: The introduction is fine as the student defines the key terms within the quotation. It could have been a bit more specific when questioning whether greater responsibility should be placed on developing countries.

Main Body: The points in the second paragraph are interesting and the student deploys her own knowledge to good effect. The final sentence in the second paragraph could usefully be adjusted to say something along the lines of "Given the greater needs of developing companies and greater resources of developed ones, developed countries may have a greater capacity to take on the higher obligation of climate change". In the third paragraph, some good points are made. The point regarding the war in Iraq and Syria makes little sense and significantly reduces the quality of the essay. It is very important to make sure that the points you make follow from each other.

Conclusion: The student does address the question in the conclusion and is very succinct. It is not clear how NATO specifically fits into the essay at all and it would have been better to leave that out.

Example Essay 5

"Developed countries have a higher obligation to tackle climate change than developing countries"
Discuss the extent to which you agree with this statement

Developed countries are the nations with mature economies and modernised environments in their states by the development starting from the 18th century, while developing countries refer to the nations which are investing most of their money into the development for economic growth and are trying to catch up to the developed ones. The recent climate changes are mainly incurred by the industrial and business processes of the economic activities in the world. These led to the emission of greenhouse gases and finally global warming. The obligation that countries should bear for this case is to eliminate the pollution of the world and allow the climate to restore. I will now look into the topic economically, historically and environmentally.

To start with, developed countries should take more responsibilities of damaging the climate because they are the starters of it. Looking back to the history, western countries, especially the UK, experienced Industrial Revolution in the 18th Century. Mass production existed by utilising machines and mining for fuels was one of the main businesses at that time. These activities led to the beginning of pollutants and greenhouse gases. This affected their air quality, such as the dark fog in the UK in the past. The businessmen were so greedy that they wanted to exploit other nations' resources for making profits and invested money for further development of new technologies to enlarge the size of production. These behaviours caused even more pollution to be emitted and started changing the climate and damaging nature. Therefore, they should be the first to respond to global warming.

Furthermore, most of the developed countries caused the huge financial and economic gap between them and the developing ones. This forced the developing nations to further increase their economic activities by ignoring the environmental and climatic impacts. It is no longer news when we hear that a developing state has taken on huge debt from a developing one. With the 'good will' of lending other countries in need money to strengthen their economic power by investment in infrastructure and the like, the developed countries always adopt a high interest rate and the debt seems impossible to return. This makes the poorer ones worse because they risk everything, including neglecting the severe consequence of climate change, to produce their economic goods in the cheapest way, which means without any costs on filtering such pollutants. This is actually not directly caused by the privileged countries.

However, it is argued that the rich nations put efforts to start cutting down the emission such as implementing EU emission quotas and keep investigating in new methods to make the production cycle cleaner. Yet, EU emission quotas are actually a failure that many nations persuaded the EU committees for more quotas and this led to the failure of the plan. In addition, those products from investigations are usually expensive and not many products from companies in developed nation will apply it. It ends up failing because of a lack of effectiveness.

To conclude, it is inevitable that developed countries are recognised as the main cause of today's climatic problems. Thus they have to bear the responsibilities more instead of the developing nations.

Examiner's Comments:

Introduction: The introduction is too long and would thus have taken up valuable time in the exam. Nonetheless, it captures the main themes of the question and sets the scene well for the essay.

Main Body: The second paragraph makes a very good point but waffles a bit much and goes off the point when talking about businessmen being greedy and about the dark fog in the UK – these two points are not relevant to the candidate's line of argument. Accordingly, does not gain marks and weakens the essay.

It would have saved a lot of time if the candidate simply stated the following:

- Developed countries have already emitted enormous amounts such as in the industrial revolution,
- So it would only be fair to expect them to do more to clean up the mess which they caused.

In the third paragraph, the student needs to be clearer as to what she means. The implication is that developing countries are hard done by the developed ones, but the student needs to state this clearly. The student also uses a weak link here. The final sentence of the third paragraph didn't make sense and contradicts the rest of the paragraph. The fourth paragraph does not add anything new to the argument. The candidate describes the failure of the EU quotas but it's not clear how this relates to the question. Surely it doesn't matter (for the purposes of this essay) whether the EU have failed with their emission quotas or not. The essay question is asking whether developed countries have a higher obligation to tackle climate change than developing countries. As the paragraph does not advance an argument as to whether developed countries should or should not take on a higher obligation than developing countries, it wastes time and reduces the quality of one's essay

Conclusion: The conclusion is succinct and follows from the main body.

Example Essay 6

"Developed countries have a higher obligation to tackle climate change than developing countries" Discuss the extent to which you agree with this statement

Climate change is a global issue that affects all nations and its peoples, and in light of the newly released global sustainability goals, perhaps we should focus on what actions should be taken to effect a change rather arguing who should take responsibility. Hence, I disagree with this statement and will be presenting my argument in this essay.

Firstly, climate change is a global issue and all nations are obligated to combat it. We must abandon the attitude that developing nations are somehow inferior to developed nations simply because of their global position. With this approach in mind, all nations therefore must be taken as accountable for this global crisis that affects us all. Perhaps the view that combatting climate change is an 'obligation' should be abandoned. Improving the condition of our world and fixing our mistakes should be regarded not as a chore, but as a responsibility to future generations. After we have confronted these issues and changed our perceptions, will a global effort truly be effectively carried forward?

Secondly, whilst it is true that developed nations have a greater capacity financially and structurally to enact a change, efforts to improve the infrastructure of a country to make it more green can be done by developing countries. Rather than seeing sustainability as an expensive undertaking, requiring new carbon capturing machines, knowledge of other ways to lesson our carbon footprint should be made clear. These simple methods such as planting more trees than the number being cut down or effective garbage disposable and recycling to minimise burning of garbage. Such inexpensive methods could easily be undertaken by developing countries and eliminating the idea that climate change is a concern of the rich.

Thirdly, to separate countries into two spheres is damaging. This segregation lead to the belief that 'developing nations' are somehow able to 'get away' with releasing high amount of greenhouse gases or deforestation by simply claiming that they don't have the capacity to make such a change. It is not enough for the developed countries to take the initiative; developing nations are equally obligated to combat climate change.

In conclusion, no country should be viewed as having a higher obligation towards alleviating climate change.

Examiner's Comments:

Introduction: The introduction is excellent. The candidate states her main view concisely and proceeds to continue with the main body. The candidate also adopts a unique take on the question, which is even better and will signal green lights in the heads of admissions tutors.

Main Body: The second paragraph raises interesting points but it is not clear how it relates to the question. A running theme throughout the essay is that every country shares a responsibility to be sustainable and reduce climate change. However, counter-arguments are not readily considered, accordingly the essay is not as persuasive as it might be.

In the third paragraph, the student makes the (very good) point about developing countries still being able to plant trees. This could be framed in a different way and incorporate a counter argument. For example:

- Climate change affects every country and, thus, every country should have an obligation to tackle climate change
- **[Counter Argument]** Some argue though that richer countries have far more resources than developing countries and, thus, can spend money and develop non-renewable energy sources (e.g. solar panels), whereas poorer countries would not have the finances to do this.
- **[Rebuttal of the counter argument]** Nonetheless, poorer countries can still do their part by planting trees and should not feel that they're 'off the hook'. Climate change affects everyone and, therefore, every country should do what they can to tackle it.
- [An example of a policy might be that each country pays a certain percentage of GDP to tackle climate change – this way, it's proportionate to each country]

Conclusion: The candidate succinctly presents her final response to the question in the conclusion. This could have been elaborated on a little more but is still fine nonetheless.

Example Essay 7

"Abortion should only be permitted in certain circumstances" Discuss.

Abortion means the mother decides to take off her foetus from her body in the form of taking away the possibility that the foetus can grow and finally become a baby which is ready to be born. With the permission of doing so, it means that the mother is taking off her foetus legally and she should bear no response afterwards. In my opinion, several circumstances should be raised and some of them should be given the chance to the mother to take her foetus off while some should not be allowed.

First of all, the victims of sexual assault or sexual abuse should have the right to abort. This mainly concerns their willingness of having the sexual activity and being pregnant. The victims are not willing to be raped by someone she did not fall in love with or someone other than her partner. Therefore, it is even more unlikely that she would further agree to be pregnant. The abuser, firstly, has this conviction of sexually assaulting someone who disagrees with his actions. Because it is a criminal action, the victim should not bear the consequences that the baby will bring such as nurturing the baby with her economic ability, which has a chance that it is insufficient to do so. Therefore, abortion should be permitted here.

Other than the above reason, a mother who has a baby which is inherently with problems should be allowed to abandon the foetus. Having children with inherent deficiency such as Down syndrome is not a choice of the parents: no one is a wrongdoer in this situation. While the parents have to bear the heavy burden to spend a lot of money on the medical caring of the baby, they may need to take care of them for their whole life. For these accidents, the authority should give them a chance to choose whether to keep their children or not. Abortion should be permitted in this circumstance. Almost all countries in the world give this choice to the parents with this problem.

However, babies which accidentally created during the illegal acts should not be permitted to abort, unless there is a medical issue raised. Increasing numbers of teenagers start to have sex at an early age such as 12. When they attempt to do these activities, they do not consider any possibilities may occur in the future and most of them do not care about the consequences. Not allowing them to have an abortion can prevent the teenagers from acting unconsciously, such as by having sex early or having sex without proper protection, even though special cases such as too young to give birth to a baby should be also under the consideration.

Furthermore, parents who want to abandon their children randomly should not be allowed. A wrong message may be given to the society that having foetus is not a real matter and we can abandon it anyway. It may also raise the moral issues such as selecting a perfect foetus in the laboratory to give birth. A random abortion also easily damages women's bodies which may affect their ability to have a baby in the future. This may lead to a decline in the birth rates. It can hamper our imbalance social structure seriously that our future generation has to bear all the welfare we need. Therefore, no permission on random abortions should be given.

To conclude, circumstances whereby the parents or the mother do not have the responsibility of having a baby inappropriately should be permitted to have abortion, whilst the others should not do so.

Examiner's Comments:

Introduction: The introduction attempts a definition of abortion, which is good. The final sentence of the introduction could have been more concise though, for example: "this essay argues that the mother should be allowed to abort in certain circumstances" – this says exactly the same thing but uses fewer words and looks better.

Main Body: The second paragraph makes a valid point but too long is spent on it. It was also quite basic and one-sided. If the student made reference to the countervailing principle based on the rights of the foetus, it would have been a more convincing paragraph (e.g. explicitly suggest that the right of the mother here should outweigh that of the foetus).

At each paragraph, the student relates it back to the question by considering whether abortion should be permitted in that circumstance. However, the essay is mainly one-sided and does not consider the possible right to life of the foetus. The student also does not consider why abortion should not be allowed in all other circumstances in enough detail.

In the penultimate paragraph, assertions, such as abortions easily damaging women's bodies are made, but this is not true if carried out by medical professionals. It is important not to make up facts and only use genuine knowledge.

Conclusion: The conclusion is not specific enough but the candidate does come to a reasoned judgement. Nonetheless, since the main body was generally one-sided, the conclusion does not feel like it is sufficiently balanced.

Example Essay 8

"Abortion should only be permitted in certain circumstances" Discuss.

Abortion is an act of ending the life of an embryo before birth. In my opinion I think abortion should be allowed when parents have a disability to take care of the child or the child itself is predicted to have a disability after he or she is born.

Firstly, if the child is detected to have a disability such as a cancer or similar life threatening disease, parents should have the choice to choose if they want the baby or not as the child may not be able to survive long. It might also bring the child discrimination which is bad for life development. However, it could be argued that every child is a gift from god and abortion is morally wrong. It's against the human right of the child itself. Moreover, through the difficulties in the process of early stage of the child, such as heavy medical treatment and discrimination from the public might train the child to be a stronger and more determined individual. Instead of a disadvantage, it might be a special advantage and experience to the child.

On the other hand, it might be argued that the inability of the parents to educate the child might be a legitimate reason for abortion. If the mother is too young to educate the child and needs huge financial support, she may be unable to care for the child. It might also be case if the parents are in prison.

In my opinion, parents should take up the responsibility of having a baby. If the mother is too young and still needs to continue her studies, the baby could be put into a foster home, who can be taken care of by a specialist. The government can consider giving out loans to these young mothers until they finish their education and have the ability to earn money themselves. If the parents are in prison, they can also send their children to a foster home and ask for permission to see their child frequently to keep the bond within the family.

In conclusion, the only permission for abortion should be when the child has a permanent disability and the parents can get to choose whether or not to give birth to the baby.

It might be inhuman to kill the embryo, but it is also not virtuous for the parents to see the child suffering. However, if the problem comes from the parent itself, the child as individuals should have the right to live, regardless of the fact that care homes might have less support to theme than normal homes, it's still a chance for them to explore the beauty of life.

Examiner's Comments:

Introduction: A clear and crisp definition in the first sentence and a nice introduction. It appears that the student is only considering a few circumstances from the introduction.

Main Body: The second paragraph involves assumptions. What if the child can live long enough, though?

The essay launches straight into specific and niche circumstances and considers remote points, such as the life development of the child. Given the time available, it would be better to stick to the main points.

The essay does not consider in much detail the alternatives and why abortion shouldn't be allowed generally apart from a brief sentence in the second paragraph. Considering the alternatives is important as that leads to a more balanced and persuasive essay and, thus, higher marks!

Conclusion: The initial conclusion is very good and succinct. However, the student also makes an additional point after the conclusion. Sometimes, this works but here it does not fit in. It's normally best to introduce completely new arguments in the main body.

Example Essay 9

"Abortion should only be permitted in certain circumstances" Discuss.

Abortion occurs when a pregnant woman decides to no longer carry her child and in turn kills the foetus. By law, pregnancy must be under a certain age limit. There are three main circumstances I believe abortion should be permitted: where the parent(s) cannot financially support their child, where the parent(s) would raise the child in an unsafe environment and finally, under the circumstance that the health of the mother is at risk. However, the law preventing abortion after a specific number of weeks should still be implemented at each instance.

Firstly, if there is evidence that parent(s) of the child are not financially capable of supporting their child in the future, then an abortion should be permitted. This is because a lack of food, shelter or clothing – seen as basic necessities – should be provided in order to ensure the child remains health. Although it can be argued that the child could be sent to adoption where these necessities can be provided, psychological impact on the family can be forgotten. The emotional connection of a mother to her unborn foetus must be less than her to her newborn, hence for the health of the mother, abortion should be permitted. It is not to be assumed however that there will not be mental consequences of abortion.

Secondly, the environment which a child is raised in has been scientifically linked to the future behaviour of said child. An abusive environment is undoubtedly unsafe for any child, both for their physical and mental wellbeing. This sort of environment can involve similar behaviour in the child which wants to be just like their parents may eventually lead to a life of crime. However, this cannot be said for all children of course. Where abortion is not an option raised by the parents themselves, should it be enforced by a governing authority? It must be vital for examination of home environments to be conducted on an equal level to ensure justice.

Finally, the health of a mother is important. The life of an unborn foetus should not be considered over the life of the woman. It is said that the right to life is of the utmost importance, hence this should be followed. When considering the health of the women, the physical and mental health must be considered equally. This is to ensure the safety of the unborn child as well as the mother.

I believe these are the circumstances that should be permitted. In turn this could reduce the crime rate, protests by those against abortion and can encourage safe sex, especially by teenagers. Although these circumstances may function in countries such as the UK, China, for instance, would permit abortion outside these guidelines due to the implementation of the 'One Child Policy'. However, I believe such policies reduce the freedoms of citizens which should be considered.

Examiner's Comments:

Introduction: The candidate points out that abortion should be allowed in three specific circumstances but does not consider why abortion shouldn't be allowed in any other circumstances (or be allowed generally). Other than this, the introduction is good, very clear, and sets the scene well for the essay.

Main Body: The third paragraph is unclear and does not consider the issue from enough perspectives to be balanced – what about the right of the child to live? Does the foetus not have that right? Or if it does, does the potential for the child to enter into crime outweigh that right? Consideration of such issues will add a greater depth to the essay and make one's argument more persuasive. It is crucial to consider alternative points of view to have a balanced essay. The candidate then digresses and considers whether abortion should be enforced on people and doesn't actually consider that issue properly – she implies that it's important (by saying that there should be 'home examination' but it's not clear what she is saying). The fourth paragraph could be improved by considering what rights, if any, should be given to the foetus and then whether the mother's right to life outweighs this. As it stands, the paragraph is a bit one-sided.

Conclusion: The conclusion is satisfactory but not great. It introduces a few new assertions (such as reducing protests and encouraging safe sex) which do not follow from the rest of the essay. It also introduces a completely new point regarding the One Child Policy in China: while this is an interesting point, the candidate has not demonstrated how it is/could be relevant to the question and so this point is a waste of space. The conclusion should be used to weigh up the pros/cons of the arguments you've already addressed in the main body and to bring everything together (and generally not to introduce new ones).

Example Essay 10

"The government should legalise the sale of human organs" Discuss.

With the lack of available organs for transplant in hospitals, many patients lost the change of survival for a longer period of time. To a large extent, government should legalise the sale of human organs, in order to boost the amount of organs available for replacement and might help the poor to gain some extra money as well.

Firstly, the sale of human organs involves buying and selling. One can gain money in exchange for given out extra/not necessary organs in their bodies (such as kidneys). This is also a more efficient use of resources while saving lives at the same time. However, it could be argued that the action creates bad incentives especially for the poor to sell as much organs as possible, without looking after their own health. This may cause serious damage to their health and even causing more deaths. On the other hand, monitory controls can be done before organs are sold. Compulsory health checks on the seller should be enforced to see whether he/she is capable of giving away the organs and also whether the organ is suitable for transplant at the same time.

Secondly, the selling of organs of organs generates tax revenue for the Government. This extra amount of revenue could be used on investment in healthcare to cure disease, which could in turn reduce the demand on organ transplants. It could also be used to hire more doctors to meet the increasing demand in the NHS. However, selling organs are morally wrong and our bodies are gifts from God and shouldn't be re-used for commercial transactions. Also, sellers might set high prices and widen the gap between rich and poor, as only rich people can afford the organs, thereby deepening inequality in society. Nonetheless, organs are property of individuals and we should full control on how we use them. We're allowed to engage in other potentially harmful activities, such as smoking and drinking. Furthermore, the government can set up a maximum price for organs to avoid the situation of overpriced organs. Accordingly, strong monitoring should be used in order to ensure everyone has an equal chance of getting suitable organs and organs should be arranged for those who are most in need of them.

In conclusion, the government should legalise the sale of human organs in order to increase the amount of organs available for transplant to save more lives, as people would have more incentive to give off their organs. This can also generate more revenue for the government under tax, which could be used in the NHS to help more people in need. Monitoring is also essential, such as setting up maximum prices and ensuring everyone has the equal chance of getting the organ they need.

Examiner's Comments:

Introduction: This is concise and the student directly addresses the question, which is good.

Main Body: The quality of written communication is not particularly good but otherwise, a number of interesting arguments are made and evaluated.

The point regarding tax was a bit remote (and, thus, did not seem entirely relevant in the context of the debate on human organs). It's not clear that would be taxed in the same way as goods (and would probably be too insignificant to make much of a difference to the government's tax revenues).

That time could have instead been used to delve deeper into evaluating the main pros and cons of legalising human organ sales. For example, the candidate raised the point that *"our bodies are gifts from God and shouldn't be re-used for commercial transactions."* This is a good point, but it could have been elaborated on further and critiqued on the basis that not all individuals follow a religion. This would have reinforced the candidate's conclusion and showed a greater depth of analysis.

Nonetheless, a variety of interesting and directly relevant arguments and counter-arguments are made, which makes this a very decent essay on the whole.

Conclusion: This is a good conclusion which directly addresses the question and the candidate elaborates on her view. However, the point about tax seems out of place as it is a new piece of information. The monitoring point would have fit well in the conclusion with a linking word, such as 'Nonetheless'.

For example:

> - In conclusion, the government should legalise the sale of human organs in order to increase the amount of organs available for transplant to save more lives, as people would have more incentive to give off their organs.
> - Nonetheless, this must be accompanied with an effective monitoring system, including the use of maximum prices, to ensure fairness.

Example Essay 11

"The government should legalise the sale of human organs" Discuss.

The question as to whether the sale of human organs should be legalised in countries has always been a hot debate throughout the centuries. As far as I am concerned, this is illegal in most of the major countries and in this essay I am going to outline the reasons.

First and foremost, moral issues are raised in the sale of human organs because many regard it as inhumane and it is not morally acceptable. As I don't see it as a proper way to earn money in a civilised country, where people earn money by selling their organs. I believe life is sacred and should be treated with great care. The sale of human organs implies that money is more important than the protection of lives.

Personally, I am in favour of organ donations which is completely different from selling organs as this does not involve the transfer of money and the meaning behind it is people really want to help others out of compassion but not for the benefits they can receive afterwards.

In addition, legalising the sale of human organs can exploit the poor, particularly in developing countries because they are vulnerable groups which can be exploited by the rich. In developing countries, the majority are not fully educated and they are poor. There is a potential that the rich in educated countries will exploit their advantages to purchase organs from them. This is unjust and unequal. Allowed to continue, this can lead to dire consequences in the long run which cannot be easily stopped.

In my opinion, the government role is to protect the welfare of citizens, so especially in developing countries, the government should not legalise the sale of human organs.

Examiner's Comments:

Introduction: The introduction appears to miss the point slightly. The quote wants the candidate to consider whether the sale of human organs *should* or *should not* be legalised. The candidate, though, says that he is going to outline the 'reasons' why it is illegal in most countries, when actually, the question wants the candidate's view as to whether it should be legal or not (and not an explanation for the present state of affairs).

Main Body: This essay is very basic, considers arguments in little depth, and is only one-sided with no consideration of counter-arguments. The candidate highlights some serious issues about allowing organ sales but does not adequately consider the issues at stake – e.g. what can be done about the current organ shortage? Highlighting this point and then evaluating it, by arguing that you don't (for example) think legalising organ sales would solve it, would make for a more persuasive essay as it shows the reader that you have considered alternative perspectives. Merely stating a bunch of opinions such as "I believe...." and "I think...." is not helpful and does not advance an argument <u>unless</u> they're backed up with reasons.

Conclusion: The conclusion, though, is satisfactory and very succinct but since it does not follow from a balanced or well-argued main body, the essay as a whole is poor.

Example Essay 12

"Sufferers of anorexia nervosa should be force-fed" Do you agree with this statement? If so, evaluate at what point of an individuals' disease this measure should be taken.

Anorexia nervosa is a term used to describe individuals who are unhealthily skinny. Some may say that anorexia is a major issue which needs to be addressed and force feeding seems to be a solution to prevent anorexia. In this essay I will be looking at the points for and against force feeding people suffering with anorexia, and I will come up with a constructive conclusion giving my personal opinion on this controversial topic.

Particular diseases often have a domino effect which results in other diseases, meaning that sufferers from anorexia may have the risk of developing other diseases as well. If an individual's anorexia reaches a limit where their daily lives are impacted, then indeed, sufferers of anorexia should be force-fed

Similarly, sufferers from anorexia may be suffering from social anxiety and insecurity due to their body structure, so in order to help improve their quality of life, sufferers should be force-fed in order to prevent sufferers' life from deteriorating.

On the other hand, one would say that force feeding sufferers of anorexia would be unideal since you would be forcing someone to do something against their own will, even if it was benefiting the sufferers. Instead, other alternatives should be explored, such as psychiatric and medical help, or other programmes which could help track the progress of the sufferer's health, rather than force feeding them. This is why some people believe that force feeding sufferers of anorexia would be unideal.

In addition, it would be difficult to distinguish the severity of anorexia and hence force feeding would be unideal because some sufferers of anorexia would be force-fed, when they really didn't need to be. Finding the cut-off point to where sufferers would need to be force-fed would be unrealistic and so other alternatives such as medical help should be explored. This is why sufferers of anorexia should not be force-fed.

In conclusion, force feeding sufferers of anorexia would be a way to tackle this disease, however I personally believe that there are other better alternatives to tackle this disease such as receiving medical treatment or seeking long term help with a professional, which would benefit sufferers in the long run.

Examiner's Comments:

Introduction: The introduction starts straight off with an attempted definition of anorexia nervosa. It's not entirely correct but given that the PBSAA exam is not a test of knowledge, it is a good enough approximation. It's really not necessary for the student to say: "I will be looking at the points for and against force feeding" or that "I will come up with a constructive conclusion giving my personal opinion" – these are both obvious and add zero marks, so the time could be better spent writing something more constructive to the essay.

Main Body: The second and third paragraphs (the beginning of the main body) are certainly valid points and they do indicate force feeding as a treatment, but the student uses the word 'should' as if it was a final conclusion in both of these paragraphs. This contradicts the student's actual conclusion at the end of the essay, which is a poor essay technique. Instead, as interim conclusions, the student should be more tentative within the main body and just say 'therefore, force feeding <u>may</u> be an option to resolve this' or 'some may, thus, argue that sufferers should be force-fed'. The fourth paragraph is very good.

A further point that links with the point on consent is that, since force feeding is against a person's free will, it would not solve the underlying problem of anorexia nervosa and a person may need to be continuously force-fed against their will, which surely does not respect their personal autonomy and capacity to think as a human being. Accordingly, alternatives such as psychiatric help to solve the underlying problem would both be more effective and accord with the patient's free will.

Conclusion: The conclusion is sufficient: it is comprehensive, clear and concise. On the whole, this is a very good essay.

Final Advice

- Use linking words.
- Do NOT use long introductions – they just waste time.
- Answer the Question – a surprisingly common issue is where students don't answer the question. This is by either misinterpreting the question, answering a different question, or only answering part of it. It is absolutely <u>critical</u> to answer the question and it is not something you can just assume you are doing. At the end of each paragraph, it would be useful to ask yourself whether you're answering the question. A good plan would help with this. If you are not answering the question, you are not gaining marks on what you're writing and it will not be impressive to the admissions tutors reading your work.
- Give a judgement – if the question asks "Do you agree?" make sure that you say whether you agree or disagree with the quote. Feel free to take a midpoint and say that you agree with it in x, y, z circumstances but disagree with it in other circumstances.
- Do not give a rant of opinions – it is important to advance an argument throughout your response.
- Do not add completely new arguments in the conclusion – it is ideal to weigh up the pros and cons that you've raised in the conclusion.
- Consider counter-arguments – even when you're heavily committed to one side of the debate or argument, considering alternative arguments (and then rebutting the counter arguments) makes your essay more persuasive.
- Signposting language – using signposting language helps make your essay clearer and more readable for the admissions tutors. For example, using connectives such as 'however' or 'nonetheless' can be used to highlight contrasting points. Words such as 'therefore' help to indicate either an interim conclusion in the middle of the essay or the final conclusion at the end.

Example Questions:

- Where does neuroscience begin and psychology end?
- Is intelligence due to nature or nurture?
- Why is love so difficult to define?
- "Chimpanzees should not have human rights". Discuss.
- "We will never make a computer as complex as the human brain". Discuss.
- "There is no such thing as free will". Discuss
- "Colour is perceived culturally". Discuss.

ANSWERS

Answer Key

Question	Answer	Question	Answer	Question	Answer	Question	Answer
1	A	51	A	101	C	151	B
2	C	52	B	102	D	152	C
3	A	53	D	103	C	153	B
4	A	54	A	104	E&F	154	C
5	C	55	C	105	D	155	D
6	D	56	D	106	C	156	D
7	D	57	C	107	B	157	C
8	A	58	A	108	A	158	C
9	A	59	D	109	C	159	C
10	B	60	D	110	B	160	A
11	D	61	D	111	C	161	C
12	C	62	B	112	D	162	A
13	D	63	C	113	B & C	163	E
14	A	64	B	114	B	164	C
15	D	65	B	115	B & D	165	B
16	A	66	D	116	D	166	B
17	B	67	E	117	F	167	C
18	B	68	C	118	D	168	B
19	A	69	E	119	D	169	C
20	B	70	D	120	B & D	170	E
21	A	71	F	121	B	171	D
22	C	72	B	122	C	172	C
23	C	73	A	123	C	173	B
24	A	74	C	124	D	174	E
25	B	75	D	125	B	175	D
26	A	76	A	126	C	176	A
27	D	77	B	127	B	177	C
28	A	78	D	128	E	178	A
29	A	79	A	129	B	179	B
30	B	80	B	130	D	180	C
31	A	81	E	131	D	181	A
32	C & E	82	B	132	C	182	B
33	B	83	C	133	C	183	F
34	B	84	C	134	B	184	C
35	D	85	D	135	C	185	E
36	A	86	C	136	C	186	B
37	A	87	C	137	C	187	B
38	B	88	A	138	D	188	C
39	D	89	C	139	C	189	C
40	A	90	C	140	E	190	C
41	B	91	A	141	D	191	F
42	B	92	A	142	C	192	C
43	E	93	D	143	A	193	A
44	B	94	B	144	A	194	C
45	D	95	E	145	C & E	195	A
46	E	96	E	146	D	196	B
47	B	97	D	147	D	197	B
48	D	98	E	148	B	198	E
49	B	99	E	149	D	199	E

| 50 | D | 100 | A | 150 | A | 200 | C |

Question	Answer	Question	Answer	Question	Answer	Question	Answer
201	B	251	C	301	A	351	D
202	C	252	D	302	B	352	D
203	D	253	B	303	C	353	F
204	C	254	A	304	B	354	B
205	B	255	D	305	F	355	C
206	D	256	D	306	E	356	B
207	C	257	A	307	F	357	C
208	C	258	C	308	A	358	A
209	A	259	A	309	A	359	A
210	C	260	E	310	A	360	C
211	B	261	D	311	C	361	B
212	E	262	A	312	A	362	D
213	D	263	D	313	A	363	C
214	C	264	D	314	F	364	A
215	B	265	B	315	E	365	C
216	E	266	A	316	D	366	C
217	C	267	E	317	B	367	C
218	C	268	D	318	D	368	B
219	E	269	F	319	A	369	D
220	B	270	F	320	F	370	E
221	D	271	F	321	B	371	D
222	C	272	D	322	C	372	D
223	D	273	C	323	C	373	B
224	E	274	E	324	C	374	E
225	B	275	E	325	E	375	E
226	C	276	C	326	A	376	B
227	C	277	C	327	C	377	C
228	D	278	A	328	E	378	A
229	B	279	E	329	E	379	C
230	E	280	A	330	C	380	B
231	C	281	A	331	E	381	B
232	A	282	C	332	E	382	B
233	C	283	A	333	E	383	C
234	C	284	F	334	B	384	C
235	D	285	H	335	C	385	A
236	A	286	C	336	B	386	C
237	D	287	H	337	B	387	D
238	D	288	B	338	C	388	C
239	C	289	F	339	D	389	D
240	C	290	E	340	C	390	A
241	C	291	B	341	B	391	C
242	E	292	A	342	A	392	B
243	D	293	I	343	F	393	B
244	C	294	C	344	D	394	A
245	B	295	B	345	A	395	C
246	A	296	D	346	B	396	B
247	F	297	A	347	A	397	B

248	F	298	B	348	F	398	E
249	A	299	C	349	D	399	C
250	C	300	C	350	A	400	A

Question	Answer	Question	Answer	Question	Answer	Question	Answer
401	D	451	A	501	B	551	B
402	A	452	D	502	C	552	A
403	D	453	A	503	B	553	B
404	C	454	B	504	C		
405	E	455	C	505	A		
406	B	456	D	506	E		
407	E	457	D	507	D		
408	C	458	D	508	C		
409	A	459	E	509	C		
410	C	460	D	510	E		
411	A	461	C	511	A		
412	C	462	C	512	D		
413	C	463	E	513	E		
414	E	464	A	514	C		
415	C	465	D	515	B		
416	D	466	C	516	A		
417	C	467	D	517	B		
418	D	468	C	518	D		
419	D	469	B	519	C		
420	B	470	E	520	E		
421	B	471	A	521	D		
422	B	472	D	522	B		
423	E	473	E	523	E		
424	C	474	C	524	C		
425	C	475	D	525	A		
426	C	476	E	526	E		
427	B	477	A	527	C		
428	E	478	E	528	A		
429	D	479	D	529	C		
430	D	480	D	530	C		
431	B	481	C	531	C		
432	A	482	D	532	A		
433	E	483	A	533	A		
434	A	484	E	534	B		
435	E	485	D	535	A		
436	A	486	C	536	E		
437	C	487	B	537	D		
438	B	488	B	538	E		
439	B	489	B	539	D		
440	A	490	E	540	B		
441	B	491	D	541	E		
442	A	492	D	542	D		
443	C	493	A	543	B		
444	E	494	C	544	C		
445	C	495	B	545	C		
446	B	496	D	546	E		
447	A	497	B	547	D		
448	B	498	E	548	C		
449	D	499	C	549	A		
450	D	500	A	550	E		

Worked Answers

Question 1: A
Whilst **B**, **C** and **D** may be true, they are not completely stated, **A** is clearly stated and so is the correct answer.

Question 2: C
The main argument of the first paragraph is to propose the point that it is more society that controls gender behaviour not genetics. **A** and **D** do not indicate either as they only allude to the end result of gender behaviour and so are incorrect. Hormonal effects are not mentioned in the first paragraph and so **B** is incorrect. **C** would undermine the argument that society *predominately* controls gender, and so is correct.

Question 3: A
B, **C** and **D** are not stated and so are incorrect. **A** is directly stated and so is correct.

Question 4: A
B and **D** are contraindicated by the statement and so are incorrect. **C** could be true but implies children always like the same thing as their same-gendered parent irrelevant of how they are treated as a child, which is contrary to the statement and so is not correct. **A** is correct as is the overall message.

Question 5: C
D may help prevent problems with sexual identity but does not prevent stereotyping and so is incorrect. **A** is not stated, and **B** is implied but not stated and so are incorrect. **C** is the end message of how to prevent gender stereotyping and so is correct.

Question 6: D
A, **B** and **C** may be true but are not mentioned in the statement and so are incorrect. The statement implies that children born with different external organs to those that their sex chromosomes would match may find it difficult to accept this difference and be uncomfortable.

Question 7: D
The text states that 'Those who regularly took 30-minute naps were more than twice as likely to remember simple words such as those of new toys.' Which means those who napped were twice as likely to remember teddy's name than the 5% who did not, 5% x 2 = 10%, which would be twice as likely, ruling out **A** and **B**. But being 'more than twice' the only possible answer is **D**.

Question 8: A
The answer is to work out 10% (the percentage of napping toddlers more likely to suffer night disturbances) of 75% (the percentage of toddlers who regularly nap). Hence 10 % of 75% is 7.5%.

Question 9: A
B, **C** and **D** may be true but there is nothing in the text to support them. **A** is suggested, as the passage states 'non-napping counterparts, who also had higher incidences of memory impairment, behavioural problems and learning difficulties'. If the impaired memory were the cause, as opposed to the result, of irregular sleeping then it would offer an alternative reason why those who nap less remember less.

Question 10: B
A and **C** are possible implications but not stated and so are incorrect. It is said that parents cite napping having 'the benefits of their child having a regular routine' so hence **B** is more correct than **D** as it refers to the benefit to the toddlers' rather than the parents.

Question 11: D
B, if true would counteract the conclusion, as it would imply that, the study is skewed. The same is true of **C**, which if true would imply unreliable results as the toddler sample are all the same age within a year, but not within a few weeks. **A**, if true, would not provide any additional support to the conclusion and so is incorrect. **D** if true would provide the most support for the conclusion as it proposes using groups with a higher incidence of napping in comparison to those with a lower incidence.

Question 12: C
Although it can be argued that **A, B, D** and **E** are true they are not the best answer to demonstrate a flaw in Tom's father's argument. **C** is the best because it accounts for other factors determining success for the Geography A-level exam such as aptitude for the subject.

Question 13: D
A is never stated and is incorrect. **B** and **C** are referred to being 'many people's' beliefs, and are cited as others' opinions not an argument supported by evidence in the passage, and so are not valid conclusions. It is implied that the NHS may have to reduce its services in the future, some of which could be fertility treatments hence **D** is the most correct answer.

Question 14: A
C does not severely affect the strength of the argument, as it is only relevant to the length of the time taken for the effects of the argument to come into place.
D is incorrect, as people breaking speed limits already would not negate the argument that speed limits should be removed, but could even be seen as supporting it. These people may count as the 'dangerous drivers' who would be ultimately weeded out of the population.

B may affect part of the argument's logic (as it undermines the idea that dangerous drivers are born to dangerous drivers), but the final conclusion that dangerous drivers will end up killing only themselves still stands, and so the ultimate population of only safe drivers may be obtained. The fact that one dead dangerous driver could have produced a safe one does not necessarily challenge the main point of this argument.
A if true would most weaken the argument as it states that fast driver is more likely to harm others and not the driver itself, which would negate the whole argument.

Question 15: D
Whilst is it stated that the Government assesses risk it is not described as an obligation, hence **A** is incorrect. The overall conclusion of the statement is that on balance the Government was justified in not spending money on flooding preparation, as it was unlikely to occur, so **C, B** and **E** are incorrect and **D** is correct.

Question 16: A
C is incorrect and **D** is a possible course of action rather than a conclusion. **B** and **E** are possible inferences but not the conclusion of the statement. The overall conclusion of the statement is that the way that children interact has changed to the solitary act of playing computer games.

Question 17: B
The passage does state that in this case the £473 million could have been put to better use, however, there is no mention that no drug should ever be stockpiled for a similar possible pandemic. The passage discusses the lack of evidence behind Tamiflu and therefore is stating that in a situation where there is a lack of evidence, there may not be justification for stockpiling millions of pounds worth of the drug. Stockpiling in the case of drugs with high effectiveness is not discussed so we should not assume this is a generic argument against preparation for any pandemic and stockpiling of any drug.

Question 18: B
The passage discusses the fact that unhealthy eating is associated with other aspects of an unhealthy lifestyle so the argument that tackling only the unhealthy eating aspect does not logically follow. The other statements are all possible reasons why the solution given may not be optimal, but are not directly referred to in the passage.

Question 19: A
This is a tricky question in which **A, B, C** and **D** are all true. However, the question asks for the conclusion of the passage, which is best represented by **A**.
B is a premise that gives justification for why the elderly should take care of themselves and **C** provides a justification for why they may not.
D is implied in the text but statement **A** is explicitly stated.
E is incorrect as the passage implies that people should spend the money that they have in old age, not stop saving altogether.

Question 20: B

The passage states stem cell research is an area where there are possible high financial and personal gains, however there is no mention of these being the main driving factors in either this area of research or others. Although rivalry between groups may be a reason driving publishing, this is not mentioned in the passage. The image discrepancies were in only one paper but the passage implies the protocol and replication problems were in both papers.

Question 21: A

D actually weakens the argument, and is therefore not a conclusion. **C** is simply a fact stated to introduce the argument, and is not a conclusion. **B** is a reason given in the passage to support the main conclusion. If we accept **B** as being true, it helps support the statement in **A**. **E** is not discussed in the passage. **A** is the main conclusion of this passage

Question 22: C

The passage describes improved safety features and better brakes in cars, and concludes that this means the road limit could be increased to 80mph without causing more road fatalities. However, if **C** is not true, this conclusion no longer follows on from this reasoning. At no point is it stated that **C** is true, so **C** is therefore the assumption in the passage. The statements in **B** and **D** are not *required* to be true for the argument's conclusion to lead on from its reasoning. **A** is a statement which is strengthened by this passage, and is not an assumption from the passage. **E** is not relevant to the conclusion or mentioned in the passage.

Question 23: C

Answers **A** and **D** are both reasons given to explain fingerprints under the theory of evolution, and contribute towards the notion given in **C**, that they do not offer support to intelligent design. Thus, **A** and **D** are reasons given in the passage, and **C** is the main conclusion. **B** is simply a fact stated to introduce the passage, whilst **E** actually contradicts something mentioned in the argument (namely that Intelligent Design is religious-based, and scientifically discredited). Neither of these options are conclusions.

Question 24: A

Answers **C**, **D** and **E** obviously present ways in which the conclusions drawn from the study could be wrong, without any mistakes being made by those carrying out the study, and thus are potential reasons. **B** is also a potential reason, because those with a low alcohol consumption could have many other risk factors for cancer, and end up with a higher *overall* risk. If the study does not take account of these, it could produce erroneous conclusions. **A** cannot be a valid reason because the passage *states* that it is '*proven*' that alcohol increases the risk of cancer. Thus, we must accept this as true, so **A** is not a potential reason.

Question 25: B

The passage states that the average speed *including* time spent stood still at stations was 115mph. Thus, **A** is incorrect, as the stopping points have already been included in the calculations of journey time. Similarly, the passage states that the train completes its journey at Kings cross, so **D** is incorrect. **C** is not correct because we have been given the total length of the journey. Whether it took the most direct route is irrelevant. **E** is completely irrelevant and does not affect the answer. **B** is an assumption, because we have only been given the *scheduled* time of departure. If the train was delayed in leaving, it would not have left at 3:30, and so would have arrived *after* 5:30.

Question 26: A

The argument discusses healthcare spending in England and Scotland, and whether this means the population in Scotland will be healthier. It says nothing about whether this system is fair, and does not mention the expenditure in Wales. Thus, **C** and **D** are incorrect. Similarly, the argument makes no reference to whether healthcare spending should be increased, so **B** is incorrect. **E** is true but not the main message of the passage. The passage does suggest that the higher healthcare expenditure per person in Scotland does not necessarily mean that the Scottish population will be healthier, so **A** is a conclusion from this passage.

Question 27: D

C is an incorrect statement, as the passage says that Polio *hasn't* been eradicated yet. **A** and **B** are reasons given to support the conclusion, which is that given in **D**. **E**, meanwhile, is an opinion given in the passage, and is not relevant to the passage's conclusion.

Question 28: A
This passage provides various positive points of the Y chromosome, before describing how all of this means it is a fantastic tool for genetic analysis. Thus, the conclusion is clearly that given in **A**. The statement in **B** is a further point given to provide evidence of its utility, as stated in the passage. Thus **B** is not a conclusion in itself, but further evidence to support the main conclusion, given in **A**. **C** is also a reason given to support the conclusion in **A**, whilst **D** is simply a fact stated to introduce the passage. As for **E**, there is no mention of Genghis Khan's children (only his descendants).

Question 29: A
Answers **C** and **E** are not valid assumptions because the argument has *stated* that a patient *must* be treated with antibiotics for a bacterial infection to clear. B is not a flaw, because this does not affect whether the antibiotics would clear the infection if it were bacterial. D is an irrelevant statement, and also disagrees with a stated phrase in the passage (that antibiotics are required to clear a bacterial infection). A is a valid flaw, because the passage does not say that antibiotics are *sufficient* or *guaranteed* to clear a bacterial infection, simply that they are *necessary*. Thus, it is possible that the infection *is* bacterial but the antibiotics failed to clear it.

Question 30: B
A, C and D, if accepted as true, all contribute towards supporting the statement given in **B**, which is a valid conclusion given in this passage. Thus, **A**, **C** and **D** are all reasons given to support the main conclusion, which is the statement given in **B**. **E** is not a valid conclusion, as the passage makes no reference to action that should be taken relating to smoking, it simply discusses its position as the main risk factor for lung cancer.

Question 31: A
D is only given as a method, with no mention of its effectiveness. We do not know if **C** is true because it is not stated. **B** is not discussed in the passage. Whilst statement **E** is true, it is supporting evidence for the conclusion, not the conclusion itself.

Question 32: C & E
Whilst **A** and **B** may be true, cost is not mentioned as a deterring factor and we are only concerned with use in the UK, so they are irrelevant. Whether cannabis was the only class C drug is not important to the argument so **D** is not correct. **C** and **E** are the correct answers because the statement concerns the use of cannabis in the UK, directly stating use will decrease from people knowing it has been upgraded to a more dangerous category and from fearing longer prison sentences from higher-class drugs.

Question 33: B
Whilst **A** and **C** may be true, they are not part of the argument. **D** is a possible, but cannot be logically proposed from the information above. **E** would be a flaw if the argument were 'all levels of sports teams reduce bullying' but the passage explicitly states 'well-performing' teams. Hence **B** is correct as it undermines the whole argument, reversing the cause and effect.

Question 34: B
Options **A**, **C** and **D** do not directly weaken the argument as if any 16 year olds were buying/drinking alcohol (whether the minority or majority) – police would still be spending time catching them. The suggested benefit to reduce police time spent catching underage drinkers would be negated if **B** were true, hence it is the correct answer.

Question 35: D
A is an interpretation of the last sentence and doesn't accurately summarise the argument in the passage. B is untrue as there is no mention of if the government can afford to give grants or not. C and E are incorrect as the passage only talks about small businesses. **D** is correct as it best summarises the change in government policy regarding small businesses.

Question 36: A
The statement discusses a case that was reported, but aims to argue that there may be important errors occurring everyday in medicine that go unreported. Option **A** if true, would significantly weaken this argument as would negate it being a possibility. **B**, **C**, **D** and **E** may be true, but they do not negate the argument – if doctors are trained, accidents like the above may still occur. Operations that are successful do not affect those that are not, nor do unavoidable errors have any relation to avoidable ones. That the patient may have died without these errors similarly does not mean that errors, when they do occur, should not be considered errors.

Question 37: A
The main point of the statement is to highlight that although there are numerous safety precautions in place to protect patients, when the weaknesses in these precautions align big errors can occur. So **A** is correct. While **E, C, B** and **D** may well be true, they are not the overall conclusion of the statement.

Question 38: B
Though not the first to be cited, the original error is cited as being the incorrect copying of the sidedness of the kidney to be removed, hence **B** is the correct option. The other options represent errors that in the 'Swiss cheese model' would have not been allowed to occur if the original had not taken place.

Question 39: D
In this instance the 'tip of the iceberg' refers to the number of medical errors reported, implying there may be a significantly larger proportion that go unreported, hence the correct option is **D**, and not **B**.

Question 40: A
The description given about the consultant's performance versus emotional arousal, is described as initially increasing then eventually decreasing over time, which is best represented by graph **A**.

Question 41: B
The consultant says that the 'public perception is that medical knowledge increases steadily over time' which is best represented by graph **B**. The consultant says the regarding the acquisition of medical knowledge, 'many doctors [reach] their peak in the middle of their careers', which is best described by the graph **D**.

Question 42: B
Obesity is not mentioned in the passage, so **E** is incorrect. There is no mention exercise specifically as it relates to old age, so **A** and **D** are also wrong. The diseases associated with lack of exercise are not specifically stated to cause early death, only that they are associated with older people, so **C** is also incorrect. The passage does, however, argue that lack of exercise is associated with illness, and so exercise would be linked to a lack of illness, or good health, so **B** is correct.

Question 43: E
The preference of women to have their babies at hospital versus home is not commented upon so **B** is incorrect. **F** is never inferred, only that midwives are capable of assisting in normal births and assessing when women need to be transferred to be to hospital, so it is wrong. **A** and **D** are possible inferences at certain points but not conclusions of the statement. **C** is never implied, only that normal home births are no more risky than those in hospital. The overall conclusion of the statement is that the home births should be encouraged where possible as they are not more risky in the cases of normal births, and hospital births are an unsustainable cost in cash-strapped NHS.

Question 44: B
While **A, C** and **D** would, if true, make the practicalities of increasing home births more difficult they would not weaken the argument as **B** would. Where the statement's whole argument rests on home births being as safe as hospital **B**, if true, would negate this.

Question 45: D
The statement says 'With the increase in availability of health resources we now, too often, use services such as a full medical team for a process that women have been completing single-handedly for thousands of years.' Thus implying **D**, 'excessive availability of health resources' is the cause of 'medicalisation of childbirth'.

Question 46: E
1 and **3** identify weaknesses in the argument. If campaigns are what help keep deaths by fire low, they can be seen as 'necessary', and their necessity may be proven by the promisingly low fire-related mortalities. If there are more people with hernias than in fires, more people can possibly die from hernias, but this does not mean the fires are less dangerous to the (fewer) individuals involved in them. **2** is irrelevant, as the argument is about how dangerous fires are in their entirety, not in relation to their constituent parts. Therefore **E**, '1 and 3 only', is correct.

Question 47: B

Since 'some footballers' that like Maths are not necessarily the same 'some' who like History we can exclude **A** and **D**. Equally, while **C** may or may not be true, we are not given any information about rugby players' preference for History, so it is incorrect. We know that all basketball players like English and Chemistry, and that none of them like History, but as we do not know about a third subject they may like **E** is incorrect. We know all of the rugby players like English and Geography and some of them Chemistry, hence there must be a section of rugby players that like all three subjects so **B** is correct.

Question 48: D

The passage discusses the problems surrounding controlling drugs, and focuses on the rapid manufacture of new 'legal highs': it is therefore implied that this is the current major problem. The passage also suggests that as the authorities cannot keep up with drugs manufacture, the legality of drugs doesn't reflect their risks.
1 is incorrect as the passage says health professionals feel legality is less relevant now, but it doesn't say that it is not still important. **3** is incorrect as the last sentence says a potential problem of legal highs is that the risks are not as clear, which contradicts the statement that the public are not concerned about any risks.

Question 49: B

The passage is discussing how banning those with the mentioned medical conditions from mountain climbing are *essential* to ensuring safety. It does not claim that this is *sufficient* to ensure safety, simply that it is *necessary*. Thus **C** is irrelevant, as risks from other activities do not affect the risk from mountain climbing. **D** is also irrelevant, because the argument discusses how it is essential to ensure safety of people on WilderTravel holidays, so those using other companies are irrelevant. **A** is an irrelevant statement because the passage is discussing what should be done *to ensure safety*, not whether this is the morally correct course of action. Thus, a discussion of whether people should choose to accept the risks is not relevant. However, **B** *is* a flaw, because the guidelines only mention those with *severe* allergies, so thinking those with less severe allergies are in danger is a false assumption that has been made by the directors.

Question 50: D

The hospital director's comments make it abundantly clear that the most important aspect of the new candidate is good surgery skills, because the hospital's surgery success record requires improvement. If we accept his reasoning as being true, then it is clear that the candidate who is most proficient at surgery should be hired, and patient interaction should not be the deciding factor. Thus, Candidate 3 should be hired, as suggested by **D**.

Question 51: A

Answers **B** and **D** are irrelevant to the argument's conclusion, since the argument only talks about how medical complications could be avoided *if* winter tyres were fitted. Whether this is possible (as in **B**) or whether there are other options (as in **D**) are irrelevant to this conclusion. C is not an assumption because the passage states that delays cause many complications, which could be avoided with quicker treatment. However, the argument does not state that winter tyres would allow ambulances to reach patients more quickly, so **A** is an assumption.

Question 52: B

The passage discusses how anti-vaccine campaigns cause deaths by spreading misinformation and reducing vaccination rates. It claims that therefore *in order to protect* people, we should block the campaigners from spreading such misinformation freely. Thus it is made clear that this action should be taken *because the campaigners cause deaths*, not simply because they are spreading misinformation. Thus, **B** is the principle embodied in the passage, and **C** is incorrect. **A** actually demonstrates an opposite principle, whilst **D** is a somewhat irrelevant statement, as the passage makes no reference to whether we should promote successful public health programmes.

Question 53: D

The passage states that the tumour has established its own blood supply (it says this was shown during the testing), and that a blood supply is *necessary* for the tumour to grow beyond a few centimetres. Thus **A** and **B** are not assumptions. **C** is not an assumption, as it actually disagrees with something the passage has implied. The passage has actually said that action *must* be taken, implying that something *can* be done to stop the tumour. However, at no point has it been said that a blood supply is *sufficient* for a tumour to grow larger than a few centimetres. If this is not true, then the argument's conclusion that we should expect the tumour to grow larger than a few centimetres, and that action must be taken, no longer readily follows on from its reasoning. It is possible the tumour will still fail to grow larger than a few centimetres. Thus, **D** is an assumption in the passage, and a flaw in its reasoning.

Question 54: A

D is incorrect, as the passage has stated the runners are people running to raise money for the GNAA. **B** and **C**, meanwhile, are incorrect as the passage is only talking about whether the GNAA *will be able to* get a new helicopter. Thus, references to whether it wishes to, or whether this is the best use of money, are irrelevant. **A**, however, is an assumption on the part of the passage's writer. The passage says that the GNAA will be able to get a helicopter if £500,000 is raised, but this does *not* mean that it won't be able to if the £500,000 is not raised by the runners. It could well be that they secure funding from elsewhere, or that prices drop. The money being *sufficient* to get a new helicopter does not mean it is *necessary* to get one.

Question 55: C

B and **D** somewhat strengthen this argument, suggesting that more people going on courses leads to better growth, and that people who have gone on these courses are more attractive to employers. **A** does not really affect the strength of the argument, as the current rate of growth does not affect whether government subsidies would lead to increased growth. **C**, however, weakens the argument significantly by suggesting that people would not be more likely to attend the courses if the government were to subsidise them, as the cost has little effect on the numbers of people attending.

Question 56: D

B is simply a fact stated in the passage. It does not draw upon any other reasons given in the passage, so it is not a conclusion. **C** is not a conclusion because it does not follow on from the passage's reasoning. The passage discusses what should be done *if* Pluto is to be classified as a planet, it does not make any mention of whether this *should* happen. **A** and **D** are both valid conclusions from the passage. However, on closer examination we can see that if we accept **A** as being true, it gives us good reason to believe the statement in **D**. Thus, **D** is the *main* conclusion in the passage, whilst **A** is an *intermediate* conclusion, which goes on to support this main conclusion.

Question 57: C

A, **B** and **D** would all affect whether the calculation of the Glasgow train's arrival time is correct, but none are assumptions because all of these things have been stated in the passage. However, the passage has *not* stated that the trains will travel at the same speed, and if this is not true, then the conclusion that the Glasgow train will arrive at 8:30pm is no longer valid. Thus, **C** is an assumption.

Question 58: A

C can actually be seen to be probably untrue, as the passage mentions a need to escape immune responses, suggesting that the immune system *can* tackle these cells. **E** is true but not representative of the main argument made in the passage. **B** and **D** are not *definitely* true. The passage mentions several *essential* steps that *must* occur, but this does not mean that they are *sufficient* for carcinogenesis to occur, or guaranteed to allow it. Equally, the passage makes no reference to multiple mechanisms by which carcinogenesis can occur. It could be there is only one pattern in which these steps can occur. **A**, however, can be reliably concluded, because the passage does mention several steps that are *essential* for carcinogenesis to occur.

Question 59: D

Answers **A** and **C** are stated in the passage (the passage states 'deservedly known'), so these can be reliably concluded. **B** can also be concluded, as it is stated that in over 50% of cancers, a loss of functional P53 is identified. **D** however, cannot be concluded, as the passage simply states that any cell that has a mutation in P53 *is at risk* of developing dangerous mutations. Thus, it cannot be concluded that a given cell *will* develop such a mutation.

Question 60: D

D is not an assumption because Sam's calculations are based on the *cost per 1000 miles*, not on a given amount of fuel being used up. Thus, he has *not* assumed anything about whether the fuel usage is the same for each car. All of the others are assumptions, which have not been considered. Each of these will affect the total saving he will make if they are not true. For example, if the Diesel car costs £100 more than the Petrol car, the total saving will be £1700, *not* £1800 as calculated.

Question 61: D

The passage discusses how alcohol is more dangerous than cannabis, and states that this highlights the gross inconsistencies in UK drugs policy. Thus, **D** is the main conclusion of the passage, whilst **A** is a reason given to support this conclusion. The passage simply highlights that the policy is grossly inconsistent, and does not mention whether it should be changed, or how (whether alcohol should be banned or cannabis allowed).

Thus, **B** and **C** are not valid conclusions from this passage. The fact alcohol is freely advertised only mentioned briefly in the passage to add strength to the argument that alcohol is more accessible than cannabis, but no judgment is made on whether this should not be so, so **E** is also not a valid conclusion from this passage.

Question 62: B
The passage discusses how if first aid supplies were available, many accidents could be avoided. B correctly points out that this is a flaw – first aid supplies may help treat accidents and reduce the prevalence of *injuries and deaths*, but there is no reason why first aid supplies should reduce the incidence of *accidents*. Answers **C** and **D** are irrelevant, since the argument is talking about how first aid supplies could reduce *accidents*, not *injuries* or deaths. Thus, discussing cases in which they could not treat the injuries, or whether they need other components to do so is irrelevant. Equally A is irrelevant, as the argument is simply talking about what could happen *if* first aid supplies were stocked in homes, and makes no reference to whether this is financially viable.

Question 63: C
Answers **A** and **D** are not flaws because the passage does not conclude the things mentioned in these. No mention is made to the safety of the drug, and the argument only states that it is thought the compound *may* be of use in combating cancer. No premature conclusions are drawn, only suggestions are made. **B** is not a flaw because we can see that the experiments *may* produce misleading results if the wrong solutions are used, suggesting that DNA replication is inhibited even if it is not. **C**, however, is a valid flaw because the argument erroneously concludes that the wrong solutions must have been used when it says the experiments *do not reflect what is actually happening*. This clearly indicates a conviction that the wrong solutions were used, which does not follow on from the experiments being old.

Question 64: B
The passage has not said anything about who scored the winning goal, so **A** is not an assumption. **C** is also incorrect, because the passage states that South Shields won the game. **B** correctly identifies that whilst beating South Shields was *sufficient* to win the league, it was *not* necessary. If Rotherham wins their other 2 games, they will still win the league, so **B** demonstrates an assumption in the passage. **D** is not relevant, as it does not affect the erroneous nature of the claim that Rotherham *will not* win the league having lost the match to South Shields.

Question 65: B
C and **D** actually strengthen or reinforce the CEO's reasoning, with **C** suggesting as time progresses Middlesbrough will have more and more people compared to Warrington, whilst **D** suggests that the market share in Warrington may not be as high as suggested, adding further reasons to build in Middlesbrough. **A** somewhat weakens the CEO's argument, but it is not a flaw in the reasoning, because the CEO is simply talking about how Middlesbrough will bring them within the range of more people, so the market share comment is a counterargument, not a flaw in his reasoning. **B**, however, is a valid flaw in this argument. Just because Warrington's population is falling, and Middlesbrough's is rising, does not necessarily mean that Middlesbrough's will be higher.

Question 66: D
1 and 2 are assumptions. The information given does *not* necessarily lead on to the conclusion that these extinction events will continue without further conservation efforts. Equally, there is nothing in the passage that says conservation efforts cannot be stepped up without increased funding. However, 3 is not an assumption, because the passage *states* that global warming has caused changed weather patterns, which have caused destruction of many habitats, which have led to many extinction events. Thus, it is given that global warming has indirectly caused these extinctions, and so the answer is **D**.

Question 67: E
The argument is suggesting that in Austria, the rail service's high passenger numbers and approval ratings are accounted for by the fact that road travel is difficult in much of Austria. It then concludes that the public subsidies have no effect. We can see that **1** instantly weakens this argument by providing evidence to the contrary, (in France, difficult road travel is not prevalent and so cannot account for the high passenger numbers/approval ratings the country possesses). **3** also weakens this conclusion by suggesting multiple factors affect the situation. This makes the conclusion based on the evidence from Austria less strong. Thus, the answer is **E**. **2** actually strengthens the argument that the public subsidies do not cause high passenger numbers/approval ratings, as Italy has high subsidies but low passenger numbers/approval ratings.

Question 68: C
A is incorrect, in 2011 24% of men and 26% of women were obese (one should not confuse this with the rates of combined obese and overweight). B is also incorrect, as what it states is true for adults; however, the figures for children aged 2-15 have changed little over the past year. D is not stated or implied by the passage.
C is implied in the last two sentences of the article, and so the correct answer.

Question 69: E
All of the statements cannot be concluded from the reference passage.

Question 70: D
Be careful of using your own knowledge here! Whilst A and B may be true, they are not the main message of the passage. C may be true but is not discussed in the passage. E is speculative, as the passage does not say if the transplant would be a 'good alternative'. D is correct as it echoes the main message of the passage.

Question 71: F
Smoking and Diabetes are risk factors for vascular disease (not a cause). Vascular disease does not always lead to infarction. The passage does not give sufficient detail about necrotic tissue to conclude C or D.

Question 72: B
A is irrelevant to the argument's conclusion. Meanwhile E does nothing to alter the conclusion, as the fact that schools receive similar funds does not affect the fact that more funding could provide better resources, and thus improve educational attainment. C actually weakens the argument; by implying that banning the richer from using the state school system would not raise many funds, as most do not use it anyway. D does not strengthen the conclusion as stating that a gap exists does not do anything to suggest that more funding will help close it. B clearly supports the conclusion that more funding, and better resources, would help close the gap in educational attainment.

Question 73: A
D and E are irrelevant to the argument's conclusion. C is actually contradicting the argument. B is stated in the passage, so is not an assumption of the passage. A describes an assumption: the increase of DVDs does not, necessarily, cause the loss of cinema customers.

Question 74: C
The question refers to aeroplanes being the fastest form of transport, and states that this means that travelling by air will allow John to arrive as soon as possible. C correctly points out that the argument has neglected to take into account other delays induced by travelling by aeroplane. Cost and legality are irrelevant to the question, so B and E are incorrect. Meanwhile, D actually reinforces the argument, and A refers to future possible developments that will not affect John's current journey.

Question 75: D
The argument states that people should not seek to prevent spiders from entering their homes. It does not say anything about whether people should like spiders being in their home, so A is incorrect. The argument also makes no allusion to the notion of people preventing flies from entering their homes, so B is incorrect. The argument also does not mention or implies that any efforts should be made to encourage spiders to enter homes, or that they should be cultivated, so C and E are also incorrect.

Question 76: A
A correctly identifies an assumption in the argument. At no point is it stated that bacterial infections in hospitals are resulting in deaths. B, C, D and E are all valid points but they do not affect the notion that pressure for more antibiotic research would save lives. Therefore, none of these statements affect the conclusion of the argument and as such they are not assumptions in this context.

Question 77: B
The passage does not state that John disregards arguments because of the gender of the speaker, so D is incorrect. A and C are also wrong, as John states he finds women with armpit hair necessarily unattractive, so a different face or the knowledge of concealed hair would not make him find the female in question more appealing to his aesthetic. John does not state Katherine wants other women to stop shaving, so E is incorrect.
B is the correct answer, as Katherine was simply speaking about societal norms, and at no point is it said she was trying to convince John to find her, with armpit hair, attractive.

Question 78: D
A is irrelevant to the argument, which says nothing about what will happen to Medicine in the future. The argument is describing how Sunita is incorrect, and how better medicine is not responsible for a high death rate from infectious disease in third world countries, and how better medicine will actually decrease this rate. C is a direct contradiction to this conclusion, so is incorrect. E is a fact stated in the argument to explain some of its reasoning, and is not a conclusion, therefore E is incorrect.

Both B and D are valid conclusions from the argument. However, B is not the main conclusion, because the fact that 'Better medicine is not responsible for a high death rate from infectious disease in third world countries' actually supports the statement in D, 'Better medicine will lead to a decrease in the death rate from infectious disease in third world countries'. Therefore, B is an example of an intermediate conclusion in this argument, which contributes to supporting the main conclusion, which is that given in D.

Question 79: A
The statement in A, that housing prices will be higher if demand for housing is higher, is not stated in this argument. However, it is implied to be true, and if it is not true, then the argument's conclusion is not valid from the reasoning given. Therefore A correctly identifies an assumption in the argument. The other statements do not affect how the reasons given in the argument lead to the conclusion of the argument, and are therefore not assumptions in the argument.

Question 80: B
A and E are both contradictory to the argument, which concludes that because of the new research, Jellicoe motors should hire a candidate with good team-working skills. C refers to an irrelevant scenario, as the argument is referring to only one candidate being hired, and at no point does it state or imply that several should be hired.
B correctly identifies the conclusion of the argument that Jellicoe motors should hire a new candidate with good team-working skills in order to boost their productivity and profits. D meanwhile exaggerates the consequences of not following this course of action. The argument does not make any reference to the notion that Jellicoe motors will struggle to be profitable if they do not hire a candidate with good team-working skills.

Question 81: E
D is in direct contradiction to the argument, so is not the main conclusion. Meanwhile, B is a reason stated in the argument to explain some of the situations described. It is not a conclusion, as it does not follow on from the reasons given in the argument.

A and E are both valid conclusions from the argument. However, only E is the *main* conclusion. This is because both A goes on to support the statement in E. If bacterial resistance to current antibiotics could result in thousands of deaths, this supports the notion that the UK government must provide incentives for pharmaceutical firms to research new antibiotics if it does not wish to risk thousands of deaths.

Meanwhile, C appears to be another intermediate conclusion in the argument that also supports the main conclusion. However, on close inspection this is not the case. C refers to the UK government directly investing in new antibiotic research, whilst the argument refers to the government providing incentives for pharmaceutical firms to do so. Therefore, C is not a valid conclusion from the argument.

Question 82: B
E is completely irrelevant because the question is referring to an unsustainable solution *if* the UN's development targets are met, so the likelihood of them being met is irrelevant. C is irrelevant because they do not affect the fact that the situation would be unsustainable if everybody used the amount of water used by those in developed countries, as stated in the question. A is also irrelevant, as the passage does not mention price as a factor to be considered within the argument.

Meanwhile, D would actually strengthen the argument's conclusion.
Therefore, the answer is B. B correctly identifies that if those in developed countries use less water, it may be possible for everyone to use the same amount as these people and still be in a sustainable situation.

Question 83: C

There is no mention of treatment, so **A** is incorrect. A need to travel abroad for the post is not stated either, so **B** is incorrect. The need for a cool head is stated explicitly, but not necessarily that this be a leader, so **D** is also wrong. Other qualities are irrelevant to the argument, so **E** is also incorrect. **C** would only be relevant if there was indeed a link between 'a specific phobia' and 'a general tendency to panic'. Thus, **C** highlights the flaw: if a fear of flying does not necessitate a general disposition of panic, the argument for not hiring this employee crumbles.

Question 84: C

The passage does not suggest there are no more university places, nor does it make a distinction between the qualities of different universities, so **A** is incorrect and **D** is irrelevant. The argument does not deny the fact that people can be successful without a university education, so **B** is also wrong. **C** is correct, as the passage specifically states 'many more graduates', but not all, are equipped with better skills and better earning potential. This suggests not all degrees produce these skill-sets in their graduates, and so not all university places will create high-earning employees.

Question 85: D

B is unrelated to the argument, as other contributing factors would not negate the damaging potential of TV. Watching sport on television would not be akin to actually playing sport, so **A** is also incorrect. The possibility of eye damage is stated as caused by TV, so **C** is incorrect. However, if people watch television *and* partake in sport, which the passage seems to imply cannot happen, they may not suffer the negative effects of obesity and social exclusion. For example, they may play sport during the day and watch television in the evening, thus experiencing the benefits of exercise and also enjoying the sedentary activity. Therefore, various potential threats supposedly posed by watching excessive television are undermined, and **D** is correct.

Question 86: C

D directly counters the above argument, and so is incorrect. Though **A**, **B** and **D** are all suggested or stated by the passage, they each act as evidence for the main conclusion, **C**, describing the 'multiple reasons to legalise cannabis'.

Question 87: C

C is not an assumption as it has been explicitly stated in the question that the salary is fixed, and therefore it will not change. The rest of the statements are all assumptions that Mohan has made. At no point has it been stated that any of the other statements are true, but they are all required to be true for Mohan's reasoning to be correct. Therefore, they are all assumptions Mohan has made.

Question 88: A

The answer is not **B** because, although the Holocaust was a tragedy, this is not explicitly stated in the passage. It cannot be **C** or **E**, as these are also not directly stated above. **D** provides an intermediary conclusion that leads to the main conclusion of **A**: we should not let terrible things happen again, and through teaching we can achieve this, so therefore 'we should teach about the Holocaust in schools'.

Question 89: C

DVDs are irrelevant – though one could access disturbing material through a DVD, this does not mean the material to be seen on TV is less disturbing. The argument also is not concerned with adults, and the suggestion is that violence in any quantity may have a detrimental effect, even if a show is not entirely made up of it. **A**, **B** and **D** are thus not the correct answers. **C** contradicts the argument, as it suggests there is no link between witnessing and re-enacting what one has witnessed. Children may watch the scenes of rape and recognise the horror of the action, and so be sworn off ever committing that crime.

Question 90: C

A is irrelevant, as the passage states it *could* teach children, not that it necessarily would. **B** and **C** are also irrelevant, as the entertainment quality of the show or the likeability of its protagonist would not undermine the logic of the argument. **C** is the correct answer, as it shows how the question uses one model of success and projects it onto all other models, which is illogical: just because Frank succeeds without morality, does not mean all others must reject morality to succeed.

Question 91: A

B, C, D and E are all irrelevant to Freddy's argument that he cannot say a sexist thing because he is a feminist. The woman's discomfort, Neil's feminist stance, the appropriateness of making comments about men, or lewd comments in general do not affect his claim. The presumed link between the two (inability to say something sexist, and feminist self-description) is the flaw in Freddy's argument: someone may believe in equal rights for the genders, and still say a sexist thing.

Question 92: A

At no point is it stated or implied that car companies should prioritise profits over the environment, so C) is incorrect. Neither is it stated that the public do not care about helping the environment, so E) is incorrect.

B) is a reason given in the argument, whilst D) is impossible if we accept the argument's reasons as true, so neither of these are conclusions.

Question 93: D

The easiest thing to do is draw the relative positions. We know Harrington is north of Westside and Pilbury. We know that Twotown is between Pilbury and Westside. Crewville is south of Twotown, Westside and Harrington but we do not know but its location relative to Pilbury.

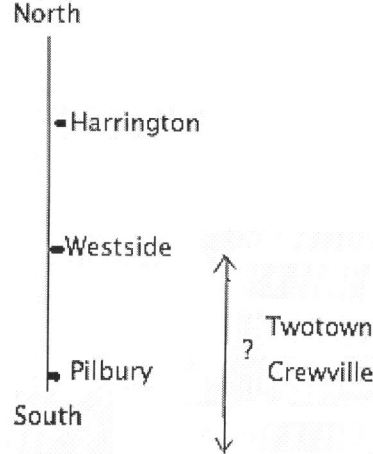

Question 94: B

By making a grid and filling in the relevant information the days Dr James works can be deduced:

	Sunday	Monday	Tuesday	Wednesday	Thursday	Friday	Saturday
Dr Evans	X	√	X	X	√	√	√
Dr James	X	√	√	√	√	X	√
Dr Luca	X	X	√	√	X	√	√

- No one works Sunday.
- All work Saturday.
- Dr Evans works Mondays and Fridays.
- Dr Luca cannot work Monday or Thursday.
- So, Dr James works Monday.
- And, Dr Evans and Dr James must work Thursday.
- Dr Evans cannot work 4 days consecutively so he cannot work Wednesday.
- Which means Dr James and Luca must work Wednesday.
- (mentioned earlier in the question) Dr Evans only works 4 days, so cannot work Tuesday.
- Which means Dr James and Luca work Tuesday.
- Dr James cannot work 5 days consecutively so cannot work Friday.
- Which means Dr Luca must work Friday.

Question 95: E
Working algebraically, using the call out rate as C, and rate per mile as M.
So,   C + 4m = 11
C + 5m = 13
Hence; (C + 5m) – (C + 4m) = £13 - £11
M = £2
Substituting this back into C + 4m = 11
C + (4 x 2) = 11
Hence, C = £3
Thus a ride of 9 mile will cost £3 + (9 x £2) = £21.

Question 96: E
Use the information to create a Venn diagram.
We don't know the exact position of both Trolls and Elves, so **A** and **D** are true. Goblins are mythical but not magical, so **C** is true. Gnomes are neither so **B** is true. But **E** is not true.

Question 97: D
The best method may be work backwards from 7pm. The packing (15 minutes) of all 100 tiles must have started by 6:45pm, hence the cooling (20 minutes) of the last 50 tiles started by 6:25pm, and the heating (45 minutes) by 5:40pm. The first 50 heating (45 minutes) must have started by 4:35pm, and cooling (20 minutes) by 5:20pm. The decoration (50 minutes) of the second 50 can occur anytime during 4:35pm- 5:40pm as this is when the first 50 are heating and cooling in the kiln, and so does not add time. The first 50 take 50 minutes to decorate and so must be started by 3:45pm.

Question 98: E
Speed = distance/time. Hence for the faster, pain impulse the speed is 1m/ 0.001 seconds. Hence the speed of the pain impulse is 1000 metres per second. The normal touch impulse is half this speed and so is 500 metres per second.

Question 99: E
Using the months of the year, Melissa could be born in March or May, Jack in June or July and Alina in April or August. With the information that Melissa and Jack's birthdays are 3 months apart the only possible combination is March and June. Hence Alina must be born in August, which means it is another 7 months until Melissa's birthday in March.

Question 100: A
PC Bryan cannot work with PC Adams because they have already worked together for 7 days in a row, so **C** is incorrect. **B** is incorrect because if PC Dirk worked with PC Bryan that would leave PC Adams with PC Carter who does not want to work with him. PC Carter can work with PC Bryan.

Question 101: C
Paying for my next 5 appointments will cost £50 per appointment before accounting for the 10% reduction, hence the cost counting the deduction is £45 per appointment. So the total for 4 appointments = 5 x £45 = £225 for the hair. Then add £15 for the first manicure and £10 x 2 for the subsequent manicures using the same bottle of polish bringing an overall total of £260.

Question 102: D
Elena is married to Alex or David, but we are told that Bertha is married to David and so Alex must be married to Elena. Hence David, Bertha, Elena and Alex are the four adults. Bertha and David's child is Gemma. So Charlie and Frankie must be Alex and Elena's two children. Leaving only options **A** or **D** as possibilities. Only Frankie and Gemma are girls so Charlie must be a boy.

Question 103: C

Using, x (minutes) as the, unknown amount of time, the second student took to examine, we can plot the time taken with the information provided thus:

	1st student		2nd student		3rd student
1st examination:	4x	1	2x	1	2x
		Break: 8 minutes			
1st examination:	x	1	x	1	x

Hence the total time taken, 45minutes (14:30-15:15)
Is represented by, $4x + 2x + 2x + x + x + x + 1+1+ 8+1+1$
$$45 \text{ minutes} = 11x \text{ (minutes)} + 12 \text{ minutes}$$
$$33 \text{ minutes} = 11x \text{ (minutes)}$$

Hence, x = 3 minutes, so the amount of time the second student took the first time, 2x, is 6 minutes.

Question 104: E & F

To work out the amount of change is the sum £5 - (2 x £1.65), which = £3.30. Logically we can then work out that the 3 coins in the change that are the same must be 1p as no other 3 coin combination can yield £1.70 when made up with 5 more coins. Thus we know that 3 of the coins are 1p, 1p & 1p. We can then deduce that there must also have been 2p and 5p coins in the change as £1.70 is divisible by ten. The only way then to make up the remaining £1.60 in 3 different coins is to have £1, 50p and 10p, Hence the change in coins is 1p, 1p, 1p, 2p, 5p, 10p, 50p and £1. So the two coins not given in change are £2 and 20p.

Question 105: D

If we express the speed of each train as W ms^{-1}. Then the relative speed of the two trains is 2W ms^{-1}.
Using Speed=distance/time: 2W = (140 + 140)/ 14.
Thus, 2W = 20, and W = 10. Thus, the speed of each train is 10 ms^{-1}.
To convert from metres to kilometres, divide by 1,000. To convert from seconds to hours, divide by 3,600.
Therefore, the conversion factor is to divide by 1,000/3,600 = 10/36 = 5/18
Thus, to convert from ms^{-1} to kmph, multiply by 18/5. Therefore, the final speed of the train is 18/5 x 10 = 36km/hr.

Question 106: C

Taking the day to be 24 hours long, this means the first tap fills 1/6 of the pool in an hour, the second 1/48, the third $\frac{1}{72}$ and the fourth $\frac{1}{96}$.

Taking 288 as the lowest common denominator, this gives: $\frac{48}{288} + \frac{6}{288} + \frac{4}{288} + \frac{3}{288}$ which = $\frac{61}{288}$ full in one hour. Hence the pool will be $\frac{244}{288}$ full in 4 hours.

The pool fills by approximately $\frac{15}{288}$ every 15 minutes.

Thus, in 4 Hours 15: $\frac{244 + 15}{288} = \frac{249}{288}$

Thus, in 4 Hours 30: $\frac{244 + 30}{288} = \frac{274}{288}$

Thus, in 4 Hours 45: $\frac{244 + 45}{288} = \frac{289}{288}$

Question 107: B

Every day up until day 28 the ant gains a net distance of 1cm, so at the end of day 27 the ant is at 27cm height and therefore only 1cm below the top. On day 28 the 3cm the ant climbs in the day is enough to take it to the top of the ditch and so it is able to climb out.

Question 108: A

To solve this question three different sums are needed to use the information given to deduce the costs of the various items. With the information that 30 oranges cost £12, £12/30 = 40p per orange with the 20% discount, hence oranges must cost 50p at full price. With the information that 5 sausages and 10 oranges cost £8.50, we know that the oranges at a 10% discount account for 10 x 45p = £4.50 so 5 undiscounted sausages cost £4 so each full price sausage is £4/5 = 80p. Finally we know that 10 sausages and 10 apples cost £9, at 10% discount the sausages cost 72p each thus accounting for 10 x 72p = £7.20 of the £9, hence the 10 apples at a 10% discount must cost £1.80, so each apple costs 18p at 10% discount. So an apple is 20p full price. Now to add up the final total: 2 oranges + 13 sausages + 2 apples = (2 x 50p) + (13 x 72p) + (12 x 18p) = £12.52.

Question 109: C

If we take the number of haircuts per year to be x, the information we have can be shown:

Membership	Annual Fee	Cost per cut	Total Yearly cost
None	None	£60	60x
VIP	£125	£50	£125 + 50x
Executive VIP	£200	£45	£200 + 45x

As we know that changing to either membership option would cost the same for the year, we can express the cost for the year, y as;

VIP: $y = £125 + 50x$

Executive VIP: $y = £200 + 45x$

Therefore: $£125 + 50x = £200 + 45x$

Simplified $5x = £75$, therefore the number of haircuts a year, x is 15.

Substituting in x, we can therefore work out:

Membership	Annual Fee	Cost per cut	Total Yearly cost
None	None	£60	£900
VIP	£125	£50	£875
Executive VIP	£200	£45	£875

Hence the amount saved by buying membership is £25.

Question 110: B

All thieves are criminals. So the circle must be fully inside the square, we are told judges cannot be criminals so the star must be completely separate from the other two.

Question 111: C

We are told that March and May have the same last number, which must be either 3 or 13. Taking the information from the question that one of the factors is related to the letters of the month names, we can interpret that 13 represents the M which starts both March and May. Therefore we know the rule is that the last number is the position of the starting letter. Knowing that there is another factor about the letters of the month that controls the code we can work out that one of the number may code for the number of letters. Which in March would be 5, which is the second letter, so we have the rule of the 2nd number. Finally through observation we may note that the first number codes for the months' relative position in the year. Hence the code of April will be 4, (for its position), 5 (for the number of letters in the name) and 1 for the position of the starting letter 'A') and so 451 is the code.

Question 112: D

If *b* is the number of years older than 5, and *a* the number of A*s, the money given to the children can be expressed:
£5 + £3b + £10a
Hence for Josie £5 + (£3 x 11) + (£10 x 9) = £128
We know that Carson receives £44 less yearly, and his b value is 13, so his amount can be expressed:
£5 + (£3 x 13) + (£10a) = £84
Simplified: £44 + £10a = £84
I.e. £10a = £40,
So Carson's 'a' value, i.e. his number of A*s is 4, so the difference between Josie and Carson is **5**.

Question 113: B & C

Using the information to make a diagram:

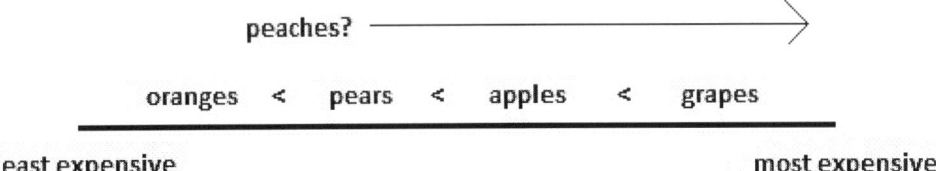

Hence **A** is incorrect. **D** and **E** may be true but we do not have enough information to say for sure. **B** is correct as we know peaches are more expensive than oranges but not about their price relative to pears. Equally we know **C** to be true as grapes are more expensive than apples so they must be more expensive than pears.

Question 114: B

It's easy to assume all the cuts should be in the vertical plane as a cake is usually sliced, however there is a way to achieve this with fewer cuts. Only three cutting motions are needed. **Start by cutting in the horizontal plane** through the centre of the cake to divide the top half from the bottom half. Then slice in the vertical plane into quarters to give 8 equally sized pieces with just three cuts.

Question 115: B & D

After the changes have been made, at 12 PM (GMT +1):
- Russell thinks it is 11 AM
- Tom thinks it is 12 PM
- Mark thinks it is 1 PM

Thus, in current GMT+1 time zone, Mark will arrive an hour early at 11 AM, Russell an hour late at 1 PM and Tom on time at 12 PM. There is therefore a two hour difference between the first and last arrival. For options E and F, be careful: the time zone listed is **NOT** GMT +1 that everyone else is working in. 1PM in GMT +3 = 11am GMT +1 (the summer time zone just entered) so that is Mark's actual arrival time; 12pm GMT +0 is the old time zone that Russell didn't change out of so that is Russell's correct arrival time.

Question 116: D

Using Bella's statements, as she must contradicted herself with her two statements, as one of them must be true, we know that it was definitely either Charlotte or Edward. Looking to the other statements, e.g. Darcy's we know that it was either Charlotte or Bella, as only one of the two statements saying it was both of them can have been a lie. Hence it must have been Charlotte.

Question 117: F

The only way to measure 0.1 litres or 100ml, is to fill the 300ml beaker, pour into the half litre/ 500 ml beaker, fill the 300ml again and pour (200ml) into the 500ml, which will make it full, leaving 100ml left in the 300ml beaker. The process requires 600ml of solution to fill the 300ml beaker twice.

Question 118: D

If you know how many houses there are on the street it is possible to work out the average, which then you can round up and down and to find the sequence of number, e.g. if you know there are 6 houses in the street 870/ 6 = 145. Which is not a house number because they are even so going up and down one even number consequentially one discovers that the numbers are 146, 144, 148, 150, 142 and 140. But it is not possible to determine Francis' house number without knowing its relative position i.e. highest, 3rd highest, lowest etc.

Question 119: D

Expressed through time:

Event	People Present
There were 20 people exercising in the cardio room	20
Four people were about to leave	20
A doctor was on the machine beside him (one of the original 20)	20
Emerging from his office one of the personal trainers called an ambulance.	21
Half of the people who were leaving, left (-2)	19
Eight people came into the room to hear the man being pronounced dead. (+8)	27
the two paramedics arrived, (+2)	29
the man was pronounced dead (-1)	28

Question 120: B & D

Blood loss can be described as 0.2 L/min.
For the man:
8 litres – 40% (3.2 L) = 4.8 L When he collapses, taking 16 minutes (3.2 / 0.2 = 16)
For the woman:
7 litres – 40% (2.8L) = 4.2: when she collapses, taking 14 minutes (2.8 / 0.2 = 14)

Hence the woman collapses 2 minutes before the man so **B** is correct, and **A** is incorrect. The total blood loss is 3.2L + 2.8L which = 6L so **C** is incorrect. The man's blood loss is 3.2L when he collapses so **E** is incorrect. The woman has a remaining blood volume of 4.2L when she collapses so **D** is correct. Blood loss is 0.2 L/min, which equates to 5 minutes per litre, which is 10 minutes per 2 litres not 12 L, so **F** is incorrect.

Question 121: B

Work out the times taken by each girl – (distance/pace) x 60 (converts to minutes) + lag time to start
Jenny: (13/8) x 60 = 97.5 minutes
Helen: (13/10) x 60 + 15 = 93 minutes
Rachel (13/11) x 60 + 25 = 95.9 minutes

Question 122: C

Work through each statement and the true figures.
A. Overlap of pain and flu-like symptoms must be at least 4% (56+48-100). 4% of 150: 0.04 x 150=6
B. 30% high blood pressure and 20% diabetes, so max percentage with both must be 20%. 20% of 150: 0.2*150 = 30
C. Total number of patients – patients with flu-like symptoms – patients with high blood pressure. Assume different populations to get min number without either. 150 – (0.56 x 150) – (0.3 x 150) = 21
D. This is an obvious trap that you might fall into if you added up the percentages and noted that the total was >100%. However, this isn't a problem as patients can discussed two problems.

Question 123: C

This is easiest to work out if you give all products an original price, I have used £100. You can then work out the higher price, and the subsequent sale price, and thus the discount from the original £100 price. As the price increases and decreases are in percentages, they will be the same for all items regardless of the price so it does not matter what the initial figure you start with is.

Marked up price: 100 x 1.15 = £115
Sale price: 115 x 0.75 = £86.25
Percentage reduction from initial price is 100 – 86.25 = 13.75%

Question 124: D
The recipe states 2 eggs makes 12 pancakes, therefore each egg makes 6 pancakes, so the number Steve must make should be a multiple of 6 to ensure he uses a whole egg.
Steve requires a minimum of 15 x 3 = 45 pancakes. To ensure use of whole eggs, this should be increased to 48 pancakes.
The original recipe is for 12 pancakes, therefore to make 48 pancakes, require 4x recipe (48/12).
Therefore quantities: 8 eggs, 400g plain flour and 1200 ml milk.

Question 125: B
Work through the question backwards.
In 6 litres of diluted bleach, there are 4.8 litres of water and 1.2 litres of partially diluted bleach.
In the 1.2 litres of partially diluted bleach, there is 9 parts water to one part original warehouse bleach. Remember that a ratio of 1:9 means 1/10 bleach and 9/10 water. Therefore working through, there is 120ml of warehouse bleach needed.

Question 126: C
We know that Charles is born in 2002, therefore in 2010 he must be 8. There are 3 years between Charles and Adam, and Charles is the middle grandchild. As Bertie is older than Adam, Adam must be younger than Charles so Adam must be 5 in 2010. In 2010, if Adam is 5, Bertie must be 10 (states he is double the age of Adam).
The question asks for ages in 2015: Adam = 10, Bertie = 15, Charles = 13

Question 127: B

Make the statements into algebraic equations and then solve them as you would simultaneous equations. Let a denote the flat fixed rate for hire, and b the price per half hour.
Cost = a + b(time in mins/30)
Peter: a + 6b (6 half hours) = 14.50 (equation 1)
Kevin: 2a + 18b = 41, or this can be simplified to give cost per kayak, a + 9b = 20.5 (equation 2)
If you subtract equation 1 from equation 2:
3b = 6, therefore b = 2

Substitute b into either equation to calculate a, using equation 1, a + 12 = 14.50, therefore a = 2.50
Finally use these values to work out the cost for 2 hours:
2.50 (flat fee) + 4 x 2 (4half hours x cost/half hour) = £10.50

Question 128: E
It is most helpful to write out all the numbers from 0 – 9 in digital format to most easily see which light elements are used for each number. You can then cross out any numbers which don't use all the lights from the digit 7.

Go through the digits methodically and you can cross out: 1, 2, 4, 5, and 6. These numbers don't contain all three

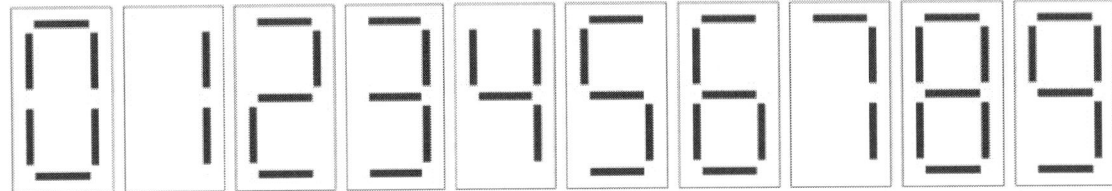

bars from the digit 7.

Question 129: B
In this question it is worth remembering it will take more people a shorter amount of time.
Work out how many man hours it takes to build the house. Days x hours x builders
12 x 7 x 4 = 336 hours
Work out how many hours it will take the 7man workforce: 336/7 = 48 hours

Convert to 8 hour days: 48/8 = 6 days

Question 130: D

By far the easiest way to do these type of questions is to draw a Venn diagram (use question marks if you are unsure about the exact position):

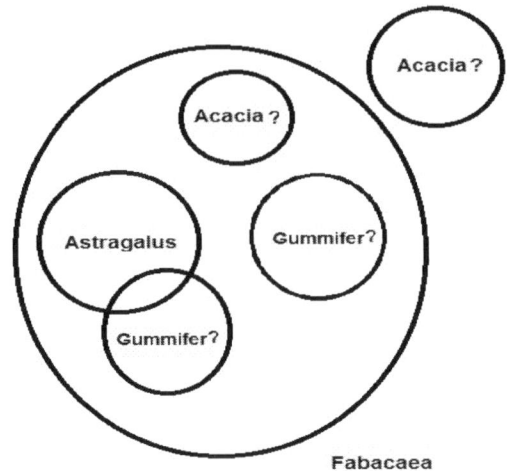

Now, it is a case of going through each statement:

A. Incorrect - Acacia may be fabacaea. Acacia are not astragalus, but does not logically follow that they therefore can't be fabacaea.
B. Incorrect – astragalus and gummifer are not necessarily separate within fabacaea.
C. Incorrect – the statement is not reversible so the fact that all astragalus and gummifer are fabacaea does not mean all facacaea are gummifer and/or astragalus. E.g. Fabacaea could be acacia.
D. Correct
E. Incorrect – Whilst some acacia could be gummifer, there is no certainty that they are.

Question 131: D

Area of a trapezium = (a+b)/2 x h
Area of cushion = (50+30)/2 x 50 = 2000cm²
Since each width of fabric is 1m wide, both sides of one cushion can fit into one width. The required length is therefore 75cm x 4 = 3m with a cost of 3 x £10 = £30.
Cost of seamstress = £25 x 4 = £100
Total cost is £130

Question 132: C

There are 30 days in September, so Lisa will buy 30 coffees.
In Milk, every 10th coffee is free, so Lisa will pay for 27 coffees at 2.40 = £64.80
In Beans, Lisa gets 20 points each day and needs 220 points to get a free coffee, which is 11 days, with 5 points left over. Therefore, in 30 days she will get 2 free coffees. The cost for 28 coffees at 2.15 is £60.20
Beans is cheaper, and the difference is £64.80 - £60.20 = £4.60.

Question 133: C

Work backwards and take note of how often each bus comes.
Must get off 220 bus at 10.57 latest. Can get 10.40 bus therefore (arrive at 10.54).
Latest can get on 283 bus is 10.15 as to make the 220 bus connection. 283 comes every 10mins (question doesn't state at what points past the hour), so Paula should be at the bus stop at 10.06 to ensure a bus comes by 10.15 at the latest. If the bus comes every 10mins, even if a bus comes at 10.05 which Paula will miss, the next bus will come at 10.15 and therefore she will still be on time.
Therefore Paula must leave at 10.01

Question 134: B

You are working out the time taken to reach the same distance (D). Make sure to take into account changing speeds of train A, and that train B leaves 20 minutes earlier.

$$Speed = \frac{distance}{time}$$

Make sure you keep the answers consistent in the time units you are using, the worked answer is all in minutes (hence the need to multiply by 60).

Train A: time for first $20km = \frac{20}{100} \times 60 = 12\ minutes$

So the distance where it equals B is $12 + (\frac{D-20}{150}) \times 60$

You need to use D-20 to account for the fact you have already calculated the time at the slower speed for the first 20km

Train B: $(\frac{D}{90}) \times 60 - 20$

Make the equations equal each other as they describe the same time and distance, and solve.

Simplifies to $32 + \frac{2D}{5} - 8 = \frac{2D}{3}$ so $D = 90km$

Train B will take 60 minutes to travel 90 km and train A will take 40 minutes (but as it leaves 20 minutes later, this will be point at which it passes).

Question 135: C

Work out the annual cost of local gym: 12 x 15 = £180
Upfront cost + class costs of university gym must therefore be >£180.
Subtract upfront cost to find number of classes: 180 – 35 = £145
Divide by cost per class (£3) to find number of classes: 145/3 = 48 1/3
48 1/3 classes would make the two gyms the same price, so for the local gym to be cheaper, you would need to attend 49 classes.

Question 136: C

A is definitely true, since the question states that all herbal drugs are not medicines. **B** is also definitely true as all antibiotics are medicines which are all drugs. **C** is definitely false, because all antibiotics are medicine, yet no herbal drugs are medicines. **D** is true as all antibiotics are medicines.

Question 137: C

Answer **A** cannot be reliably concluded, because from the information given a non-"Fast" train could stop at Newark, but not at Northallerton or Durham. We have no information on whether *all* trains stopping at Newark also stop at Northallerton.

Answer **B** is not correct because 8 is the *average* number of trains that stop at Northallerton. It is possible that on some days more than 16 trains run, and more than 8 will thus stop at Northallerton. Answer **D** is incorrect because it is mentioned that *all* trains stopping at Northallerton also stop at Durham, giving a total 6 stops as a minimum for a train stopping at Northallerton (the others being the 4 stops which *all* trains stop at).

Answer **E** is incorrect for a similar reason to **A**. We have no information on whether all trains stopping at Newark also stop at Northallerton, so cannot determine that they must also stop at Durham.

Answer **C** is correct because "Fast" trains make less than 5 stops. Since all trains already stop at 4 stops (Peterborough, York, Darlington and Newcastle), they cannot then stop at Durham, as this would give 5 stops.

Question 138: D
From the information we are given, we can compose the following image of how these towns are located (not to scale, but shows the direction of each town with respect to the others):

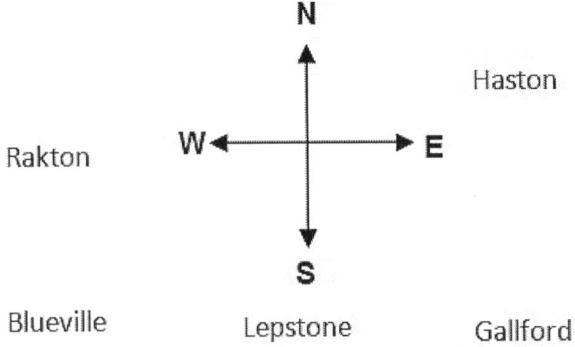

From this "map", we can see that all statements apart from **D** are true. Statement **D** is definitely *not true*, since Blueville is south west of Haston it cannot be East of Haston.

Question 139: C
We are told that in order to form a government, a party (or coalition) must have *over* 50% of seats. Thus, they must have at least 50% of the total seats plus 1, which is 301 seats.
We are told that we are looking for the *minimum* number of seats the greens can have in order to form a coalition with red and orange. Thus, we are seeking for Red and Orange to have the *maximum* number of seats possible, under the criteria given.

Thus we can calculate as follows:
- No party has over 45% of seats, so the maximum that the Red party can have is 45%, which is 270 seats.
- No party except for red and blue has won more than 4% of seats. We are told that the green party won the 4th highest number of seats, so it is possible that the Orange party won the 3rd highest.
- Thus, the maximum number of seats the orange party can have won is 4% of the total, which is 24 seats.
- Thus, the maximum possible combined total of the Red and Orange party's seats won is 294.

Thus, in order to achieve a total of 301 seats in a Red-Orange-Green coalition, the Green party have to have won at least 7 seats.

Question 140: E
Expressing the amount each child receives:

Youngest	M
2nd youngest	$M + D$
3rd youngest/ 3rd oldest	$M + 2D$
4th youngest/ 2nd oldest	$M + 3D$
Oldest	$M + 4D$

Question 141: D
The total amount of money received;
£100, = M + M + D + M + 2D + M + 3D + M + 4D
Simplified, thus is:
£100 = *5M + 10D*

Question 142: C
The two youngest are expressed as *M* and *M + D*. Simplified as *2M + D*.
The three oldest are expressed as *M + 2D, M + 3D* and *M + 4D*, Simplified as *3M + 9D*
Hence 7 times the two youngest together is expressed 7(2M + D), so altogether the Answer is 7(2M + D) = 3M + 9D.

Question 143: A

To work this out, simplify the two equations:

$7(2M + D) = 3M + 9D$
$14M + 7D = 3M + 9D$
$11M = 2D$
$M = \dfrac{2D}{11}$

Question 144: A

Substitute M into the equation $£100 = 5M + 10D$

$5\left(\dfrac{2D}{11}\right) + 10D = £100$

$\dfrac{10D}{11} + 10D = \dfrac{10D}{11} + \dfrac{110D}{11} = \dfrac{120D}{11}$

Question 145: C & E

The easiest way to work this out is using a table. With the information we know:

1st		Madeira
2nd		
3rd	Jaya	
4th		

Ellen made carrot cake and it was not last. It now cannot be 1st or 3rd as these places are taken so it must be second:

1st		Madeira
2nd	Ellen	Carrot cake
3rd	Jaya	
4th		

Aleena's was better than the tiramisu, so she can't have come last, therefore Aleena must have placed first

1st	Aleena	Madeira
2nd	Ellen	Carrot cake
3rd	Jaya	
4th		

And the girl who made the Victoria sponge was better than Veronica:

1st	Aleena	Madeira
2nd	Ellen	Carrot cake
3rd	Jaya	Victoria Sponge
4th	Veronica	Tiramisu

Question 146: D

The information given can be expressed to show the results that the teams must have had to make their points total.

Team	Points	Game Results			
Celtic Changers	2	L	L	D	D
Eire Lions	?	?	?	?	?
Nordic Nesters	8	W	W	D	D
Sorten Swipers	5	W	D	D	L
Whistling Winners	1	D	L	L	L

The results so far total 3 wins, 6 losses and 7 draws. Since, the number of draws must be even, there must have been another draw. So we know one of the Eire Lions results is a draw.

The difference between wins (3) and losses (6) is 3. Thus, there must be another 3 wins to account for this difference. So the Eire Lions results must be 3 wins and 1 draw. Thus, they scored 3 x 3 + 1 = 10.

Question 147: D
Remember to consider the gender of each person. Then draw a quick diagram to show the given information you can see that only D is correct.

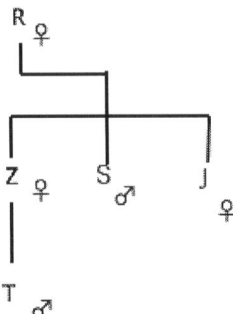

Question 148: B
After the first round; he knocks off 8 bottles to leave 8 left on the shelf. He then puts back 4 bottles. There are therefore 12 left on the shelf. After the second round, he has hit 3 bottles and damages 6 bottles in total, and an additional 2 at the end. He then puts up 2 new bottles to leave 12 − 8 + 2 = 6 bottles left on the shelf. After the final round, John knocks off 3 bottles from the shelf to leave 3 bottles standing.

Question 149: D
Based on the information we have we can plot the travel times below. Change over times are in a smaller font.

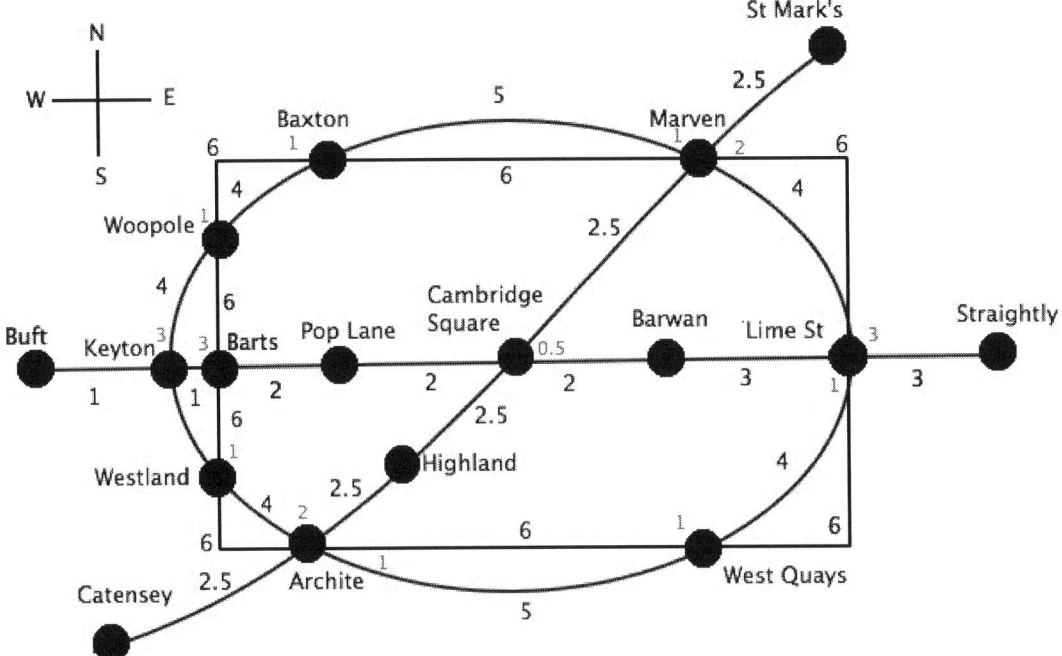

Hence on the St Mark's line, St Mark's to Archite takes 4 x 2.5 minutes = 10 minutes.

Question 150: A
Going from stop to stop on the Straightly line end Buft to Straightly would take 14 minutes, but we are told earlier on there is an express train that goes end to end and only takes 6.

Question 151: B
The quickest route from Baxton to Pop Lane is via Marven and Cambridge Square, which takes 5 + 2 + 2.5 + 0.5 + 2 = 12 minutes. Baxton to Pop Lane via Barts would take 4 + 1 + 6 + 3 + 2 = 16 minutes, which is longer so **E** is incorrect. Other options include times failing to take account of, or incorrectly adding changeover times, and so are incorrect.

Question 152: C
From Cambridge Square:

- Catensey is (2.5 x 3 =) 7.5 minutes away.
- Woopole, is (4 + 3 + 1 +2 + 2 =) 12 minutes.
- Buft is (1 + 1 + 2 + 2 =) 6 minutes.
- Westland is (4 + 2 + 2.5 + 2.5 =) 11 minutes.

Question 153: B

With the new delay information we can plot the travel times as before, adjusted for the delays. Plus a 5 minute delay on the platforms when waiting on any platform for a train.

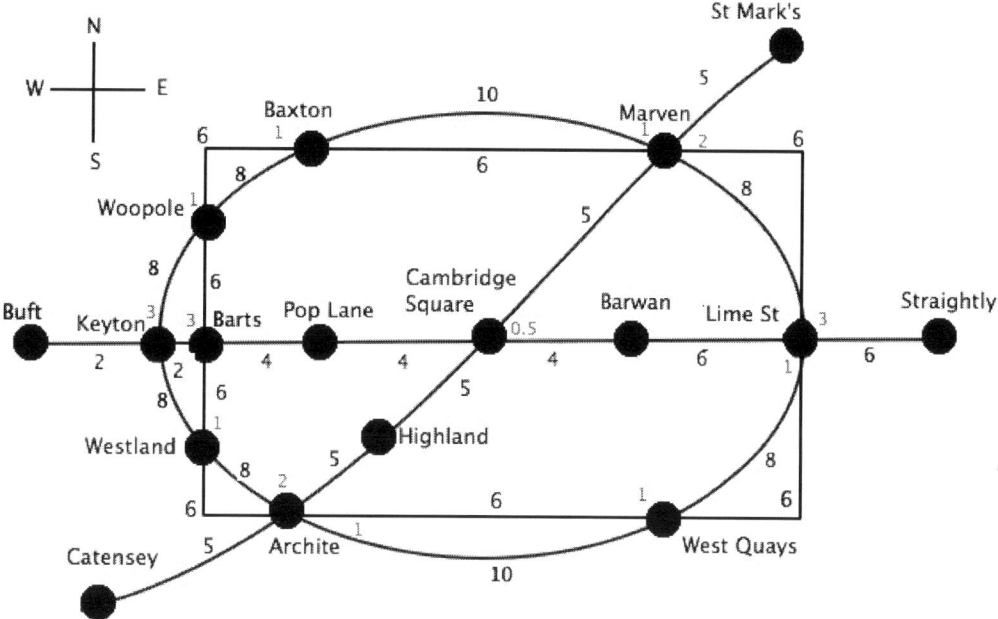

The quickest way from Westland to Marven now uses the non-delayed reliable rectangle line. Four stops on the rectangle line take 6 mins each so 24 minutes in total on the train. Add to this the additional 5 minutes platform waiting time to give a total journey time of 29 minutes.

Question 154: C

- Baxton to Archite via Barts using only the Rectangle line takes (5 + 6 +6+ 6 +6=) 29 minutes.
- Baxton to Woopole on the Rectangle line, then Oval to Archite via Keyton takes (5 + 6 + 1 + 5 + 8 + 8 + 8 =) 41 minutes
- Baxton to Archite on the Oval line only takes (5 + (8 x 4) =) 37 minutes
- Baxton to Woopole on the Oval line, then Rectangle to Archite via Barts takes (5 + 8 + 1 + 5 + 6 + 6 + 6 =) 37 minutes
- As the bus takes 27-31 minutes, it is not possible to tell from between the options which will be slower/quicker so option **C** is the right answer.

Question 155: D

Remember the 5-minute platform wait. We are not told that the St Mark's express train from end to end is no longer running so we must assume that it is, which takes 5 minutes (plus the wait at St Mark's to go to Catensey).

Then, there is a 5 minute wait at Catensey to Archite, and a 2 + 5 minute changeover at Archite onto the Rectangle line which then takes 6 minutes to West Quays. 5 + 5 + 5 + 5 + 2 + 5 + 6 = 33 minutes. Via Lime St the journey takes 5 + 5 + 5+ 2 + 5 + 6+ 6 = 29 minutes.

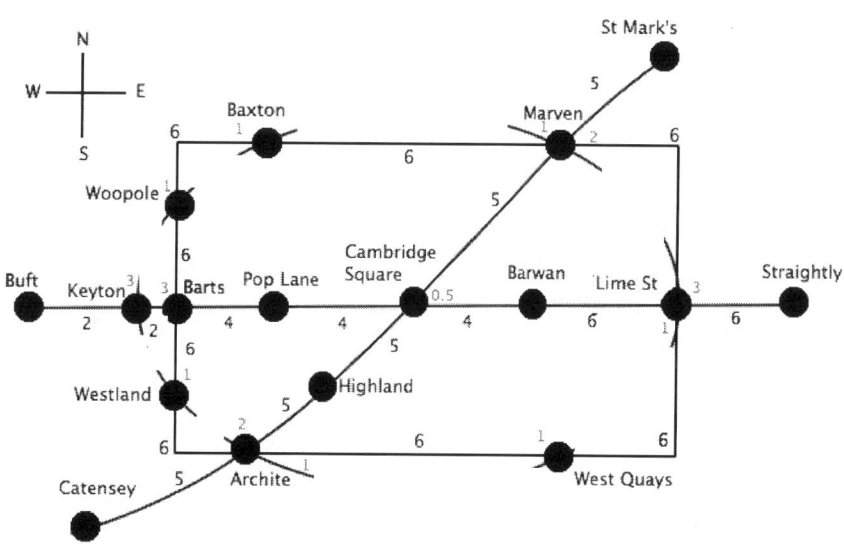

Question 156: D

From the information:
- "Simon's horse wore number 1."
- "..the horse that wore 3, which was wearing red.."
- "the horse wearing blue wore number 4."

We can plot the information below:

Place	Owner	Number	Colours
	Simon	1	
		2	
		3	Red
		4	Blue

In addition: "The horse wearing green; Celia's, came second"

Which means Celia's horse must have worn number two because it cannot have worn number 1 because that is Simon's horse. Also it cannot have worn number three or four because they wore red and blue respectively. So we can plot this further deduction:

Place	Owner	Number	Colours
	Simon	1	
2nd	Celia	2	Green
		3	Red
		4	Blue

We also know that
- "Arthur's horse beat Simon's horse"
- "Celia's horse beat the horse that wore number 1." i.e. Simon's

We know Celia's horse came second, and that both Celia's and Arthur's horses beat Simon's. This means that Simon's horse must have come last. So;

Place	Owner	Number	Colours
4th	Simon	1	
2nd	Celia	2	Green
		3	Red
		4	Blue

And knowing that:
- "Only one horse wore the same number as the position it finished in."

The horses wearing numbers 3 and 4 must have placed 1st and 3rd respectively. Hence:

Place	Owner	Number	Colours
4th	Simon	1	
2nd	Celia	2	Green
1st		3	Red
3rd		4	Blue

"Lila's horse wasn't painted yellow nor blue"

So Lila's must have been red, and Simon's yellow. Leaving the only option for Arthur's to be blue. So we now know:

Place	Owner	Number	Colours
4th	Simon	1	Yellow
2nd	Celia	2	Green

1st	Lila	3	Red
3rd	Arthur	4	Blue

Question 157: C
Year 1 – 40 x 1.2 = 48
Year 2 – 48 x 1.2 = 57.6
Year 3 – 57.6 x 1.1 = 63.36
Year 4 – 63.36 x 1.1 = 69.696.

Question 158: C
To minimise the total cost to the company, they want the wage bills for each site to be less than £200,000. Working this out involves some trial and error; you can speed this up by splitting employees who earn similar amounts between the sites e.g. Nicola and John as they are the top two earners.
Nicola + Daniel + Luke = £ 198,500 and John + Emma + Victoria = £ 199,150

Question 159: C
Remember that pick up and drop off stops may be the same stop, therefore the minimum number of stops the bus had to make was 7. This would take 7 x 1.5 = 10.5 minutes.
Therefore the total journey time = 24 + 10.5 = 34.5 minutes.

Question 160: A
The best method here is to work backwards. We know the potatoes have to be served immediately, so they should be finished roasting at 4pm, so they should start roasting 50 minutes prior to that, at 3:10. We also know they have to be roasted immediately after boiling, so they should be prepared by 3:05, in order to boil in time. She should therefore start preparing them no later than 2:47, though she could prepare them earlier.
The chicken needs to be cooked by 3:55 to give it time to stand, so it should begin roasting at 2:40, and Sally should begin to prepare it no later than 2:25.
You can construct a rough timeline:

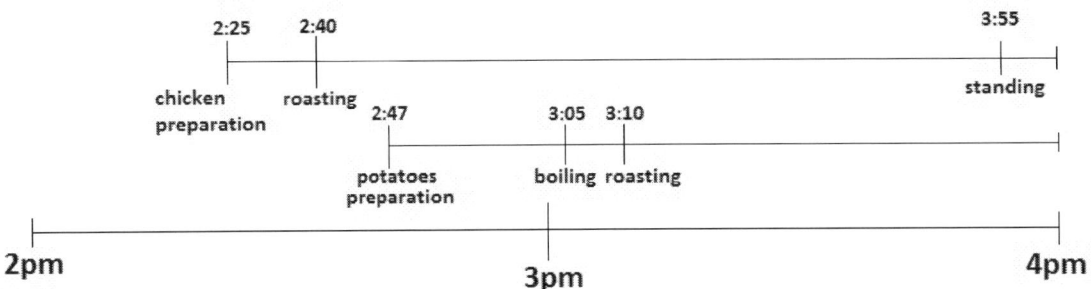

We can see from this timeline that from 2:40 onwards, there will be no long enough period of time in which there is a free space in the cooker for the vegetables to be boiled. They therefore must be finished cooking at 3:05. The latest time prior to this that Sally has time to prepare them (5 minutes) is at 2:40, between preparing the chicken and the potatoes. She should therefore begin preparing the vegetables at 2:42, then begin boiling at 2:47, so they can be finished cooking by 2:55, in time for the potatoes to boil at 3:05.
Chicken: 2:25
Potatoes: 2:47
Vegetables: 2:42

Question 161: C

The quickest way to do this is via trial and error. However, for the sake of completion: let each child's age be denoted by the letter of their name, and form an equation for their total age:

$P + J + A + R = 80$

The age of each child can be written in terms of Paul's age.

$P = 2J$, therefore $J = \dfrac{P}{2}$

$A = \dfrac{P + J}{2}$

Now substitute in $J = \dfrac{P}{2}$ to get in terms of P only: $A = \dfrac{P + \dfrac{P}{2}}{2} = \dfrac{P}{2} + \dfrac{P}{4} = \dfrac{3P}{4}$

$R = P + 2$

Thus: $P + \dfrac{P}{2} + \dfrac{3P}{4} + P(+2) = 80$

Simplify to give: $\dfrac{13P}{4} = 78$

$13P = 312$. Thus, $P = 24$

Substitute P = 24 into the equations for the other children to get: J = 12, A = 18, R = 26

Question 162: A

The total number of buttons is 71 + 86 + 83 = 240. The total number of suitable buttons is 22 + 8 = 30. Thus, she will have to remove a maximum of 210 buttons in order to guarantee picking a suitable button on the next attempt.

Question 163: E

This question requires you to calculate the adjusted score for Ben for each segment. If Ben has a 50% chance of hitting the segment he is aiming for, we can assume he hits each adjacent segment 25% of the time. Thus:

$$Adjusted\ Score = \dfrac{Segment\ aimed\ at}{2} + \dfrac{First\ Adjacent\ Segment}{4} + \dfrac{Second\ Adjacent\ Segment}{4}$$

$$Adjusted\ Score = \dfrac{Segment\ aimed\ at}{2} + \dfrac{Sum\ of\ Adjacent\ Segments}{4}$$

E.g. if he aims at segment 1: He will score $\dfrac{1}{2} + \dfrac{18 + 20}{4} = 10$

Now it is a simple case of trying the given options to see which segment gives the highest score. In this case, it is segment 19: $\dfrac{19}{2} + \dfrac{7 + 3}{4} = 12$

Question 164: C

The total cost is £8.75, and Victoria uses a £5.00 note, leaving a total cost of £3.65 to be paid using change.
Up to 20p can be paid using 1p and 2p pieces, so she could use 20 1p coins to make up this amount.
Up to 50p can be paid using 5p and 10p pieces, so she could use 10 5p pieces to make up this amount. This gives a total of 30 coins, and a total payment of £0.70.
Up to £1.00 can be paid using 20p pieces and 50p pieces. Thus, she could use up to 5 20p pieces, giving a total of 35 coins used, and a total payment of £1.70.

The smallest denomination of coin that can now be used is a £1.00 coin. Hence Victoria must use 2 £1.00 coins, giving a total of 37 coins, and a total payment of £3.70. However, we know that the total cost to pay in change was £3.65, and that Victoria paid the exact amount, receiving no change. Thus, we must take away coins to the value of 5p, removing the smallest number of coins possible. This is achieved by taking away 1 5p piece, giving a grand total of 36 coins.

Question 165: B
The time could be 21:25, if first 2 digits were reversed by the glass of water (21 would be reversed to give 15). **A** cannot be the answer, because this would involve altering the last 2 digits, and we can see that 25 on a digital clock, when reversed simply gives 25 (the 2 on the left becomes a 5 on the right, and the 5 on the right becomes a 2 on the left). **C** cannot be the answer, as this involves reversing the middle 2 digits. As with the right two digits, the middle 2 digits of 2:5 would simply reverse to give itself, 2:5. **D** could be the time if the 2nd and 4th digits were reversed, as they would both become 2's. However, the question says that 2 *adjacent* digits are reversed, meaning that the 2nd and 4th digits cannot be reversed as required here. **E** is not possible as it would require all four numbers to be reversed.
Thus, the answer is **B**.

Question 166: B
We can see from the question that Lorkdon is a democracy and therefore cannot have been invaded by a democracy because of the treaty (we are assuming this treaty is upheld, as said in the question). Thus, Nordic (which has invaded Lorkdon) *must* be a dictatorship. Now, we can see that Worsid has been invaded by a dictatorship, *and* has invaded a dictatorship. The question states that no dictatorship has undergone both of these events. Thus, we know that Worsid cannot be a dictatorship. We also know from the question that each of these countries is *either* a dictatorship or a democracy. Thus, Worsid must be a democracy.

Question 167: C
The total price of all of these items would usually be £17. However, with the DVD offer, the customer saves £1, giving a total cost of £16. Thus, the customer will need to receive £34 in change.

Question 168: B
To answer this, we simply calculate how much total room in the pan will be taken up by the food for each guest:
- 2 rashers of bacon, giving a total of 14% of the available space.
- 4 sausages, taking up a total of 12% of the available space.
- 1 egg takes up 12% of the available space.

Adding these figures together, we see that each guest's food takes up a total of 38% of the available space.
Thus, Ryan can only cook for 2 guests at once, since 38% multiplied by 3 is 114%, and we cannot use up more than 100% of the available space in the pan.

Question 169: C
To calculate this, let the total number of employees be termed "Y".
We can see that £60 is the total cost for providing cakes for 40% of "Y".
We know that £2 is required for each cake. Thus, we can work out that 30 must be 40% of Y.

$0.4Y = 60/2$
$0.4Y = 30$
$Y = 75$

Thus, we can calculate that the total number of employees must be 75.

Question 170: E
The normal waiting time for treatment is 3 weeks. However, the higher demand in Bob's local district mean this waiting time is extended by 50%, giving a total of 4.5 weeks.
Then, we must consider the delay induced because Bob is a lower risk case, which extends the waiting time by another 20%. 20% of 4.5 is 0.9, so there is a delay of another 0.9 weeks for treatment.
Thus, Bob can expect to wait 5.4 weeks for specialist treatment on his tumour.

Question 171: D
In the class of 30, 40% drink alcohol at least once a month, which is 12. Of these, 75% drink alcohol once a week, which is 9. Of these, 1 in 3 smoke marijuana, which is 3.
In the class of 30, 60% drink alcohol less than once a month, which is 18. Of these, 1 in 3 smoke marijuana, which is 6.

Therefore the total number of students who smoke marijuana is 3+6, which is 9.

Question 172: C
The sequence can either be thought of as doubling the previous number then adding 2, or adding 1 then doubling. Double 46 is 92, plus 2 is 94.

Question 173: B
If the mode of 5 numbers of 3, it must feature at least two threes. If the median is 8, we know that the 3rd largest number is an 8. Hence we know that the 3 smallest numbers are 3, 3, and 8. Because the mean is 7, we know that the 5 numbers must add up to 35. The three smallest numbers add up to 14. Hence the two largest must add up to 21.

Question 174: E
The biggest difference in the weight of potatoes will be if the bag with only 5 potatoes in weighs the maximum, 1100g, and the bag with 10 potatoes weighs the minimum, 900g. If there are 5 equally heavy potatoes in a bag weighing 1100g, each weighs 220g. If there are 10 equally heavy potatoes in a 900g bag, each weighs 90g. The difference between these is 130g.

Question 175: D
There are 60 teams, and 4 teams in each group, so there are 15 groups. In each group, if each team plays each other once, there will be 6 matches in each group, making a total of 90 matches in the group stage. There are then 16 teams in the knockout stages, so 8 matches in the first round knockout, then 4, then 2, then 1 final match when only two teams are left. Hence there are 105 matches altogether (90 + 8 + 4 + 2 + 1 = 105).

Question 176: A
We know the husband's PIN number must be divisible by 8 because it has been multiplied by 2 3 times and had a multiple of 8 added to it. The largest 4 digit number which is divisible by 8 is 9992. Minus 200 is 9792. Divide by 2 is 4896. Hence the largest the husband's last 4 card digits can be is 4896. Minus 200 is 4696. Divide by 2 is 2348. Hence the largest my last 4 card digits can be is 2348. Minus 200 is 2148. Divide by 2 is 1074. Hence the largest my PIN number can be is 1074.

Question 177: C
If the first invitation is sent as early as possible, it will be sent on the 50th birthday. It will be accepted after 2 reminders and hence conducted at 50 years 11 months. The time between each screening will be 3 years 11 months. Hence, the second screening will be at 54 years 10 months. The third screening will be at 58 years 9 months. Hence, the fourth screening will be at 62 years 8 months.

Question 178: A
Ellie has worked for the company for more than five but less than six whole years. At the end of each whole year she receives a pay rise in thousands equal to the number of years of her tenure. Therefore at the end of the first year the raise is £1,000, then at the end of the second year it is £2,000 and so on to year 5. Thus the total amount of her pay comprised by the pay rises is £15,000, so the basic pay before accounting for these rises was £40,000 - £15,000 = £25,000.

Question 179: B
The trains come into the station together every 40 minutes, as the lowest common multiple of 2, 5 and 8 is 40. Hence, if the last time trains came together was 15 minutes ago, the next time will be in 25 minutes.

Question 180: C
If you smoke, your risk of getting Disease X is 1 in 24. If you drink alcohol, your risk of getting Disease X is 1 in 6. Each tablet of the drug halves your risk. Therefore a drinker taking 1 tablet means their risk is 1 in 12, and taking 2 tablets means their risk is 1 in 24, the same as someone who smokes.

Question 181: A
There are 10 red and 8 green balls. Clearly the most likely combination involves these colours only. Since there are more red balls than green, the probability of red-red is greater than green-green. However, there are **two** possible ways to draw a combination, either the red first followed by green or green first followed by red. The probability of red-red = $\left(\frac{10}{20} x \frac{9}{19}\right) = \frac{9}{38}$.

The probability of red and green = $\left(\frac{8}{20} \times \frac{10}{19}\right) + \left(\frac{10}{20} \times \frac{8}{19}\right) = \frac{8}{38} + \frac{8}{38} = \frac{16}{38}$. Therefore the combination of red and green is more likely.

Question 182: B

The least likely combination of balls to draw is blue and yellow. You are much more likely to draw a green ball than either a blue or yellow one because there are many more in the bag. Since the draw is taken without replacement, yellow and yellow is impossible because there is only one yellow ball.

Question 183: F

Since there is only 1 blue and 1 yellow ball, it is possible to take 18 balls which are red or green. You would need to take 19 of the 20 balls to be certain of getting either the blue ball or the yellow ball.

Question 184: C

The smallest number of parties required would theoretically be 3 – Namely Labour, the Liberal Democrats and UKIP, giving a total of 355 seats. However, the Liberal Democrats will not form a coalition with UKIP, so this will not be possible. Thus, there are 2 options:

➢ Labour can form a coalition with the Greens and UKIP, which is not contradictory to anything mentioned in the question. This would give a total of 325 seats, and would thus need the next 2 largest parties (The Scottish National Party and Plaid Cymru) in order to get more than 350 seats, meaning 5 parties would need to be involved.
➢ Alternatively, Labour can form a coalition with the Liberal Democrats and the Green Party. This would give a total of 340 seats. Only one more party (e.g. the Scottish National Party) would be required to exceed 350 seats, giving a grand total of 4 parties.

Thus, the smallest number of parties needed to form a coalition would be 4.

Question 185: E

360 appointments are attended and only 90% of those booked are attended, meaning there were originally 400 appointments booked in and 40 have been missed. 1 in 2 of the booked appointments were for male patients, so 200 appointments were for male patients. Male patients are three times as likely to miss booked appointments, so of the 40 that were missed, 30 were missed by men. Given that of 200 booked appointments, 30 were missed, this means 170 were attended.

Question 186: B

If every one of 60 students studies 3 subjects, this is 180 subject choices altogether. 60 of these are Maths, because everyone takes Maths. 60% of 60 is 36, so 36 are Biology. 50% of 60 is 30, so 30 are Economics and 30 are Chemistry. 60+36+30+30=156, so there are 24 subject choices left which must be Physics.

Question 187: B

If 100,000 people are diagnosed with chlamydia and 0.6 partners are informed each, this is 60,000 people, of which 80% (so 48,000) have tests. 12,000 of the partners who are informed, as well as 240,000 who are not (300,000 – 60,000) do not have tests. This makes 252,000 who are not tested. We can assume that half of these people would have tested positive for chlamydia, which is 126,000. So the answer is 126,000.

Question 188: C

Tiles can be added at either end of the 3 lines of 2 tiles horizontally or at either end of the 2 lines of 2 tiles vertically. This is a total of 10, but in two cases these positions are the same (at the bottom of the left hand vertical line and the top of the right hand vertical line). So the answer is 10 – 2 = 8.

Question 189: C

Harry needs a total of 4000ml + 1200ml = 5200ml of squash. He has 1040ml of concentrated squash, which is a fifth of the total dilute squash he needs. So he will need 4 parts water to every 1 part concentrated squash, therefore the resulting liquid is 1/5 squash and 4/5 water.

Question 190: C

There are 24 different possible arrangements (4 x 3 x 2 x 1), which means that there are 23 other possible arrangements than Alex, Beth, Cathy, Daniel.

Question 191: F
A is incorrect because the distance travelled is only 10 miles. **B** is incorrect because the distance travelled is 19 miles. **C** is incorrect because no town is visited twice. **D** is incorrect because Hondale and Baleford are both visited twice. **E** is incorrect because no town is visited twice. Therefore **F** is the correct answer.

Question 192: C
Georgia is shorter than her Mum and Dad, and each of her siblings is at least as tall as Mum (and we know Mum is shorter than Dad because Ellie is between the two), so we know Georgia is the shortest. We know that Ellie, Tom and Dad are all taller than Mum, so Mum is second shortest. Ellie is shorter than Dad and Tom is taller than Dad, so we can work out that Ellie must be third shortest.

Question 193: A
Danielle must be sat next to Caitlin. Bella must be sat next to the teaching assistant. Hence these two pairs must sit in different rows. One pair must be sat at the front with Ashley, and the other must be sat at the back with Emily. Since the teaching assistant has to sit on the left, this must mean that Bella is sat in the middle seat and either Ashley or Emily (depending on which row they are in) is sat in the right hand seat. However, Bella cannot sit next to Emily, so this means Bella and the teaching assistant must be in the front row. So Ashley must be sat in the front right seat.

Question 194: C
The dishwasher is run 2+p times a week, where p is the number of people in the house. Let the number of people in the house when the son is not home be s, and when the son is home it is s+1. In 30 weeks when the son is home, she would buy 6 packs of dishwasher tablets. In 30 weeks when the son is not home, she would buy 5 packs of dishwasher tablets. So 1.2 times as many packs of dishwasher tablets are bought when he is home. So 2+s+1 is 1.2 time 2+s.
i.e. $2.4 + 1.2s = 2 + s + 1$
Therefore 0.2s = 0.6
s = 3
When her son is home, there are s + 1 = 4 people in the house.

Question 195: A
No remaining days in the year obey the rule. The next date that does is 01/01/2015 (integers are 0, 1, 2, 5). This is 6 days later than the specified date.

Question 196: B
If each town is due North, South, East or West of at least 2 other towns and we know that one is east and one is north of a third, then they must be arranged in a square. So Yellowtown is 4 miles east of Bluetown to make a square, which means it must be 5 miles north of Redtown. So Redtown is 5 miles south of Yellowtown.

Question 197: B
Jenna pours 4/5 of 250 ml into each glass, which is 200 ml. Since she has 1500 ml of wine, she pours 100 ml into the last glass, which is 2/5 of the 250 ml full capacity.

Question 198: E
The maximum number of girls in Miss Ellis's class with brown eyes and brown hair is 10, because the two thirds of the girls with brown eyes could also all have brown hair. The minimum number is 0 because it could be that all the boys, and the third of the girls without brown eyes, all had brown hair, which would be 2/3 of the class.

Question 199: E
A negative "score" results from any combination of throws which includes a 1 but from no other combination. Given that a negative score has a 0.75 probability, a positive or zero score has a 0.25 probability. Therefore throwing two numbers that are not 1 twice in a row has a probability of 0.25. Hence, the probability of throwing a non-1 number on each throw is $\sqrt{0.25} = 0.5$. So the probability of throwing a 1 on an individual throw is 1 − 0.5 = 0.5.

Question 200: C
We can work out from the information given the adult flat rate and the charge per stop. Let the charge per stop be s and the flat rate be f. Therefore: 15s + f = 1.70
8s + f = 1.14
We can hence work out that: 7s = 0.56, so s = 0.08. Hence, f = 0.50
Megan is an adult so she pays this rate. For 30 stops, the rate will be 0.08 x 30 + 0.50 = 2.90.

Question 201: B
We found in the previous question that the flat rate for adults is £0.50 and the rate per stop is £0.08. We know that the child rate is half the flat rate and a quarter of the "per stop" rate, so the child flat rate is £0.25 and the rate per stop is 2p. So for 25 stops, Alice pays:
0.02 x 25 + 0.25 = 0.75

Question 202: C
We should first work out how many stops James can travel. For £2, he can afford to travel as many stops as £1.50 will take him once the flat rate is taken into account. The per stop rate is 8p per stop, so he can travel 18 stops, so he will need to go to the 18th stop from town. So he will need to walk past 7 stops to get to the stop he can afford to travel from.

Question 203: D
The picture will need a 12 inch by 16 inch mount, which will cost £8. It will need a 13 inch by 17 inch frame, which will cost £26. So the cost of mounting and framing the picture will be £8 + £26 = £34.

Question 204: C
Mounting and framing an 8 by 8 inch painting will cost £5 for the mount and £22 for the frame, which is £27. Mounting and framing a 10 by 10 inch painting will cost £6 for the mount and £26 for the frame, which is £32. The difference is £32 - £27 = £5.

Question 205: B
We found in the last question that mounting and framing a 10 by 10 inch painting will cost £6 for the mount and £26 for the frame, which is £32 total. We can calculate that each additional inch of mount and frame for a square painting costs £2.50; £2 for the frame and £0.50 for the mount. So an 11 inch painting will cost £34.50 to frame and mount, a 12 inch £37, a 13 inch £39.50, a 14 inch £42. The biggest painting that can be mounted and framed for £40 is a 13 inch painting.

Question 206: D
Recognise that the pattern is *"consonants move forward by two consonants; vowel stay the same"*. This allows coding of the word MAGICAL to PAJIFAN to RALIHAQ.

	Forward two		Forward two
M	$\Rightarrow$	O (skips to) P	$\Rightarrow$ R
A	$\Rightarrow$	Stays the same	$\Rightarrow$ A
G	$\Rightarrow$	I (skips to) J	$\Rightarrow$ L
I	$\Rightarrow$	Stays the same	$\Rightarrow$ I
C	$\Rightarrow$	E (skips to) F	$\Rightarrow$ H
A	$\Rightarrow$	Stays the same	$\Rightarrow$ A
L	$\Rightarrow$	N	$\Rightarrow$ Q

Question 207: C
If f donates the flat rate, and k denotes the rate per km, we can form simultaneous equations:
f + 5k = £6 AND f + 3k = £4.20
Subtract equation two from equation one:
(f + 5k) - (f + 3k) = £6 - £4.20
Thus, 2k = £1.80 and k = £0.90
Therefore, f + (5 x 0.90) = £6
So, f + £4.50 = £6. Thus, f = £1.50
7k will be £1.50 + 7 x £0.90 = £7.80

Question 208: C
The increase from 2001/2 to 2011/12 was 1,019 to 11,736, which equals a linear increase of 10,717 admissions. So, in 20 years, we would expect to see an increase by 10,717 x 2 = 21,434. Add this to the number in 2011 to give 33,170 admissions.

Question 209: A
As the question uses percentages, it does not matter what figure you use. To make calculations easier, use an initial price of £100. When on sale, the dress is 20% off, so using a normal price of £100, the dress would be £80. When the dresses are 20% off, the shop is making a 25% profit. Therefore: £80 = 1.25 x purchase price. Therefore, the purchase price is: $\frac{80}{1.25} = £64$. Thus, the normal profit is £100 - £64 = £36. I.e. when a dress sells for £100, the shop makes £36 or 36% profit.

Question 210: C
1. Incorrect. There must be 6 general committee clinical students, plus the treasurer, and 2 sabbatical roles, none of whom can be preclinical, so there must be a maximum of 11 preclinical students.
2. Correct. There must two general for each year plus welfare and social officers, totalling to 6.
3. Incorrect. The committee is made up of 20 students, 2 roles are sabbatical, so there are 18 studying students, and therefore there can be 3 from each year.
4. Correct. There are 18 studying students on the committee, and there must be 6 general committee members from pre-clinical, plus welfare and social, therefore there must be a minimum of 8 pre-clinical students, so there must be 10 clinical students.
5. Incorrect. You need to count up the number of specific roles on the committee, which is 5, and there must be 2 students from each year, which is 12. This leaves 3 more positions, which the question doesn't state can't be first years. Therefore there could be up to 5 first years.
6. Incorrect. There must be at least 2 general committee members from each year. However, the worked answer to 5 shows there are 15 general committee members which are split across the 6 years, and so there must be an uneven distribution.

Question 211: B
Remember 2012 was a leap year. Work through each month, adding the correct number of days, to work out what day each 13th would be on.
If a month was 28 days, the 13th would be the same day each month, therefore to work this out quickly, you only need to count on the number of days over 28. For example, in a month with 31 days, the 13th will be 3 weekdays (31-28) later.

Thus if 13th January is a Friday, 13th February is a Monday, (February has 29 days in 2012), 13th March is a Tuesday and 13th April is a Friday.

Question 212: E
There are 18 sheep in total. The question states there are 8 male sheep, which means there are 10 female sheep before some die. 5 female sheep die, so there are 5 female sheep alive to give birth to lambs. Each delivers 2 lambs, making 10 lambs in total. There are 4 male sheep and 5 mothers so the total is 10 + 4 + 5 = 19 sheep.

Question 213: D
We can see from the fact that all the possible answers end "AME" that the letters "AME" must be translated to the last 3 letters of the coded word, "JVN", under the code. J is the 10th letter of the alphabet so it is 9 letters on from A (V is the 21st letter of the alphabet and M is the 13th, and N is the 14th letter of the alphabet and E is the 5th, therefore these pairs are also 9 letters apart). Therefore P is the code for the letter 9 letters before it in the alphabet. P is the 16th letter of the alphabet, therefore it is the code for the 7th letter of the alphabet, G. Therefore from these solutions the only possibility for the original word is GAME.

Question 214: C
Let x be the number of people who get on the bus at the station.
It is easiest to work backwards. After the 4th stop, there are 5 people on the bus. At the 4th stop, half the people who were on the bus got off (and therefore half stayed on) and 2 people got on. Therefore, 5 is equal to 2 plus half the number of people who were on the bus after the 3rd stop. So half the number of people who were on the bus after the 3rd stop must be 3. Therefore, after the 3rd stop, there must have been 6 people on the bus.

We can then say that 6 is equal to 2 plus half the number of people who were on the bus after the 2nd stop. Therefore there were 8 people on the bus after the 2nd stop.
We can then say that 8 is equal to 2 plus half the number of people who were on the bus after the 1st stop. Therefore there were 12 people on the bus after the 1st stop.
We can then say that 12 is equal to 2 plus half the number of people who got on the bus at the station. Therefore the number of people who got on the bus at the station is 20.

Question 215: B
We know from the question that I have purchased small cans of blue and white paint, and that blue paint accounted for 50% of the total cost. Since a can of blue paint is 4 X the price of a can of white paint, we know I must have purchased 4 cans of white paint for each can of blue paint.
Each can of small paint covers a total of $10m^2$, and I have painted a total of $100m^2$, in doing so using up all the paint. Therefore, I must have purchased 10 cans of paint. Therefore, I must have purchased 2 cans of blue paint and 8 cans of white paint. So I must have painted $20m^2$ of wall space blue.

Question 216: E
The cost for x cakes under this offer can be expressed as: $x(42-x^2)$
Following this formula, we can see that 2 cakes would cost 76p, 3 cakes would cost 99p, and 4 cakes would cost 104p. As the number of cakes increases beyond 4, we see that the overall price actually drops, as 5 cakes would cost 85p and 6 cakes would cost 36p. This confirms Isobel's prediction that the offer is a bad deal for the baker, as it ends up cheaper for the customer to purchase more cakes. It is clear that 6 cakes is the smallest number for which the price will be under 40p, and the price will continue to drop as more cakes are purchased.

Question 217: C
Adding up the percentages of students in University A who do "Science" subjects gives:
23.50 + 6.25 + 30.25 = 60%.
60% of 800 students is 480, so 480 students in University A do "Science" subjects.
Adding up the percentages of students in University B who do "Science subjects" gives:
13.25 + 14.75 + 7.00 = 35%. 35% of 1200 students is 420, so 420 students in University B do "Science" subjects. Therefore:
480 – 420 = 60
60 more students in University A than University B take a "Science" subject.

Question 218: C
Let the number of miles Sonia is travelling be x. Because she is crossing 1 international border, travelling by Traveleasy Coaches will cost Sonia: £(5 + 0.5x)
Travelling by Europremier coaches will cost Sonia: £(15 + 0.1x).

Because we know the cost is the same for both companies, the number of miles she is travelling can be found by setting these two expressions equal to each other: 5 + 0.5x = 15 + 0.1x.
This equation can be rearranged to give: 0.4x = 10
Therefore: x = 10/0.4 = 25

Question 219: E
To find out whether many of these statements are true it is necessary to work out the departure and arrival times, and journey time, for each girl.

Lauren departs at 2:30pm and arrives at 4pm, therefore her journey takes 1.5 hours
Chloe departs at 1:30pm and her journey takes 1 hour longer than 1.5 hours (Lauren's journey), therefore her journey takes 2.5 hours and she arrives at 4pm
Amy arrives at 4:15pm and her journey takes 2 times 1.5 hours (Lauren's journey), therefore her journey takes 3 hours and she departs at 1:15pm.
Looking at each statement, the only one which is definitely true is **E**: Amy departs at 1:15pm and Chloe departs at 1:30pm therefore Amy departed before Chloe.

D *may* be true, but nothing in the question shows it is *definitely* true, so it can be safely ignored.

Question 220: B
First consider how many items of clothing she can take by weight. The weight allowance is 20kg. Take off 2kg for the weight of the empty suitcase, then take off another 3kg (3 X 1000g) for the books she wishes to take. Therefore she can fit 15kg of clothes in her suitcase. To find out how many items of clothing this is, we can divide 15kg=15000g by 400g: 15000/400 = 150/4 = 37.5
So she can pack up to 37 items of clothing by weight.

Now consider the volume of clothes she can fit in. The total volume of the suitcase is:
50cm x 50cm x 20cm = 50000cm^3
The volume of each book is: 0.2m x 0.1m x 0.05m = 1000cm^3

So the volume of space available for clothes is: 50000 – (3 x 1000) = 47000cm^3
To find out how many items of clothing she can fit in this space, we can divide 47000 by 1500:
47000/1500 = 470/15 = 31 1/3
So she can pack up to 31 items of clothing by volume.

Although she can fit 37 items by weight, they will not fit in the volume of the suitcase, so the maximum number of items of clothing she can pack is 31.

Question 221: D
We can work out the Answer by considering each option:
Bed Shop A: £120 + £70 = £190
Bed Shop B: £90 + £90 = £180
Bed Shop C: £140 + (1/2 x £60) = £170
Bed Shop D: (2/3) x (£140+£100) = (2/3) x (£240) = £160
Bed Shop E: £175
Therefore the cheapest is Bed Shop **D**.

Question 222: C
The numbers of socks of each colour is irrelevant, so long as there is more than one of each (which there is). There are only 4 colours of socks, so if Joseph takes 5 socks, it is guaranteed that at least 2 of them will be the same colour.

Question 223: D
Paper comes in packs of 500, and with each pack 20 magazines can be printed. Each pack costs £3.
Card comes in packs of 60, and with each pack 60 magazines can be printed. Each pack costs £3 x 2 = £6.
Each ink cartridge prints 130 sheets, which is 130/26 = 5 magazines. Each cartridge costs £5.

The lowest common multiple of 20, 60 and 5 is 60, so it is possible to work out the total cost for printing 60 magazines. Printing 60 magazines will require 3 packs of paper at £3, 1 pack of card at £6 and 12 ink cartridges at £5. So the total cost of printing 60 magazines is: (3 x 3) + 6 + (12 x 5) = £75.

The total budget is £300.
£300/£75 = 4
So we can print 4x60 magazines in this budget, which is 240 magazines.

Question 224: E
We can express the information we have as: $\frac{1}{4} - \frac{1}{5} = \frac{1}{20}$
So the six additional lengths make up 1/20 of Rebecca's intended distance. So the number of lengths she intended to complete was: 20 x 6 = 120.

Question 225: B
Sammy has a choice of 3 flavours for the first sweet that he eats. Each of the other sweets he eats cannot be the same flavour as the sweet he has just eaten. So he has a choice of 2 flavours for each of these four sweets. So the total number of ways that he can make his choices is:
$3 \times 2 \times 2 \times 2 \times 2 = 48$

Question 226: C
Suppose that today Gill is x years old. It follows that Granny is 15x years old. In 4 years' time, Gill will be (x+4) years old and Granny will be 15x+4 years old. We know that in 4 years' time, Granny's age is equal to Gill's age squared, so: $15x + 4 = (x + 4)^2$
Expanding and rearranging, we get: $x^2 - 7x + 12 = 0$
We can factorise this to get: $(x - 3)(x - 4)$

So x is either 3 or 4. Gill's age today is either 3 or 4 so Granny is either 45 or 60. We know Granny's age is an even number, so she must be 60 and hence Gill must be 4. So the difference in their ages is 56 years.

Question 227: C
If Pierre is telling the truth, everyone else is not telling the truth. But, also in this case, what Qadr said is not true, and hence Ratna is telling the truth. So we have a contradiction. So we deduce that Pierre is not telling the truth. Therefore, Qadr is telling the truth, and so Ratna is not telling the truth. So Sven is also telling the truth, and hence Tanya is not telling the truth. So Qadr and Sven are telling the truth and the other three are not telling the truth.

Question 228: D
Angus walks for 20 minutes at 3 mph and runs for 20 minutes at 6 mph. 20 minutes is one-third of an hour. So the number of miles that Angus covers is: $3 \times 13 + 6 \times 13 = 6$
Bruce covers the same distance. So Bruce walks 12×3 miles at 3 mph which takes him 30 minutes and runs the same distance at 6 mph which takes him 15 minutes. So altogether it takes Bruce 45 minutes to finish the course.

Question 229: B
Although you could do this quickly by forming simultaneous equations, it is even quicker to note that 72 x 4 = 288. Since Species 24601 each have 4 legs; it leaves a single member of species 8472 to account for the other 2 legs.

Question 230: E
None of the options can be concluded for certain. We are not told whether any chicken dishes are spicy, only that they are all creamy. Whilst all vegetable dishes are spicy, some non-vegetable dishes could also be spicy. There is no information on whether dishes can be both creamy and spicy, nor on which, if any, dishes contain tomatoes. Remember, if you're really stuck, draw a Venn diagram for these types of questions.

Question 231: C
At 10mph, we can express the time it takes Lucy to get home as: 60 x 8/10 = 48
Since Simon sets off 20 minutes later, his time taken to get home, in order to arrive at the same time, must be:
48 – 20 = 28
Therefore his cycling speed must be: 48/28 x 10 = 17mph

Question 232: A
The total profit from the first transaction can be expressed as: 2000 x 8 = 16,000p
The total profit from the second transaction is: 1000 x 6 = 6,000p

Therefore the total profit is 22,000p or £220 before charges. There are four transactions at a cost of £20 each, therefore the overall profit is: £220 – (20 x 4) = £140

Question 233: C
For the total score to be odd, there must be either three odd or one odd and two even scores obtained. Since the solitary odd score could be either the first, second or third throw there are four possible outcomes that result in an odd total score. Additionally, there are the same number of possibilities giving an even score (either all three even or two odd and one even scores obtained), and the chance of throwing odd or even with any given dart is equal. Therefore, there is an equal probability of three darts totalling to an odd score as to an even score, and so the chance of an odd score is ½.

Question 234 C
This is a compound interest question. £5,000 must be increased by 5%, and then the answer needs to be increased by 5% for four more iterations. After one year: £5,000 x 1.05 = £5,250
Increasing sequentially gives 5512, 5788, 6077 and 6381 after five years. Therefore the answer is £6,381.

Question 235: D
If in 5 years' time the sum of their ages is 62, the sum of their ages today will be: 62 – (5 x 2) = 52
Therefore if they were the same age they would both be 26, but with a 12 year age gap they are 20 and 32 today. Michael is the older brother, so 2 years ago he would have been aged 30.

Question 236: A
Tearing out every page which is a multiple of 3 removes 166 pages. All multiples of 6 are multiples of 3, so no more pages are torn out with that instruction. Finally, half of the remaining pages are removed, which equates to an additional 167 pages. Therefore 333 pages are removed in total. The total surface area of these pages is 15 x 30 x 333 = 149,850 cm^2 = 14.9m^2. At 110 gm^2, 14.9 m^2 weighs 14.9 x 110 = 1,650g (1,648g unrounded)

Question 237: D
The cost of fertiliser is 80p/kg = 8p/100g. At 200g the incremental increase in yield is 65 pence/m. At each additional 100g it will be reduced by 30%, therefore at 300g/m it is 45.5p, at 400g/m it is 31.8p, at 500g/m it is 22.3p, at 600g/m it is 15.6p, at 700g/m it is 10.9p, and at 800g it is 7.6p. So at 800g the gain in yield is less than the cost of the fertiliser to produce the gain, and so it is no longer cost effective to fertilise more.

Question 238: D
Statements **A**, **C** and **E** are all definitely true. Meanwhile, statement **B** may be not true but is not definitely untrue, as this depends on the number of cats and rabbit owned.
Only statement **D** is definitely untrue. The type of animal requiring the most food is a dog, and as can be seen from the tables, Furry Friends actually sells the most expensive dog food, not the cheapest.

Question 239: C
The largest decrease in bank balance occurs between January 1st and February 1st, totalling £171, reflecting the amount spent during the month of January, £1171. However, because there is a pay rise beginning on March 10th, we need to consider that from April onwards, the bank balance will have increased by £1100, not £1000. This means that the same decrease in bank balance reflects £100 more spending if it occurs after March. This means that 2 months now have seen more spending than February. Between March 1st and April 1st, the bank balance has decreased by £139. With the salary increase, the salary is now £1100, so the total spending for the month of March is £1239. This is greater than the total spending during the month of January.
Similarly, the month of April has also seen more spending than January once the pay rise is considered, a total of £1225 of spending. However, this is still less than the month of March.

Question 240: C
If Amy gets a taxi, she can set off 100 minutes before 1700, which is 1520.
If Amy gets a train, she must get the 1500 train as the later train arrives after 1700, so she must set off at 1500.
Since Northtown airport is 30 minutes from Northtown station, there is no way Amy can get the flight and still arrive at Northtown station by 1700. Therefore Amy should get a taxi and should leave at 1520.

Question 241: C

We can decompose the elements of the multiplication grid into their prime factors, thus:

	C	D
A	2 x 2 x 2 x 3 x 7	2 x 2 x 2 x 2 x 3 x 3 x 5
B	7 x 17	2 x 3 x 5 x 17

bc = 7 x 17, so one of b and c must be 7 and the other must be 17. b must be 17 because bd is a multiple of 17 and not of 7, and c must be 7 because ac is a multiple of 7 and not of 17. ac is 168, so a must be 168 divided by 7, which is 24. ad is 720 so d must be 720 divided by 24, which is 30. Hence the answer is 30.
Alternatively approach the question by eliminating all answers which are not factors of both 720 and 510.

Question 242: E
48% of the students are girls, which is 720 students. Hence 80 is 1/9 of the girls, so 1/9 of boys are mixed race. The remaining 780 students are boys, so 87 boys are mixed race to the nearest person. There is a shortcut to this question. Notice that 80 girls are mixed race, and the proportion is the same for boys. As there are more boys than girls we know the answer is greater than 80. Option **E** 90 is the only option for which this holds true.

Question 243: D
Don't be fooled – this is surprisingly easy. We can see that between Monday and Thursday, Christine has worked a total of 30 hours. We can also calculate how long her shift on Friday was supposed to be. She is able to make up the hours by working 3 extra hours next week, and 5 hours on Sunday. Thus, the Friday shift must have been planned to be 8 hours long. Adding this to the other 30 hours, we see that Christine was supposed to work 38 hours this week.

Question 244: C
130°. Each hour is 1/12 of a complete turn, equalling 30°. The smaller angle between 8 and 12 on the clock face is 4 gaps, therefore 120°. In addition, there is 1/3 of the distance between 3 and 4 still to turn, so an additional 10° must be added on to account for that.

Question 245: B
The total price of all of these items would usually be £17. However, with the DVD offer, the customer saves £1, giving a total cost of £16. Thus, the customer will need to receive £34 in change.

Question 246: A
DNA consists of 4 bases: adenine, guanine, thymine and cysteine. The sugar backbone consists of deoxyribose, hence the name DNA. DNA is found in the cytoplasm of prokaryotes.

Question 247: F
Mitochondria are responsible for energy production by ATP synthesis. Animal cells do not have a cell wall, only a cell membrane. The endoplasmic reticulum is important in protein synthesis, as this is where the proteins are assembled.

Question 248: F
If you aren't studying A-level biology, this question may stretch you. However, it is possible to reach an answer by process of elimination. Mitochondria are the 'powerhouse' of the cell in aerobic respiration, responsible for cell energy production rather than DNA replication or protein synthesis. As energy producers they are required in muscle cells in large numbers, and in sperm cells to drive the tail responsible for movement. They are enveloped by a double membrane, possibly because they started out as independent prokaryotes engulfed by eukaryotic cells.

Question 249: A
The majority of bacteria are commensals and don't lead to disease.

Question 250: C
Bacteria carry genetic information on plasmids and not in nuclei like animal cells. They don't need meiosis for replication, as they do not require gametes. Bacterial genomes consist of DNA, just like animal cells.

Question 251: C
Active transport requires a transport protein and ATP, as work is being done against an electrochemical gradient. Unlike diffusion, the relative concentrations of the materials being transported aren't important.

Question 252: D
Meiosis produces haploid gametes. This allows for fusion of 2 gametes to reach a full diploid set of chromosomes again in the zygote.

Question 253: B
Mendelian inheritance separates traits into dominant or recessive. It applies to all sexually reproducing organisms. Don't get confused by statement C – the offspring of 2 heterozygotes has a 25% chance of expressing a recessive trait, but it will be homozygous recessive.

Question 254: A
Hormones are released into the bloodstream and act on receptors in different organs in order to cause relatively slow changes to the body's physiology. Hormones frequently interact with the nervous system, e.g. Adrenaline and Insulin, however, they don't directly cause muscles to contract. Almost all hormones are synthesised.

Question 255: D
Neuronal signalling can happen via direct electrical stimulation of nerves or via chemical stimulation of synapses which produces a current that travels along the nerves. Electrical synapses are very rare in mammals, the majority of mammalian synapses are chemical.

Question 256: D
Remember that pH changes cause changes in electrical charge on proteins (= polypeptides) that could interfere with protein – protein interactions. Whilst the other statements are all correct to a certain extent, they are the downstream effects of what would happen if enzymes (which are also proteins) didn't work.

Question 257: A
The bacterial cell wall is made up of cellulose and protects the bacterium from the external environment, in particular from osmotic stresses, and is important in most bacteria.

Question 258: C
Sexual reproduction relies on formation of gametes during **meiosis**. Mitosis doesn't produce genetically distinct cells. Mitosis is, however, the basis for tissue growth.

Question 259: A
A mutation is a permanent change in the nucleotide sequence of DNA. Whilst mutations may lead to changes in organelles and chromosomes, or even be harmful, they are strictly defined as permanent changes to the DNA or RNA sequence.

Question 260: E
Mutations are fairly common, but in the vast majority of cases do not have any impact on phenotype due to the redundancy of the genome. Sometimes they can confer selective advantages and allow organisms to survive better (i.e. evolve by natural selection), or they can lead to cancers as cells start dividing uncontrollably.

Question 261: D
Antibodies represent a pivotal molecule of the immune system. They provide very pointed and selective targeting of pathogens and toxins without causing damage to the body's own cells.

Question 262: A
Kidneys are not involved in digestion, but do filter the blood of waste products. Glucose is found in high concentrations in the urine of diabetics, who cannot absorb it without working insulin.

Question 263: D
Hormones are slower acting than nerves and act for a longer time. Hormones also act in a more general way. Adrenaline is also a hormone released into the body causing the fight-or-flight response. Although it is quick acting, it still lasts for a longer time than a nervous response, as you can still feel its effects for a time after the response, e.g. shaking hands.

Question 264: D
Homeostasis is about minimising changes to the internal environment by modulating both input and output.

Question 265: B
There is less energy and biomass each time you move up a trophic level. Only 10% of consumed energy is transferred to the next trophic level, so only one tenth of the previous biomass can be sustained in the next trophic level up.

Question 266: A
In asexual reproduction, there is no fusion of gametes as the single parent cell divides. There is therefore no mixing of chromosomes and, as a result, no genetic variation.

Question 267: E
The image is first formed on the retina which conveys it to the brain via a sensory nerve. The brain then sends an impulse to the muscle via a motor neuron.

Question 268: D
Blood from the kidney returns to the heart via the renal (kidney-related) vein, which drains into the inferior vena cava. The blood then passes through the pulmonary vasculature (veins carry blood to the heart, arteries away from the heart) before going into the aorta and eventually the hepatic (liver-related) artery.

Question 269: F
Clones are genetically identical by definition, and a large number of them could conceivably reduce the gene pool of a population. In adult cell cloning, the genetic material of an egg is replaced with the genetic material of an adult cell. Cloning is possible for all DNA based life forms, including plants and other types of animals.

Question 270: F
Gene varieties cause intraspecies variation, e.g. different eye colours. If mutations confer a selective advantage, those individuals with the mutation will survive to reproduce and grow in numbers. Genetic variation is caused by mixing of parent genomes and mutations. Species with similar characteristics often do have similar genes.

Question 271: F
Alleles are different versions of the same gene. If you are a homozygous for a trait, you have two identical alleles for that particular gene, and if you are heterozygous you have two different alleles of that gene. Recessive traits only appear in the phenotype when there are no dominant alleles for that trait, i.e. two recessive alleles are carried.

Question 272: D
Remember that red blood cells don't have a nucleus and therefore have no DNA. In meiosis, a diploid cell divides in such a way so as to produce four haploid cells. Any type of cell division will require energy.

Question 273: C
The hypothalamus detects too little water in the blood, so the pituary gland releases ADH. The kidney maintains the blood water level, and allows less water to be lost in the urine until the blood water level returns to normal.

Question 274: E
Venous blood has a higher level of carbon dioxide and lower oxygen. Carbon dioxide forms carbonic acid in aqueous solution, thus making the pH of venous blood slightly more acidic than arterial blood. This leaves only E and F as possibilities, but releasing pH levels cannot fluctuate significantly gives pH 7.4.

Question 275: E
The cytoplasm is 80% water, but also contains, among other things, electrolytes and proteins. The cytoplasm doesn't contain everything, e.g. DNA is found in the nucleus.

Question 276: C
ATP is produced in mitochondria in aerobic respiration and in the cytoplasm during anaerobic respiration only.

Question 277: C
The cell membrane allows both active transport and passive transport by diffusion of certain ions and molecules, and is found in eukaryotes and prokaryotes like bacteria. It is a phospholipid bilayer.

Question 278: A
1 and 2 only: 223 PAIRS = 446 chromosomes; meiosis produces 4 daughter cells with half of the original number of chromosomes each, while mitosis produces two daughter cells with the original number of chromosomes each.

Question 279: E
If Bob is homozygous dominant (RR) the probability of having a child with red hair is 0%. However, if Bob is heterozygous (Rr), there is a 50% chance of having a child with red hair, since Mary must be homozygous recessive (rr) to have red hair. As we do not know Bob's genotype, both possibilities must be considered.

Question 280: A
If an offspring is born with red hair, it confirms Bob is heterozygous (Rr). He cannot have a red-haired child if he is homozygous dominant (RR), and would himself have red hair were he homozygous recessive (rr).

Question 281: A
Monohybrid cross rr and Rr results in 50% Rr and 50% rr offspring. 50% of offspring will have black hair, but they will be heterozygous for the hair allele.

Question 282: C
When the chest walls expand, the intra-thoracic pressure decreases. This causes the atmospheric pressure outside the chest to be greater than pressure inside the chest, resulting in a flow of air into the chest.

Question 283: A
Producers are found at the bottom of food chains and always have the largest biomass.

Question 284: F
All the statements are true; the carbon and nitrogen cycles are examinable in Section 2, so make sure you understand them! The atmosphere is 79% inert N_2 gas, which must be 'fixed' to useable forms by high-energy lightning strikes or by bacterial mediation. Humans also manually fix nitrogen for fertilisers with the Haber process.

Question 285: H
None of the above statements are correct. Mutations can be silent, cause a loss of function, or even a gain in function, depending on the exact location in the gene and the base affected. Mutations only cause a change in protein structure if the amino acids expressed by the gene affected are changed. This is normally due to a shift in reading frame. Whilst cancer arises as a result of a series of mutations, very few mutations actually lead to cancer.

Question 286: C
Remember that heart rate is controlled via the autonomic nervous system, which isn't a part of the central nervous system.

Question 287: H
None of the above are correct. There is no voluntary input to the heart in the form of a neuronal connection. Parasympathetic neurones slow the heart and sympathetic nervous input accelerates heart rate.

Question 288: B
If lipase is not working, fat from the diet will not be broken down, and will build up in the stool. Lactase, for instance, is responsible for breaking down lactose, and its malfunctioning causes lactose-intolerance.

Question 289: F
Oxygenated blood flows from the lungs to the heart via the pulmonary vein. The pulmonary artery carries deoxygenated blood from the heart to the lungs. Animals like fish have single circulatory systems. Deoxygenated blood is found in the superior vena cava, returning to the heart from the body. Veins in the arms and hands frequently don't have valves.

Question 290: E
Enzymatic digestion takes place throughout the GI tract, including in the mouth (e.g. amylase), stomach (e.g. pepsin), and small intestine (e.g. trypsin). The large intestine is primarily responsible for water absorption, whilst the rectum acts as a temporary store for faecal matter (i.e. digestion has finished by the rectum).

Question 291: B
This is an example of the monosynaptic stretch reflex; these reflexes are performed at the spinal level and therefore don't involve the brain.

Question 292: A
Statement 2 describes diffusion, as CO_2 is moving with the concentration gradient. Statement 3 describes active transport, as amino acids are moving against the concentration gradient.

Question 293: I
3 is the correct equation for animals, and 4 is correct for plants.

Question 294: C
The mitochondria are only the site for aerobic respiration, as anaerobic respiration occurs in the cytoplasm. Aerobic respiration produces more ATP per substrate than anaerobic respiration, and therefore is also more efficient. The chemical equation for glucose being respired aerobically is: $C_6H_{12}O_6 + 6O_2 \rightarrow 6CO_2 + 6H_2O$. Thus, the molar ratio is 1:6 (i.e. each mole glucose produces 6 moles of CO_2).

Question 295: B
The nucleus contains the DNA and chromosomes of the cell. The cytoplasm contains enzymes, salts and amino acids in addition to water. The plasma membrane is a bilayer. Lastly, the cell wall is indeed responsible for protecting vs. increased osmotic pressures.

Question 296: D
When a medium is hypertonic relative to the cell cytoplasm, it is more concentrated than the cytoplasm, and when it is hypotonic, it is less concentrated. So, when a medium is hypotonic relative to the cell cytoplasm, the cell will gain water through osmosis. When the medium is isotonic, there will be no net movement of water across the cell membrane. Lastly, when the medium is hypertonic relative to the cell cytoplasm, the cell will lose water by osmosis.

Question 297: A
Stem cells have the ability to differentiate and produce other kinds of cells. However, they also have the ability to generate cells of their own kind and stem cells are able to maintain their undifferentiated state. The two types of stem cells are embryonic stem cells and adult stem cells. The adult stem cells are present in both children and adults.

Question 298: B
All of the following statements are examples of natural selection, except for the breeding of horses. Breeding and animal husbandry are notable methods of artificial selection, which are brought about by humans.

Question 299: C

Enzymes create a stable environment to stabilise the transition state. Enzymes do not distort substrates. Enzymes generally have little effect on temperature directly. Lastly, they are able to provide alternative pathways for reactions to occur.

Question 300: C

A negative feedback system seeks to minimise changes in a system by modulating the response in accordance with the error that's generated. Salivating before a meal is an example of a feed-forward system (i.e. salivating is an anticipatory response). Throwing a dart does not involve any feedback (during the action). pH and blood pressure are both important homeostatic variables that are controlled via powerful negative feedback mechanisms, e.g. massive haemorrhage leads to compensatory tachycardia.

Question 301: A

One of the major functions of white blood cells is to defend the body against bacterial and fungal infections. They can kill pathogens by engulfing them and also use antibodies to help them recognise pathogens. Antibodies are produced by white blood cells.

Question 302: B

The CV system does indeed transport nutrients and hormones. It also increases blood flow to exercising muscles (via differential vasodilatation) and also helps with thermoregulation (e.g. vasoconstriction in response to cold). The respiratory system is responsible for oxygenating blood.

Question 303: C

Adrenaline always increases heart rate and is almost always released during sympathetic responses. It travels primarily in the blood and affects multiple organ systems. It is also a potent vasoconstrictor.

Question 304: B

Protein synthesis occurs in the cytoplasm. Proteins are usually coded by several amino acids. Red blood cells lack a nucleus and, therefore, the DNA to create new proteins. Protein synthesis is a key part of mitosis, as it allows the parent cell to grow prior to division.

Question 305: F

Remember that most enzymes work better in neutral environments (amylase works even better at slightly alkaline pH). Thus, adding sodium bicarbonate will increase the pH and hence increase the rate of activity. Adding carbohydrate will have no effect, as the enzyme is already saturated. Adding amylase will increase the amount of carbohydrate that can be converted per unit time. Increasing the temperature to 100° C will denature the enzyme and reduce the rate.

Question 306: E

Taking the normal allele to be C and the diseased allele to be c, one can model the scenario with the following Punnett square:

		Carrier Mother	
		C	c
Diseased Father	c	Cc	cc
	c	Cc	cc

The gender of the children is irrelevant as the inheritance is autosomal recessive, but we see that all children produced would inherit at least one diseased allele.

Question 307: F

All of the organs listed have endocrine functions. The thyroid produces thyroid hormone. The ovary produces oestrogen. The pancreas secretes glucagon and insulin. The adrenal gland secretes adrenaline. The testes produce testosterone.

Question 308: A
Insulin works to decrease blood glucose levels. Glucagon causes blood glucose levels to increase; glycogen is a carbohydrate. Adrenaline works to increase heart rate.

Question 309: A
The left side of the heart contains oxygenated blood from the lungs which will be pumped to the body. The right side of the heart contains deoxygenated blood from the body to be pumped to the lungs.

Question 310: A
Since Individual 1 is homozygous normal, and individual 5 is heterozygous and affected, the disease must be dominant. Since males only have one X-chromosome, they cannot be carriers for X-linked conditions. If Nafram syndrome was X-linked, then parents 5 and 6 would produce sons who always have no disease and daughters that always do. As this is not the case shown in individuals 7-10, the disease must be autosomal dominant.

Question 311: C
We know that the inheritance of Nafram syndrome is autosomal dominant, so using N to mean a diseased allele and n to mean a normal allele, 5, 7 and 8 must be Nn because they have an unaffected parent. 2 is also Nn, as if it was NN all its progeny would be Nn and so affected by the disease, which is not the case, as 3 and 4 are unaffected.

Question 312: A
Since 6 is disease free, his genotype must be nn. Thus, neither of 6's parents could be NN, as otherwise 6 would have at least one diseased allele.

Question 313: A
Urine passes from the kidney into the ureter and is then stored in the bladder. It is finally released through the urethra.

Question 314: F
Deoxygenated blood from the body flows through the inferior vena cava to the right atrium where it flows to the right ventricle to be pumped via the pulmonary artery to the lungs where it is oxygenated. It then returns to the heart via the pulmonary vein into the left atrium into the left ventricle where it is pumped to the body via the aorta.

Question 315: E
During inspiration, the pressure in the lungs decreases as the diaphragm contracts, increasing the volume of the lungs. The intercostal muscles contract in inspiration, lifting the rib cage.

Question 316: D
Whilst A, B, C and E are true of the DNA code, they do not represent the property described, which is that more than one combination of codons can encode the same amino acid, e.g. Serine is coded by the sequences: TCT, TCC, TCA, TCG.

Question 317: B
The degenerate nature of the code can help to reduce the deleterious effects of point mutations. The several 3-nucleotide combinations that code for each amino acid are usually similar such that a point mutation, i.e. a substitution of one nucleotide for another, can still result in the same amino acid as the one coded for by the original sequence.

The degenerate nature of the code does little to protect against deletions/insertions/duplications, which will cause the bases to be read in incorrect triplets, i.e. result in a frame shift.

Question 318: D
The hypothalamus is the site of central thermoreceptors. A decrease in environmental temperature decreases sweat secretion and causes cutaneous vasoconstriction to minimise heat loss from the blood.

Question 319: A
The movement of carbon dioxide in the lungs and neurotransmitters in a synapse are both examples of diffusion. Glucose reabsorption is an active process, as it requires work to be done against a concentration gradient.

Question 320: F

Some enzymes contain other molecules besides protein, e.g. metal ions. Enzymes can increase rates of reaction that may result in heat gain/loss, depending on if the reaction is exothermic or endothermic. They are prone to variations in pH and are highly specific to their individual substrate.

Question 321: B

Each three-block combination is mutually exclusive to any other combination, so the probabilities are added. Each block pick is independent of all other picks, so the probabilities can be multiplied. For this scenario there are three possible combinations:

P(2 red blocks and 1 yellow block) = P(red then red then yellow) + P(red then yellow then red) + P(yellow then red then red) =

$(\frac{12}{20} x \frac{11}{19} x \frac{8}{18}) + (\frac{12}{20} x \frac{8}{19} x \frac{11}{18}) + (\frac{8}{20} x \frac{12}{19} x \frac{11}{18}) =$

$\frac{3 \ x \ 12 \ x \ 11 \ x \ 8}{20 \ x \ 19 \ x \ 18} = \frac{44}{95}$

Question 322: C

Multiply through by 15: $3(3x + 5) + 5(2x - 2) = 18 \ x \ 15$

Thus: $9x + 15 + 10x - 10 = 270$

$9x + 10x = 270 - 15 + 10$

$19x = 265$

$x = 13.95$

Question 323: C

This is a rare case where you need to factorise a complex polynomial:

(3x)(x) = 0, possible pairs: 2 x 10, 10 x 2, 4 x 5, 5 x 4

(3x - 4)(x + 5) = 0

3x - 4 = 0, so x = $\frac{4}{3}$

x + 5 = 0, so x = -5

Question 324: C

$\frac{5(x-4)}{(x+2)(x-4)} + \frac{3(x+2)}{(x+2)(x-4)}$

$= \frac{5x - 20 + 3x + 6}{(x+2)(x-4)}$

$= \frac{8x - 14}{(x+2)(x-4)}$

Question 325: E

p α $\sqrt[3]{q}$, so p = k $\sqrt[3]{q}$

p = 12 when q = 27 gives 12 = k $\sqrt[3]{27}$, so 12 = 3k and k = 4 so p = 4 $\sqrt[3]{q}$

Now p = 24:

24 = 4$\sqrt[3]{q}$, so 6 = $\sqrt[3]{q}$ and q = 6^3 = 216

Question 326: A

8 x 9 = 72

8 = (4 x 2) = 2 x 2 x 2

9 = 3 x 3

(2 x 2 x 2 x 3 x 3)² = 2 x 2 x 2 x 2 x 2 x 2 x 3 x 3 x 3 x 3 = 2^6 x 3^4

Question 327: C

Note that 1.151 x 2 = 2.302.

Thus: $\dfrac{2 \times 10^5 + 2 \times 10^2}{10^{10}} = 2 \times 10^{-5} + 2 \times 10^{-8}$

= 0.00002 + 0.00000002 = 0.00002002

Question 328: E

$y^2 + ay + b$

$= (y+2)^2 - 5 = y^2 + 4y + 4 - 5$

$= y^2 + 4y + 4 - 5 = y^2 + 4y - 1$

So a = 4 and y = -1

Question 329: E

Take $5(m + 4n)$ as a common factor to give: $\dfrac{4(m+4n)}{5(m+4n)} + \dfrac{5(m-2n)}{5(m+4n)}$

Simplify to give: $\dfrac{4m + 16n + 5m - 10n}{5(m+4n)} = \dfrac{9m + 6n}{5(m+4n)} = \dfrac{3(3m+2n)}{5(m+4n)}$

Question 330: C

$A \propto \dfrac{1}{\sqrt{B}}$. Thus, $= \dfrac{k}{\sqrt{B}}$.

Substitute the values in to give: $4 = \dfrac{k}{\sqrt{25}}$.

Thus, $k = 20$.

Therefore, $A = \dfrac{20}{\sqrt{B}}$.

When B = 16, $A = \dfrac{20}{\sqrt{16}} = \dfrac{20}{4} = 5$

Question 331: E

Angles SVU and STU are opposites and add up to 180°, so STU = 91°

The angle of the centre of a circle is twice the angle at the circumference so

SOU = 2 x 91° = 182°

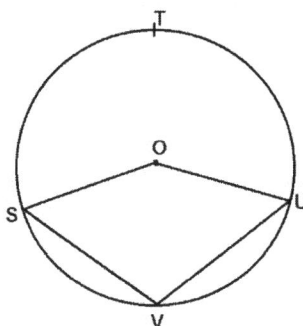

Question 332: E

The surface area of an open cylinder A = 2πrh. Cylinder B is an enlargement of A, so the increases in radius (r) and height (h) will be proportional: $\frac{r_A}{r_B} = \frac{h_A}{h_B}$. Let us call the proportion coefficient n, where $n = \frac{r_A}{r_B} = \frac{h_A}{h_B}$.

So $\frac{Area\ A}{Area\ B} = \frac{2\pi r_A h_A}{2\pi r_B h_B} = n \times n = n^2$. $\frac{Area\ A}{Area\ B} = \frac{32\pi}{8\pi} = 4$, so n = 2.

The proportion coefficient n = 2 also applies to their volumes, where the third dimension (also radius, i.e. the r^2 in $V = \pi r^2 h$) is equally subject to this constant of proportionality. The cylinder's volumes are related by $n^3 = 8$.

If the smaller cylinder has volume 2π cm³, then the larger will have volume 2π x n³ = 2π x 8 = 16π cm³.

Question 333: E

$$= \frac{8}{x(3-x)} - \frac{6(3-x)}{x(3-x)}$$

$$= \frac{8 - 18 + 6x}{x(3-x)}$$

$$= \frac{6x - 10}{x(3-x)}$$

Question 334: B

For the black ball to be drawn in the last round, white balls must be drawn every round. Thus the probability is given by $P = \frac{9}{10} \times \frac{8}{9} \times \frac{7}{8} \times \frac{6}{7} \times \frac{5}{6} \times \frac{4}{5} \times \frac{3}{4} \times \frac{2}{3} \times \frac{1}{2}$

$= \frac{9 \times 8 \times 7 \times 6 \times 5 \times 4 \times 3 \times 2 \times 1}{10 \times 9 \times 8 \times 7 \times 6 \times 5 \times 4 \times 3 \times 2 \times 1} = \frac{1}{10}$

Question 335: C

The probability of getting a king the first time is $\frac{4}{52} = \frac{1}{13}$, and the probability of getting a king the second time is $\frac{3}{51}$. These are independent events, thus, the probability of drawing two kings is $\frac{1}{13} \times \frac{3}{51} = \frac{3}{663} = \frac{1}{221}$

Question 336: B

The probabilities of all outcomes must sum to one, so if the probability of rolling a 1 is x, then:

$x + x + x + x + 2x = 1$. Therefore, $x = \frac{1}{7}$.

The probability of obtaining two sixes $P_{12} = \frac{2}{7} \times \frac{2}{7} = \frac{4}{49}$

Question 337: B

There are plenty of ways of counting, however the easiest is as follows: 0 is divisible by both 2 and 3. Half of the numbers from 1 to 36 are even (i.e. 18 of them). 3, 9, 15, 21, 27, 33 are the only numbers divisible by 3 that we've missed. There are 25 outcomes divisible by 2 or 3, out of 37.

Question 338: C

List the six ways of achieving this outcome: HHTT, HTHT, HTTH, and TTHH, THTH, THHT. There are 2^4 possible outcomes for 4 consecutive coin flips, so the probability of two heads and two tails is: $6 \times \frac{1}{2^4} = \frac{6}{16} = \frac{5}{8}$

Question 339: D

Count the number of ways to get a 5, 6 or 7 (draw the square if helpful). The ways to get a 5 are: 1, 4; 2, 3; 3, 2; 4, 1. The ways to get a 6 are: 1, 5; 2, 4; 3, 3; 4, 2; 5, 1. The ways to get a 7 are: 1, 6; 2, 5; 3, 4; 4, 3; 5, 2; 6, 1. That is 15 out of 36 possible outcomes.

	1	2	3	4	5	6
1	2	3	4	5	6	7
2	3	4	5	6	7	8
3	4	5	6	7	8	9
4	5	6	7	8	9	10
5	6	7	8	9	10	11
6	7	8	9	10	11	12

Question 340: C

There are x+y+z balls in the bag, and the probability of picking a red ball is $\frac{x}{(x+y+z)}$ and the probability of picking a green ball is $\frac{z}{(x+y+z)}$. These are independent events, so the probability of picking red then green is $\frac{xz}{(x+y+z)^2}$ and the probability of picking green then red is the same. These outcomes are mutually exclusive, so are added.

Question 341: B

There are two ways of doing it, pulling out a red ball then a blue ball, or pulling out a blue ball and then a red ball. Let us work out the probability of the first: $\frac{x}{(x+y+z)} \times \frac{y}{x+y+z-1}$, and the probability of the second option will be the same. These are mutually exclusive options, so the probabilities may be summed.

Question 342: A

[x: Player 1 wins point, y: Player 2 wins point]

Player 1 wins in five rounds if we get: yxxxx, xyxxx, xxyxx, xxxyx.

(Note the case of xxxxy would lead to player 1 winning in 4 rounds, which the question forbids.)

Each of these have a probability of p⁴(1-p). Thus, the solution is 4p⁴(1-p).

Question 343: F

$4x + 7 + 18x + 20 = 14$

$22x + 27 = 14$

Thus, $22x = -13$

Giving $x = -\dfrac{13}{22}$

Question 344: D

$r^3 = \dfrac{3V}{4\pi}$

Thus, $r = \left(\dfrac{3V}{4\pi}\right)^{1/3}$

Therefore, $S = 4\pi\left[\left(\dfrac{3V}{4\pi}\right)^{\frac{1}{3}}\right]^2 = 4\pi\left(\dfrac{3V}{4\pi}\right)^{\frac{2}{3}}$

$= \dfrac{4\pi(3V)^{\frac{2}{3}}}{(4\pi)^{\frac{2}{3}}} = (3V)^{\frac{2}{3}} \times \dfrac{(4\pi)^1}{(4\pi)^{\frac{2}{3}}}$

$= (3V)^{\frac{2}{3}}(4\pi)^{1-\frac{2}{3}} = (4\pi)^{\frac{1}{3}}(3V)^{\frac{2}{3}}$

Question 345: A

Let each unit length be x.

Thus, $S = 6x^2$. Therefore, $x = \left(\dfrac{S}{6}\right)^{\frac{1}{2}}$

$V = x^3$. Thus, $V = \left[\left(\dfrac{S}{6}\right)^{\frac{1}{2}}\right]^3$ so $V = \left(\dfrac{S}{6}\right)^{\frac{3}{2}}$

Question 346: B

Multiplying the second equation by 2 we get 4x + 16y = 24. Subtracting the first equation from this we get 13y = 17, so $y = \dfrac{17}{13}$. Then solving for x we get $x = \dfrac{10}{13}$. You could also try substituting possible solutions one by one, although given that the equations are both linear and contain easy numbers, it is quicker to solve them algebraically.

Question 347: A

Multiply by the denominator to give: $(7x + 10) = (3y^2 + 2)(9x + 5)$

Partially expand brackets on right side: $(7x + 10) = 9x(3y^2 + 2) + 5(3y^2 + 2)$

Take x terms across to left side: $7x - 9x(3y^2 + 2) = 5(3y^2 + 2) - 10$

Take x outside the brackets: $x[7 - 9(3y^2 + 2)] = 5(3y^2 + 2) - 10$

Thus: $x = \dfrac{5(3y^2 + 2) - 10}{7 - 9(3y^2 + 2)}$

Simplify to give: $x = \dfrac{(15y^2)}{(7 - 9(3y^2 + 2))}$

Question 348: F

$$3x\left(\frac{3x^7}{x^{\frac{1}{3}}}\right)^3 = 3x\left(\frac{3^3 x^{21}}{x^{\frac{3}{3}}}\right)$$

$$= 3x\frac{27x^{21}}{x} = 81x^{21}$$

Question 349: D

$$2x[2^{\frac{7}{14}} x^{\frac{7}{14}}] = 2x[2^{\frac{1}{2}} x^{\frac{1}{2}}]$$

$$= 2x(\sqrt{2}\sqrt{x}) = 2[\sqrt{x}\sqrt{x}][\sqrt{2}\sqrt{x}]$$

$$= 2\sqrt{2x^3}$$

Question 350: A

$A = \pi r^2$, therefore $10\pi = \pi r^2$

Thus, $r = \sqrt{10}$

Therefore, the circumference is $2\pi\sqrt{10}$

Question 351: D

$3.4 = 12 + (3 + 4) = 19$

$19.5 = 95 + (19 + 5) = 119$

Question 352: D

$2.3 = \frac{2^3}{2} = 4$

$4.2 = \frac{4^2}{4} = 4$

Question 353: F

This is a tricky question that requires you to know how to 'complete the square':

$(x + 1.5)(x + 1.5) = x^2 + 3x + 2.25$

Thus, $(x + 1.5)^2 - 7.25 = x^2 + 3x - 5 = 0$

Therefore, $(x + 1.5)^2 = 7.25 = \frac{29}{4}$

Thus, $x + 1.5 = \sqrt{\frac{29}{4}}$

Thus $x = -\frac{3}{2} \pm \sqrt{\frac{29}{4}} = -\frac{3}{2} \pm \frac{\sqrt{29}}{2}$

Question 354: B

Whilst you definitely need to solve this graphically, it is necessary to complete the square for the first equation to allow you to draw it more easily:

$(x + 2)^2 = x^2 + 4x + 4$

Thus, $y = (x + 2)^2 + 10 = x^2 + 4x + 14$

This is now an easy curve to draw (y = x² that has moved 2 units left and 10 units up). The turning point of this quadratic is to the left and well above anything in x³, so the only solution is the first intersection of the two curves in the upper right quadrant around (3.4, 39).

Question 355: C

By far the easiest way to solve this is to sketch them (don't waste time solving them algebraically). As soon as you've done this, it'll be very obvious that y = 2 and y = 1-x² don't intersect, since the latter has its turning point at (0, 1) and zero points at x = -1 and 1. y = x and y = x² intersect at the origin and (1, 1), and y = 2 runs through both.

Question 356: B

Notice that you're not required to get the actual values – just the number's magnitude. Thus, 897653 can be approximated to 900,000 and 0.009764 to 0.01. Therefore, 900,000 x 0.01 = 9,000

Question 357: C

Multiply through by 70: $7(7x + 3) + 10(3x + 1) = 14 \times 70$

Simplify: $49x + 21 + 30x + 10 = 980$

$79x + 31 = 980$

$x = \dfrac{949}{79}$

Question 358: A

Split the equilateral triangle into 2 right-angled triangles and apply Pythagoras' theorem:

$x^2 = \left(\dfrac{x}{2}\right)^2 + h^2$ $h^2 = \dfrac{3}{4}x^2$. Thus

$h = \sqrt{\dfrac{3x^2}{4}} = \dfrac{\sqrt{3x^2}}{2}$

The area of a triangle = ½ x base x height = $\dfrac{1}{2}x \cdot \dfrac{\sqrt{3x^2}}{2}$

Simplifying gives: $x \cdot \dfrac{\sqrt{3x^2}}{4} = x \cdot \dfrac{\sqrt{3}\sqrt{x^2}}{4} = \dfrac{x^2\sqrt{3}}{4}$

Question 359: A

This is a question testing your ability to spot 'the difference between two squares'.

Factorise to give: $3 - \dfrac{7x(5x - 1)(5x + 1)}{(7x)^2(5x + 1)}$

Cancel out: $3 - \dfrac{(5x - 1)}{7x}$

Question 360: C

The easiest way to do this is to 'complete the square':

$(x-5)^2 = x^2 - 10x + 25$

Thus, $(x-5)^2 - 125 = x^2 - 10x - 100 = 0$

Therefore, $(x-5)^2 = 125$

$x - 5 = \pm\sqrt{125} = \pm\sqrt{25}\sqrt{5} = \pm 5\sqrt{5}$

$x = 5 \pm 5\sqrt{5}$

Question 361: B

Factorise by completing the square:

$x^2 - 4x + 7 = (x-2)^2 + 3$

Simplify: $(x-2)^2 = y^3 + 2 - 3$

$x - 2 = \pm\sqrt{y^3 - 1}$

$x = 2 \pm \sqrt{y^3 - 1}$

Question 362: D

Square both sides to give: $(3x+2)^2 = 7x^2 + 2x + y$

Thus: $y = (3x+2)^2 - 7x^2 - 2x = (9x^2 + 12x + 4) - 7x^2 - 2x$

$y = 2x^2 + 10x + 4$

Question 363: C

This is a fourth order polynomial, which you aren't expected to be able to factorise at GCSE. This is where looking at the options makes your life a lot easier. In all of them, opening the bracket on the right side involves making $(y \pm 1)^4$ on the left side, i.e. the answers are hinting that $(y \pm 1)^4$ is the solution to the fourth order polynomial.

Since there are negative terms in the equations (e.g. $-4y^3$), the solution has to be:

$(y-1)^4 = y^4 - 4y^3 + 6y^2 - 4y + 1$

Therefore, $(y-1)^4 + 1 = x^5 + 7$

Thus, $y - 1 = (x^5 + 6)^{\frac{1}{4}}$

$y = 1 + (x^5 + 6)^{1/4}$

Question 364: A

Let the width of the television be 4x and the height of the television be 3x.

Then by Pythagoras: $(4x)^2 + (3x)^2 = 50^2$

Simplify: $25x^2 = 2500$

Thus: $x = 10$. Therefore: the screen is 30 inches by 40 inches, i.e. the area is 1,200 inches².

Question 365: C

Square both sides to give: $1 + \dfrac{3}{x^2} = (y^5 + 1)^2$

Multiply out: $\dfrac{3}{x^2} = (y^{10} + 2y^5 + 1) - 1$

Thus: $x^2 = \dfrac{3}{y^{10} + 2y^5}$

Therefore: $x = \sqrt{\dfrac{3}{y^{10} + 2y^5}}$

Question 366: C

The easiest way is to double the first equation and triple the second to get:

$6x - 10y = 20 \text{ and } 6x + 6y = 39$.

Subtract the first from the second to give: $16y = 19$,

Therefore, $y = \dfrac{19}{16}$.

Substitute back into the first equation to give $x = \dfrac{85}{16}$.

Question 367: C

This is fairly straightforward; the first inequality is the easier one to work with: B and D and E violate it, so we just need to check A and C in the second inequality.

C: $1^3 - 2^2 < 3$, but A: $2^3 - 1^2 > 3$

Question 368: B

Whilst this can be done graphically, it's quicker to do algebraically (because the second equation is not as easy to sketch). Intersections occur where the curves have the same coordinates.

Thus: $x + 4 = 4x^2 + 5x + 5$

Simplify: $4x^2 + 4x + 1 = 0$

Factorise: $(2x + 1)(2x + 1) = 0$

Thus, the two graphs only intersect once at $x = -\dfrac{1}{2}$

Question 369: D

It's better to do this algebraically as the equations are easy to work with and you would need to sketch very accurately to get the answer. Intersections occur where the curves have the same coordinates. Thus: $x^3 = x$

$x^3 - x = 0$

Thus: $x(x^2 - 1) = 0$

Spot the 'difference between two squares': $x(x + 1)(x - 1) = 0$

Thus there are 3 intersections: at $x = 0, 1 \text{ and } -1$

Question 370: E

Note that the line is the hypotenuse of a right angled triangle with one side unit length and one side of length ½.

By Pythagoras, $\left(\frac{1}{2}\right)^2 + 1^2 = x^2$

Thus, $x^2 = \frac{1}{4} + 1 = \frac{5}{4}$

$x = \sqrt{\frac{5}{4}} = \frac{\sqrt{5}}{\sqrt{4}} = \frac{\sqrt{5}}{2}$

Question 371: D

We can eliminate z from equation (1) and (2) by multiplying equation (1) by 3 and adding it to equation (2):

$3x + 3y - 3z = -3$	Equation (1) multiplied by 3
$2x - 2y + 3z = 8$	Equation (2) then add both equations
$5x + y = 5$	We label this as equation (4)

Now we must eliminate the same variable z from another pair of equations by using equation (1) and (3):

$2x + 2y - 2z = -2$	Equation (1) multiplied by 2
$2x - y + 2z = 9$	Equation (3) then add both equations
$4x + y = 7$	We label this as equation (5)

We now use both equations (4) and (5) to obtain the value of x:

$5x + y = 5$	Equation (4)
$-4x - y = -7$	Equation (5) multiplied by -1
$x = -2$	

Substitute x back in to calculate y:

4x + y = 7

4(-2) + y = 7

- 8 + y = 7

y = 15

Substitute x and y back in to calculate z:

x + y – z = -1

-2 + 15 – z = -1

13 – z = -1

-z = -14

z = 14

Thus: x = -2, y = 15, z = 14

Question 372: D

This is one of the easier maths questions. Take 3a as a factor to give:

$3a(a^2 - 10a + 25) = 3a(a - 5)(a - 5) = 3a(a - 5)^2$

Question 373: B

Note that 12 is the Lowest Common Multiple of 3 and 4. Thus:

-3 (4x + 3y) = -3 (48)   Multiply each side by -3

 4 (3x + 2y) = 4 (34)   Multiply each side by 4

-12x – 9y = -144

<u>12x + 8y = 136</u>   Add together

   -y = -8

   y = 8

Substitute y back in:

4x + 3y = 48

4x + 3(8) = 48

4x + 24 = 48

4x = 24

x = 6

Question 374: E

Don't be fooled, this is an easy question, just obey BODMAS and don't skip steps.

$$\frac{-(25-28)^2}{-36+14} = \frac{-(-3)^2}{-22}$$

This gives: $\frac{-(9)}{-22} = \frac{9}{22}$

Question 375: E

Since there are 26 possible letters for each of the 3 letters in the license plate, and there are 10 possible numbers (0-9) for each of the 3 numbers in the same plate, then the number of license plates would be:

$(26) \times (26) \times (26) \times (10) \times (10) \times (10) = 17,576,000$

Question 376: B

Expand the brackets to give: $4x^2 - 12x + 9 = 0$.

Factorise: $(2x - 3)(2x - 3) = 0$.

Thus, only one solution exists, x = 1.5.

Note that you could also use the fact that the discriminant, $b^2 - 4ac = 0$ to get the answer.

Question 377: C

$$= \left(x^{\frac{1}{2}}\right)^{\frac{1}{2}} \left(y^{-3}\right)^{\frac{1}{2}}$$

$$= x^{\frac{1}{4}} y^{-\frac{3}{2}} = \frac{x^{\frac{1}{4}}}{y^{\frac{3}{2}}}$$

Question 378: A

Let x, y, and z represent the rent for the 1-bedroom, 2-bedroom, and 3-bedroom flats, respectively. We can write 3 different equations: 1 for the rent, 1 for the repairs, and the last one for the statement that the 3-bedroom unit costs twice as much as the 1-bedroom unit.

(1) x + y + z = 1240

(2) 0.1x + 0.2y + 0.3z = 276

(3) z = 2x

Substitute z = 2x in both of the two other equations to eliminate z:

(4) x + y + 2x = 3x + y = 1240

(5) 0.1x + 0.2y + 0.3(2x) = 0.7x + 0.2y = 276

-2(3x + y) = -2(1240)	Multiply each side of (4) by -2
10(0.7x + 0.2y) = 10(276)	Multiply each side of (5) by 10
(6) -6x -2y = -2480	Add these 2 equations
(7) 7x + 2y = 2760	
x = 280	
z = 2(280) = 560	Because z = 2x
280 + y + 560 = 1240	Because x + y + z = 1240
y = 400	

Thus the units rent for £ 280, £ 400, £ 560 per week respectively.

Question 379: C

Following BODMAS:

$$= 5\left[5(6^2 - 5 \times 3) + 400^{\frac{1}{2}}\right]^{1/3} + 7$$

$$= 5\left[5(36 - 15) + 20\right]^{\frac{1}{3}} + 7$$

$$= 5\left[5(21) + 20\right]^{\frac{1}{3}} + 7$$

$$= 5(105 + 20)^{\frac{1}{3}} + 7$$

$$= 5(125)^{\frac{1}{3}} + 7$$

$$= 5(5) + 7$$

$$= 25 + 7 = 32$$

Question 380: B

Consider a triangle formed by joining the centre to two adjacent vertices. Six similar triangles can be made around the centre – thus, the central angle is 60 degrees. Since the two lines forming the triangle are of equal length, we have 6 identical equilateral triangles in the hexagon.

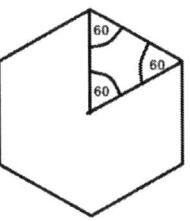

Now split the triangle in half and apply Pythagoras' theorem:

$1^2 = 0.5^2 + h^2$

Thus, $h = \sqrt{\frac{3}{4}} = \frac{\sqrt{3}}{2}$

Thus, the area of the triangle is: $\frac{1}{2}bh = \frac{1}{2} \times 1 \times \frac{\sqrt{3}}{2} = \frac{\sqrt{3}}{4}$

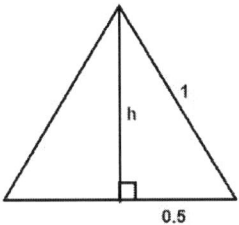

Therefore, the area of the hexagon is: $\frac{\sqrt{3}}{4} \times 6 = \frac{3\sqrt{3}}{2}$

Question 381: B

Let x be the width and x+19 be the length.

Thus, the area of a rectangle is $x(x + 19) = 780$.

Therefore:

$x^2 + 19x - 780 = 0$

$(x - 20)(x + 39) = 0$

$x - 20 = 0$ or $x + 39 = 0$

$x = 20$ or $x = -39$

Since length can never be a negative number, we disregard x = -39 and use x = 20 instead.

Thus, the width is 20 metres and the length is 39 metres.

Question 382: B

The quickest way to solve is by trial and error, substituting the provided options. However, if you're keen to do this algebraically, you can do the following:

Start by setting up the equations: Perimeter = 2L + 2W = 34

Thus: L + W = 17

Using Pythagoras: $L^2 + W^2 = 13^2$

Since L + W = 17, W = 17 - L

Therefore: $L^2 + (17 - L)^2 = 169$

$L^2 + 289 - 34L + L^2 = 169$

$2L^2 - 34L + 120 = 0$

$L^2 - 17L + 60 = 0$

$(L - 5)(L - 12) = 0$

Thus: L = 5 and L = 12

And: W = 12 and W = 5

Question 383: C

Multiply both sides by 8:	$4(3x - 5) + 2(x + 5) = 8(x + 1)$
Remove brackets:	$12x - 20 + 2x + 10 = 8x + 8$
Simplify:	$14x - 10 = 8x + 8$
Add 10:	$14x = 8x + 18$
Subtract 8x:	$6x = 18$
Therefore:	$x = 3$

Question 384: C

Recognise that 1.742 x 3 is 5.226. Now, the original equation simplifies to: $= \dfrac{3 \times 10^6 + 3 \times 10^5}{10^{10}}$

$= 3 \times 10^{-4} + 3 \times 10^{-5} = 3.3 \times 10^{-4}$

Question 385: A

$Area = \dfrac{(2 + \sqrt{2})(4 - \sqrt{2})}{2}$

$= \dfrac{8 - 2\sqrt{2} + 4\sqrt{2} - 2}{2}$

$= \dfrac{6 + 2\sqrt{2}}{2}$

$= 3 + \sqrt{2}$

Question 386: C

Square both sides: $\frac{4}{x} + 9 = (y-2)^2$

$\frac{4}{x} = (y-2)^2 - 9$

Cross Multiply: $\frac{x}{4} = \frac{1}{(y-2)^2 - 9}$

$x = \frac{4}{y^2 - 4y + 4 - 9}$

Factorise: $x = \frac{4}{y^2 - 4y - 5}$

$x = \frac{4}{(y+1)(y-5)}$

Question 387: D

Set up the equation: $5x - 5 = 0.5(6x + 2)$

$10x - 10 = 6x + 2$

$4x = 12$

$x = 3$

Question 388: C

Round numbers appropriately: $\frac{55 + (\frac{9}{4})^2}{\sqrt{900}} = \frac{55 + \frac{81}{16}}{30}$

81 rounds to 80 to give: $\frac{55 + 5}{30} = \frac{60}{30} = 2$

Question 389: D

There are three outcomes from choosing the type of cheese in the crust. For each of the additional toppings to possibly add, there are 2 outcomes: 1 to include and another not to include a certain topping, for each of the 7 toppings

Thus, the number of different kinds of pizza is: $3 \times 2 \times 2 \times 2 \times 2 \times 2 \times 2 \times 2 = 3 \times 2^7$

$= 3 \times 128 = 384$

Question 390: A

Although it is possible to do this algebraically, by far the easiest way is via trial and error. The clue that you shouldn't attempt it algebraically is the fact that rearranging the first equation to make x or y the subject leaves you with a difficult equation to work with (e.g. $x = \sqrt{1 - y^2}$) when you try to substitute in the second.

An exceptionally good student might notice that the equations are symmetric in x and y, i.e. the solution is when $x = y$. Thus $2x^2 = 1$ and $2x = \sqrt{2}$ which gives $\frac{\sqrt{2}}{2}$ as the answer.

Question 391: C

If two shapes are congruent, then they are the same size and shape. Thus, congruent objects can be rotations and mirror images of each other. The two triangles in E are indeed congruent (SAS). Congruent objects must, by definition, have the same angles.

Question 392: B

Rearrange the equation: $x^2 + x - 6 \geq 0$

Factorise: $(x + 3)(x - 2) \geq 0$

Remember that this is a quadratic inequality so requires a quick sketch to ensure you don't make a silly mistake with which way the sign is.

Thus, $y = 0$ when $x = 2$ and $x = -3$. $y > 0$ when $x > 2$ or $x < -3$.

Thus, the solution is: $x \leq -3 \text{ and } x \geq 2$.

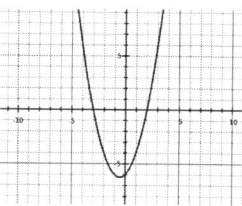

Question 393: B

Using Pythagoras: $a^2 + b^2 = x^2$

Since the triangle is equilateral: $a = b$, so $2a^2 = x^2$

Area $= \frac{1}{2} base \times height = \frac{1}{2}a^2$. From above, $a^2 = \frac{x^2}{2}$

Thus the area $= \frac{1}{2} \cdot \frac{x^2}{2} = \frac{x^2}{4}$

Question 394: A

If X and Y are doubled, the value of Q increases by 4. Halving the value of A reduces this to 2. Finally, tripling the value of B reduces this to ⅔, i.e. the value decreases by ⅓.

Question 395: C

The quickest way to do this is to sketch the curves. This requires you to factorise both equations by completing the square:

$x^2 - 2x + 3 = (x - 1)^2 + 2$

$x^2 - 6x - 10 = (x - 3)^2 - 19$ Thus, the first equation has a turning point at (1, 2) and doesn't cross the x-axis. The second equation has a turning point at (3, -19) and crosses the x-axis twice.

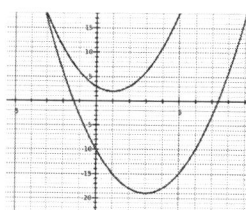

Passage 1

Question 396: B

The opponents said that drug consumption is criminogenic because a drug addiction 'can lead to other crimes'. Option A is incorrect as the passage already states that consuming drugs is in itself a criminal offence. Thus, it would be odd and circular if opponents were to argue this.

Question 397: B

It is close between A and B. In regard to A, the author merely points out a 'contrast', which may not necessarily indicate an inconsistency, whereas the author says, in the context of option B in the passage that there is 'incoherence', which clearly means there is an inconsistency. Therefore, the author *presented* B as being paradoxical.

Question 398: E

The entire article is based on the idea of controlled drugs being legalised. Each sub-argument provides an intermediate conclusion from which the main argument is inferred.

Question 399: C

The author does not argue that drug consumption would fall (as distinct from highlighting that it fell for one age group in Portugal) or increase, so A and B are incorrect. The author implied that drug consumption should be seen as a *present* public health problem in the passage – not that it would be a health concern once drugs were legalised so E is wrong. D is not a practical effect which the author believes would happen. C is explicitly stated in the passage.

Question 400: A

The author has based his argument on the fact that there aren't third party effects to taking drugs (e.g. no third party health effects & that the fact of criminalising increases secondary offences). However, if drug consumption increases one's propensity for violence, it contradicts that argument.

Passage 2

Question 401: D

The passage attacks a generalisation and shows an example that refutes one given to the 'musical' genre. Nothing is mentioned of Sondheim's talents, or what his role was in creating the musical, nor are there claims made in relation to Wheeler's literary tastes (he may just like ONE penny dreadful). This musical may deal with morbid themes, but that's not to say that most do - it could be only a select few that do.

Question 402: A

The pies make the crimes 'culinary' in nature, the mention of revenge shows Todd's illegal acts to be 'vengeful', the word 'macbre' indicates it's disturbing and the judge's rape is a 'sexual' crime. There is nothing explicitly suggesting the crimes of any party are funny, or to be considered funny.

Question 403: D

This option is essentially synonymous in the quoted belief, 'we all deserve to die', which includes both bad and good people and makes no significant reference to gender exclusion/inclusion.

Question 404: C

There are four mentioned themes, but that does not mean there are only four themes, nor does 'legal corruption' get named as the central theme. As the entirety of Sweeney Todd is not discussed in the passage, only a central plot line, one could not exclude the potential of something positive happening in the play - even a minor incident. Sadness in itself, therefore, cannot be considered the focus of the play. The themes mentioned are, however, indeed macabre.

Question 405: E

Though the original title 'A String of Pearls: A Romance' may appear to suggest a romantic relationship within the narrative, nothing in the passage states the two are a couple so A is incorrect. The passage only suggested that *some* of the songs were removed, not all of the songs, so B is incorrect. We can't be sure about D as the passage does not refer to the critical acclaim of the film. In regard to C, while some changes were made to the film, we aren't told whether the main storyline changes. Finally, E is explicitly stated in the passage, so that must be true.

Passage 3

Question 406: B

This is mentioned as an impact on the country in the passage and not mentioned as having a personal impact, whereas all others are mentioned as personal impacts. Also, as is evident from the term itself, an increase in government spending affects the government. The focus of the point was on the government's spending (rather than on any welfare benefits derived).

Question 407: E

This option is explicitly stated in the passage.

Question 408: C

This is implied as the author states the numerous benefits of high-quality education provision but also notes how 'more emphasis' should be placed on it. Crucially, it says that vocational education is 'second rate' and that it must change. A clear implication of these sentences is that more should be done to encourage vocational courses. E is already stated in the passage (as the author highlights the negative consequences). The author also explicitly states A, B, and D. Therefore, since they are all stated in the passage, they are incorrect.

Question 409: A

While the author does argue for B, it is only part of the main argument and is in the context of increasing high-quality vocational provision for young people. The skills shortage was used more as a reason to argue for A. Given the emphasis on raising vocational education, it is clear that A is the correct answer. The author does not argue for C and actually points out that the jobs are already there, it's just that young people need to be trained more. D was not argued for and E was an assertion (and, thus, not an argument, let alone a main argument).

Question 410: C

This is explicitly stated in the passage. A is not stated in the passage. While Dulux was increasing young people's skills, the author did not advocate this for businesses generally and, thus, B is incorrect. The author suggested that D and E should be done by the government, rather than by businesses.

Passage 4

Question 411: A
B, C, and D are all stated as influences in the passage but option A is stated as underlying all those reasons and thus, A is the 'ultimate' influence.

Question 412: C
The passage mentions that a son was required to secure the Tudor dynasty. Therefore, there is something familial relating to all of this. Therefore, B and E are incorrect. D doesn't follow from the sentence so it has to be either A or C. A doesn't make sense in this context as it's not clear how having a son would secure his family but C fits in well.

Question 413: C
Royal Supremacy was merely the process of getting control over the church and was not a reason for getting a son (it was the means to getting the son) so A is wrong. B is incorrect as it should be the other way round – he wanted to divorce Catherine to get a son (and not get a son to divorce Catherine). C fits in with the passage and, thus, is correct.

Question 414: E
A and D were stated in the passage, so are incorrect. Even if B and C were true, they would not weaken any of the conclusions, so they are not correct. However, E is correct as if he believed that he could get a divorce from Rome, he would have tried to get that as it was the 'straightforward' option. The author also stated that without Henry's desire for a break from Rome, it wouldn't have happened. Therefore, point E would be a necessary assumption to support the author's points.

Question 415: C
The passage never suggests that the Act of Supremacy is the royal supremacy, so E is incorrect. The passage states that the Royal Supremacy was established once Henry became the only head of the church, so C is, thus, correct as it means the King had become the leader of the church. D is, therefore, obviously incorrect as the Pope isn't the head of the English church. B is too vague and while option A had to occur for the Royal Supremacy to take place, the passage pointed out that C was, in fact, the royal supremacy.

Passage 5

Question 416: D
The passage explicitly states that charities may not need to pay corporation tax. A is not true based on the passage – as you can provide a public benefit but have not registered to be a charity. It is only after registration as a charity that an institution gets the fiscal benefits; this does not happen automatically. B and C are not proved in the passage, and E is an opinion, which can't be true or false. In regard to C specifically, it cannot be assumed that just because event X is required for event Y to occur that if Y does not occur, X does not occur – in the context of the passage, you can still provide a public benefit and not be a charity. Therefore, C is incorrect.

Question 417: C
The passage explicitly states that it's "necessary" for an institution to demonstrate that its purposes are for the public benefit.

Question 418: D
Both C and E are easily eliminated as neither of these institutions were part of the trial, which is where the argument was advanced. We're told that tribunal judges didn't consider the argument and it is, thus, clear by implication that they didn't bring it forward (therefore, B is incorrect), so we're left with either A or D. It's not A as the argument weakens their position (being independent schools) so it's unlikely they would advance it. By elimination, therefore, it must be the Education Review Group, D.

Question 419: D

Whether the law should or should not allow a free-for-all is not a point that can be tested – it is a person's opinion and cannot be true or false. All the other options can be tested.

Question 420: B

In the passage, it is stated that the tribunal said that children who couldn't afford the fees of private schools must benefit from them for there to be a 'public benefit'. Accordingly, providing scholarships to others who can't afford the fees would help with this. A is insufficient to meet the tribunal's definition. C, D, and E do not support the argument that there's a public benefit.

Passage 6

Question 421: B

Amazon is more powerful. The author said that one is more powerful than the other at the beginning of the passage and it later becomes clear that Amazon is more powerful as they were able to restrict the sales of Hatchette's books in negotiations, thus, indicating a stronger bargaining position.

Question 422: B

There is irony because Hatchette have done aggressive things, just like Amazon have and yet, they are now complaining about Amazon.

Question 423: E

This option draws all of the points expressed in the passage together. Even though Amazon engaged in aggressive tactics, others have done it too and Amazon have done beneficial things. It gets to the heart of the passage, which is considering the actions of Amazon.

Question 424: C

The word 'monstrous' implies not only that there is a big task, but that the task is too big as the word implies some dissatisfaction with all the work that authors have to do.

Question 425: C

If Hachette had offered the same services as Amazon had, it would directly contradict what the author has said – Amazon's services wouldn't be an 'innovation', Hachette (one of the 'big publishers') would not have been acting unfairly in the past and Hachette would have been acting to the benefit of small authors: this would all be contrary to the author's points in the final paragraph; therefore, point C most undermines the author's argument.

Question 426: C

The author has been positive about what Amazon has done throughout the article. Therefore, the author would most likely disagree with the suggestion that Amazon has abused their market position. The author has acknowledged A, B, and E in the article. The author isn't likely to agree with D because Hachette had engaged in a conspiracy.

Passage 7

Question 427: B

The answer here is between A and B, both undermine the author's argument that the court system limits access to justice. B *most* undermines the author's argument because if these cases are normally settled out of court, the court system's high cost does not limit access to justice as people would already be getting justice, albeit outside the court system. Option A doesn't undermine it as much because it just says that there are different options for small claimants, whereas B directly cuts at the option. C, D, and E don't necessarily undermine the author's argument.

Question 428: E

This question necessitates being able to deduce the correct information from the passage and shows whether you've understood the passage. 1 hour of legal advice is £200 and the court fee for each is £35. Therefore, the cost for each side is £235. Therefore, the cost for both sides together is £470. As the passage stated that the losing side pays the winning side's costs (as well as their own), the losing side would have to pay a total of £470.

Question 429: D

This is a statement that cannot be tested as true or false and is a normative statement. Therefore, it is an opinion.

Question 430: D

A and B are true but they are explicitly stated in the passage, so are incorrect (the question explicitly asks for an option which is *not stated*). Neither C nor E can be implied. The passage states that the TV show 'resembles' a courtroom, thereby implying that it is not actually a real courtroom but some kind of mock courtroom that looks similar.

Question 431: B

Despite discussing the Judge Rinder show, the author never advances an argument that an online court should be modelled on it – just that the TV show shows that lawyers aren't needed.

Question 432: A

B doesn't even relate to whether the justice system is inefficient or not, so that's incorrect. Again, D and E don't relate to whether the *current* justice system is efficient. On the other hand, option A points out that the author has only referred to a subset of claims (i.e. small claims) and not considered the justice system generally. In particular, no reference was made to the criminal justice system. It doesn't follow that just because one part of it is inefficient, that the rest of it is inefficient. Therefore, A is correct as it highlights why that argument was weak.

Passage 8

Question 433: E

The author made the analogy in order to demonstrate that even though the driverless car may seem strange, people will still adapt to it. Therefore, E is correct. A is wrong as the author only says that at the first part of the analogy. C doesn't necessarily follow. While D is, in essence, what the author is saying, he's applied it to driverless cars. Therefore, his *main* point is that the public will adapt to the driverless car. Since the author was not arguing that the public *should* take up the driverless car with the analogy, B is incorrect.

Question 434: A

The assumption made is that people adapt to new things.

Question 435: E

The Top Gear test doesn't suggest any of A, B, C or D in respect of the use of autonomous cars *on roads*. A, B, C are obviously not demonstrated by the passage. D is not relevant to the question and would be a generalisation as well.

Question 436: A

Throughout, the author describes different aspects of the take-up of driverless cars by car companies and governments and only considers the benefits of it to drivers in the final paragraph. The author does not point out arguments for and against, so E is incorrect. Indeed, the author's view is that the public will want to drive such a car, but this does not underlie the entire piece, so C is incorrect. The same is true with option B. Again, while D is true, it is not the underlying theme of the article.

Question 437: C

E is incorrect as it doesn't relate to the author's main argument in the final paragraph – indeed, the author even acknowledged point E in respect of luxury cars. In regard to B and D, which relate to how cars are currently (B) or the current views on it (D), the author argues that there will be an uptake of it *in the future*. B and D just relate to the present and, thus, don't undermine the author's argument. If C were true, though, this would undermine the author's argument as the public may not take it up in that case. A doesn't necessarily show that people won't take up driverless cars. Therefore, A is incorrect.

Passage 9

Question 438: B

The Society suggest that one's autonomy involves a condition to act ethically and, therefore, if one restricts euthanasia/assisted suicide (an intentional killing), it wouldn't infringe autonomy. Hence, it is assumed that euthanasia/assisted suicide is unethical so that one is not infringing another's autonomy by restricting the unethical act. Looking at it from the reverse view – if we said that an intentional killing is ethical, the conclusion above wouldn't necessarily follow from the premises.

C and E are not necessarily assumed in the argument – i.e. the argument would hold even if they are untrue. Again, in contrast to A and D, the Society actually states that acting ethically is a part of being autonomous. Therefore, it does not infringe autonomy to stop an unethical act. Hence, A and D are incorrect.

Question 439: B

A clear difference, as stated in the first paragraph, between assisted suicide/euthanasia and suicide is that the former options involve a third party, whereas the latter only involves one person. The Society just argued that euthanasia/assisted suicide should be restricted and not necessarily suicide in itself. While D is true, it does not explain the gap in the logic (which is what the question is asking for). C and E are irrelevant as the author suggested the Society argued that suicide *should* be illegal, which is suggesting an opinion, so it's not relevant that it's in fact currently legal.

Question 440: A

It's implicit that assisted suicide and euthanasia should not be allowed – the society already assumed that it's unethical and said not allowing it wouldn't restrict one's autonomy. B is an assumed assertion, but not an implied *argument*. C and D are incorrect as the Society isn't considering what the current state of the law is. E is incorrect as it did not follow that the Society made this and the author explicitly suggested this.

Question 441: B

This is a question asking for a factual response. The author has pointed out that the court has given more weight to non-maleficence and, thus, that clearly has priority. Although the arguments initially suggest the author may be in favour of autonomy, the question is not asking what the author's opinions are, but which principle, in fact, has priority. C and D are wrong as they're not principles in this context and E is wrong as it has already been shown that non-maleficence has priority.

Question 442: A

In the final paragraph, the case of Miss B was explained on the basis that the doctors were not actually harming the patient, which satisfies the definition of non-maleficence given in the passage. The author also states that non-maleficence was given a significant weighting in the case. B, C, D, and E may well have been relevant to the court's decision but the author only referred to A when discussing the case of Miss B.

Passage 10

Question 443: C

The author never suggested that the IMF should be replaced throughout the passage.

Question 444: E
Benefits of giving the loan to Ireland was explicitly stated.

Question 445: C
Some of the other options were indeed factors in the Greek debt crisis but those other factors were, according to the author, caused by the government spending more money than what it had.

Question 446: B
The author would not agree with the view that the IMF have *only* been beneficial in the world because of the issues the author has stated that they've caused. D and E follow directly from the passage, so the author would agree with those. Given the issues of the IMF in the past, the author would likely agree with A. Even though the author didn't explicitly suggest C in the passage, he is less likely to agree with B compared to C because there have been issues with the IMF, so it is more plausible to agree with C, when compared to B (in particular because B directly contradicts the passage, whereas C does not).

Question 447: A
Incompetence suggests that something was not done *as it should have been done* – accordingly, option A fits in well with the passage and more so than options B and C. Although point E was stated in the passage, it was mentioned in a different context. D is explicitly pointed out, so is incorrect.

Passage 11

Question 448: B
This was not explicitly stated but is quite clearly true as the passage states that since 1953, a UK citizen could take the UK government to the European Court.

Question 449: D
In the third paragraph, the author explicitly stated that UK citizens could sue from 2000 onwards, when the Human Rights Act came into force. While the ECHR was in force since 1950, the author never said that UK citizens could sue in domestic courts then. It was only after the UK Human Rights Act was passed that, as the author said, they could sue in domestic courts.

Question 450: D
The author makes an argument in the final paragraph, citing examples of 'positive cases' and argues that they're some of the examples of the Convention giving rights to people. Therefore, a clear argument is that the Convention is benefiting UK citizens. The author doesn't argue for A and takes the opposite position to B and C. While E is true, it is merely an assertion as opposed to an argument.

Question 451: A
C and E are clearly incorrect as they aren't stated or implied at all in the passage. D was a reason for the European Court of Human Right's decision to block the deportation but the UK still wanted to deport Qatada – they just couldn't do so legally – it was the European Court that blocked the deportation and thus, A is the correct answer.

Question 452: D
The author makes the point that the benefits of the Convention outweigh the negatives as it is pointed out that there are more positive cases than negative cases. The author acknowledges that there are sometimes bad outcomes (so B is incorrect) but that the good ones outweigh this.

Question 453: A

In the final paragraph, the author was suggesting that being a signatory to the ECHR was beneficial to the UK (as there are many more 'good' cases). Accordingly, B doesn't follow. While the author may agree with D or E, they would be inconsistent as a *main* conclusion given that the author's primary contention was that there are many more positive aspects of the system than the negative and doesn't touch on altering it (so C is incorrect).

Passage 12

Question 454: B

C is incorrect as there's no mention or implication of an organisation (and it's not a literary technique), D is incorrect as no irony (when what *appears* to be the case is not *actually* the case) is present and the author does draw a similarity between anything so E isn't correct. The author does not suggest that the invisible hand was 'like' anything, so it can't be a simile (A is incorrect). It is in fact a metaphor, option B.

Question 455: C

A is wrong as while employees are stakeholders, it was stated in the passage (and the question related to an unstated implication). People generally are not stakeholders – the passage defined stakeholders as only those who are significantly affected by a business' decision. Again, this was not implicitly suggested in the passage, so B is incorrect. Neither D nor E is implied either. Shareholders are a stakeholder that is implicitly mentioned in the passage. In paragraph 5, the author discusses moving call centres abroad when considering the impact of business decisions on 'stakeholders'. The author says that the increase in profits benefits shareholders. As shareholders are significantly affected by this (in getting more profit), they are stakeholders. Further, immediately after the profit point, the author states: "However, it negatively harms other stakeholders"; using the word 'other' also implies that shareholders are stakeholders.

Question 456: D

The author brings up the call centre example to show the effects of it but also to show that it is based on profit maximisation and what the impact of profit maximisation is (i.e. that it can lead to call centres going abroad but it might not, as in the case of BT). The author does not argue for either A, B or C and it is not clear that the author takes a position against moving call centres abroad. Therefore, E is incorrect.

Question 457: D

The author considers throughout that profit maximisation is a relevant objective but that other objectives should also be taken into account and explicitly states this. Accordingly, A and B are incorrect: the author never suggests those points. While C may be broadly true, the author points out that it isn't always beneficial. The author does not argue for or consider point E in much detail.

Question 458: D

As stated in the passage (2nd paragraph), if an individual tries to maximise profits, that will maximise the welfare of society because of the market (or the invisible hand of the market). Accordingly, Smith's view is that profit maximisation maximises the welfare of society. A is in the wrong order (profit maximisation occurs *before* the invisible hand), B and C are wrong because the invisible hand appears to discuss the automatic mechanism of the market and these options do not espouse Smith's ultimate view, which is point D. D more precisely equates with the view in the passage than E, so D is correct.

Passage 13

Question 459: E

A and C are clearly wrong as those groups are harmed. The passage doesn't mention B so that is incorrect. The choice is between D and E, both of whom receive benefits. However, according to the passage, law firms will lose out on fewer oil exploration projects, whereas the consumers have no immediate loss – just the benefit of lower prices. Therefore, E is the correct answer.

Question 460: D

A number of the options are potential reasons but the loss of £4.5 billion was cited as the *immediate* reason in the passage. Low revenues don't necessarily mean a loss is incurred and the passage cites losses as the reason for job cuts generally. Therefore, E is incorrect. Both A and B are factors but not the immediate factors and C just describes the way in which the workers were made unemployed.

Question 461: C

Obviously, to claim unemployment benefits, one cannot have a job. Therefore, it is assumed that those 7,000 individuals would not have a job if they're to seek unemployment benefits. Hence, C is correct. B is not a necessary assumption as the passage just says that the individuals would *seek* unemployment benefits – this does not require that the government actually do have benefits to give. This is a very fine distinction and you're doing very well if you have understood this. Hence, C is a necessary assumption but B is not necessary to support the statement. A, D and E are not relevant as they merely explain or describe the unemployment that has already occurred.

Question 462: C

The first paragraph explicitly attributes the reduction in oil price to the shale boom in the US, which increased supply and ultimately lowered oil prices. A and B are not cited as reasons. E is just a descriptor for the hard times that oil companies are experiencing and not a reason. The whole part of D was not suggested in the passage.

Question 463: E

The author simply points out that the oil companies will go bust if they continue to make losses, which is happening to *some* due to the oil price. Low oil prices are not a reason in and of itself to make redundancies – it is when a company is making a loss that it may need to sack workers.

Passage 14

Question 464: A

All other options are stated in the passage and this is explicitly not true based on the passage – as nuclear power is stated as a non-renewable energy source but the passage also states that it doesn't emit carbon. Therefore, A is correct as not *all* non-renewables emit carbon.

Question 465: D

The author explicitly argues for this at the end of paragraphs one and two. Option A is an assertion and not an argument. B, C and E are plainly not argued for in the passage. The author also appears to disagree with E.

Question 466: C

The author has already argued for a focus on renewable energies and has also expressed concern and doubt as to whether nuclear power is economical given the dangerous waste it produces. Therefore, C is the answer. E is incorrect as the author said that nuclear power is now mostly safe. A and B are not considered. While the author would agree with D, he would be more likely to accede to C as he said at the end of the final paragraph that nuclear power is not economical for the UK.

Question 467: D

This is clearly correct. Earlier in the passage, the author brought up the importance of effective government planning and then the High Court decision showed that the government hadn't undertaken effective planning.

Question 468: C

As the passage highlights the fact that there are issues with fossil fuels emitting carbon, just because a form of energy is cheaper in itself does not mean it will be more beneficial than nuclear power (if the cheaper form pollutes). Therefore, A doesn't necessarily weaken the author's argument based on the passage. B is too vague. While D is true, the author states that there are new safeguards now, so it doesn't necessarily apply in the present day nuclear power stations, so D is incorrect. E is incorrect as all it shows is that the government didn't do enough consideration of waste disposal – i.e. it does not indicate that nuclear power is not or is less beneficial. Either way, option C weakens the government's argument the most as other options may well be more beneficial if C is true.

Passage 15

Question 469: B

Neither A nor D is suggested in the passage. The author does suggest C, but only if B doesn't work. The author explicitly endorsed option B in the passage and believes that this would stimulate the culture change required in the final paragraph. The author did suggest E at the end of the second paragraph, but this only applies to direct wage discrimination, which the passage says does not account for the entirety of the gender pay gap. The author clearly believes that a reporting obligation would be effective to help the gender pay gap and help with direct discrimination (as stated in the final paragraph). Therefore, it is clear that option B is the preferred option of the author.

Question 470: E

The author clearly argues for this at the end of the second paragraph. B, C and D are not argued for. A is stated in the passage as an *assertion* and not an argument.

Question 471: A

In contrasting both a reporting obligation and the mandatory minimum, the author states that the mandatory minimum may not lead to a culture change and may cause resentment whereas the author states that the reporting obligation will lead to a culture change. So it is, thus, clear that this is the reason for the author's choice. D is not relevant here and E is not the main reason why the author preferred the reporting obligation – it was the culture change. The author doesn't suggest in the passage that B or C will occur from choosing the reporting obligation.

Question 472: D

Each of A, B, and C are cited as reasons for differences in the pay between genders. E is not stated as a reason for a difference.

Question 473: E

The high cost is the author's concern. While the author would agree with B, which is not the author's *concern* but merely the way in which the author would *address his concern*. A and D are not argued in the passage.

Passage 16

Question 474: C

"Oddly, even in spite of a weakening currency, the country is nowhere near to having a trade balance". The use of the words 'oddly' and 'in spite' suggest that the opposite should normally be happening. Since the country is nowhere near to having a trade balance, the opposite would be that the country would be nearer to (or have) a trade balance. Therefore, C is the correct answer as that fits in with this idea the most. E is wrong as that is the current position. A and B are wrong as they fit in with the current position as well. D is not suggested in the passage.

Question 475: D

This is explicitly explained in the passage (fourth paragraph – "As long as Britain exports to the rest of the world as much as it imports…").

Question 476: E

In the final paragraph, the author points out that de-industrialisation and a poor skills base are the wider problems linked with being a net importer. Based on the definition within the passage, being a net importer means the country doesn't have a trade balance. Thus, it is clear that the author is saying that de-industrialisation and poor skills are the reasons for the lack of exports (which mean the UK doesn't have a trade balance). B is incorrect as it means the same thing as not having a trade balance – it does not explain why there is no trade balance.

Question 477: A

This is most consistent with the entire passage. The author explicitly states that our import levels would be OK, but we just need to export more. The final paragraph also indicates that the UK's problem is too few exports as opposed to too many imports. Therefore, B is incorrect. C, D, and E do not underlie the entire passage either.

Question 478: E

A, B and C are irrelevant as they are not referred to in the last paragraph. While both D and E are true, an individual would choose the German goods because they're cheaper (as stated in the last paragraph). They wouldn't have a reason to base their choice on the lack of investment in the UK. Therefore, D is incorrect.

Passage 17

Question 479: D

The author explicitly said this is due to concerns about ESPN, a different part of the Disney Company, so D is obviously the correct answer.

Question 480: D

Ultimately, whether something is 'successful' can be a matter of opinion – some cinema goers did not particularly like the film, even though most did. All other options were facts.

Question 481: C

A prediction is, of course, an estimation of a future result. A is wrong as other companies already have produced such products and the author does not argue for D or E. While B is mentioned in the passage, the author did not predict that it would happen – the author simply stated that some analysts said it would happen. Therefore, B is incorrect. On the contrary, the author expressly predicted C in the passage.

Question 482: D

The author talks about how success does 'not stop' at the success of the box office alone but how merchandising has a role to play. Throughout the passage, the author also pointed out how the merchandising was successful. Therefore, D is the correct answer. E does not follow. Although the author asserts that an important part of *most* successful films is merchandising, that does not mean all – therefore, C is incorrect. The author did not argue for either A or B as well.

Question 483: A

This option is definitely false because the fifth paragraph explicitly states that Disney created products. It also said that Disney did not create all of the products themselves, thus implying that they created at least *some* of the products themselves and that others created some of the products.

Passage 18

Question 484: E

The author does not evince a belief as to whether society should adopt same-sex or opposite-sex marriage. The author just argues (by the end) that marriage is a social construct and, arguably, implies that adopting same-sex marriage is a reflection of society. This does not mean that the author argues for same-sex marriage – he could still disagree with society's position. The passage just doesn't refer to his personal view.

Question 485: D

The author explicitly states that the argument of the opponents (in the second paragraph) was circular and only criticises their argument, but does not take a view as to either side of the debate in the process.

Question 486: C

The author was arguing that while marriage was originally a religious construct, it was still a social construct in the 12th Century as much as now. It's just that religion had a greater role in society then.

Question 487: B

The basis for saying that marriage did not require a religious ceremony since 1837 would be that there had to be a religious ceremony before 1837.

Question 488: B

The author states that marriage has continued to evolve, even 'now' to reflect society, thereby suggesting that the recent reform which allowed for same-sex marriage (mentioned at the beginning of the passage), was a reflection of society. It is important in such questions to take a 'global' look at the whole passage while also referring to specific details when required.

Passage 19

Question 489: B

The author argues throughout that sugar should be taxed and considers potential counter-arguments, but rebuts them. E is incorrect because, while the author does consider the pros and cons, the author argues for a sugar tax throughout and thus, C is also incorrect. Indeed, the author does point out that D should be done, but that it should be done as well as a sugar tax and this was an incidental point at the end of the article, rather than underlying the entire article. Although the author does allude to point A, that is not the main point of the article, which is to reduce sugar consumption by a sugar tax – the author just deployed point A to suggest that a sugar tax is fair.

Question 490: E

If people were not to reduce consumption of sugary drinks, it would directly undermine the author's argument because imposing the sugar tax (which would increase prices) would not reduce sugar consumption, which the author highlighted as the reason for imposing the tax in the first place. D does not contradict the argument – it is, in fact, intended that prices would increase. A and C don't undermine the author's argument. While B may be an issue, the author potentially reconciles with this on the basis that those who consume it should bear the consequences of it. Therefore, E is the correct answer.

Question 491: D

This question was limited to the sixth paragraph only. If people don't get health problems from consuming sugar, they're not causing problems for society (i.e. costs to NHS); therefore, it would not be fair to tax them extra given that they aren't causing additional health costs to society. Although the author suggests that people are ignorant of the health consequences, it's not an intrinsic part of the argument that a sugar tax is fair – a sugar tax is meant to be fair (according to the author) because the people who cause the social costs would pay for it. Therefore, E is incorrect. Again, A, B, and C don't take issue with the argument that the people who cause health costs should pay for them. Accordingly, they're incorrect. While B would undermine the author's main argument, it does not undermine the argument he advanced in the sixth paragraph.

Question 492: D

While the passage implies that excess sugar consumption can cause obesity, it does not suggest that all cases of obesity are due to excess sugar consumption. Therefore, we cannot say that option D is true based on the passage. All other options are stated in the passage.

Question 493: A

A is not explicitly stated but is clearly assumed as the link between excess sugar consumption and the health consequences that the author cites (if we said option A was false, then the author's argument would be undermined - option A is a necessary assumption). None of the other options are unstated assumptions.

Question 494: C

The final sentence effectively says that prevention is better than cure, and option C is the only one which illustrates this. E is incorrect because the final sentence does not suggest that anyone is falling.

Passage 20

Question 495: B

Whether something is the 'toughest' sporting challenge is open to debate and can't be tested as being true or false.

Question 496: D

The team leader has the support of his teammates (according to the passage) and, thus, is more likely to win the race compared to if he was just one of the supporting teammates. The team leader also benefits from saving energy. This is also supported by the example stated in the passage, where the leader of Team Sky won in 2012. A, C, and E are incorrect as they don't denote an additional benefit – in particular, A and C are pre-conditions to becoming a team leader. While B is true, it's not correct as it's not necessarily a benefit that the team leader alone gets – in the passage, it was stated that the supporting rider in Team Sky came second in the race (and, by implication, beat all the other team leaders).

Question 497: B

When discussing the slipstreaming effect, the passage explicitly says that this is why cyclists tend to stay together. C is wrong because the passage says that the fact of the cyclists being in a bunch influences team strategy (not the other way round).

Question 498: E

A and B are clearly not implied in the passage. Team Sky's choice was correct for them because their rider won the race. C is stated in the passage ('it would not be possible to say that the result would have been the same') and D does not follow from the passage – the passage never said that the slipstreaming effect would make someone a better rider (just that it's a natural phenomenon that increases one's speed). Therefore, by elimination, E is the only one left. The author seems to believe this based on the fact that the supporting rider did something historic (by coming 2nd) and something 'unheard of' and that the author doubts the result if they were both equals. Hence, E is the correct answer.

Question 499: C

This is the only option that follows from the passage. In the final paragraph, it is explicitly stated that the supporting cyclist used extra energy to help his team leader. As the passage states, helping out a team leader involves keeping the team leader behind the supporting cyclists so that the team leader uses *less* energy – or conversely, the result is that the supporting cyclist may use *more* energy.

Passage 21

Question 500: A

Whether something requires *urgent* attention cannot be tested as true or false and is, therefore, an opinion as opposed to an assertion of fact. B, C, D, and E are all assertions of fact.

Question 501: B

Option A doesn't necessarily follow. The fact that there is a greater proportion of ethnic minorities in prison when compared to their proportion in the population indicates that there's a disproportionate number of ethnic minorities in prison. The government does indeed need to find out about it, but this was explicitly stated in the second paragraph (rather than being implicit) and so was the fact the statistics aren't ideal. Therefore, C and D are incorrect. E does not follow from the statistics so it is incorrect.

Question 502: C

The passage explicitly states that ethnic minorities are more likely to receive longer sentences. The passage doesn't indicate whether there is conscious discrimination, so D is incorrect. Judges don't have discretion for the guilty plea discount and it's not argued that the higher sentences are a breach of the rule of law. Finally, E is incorrect as the passage indicates that socio-economic factors are relevant.

Question 503: B

The passage states that there are a number of factors that judges consider when deciding their sentences and these form part of their discretion when deciding the sentence. The author uses this to explain why there may be different sentences for the same offence so B is the correct option. C and E show specific instances of different sentences but option B explains all the circumstances. Finally, option A does not, according to the author, appear to always explain the differences in sentences, although it sometimes might. Option D does not have an impact on sentencing so is not relevant.

Question 504: C

This option fits in best with the final paragraph and explains the higher number of ethnic minorities in the prison population. A doesn't follow from the paragraph. D doesn't explain the increase in prison population and E is just a policy suggestion (it's not an explanation) so it's not relevant.

Question 505: A

This is implicit in the final paragraph as the author cites researchers who have found that racial stereotypes do exist in the police force. B and C are explicit (and not implicit). While D is noted in the passage, it is not implied in the final paragraph and the author, if anything, would likely argue against point E and there's nothing to imply that in the paragraph, so E is incorrect as well.

Passage 22

Question 506: E

The definition of a tax inversion, according to the passage, is that a company buys another company in a different country (different jurisdiction). Therefore, the two companies have to be in different countries.

Question 507: D

The passage explicitly states that the purpose of a tax inversion is for a company to move its headquarters to get a lower tax rate. Therefore, D is the essential element. A and B are just a means to an end (the end being D). C doesn't necessarily follow (although it may be the aim of the company) as the defining feature and E doesn't follow either.

Question 508: C

Simply, the aim is to lower their tax liability, as stated in the passage.

Question 509: C

A is wrong as that isn't a benefit to society. D doesn't follow and E was not stated in the passage. However, C was explicitly stated as a potential benefit.

Question 510: E

Buffett was explicitly stating the benefits, with the implication being that businesses should pay their taxes. Therefore, C is incorrect as that is explicit. D does not follow (he was saying that there are benefits from *existing* tax rates). Neither A nor B was argued either.

Passage 23

Question 511: A

The third paragraph was saying that the Black Death transformed the position of peasants *because* ('as') they could now move to different manors. Therefore, a 'transformation' necessitates the assumption that the peasants could not move to different manors before the Black Death. Therefore, A is correct. The passage doesn't say that peasants transformed society, so B is incorrect. D is contradicted and E does not follow. While C is not contradicted, it does not fit in with the discussion in the 3rd paragraph.

Question 512: D

The passage refers to the shortage of the workforce when explaining why women's wages increased. None of the other options follow from the explanation.

Question 513: E

Although peasants moved around, that doesn't necessarily mean that they had permission to do so.

Question 514: C

This is a necessary assumption since the author points out that the population started decreasing before the Black Death due to the Great Famine.

Question 515: B

Both views agree on the point that the Black Death had a *role*.

Question 516: A

This would mean that manorial discipline did not weaken and the author's intermediate conclusion would be false.

Passage 24

Question 517: B

The passage explicitly makes the point that legal rights and obligations are lower for a cohabitation than for a marriage. While A may sometimes be true, it doesn't always hold and the passage doesn't argue for this.

Question 518: D

The fourth paragraph explicitly states that the cohabitee wouldn't receive such property "unless it was stated in the will" and the author says it's easy for a cohabiting couple to get round it by creating a will.

Question 519: C

This is the likely argument of the campaigners as their statistic was a 'retort' to the author's point on the infringing couples freedom and the statistic does provide some support (albeit weak) to point C because it shows that a number of couples would consent to the additional legal rights and responsibilities.

Question 520: E

The author expressly disagrees with A and B. C doesn't make sense as the author already stated that it is not a legal concept, so it can't really be banned. The author does not argue for D either. In the final paragraph, though, the author refers to improving the public's understanding, so it is likely that the author would agree with E.

Question 521: D

The author expressly disagrees with giving additional legal rights and responsibilities to cohabiting couples on the basis of absence of consent.

Passage 25

Question 522: B

This naturally fits in the context. Higher costs are not a benefit so point A doesn't make sense. D and E do not easily fit in the sentence either. B makes the most sense as the author is trying to say that the higher costs are resultant from the change in regulations.

Question 523: E

It is open to debate whether Mercedes should or should not be criticised and it, thus, cannot be a fact as it is not something that is provable to be either true or false.

Question 524: C

This is the best answer as the passage explicitly discusses the impact on smaller teams who have been hit by the increase in engine costs. The author does not believe A is the case. B, D and E do not directly relate to whether competition has been hampered so they are incorrect.

Question 525: A

The author simply states that Mercedes built the best car and should get the credit for that. It was not the change in the rules that caused it, but they simply exploited the new rules best.

Question 526: E

The author was not referring to Mercedes specifically, but to other teams dominating previous seasons as well. Therefore, B is wrong and so is C, as that's a recent phenomenon. Ultimately, the author points out that rule changes can increase overtaking (and, thus, competition) and explicitly states that the nature of some rules and regulations is a reason for the dominance.

Passage 26

Question 527: C

Germany paid the victims of the Nazi war crimes themselves whereas the author brings up the contention that the victims of the slave trade are no longer with us. Hence, option C is the relevant distinction between the two.

Question 528: A

This option best fits in with the argument. The company can be equated to the country and the employee being the individual victim. While the individual victims should be compensated, the passage's argument doubts whether the country as the overarching institution should benefit.

Question 529: C

The author considers arguments both for and against giving reparations throughout. It does not appear that the author takes up positions A or B.

Question 530: C

The author does not disagree with Hartley-Brewer's point but merely states that the responsibility of one of the main antagonists (i.e. the UK) should hold. D is an assumption but does not highlight the author's view.

Passage 27

Question 531: C

The passage explicitly states that the government considers the costs and benefits of animal research when deciding whether to give a license to allow it. A and E are wrong as the author was actually saying that no reasonable scientist would make animals suffer *unnecessarily*.

Question 532: A

The author seems to take the position that animal testing is beneficial by highlighting many of the positive examples of it. The author does indeed point out issues and says that a blanket allowance should not be given but that's consistent with allowing animal testing in certain circumstances.

Question 533: A

What counts as reasonable is not something that can be definitively proven to be true or false. Accordingly, it is an opinion – different people can validly disagree on the issue.

Question 534: B

This seems to be the main concern of the author.

Question 535: A

Option A undermines the author's view as, if it is true, this would mean that the government's licenses are given too frequently and that the harm to animals is not minimised.

Passage 28

Question 536: E

This was explicitly stated by the writer.

Question 537: D

This was implied by the writer when stating that unauthorised use would increase.

Question 538: E

As everyone has a natural right in what they produce, it shouldn't be used without their permission.

Question 539: D

Incentivising the production of intellectual works was explicitly stated by the author as a justification for copyright laws.

Question 540: B

This is implied in Hettinger's argument.

Question 541: C

Locke argues for natural rights, which would require copyright protection and Hettinger wants copyright protection to encourage the production of intellectual works.

Passage 29

Question 542: E

The passage explicitly states that tax evasion is illegal and that tax avoidance is legal.

It is true that Google/Starbucks have engaged in tax avoidance in the past, but that point does not indicate the difference between avoidance and evasion.

Question 543: D

The passage says that Starbucks paid zero tax. It also says that the tax rate is 20% on all declared profits. This means that Starbucks both enjoyed a declared profit and evaded tax *or* it had zero declared profits and may have avoided tax. Given that the writer explicitly stated that Starbucks were within the law, they can't have evaded tax. Therefore, they must have declared zero profits in the years they paid zero tax.

Question 544: B

Starbucks engages in tax avoidance and the author explicitly stated that this 'led' to boycotts.

Question 545: C

It is simply that companies should pay tax because they receive a benefit. The writer also points out an example of a company's use of a public service, thereby implying that companies should pay tax.

Question 546: C

Tax avoidance is where not as much tax is being paid as what should be paid. The author says this can be subjective as well. Accordingly, whether a tax payment is as it *should* be cannot be tested to be true or false. Indeed, most people may think that 20% is the correct amount to be paid but others think that as long as the law is being followed, the company is fine (and those individuals would not call it tax avoidance).

Question 547: E

The author discusses both the responsibilities of the government and the companies.

Question 548: D

This question refers to the tax system *generally* as opposed to just Starbucks' tax arrangement and the author refers to this at the final paragraph when comparing the different groups of taxpayers (large business, small business, and individuals).

Passage 30

Question 549: C

The passage explicitly states that 14 women were arrested and so were the 3 inspectors, thereby making it to a total of 17 arrests.

Question 550: A

It is clear that Anthony was brought to trial but it is not clear whether any other women or whether the 3 inspectors went to trial.

Question 551: B

Hall dissented, so it's clear that the election officers were not united but were divided, so B is the correct response. Neither, C, D nor E follow from the passage.

Question 552: A

It was explicitly discussed in the third paragraph that Anthony believed she had a lawful right to vote due to the advice from her counsel.

Question 553: B

This follows from what is stated in the passage. The passage does not say that the judge believed the jury were biased and there is nothing to suggest that either A or D follows.

Final Advice

Arrive well rested, well fed and well hydrated

The PBSAA is an intensive test, so make sure you're ready for it. Ensure you get a good night's sleep before the exam (there is little point cramming) and don't miss breakfast. If you're taking water into the exam then make sure you've been to the toilet before so you don't have to leave during the exam. Make sure you're well rested and fed in order to be at your best!

Move on

If you're struggling, move on. Every question has equal weighting and there is no negative marking. In the time it takes to answer on hard question, you could gain three times the marks by answering the easier ones. Be smart to score points- especially in section 1B where some questions are far easier than others.

Make Notes on your Essay

You may get asked questions on your essay at the interview. Given that there is sometimes more than four weeks from the PBSAA to the interview, it is really important to make short notes on the essay title and your main arguments after the essay. You'll thank yourself after the interview if you do this.

Afterword

Remember that the route to a high score is your approach and practice. Don't fall into the trap that *"you can't prepare for the PBSAA"*– this could not be further from the truth. With knowledge of the test, some useful time-saving techniques and plenty of practice you can dramatically boost your score.

Work hard, never give up and do yourself justice.

Good luck!

Acknowledgements

I would like to express my sincerest thanks to the many people who helped make this book possible, especially the dedicated Oxbridge Tutors who shared their expertise in compiling the huge number of questions and answers.

Rohan

About UniAdmissions

UniAdmissions is an educational consultancy that specialises in supporting **applications to Medical School and to Oxbridge**.

Every year, we work with hundreds of applicants and schools across the UK. From free resources to our *Ultimate Guide Books* and from intensive courses to bespoke individual tuition – with a team of **300 Expert Tutors** and a proven track record, it's easy to see why UniAdmissions is the **UK's number one admissions company**.

To find out more about our support like intensive **PBSAA tuition** check out www.uniadmissions.co.uk/PBSAA

Your Free Book

Thanks for purchasing this Ultimate Guide Book. Readers like you have the power to make or break a book – hopefully you found this one useful and informative. If you have time, *UniAdmissions* would love to hear about your experiences with this book.

As thanks for your time we'll send you another ebook from our Ultimate Guide series absolutely FREE!

How to Redeem Your Free Ebook in 3 Easy Steps

1) Either scan the QR code or find the book you have on your Amazon purchase history or your email receipt to help find the book on Amazon.

2) On the product page at the Customer Reviews area, click on 'Write a customer review'

Write your review and post it! Copy the review page or take a screen shot of the review you have left.

3) Head over to www.uniadmissions.co.uk/free-book and select your chosen free ebook! You can choose from:
- ✓ The Ultimate UKCAT Guide – 1250 Practice Questions
- ✓ The Ultimate BMAT Guide – 800 Practice Questions
- ✓ The Ultimate TSA Guide – 300 Practice Questions
- ✓ The Ultimate LNAT Guide – 400 Practice Questions
- ✓ The Ultimate HSPSAA Guide – 400 Practice Questions
- ✓ The Ultimate NSAA Guide – 400 Practice Questions
- ✓ The Ultimate ECAA Guide – 300 Practice Questions
- ✓ The Ultimate ENGAA Guide – 250 Practice Questions
- ✓ The Ultimate PBSAA Guide – 550 Practice Questions
- ✓ The Ultimate FPAS SJT Guide – 300 Practice Questions
- ✓ The Ultimate Oxbridge Interview Guide
- ✓ The Ultimate Medical School Interview Guide
- ✓ The Ultimate UCAS Personal Statement Guide
- ✓ The Ultimate Medical Personal Statement Guide
- ✓ The Ultimate Medical School Application Guide
- ✓ BMAT Past Paper Solutions
- ✓ TSA Past Paper Worked Solutions

Your ebook will then be emailed to you – it's as simple as that!
Alternatively, you can buy all the above titles at **www.uniadmissions.co.uk/our-books**

Printed in Poland
by Amazon Fulfillment
Poland Sp. z o.o., Wrocław